£15.00

DEFOE'S EARLY LIFE

DEFOE'S EARLY LIFE

F. Bastian

First published 1981 by
THE MACMILLAN PRESS LTD
London and Basingstoke
Companies and representatives
throughout the world

ISBN 0 333 27432 6

Typeset in 11/12 Baskerville by
STYLESET LIMITED
Salisbury · Wiltshire

Printed in Hong Kong

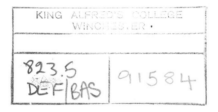

To Mary

Contents

viii   *Contents*

List of Illustrations

Acknowledgements

Anyone writing about Defoe inevitably owes much to previous biographers, and to the army of scholars who have made specialised studies of various aspects of his life and works. It is only possible here to express my indebtedness to those from whom I have received something more than can be found on the printed page.

I find it difficult to say how much I owe to the late Professor John Robert Moore, of Indiana University, whose unfailing kindness and generosity over some twenty years encouraged me to pursue my interest in Defoe. Warm thanks are also due to Professor Manuel Schonhorn, of Southern Illinois University, for friendship and for moral support that has meant more than he may have realised.

I am greatly indebted to Wadham College, Oxford, for a Schoolmaster Studentship, which enabled me to spend several months familiarising myself with material in the Bodleian Library. I am grateful to the staff of this and other libraries, and especially to that of the Central Reference Library, Bath, for their willing assistance over many years.

I also wish to thank the following, who were good enough to answer my enquiries on a variety of topics, sometimes on several occasions and at considerable length, although of course I alone am responsible for any errors I may have made in using their information: Mr J. H. Andrews (for dating Defoe's journeys in England); Professor C. R. Boxer (late seventeenth-century Portugal); Professor Harold F. Brooks (John Oldham); Mr G. V. S. Bucknall (translation from the Portuguese); Mr F. J. Dallett (Charles Lodwick and his relatives); Professor Frank H. Ellis (Defoe's satirical verse); Mr D. F. Foxon (Defoe's publisher); Mr A. H. Hall (records of the Butchers' Company); Mr A. J. Holland (shipbuilding on the Hamble); Mr James McQueen (Alexander Lauder); Miss Julia de L. Mann (the seventeenth-century economic background); Mrs Rosalind Mitchison (Scottish customs officials), Mr P. C. D. Mundy (genealogy of the Foe and Tuffley families); Mr Stephen R. Parkes (John Dunton); Professor Nesca A. Robb (the political situation in England in 1701); Professor Pat Rogers (contemporary periodical publications); Mrs Vivian Salmon (the Lodwick family); Mr A. D. Saunders (Tilbury Fort); Professor T. C. Smout (Scottish merchants in Holland); Professor G. A. Starr (a contempory but unrelated Defoe family).

Finally I am grateful to my son, Christopher Bastian, and to my former colleague, Stephen Lycett, for reading the typescript at an early stage and for their very constructive comments.

F. B.

Introduction

Born in 1660, the year of Charles II's restoration, Daniel Defoe was to outlive the same five monarchs as the Vicar of Bray, and to experience similar problems of survival in changing times. If, near the end of his life in 1731, he had looked back on its many vicissitudes, there is no doubt what he would have considered its highest peak — his service for King William III. After the death of his royal master in 1702, his remaining years were in many ways an anti-climax. Ironically, it is these years that have been most fully treated by his biographers, while his earlier life has been comparatively neglected.

This distortion reflects the uneven distribution of source material. The whole of his surviving correspondence, his entire journalistic output, and nine-tenths of his other writings date from the last three decades of his life. However, information about his earlier life is not entirely lacking: these years saw the appearance of one full-length book, his *Essay upon Projects* (1697), a fair sprinkling of tracts, and several long poems, including *The True-Born Englishman* (1701) which first made him known to the general public. There is also archive material, notably a rich vein struck by Professor James Sutherland, who found legal documents relating to a number of commercial disputes in which he was involved during the 1690s.[1] Yet, if he had died before his marriage in his twenty-fourth year, there would be nothing to show that he had ever existed. Fortunately there is a further source of information which helps to fill this early gap, and also to put flesh on the bare bones of the official records during the two following decades — the autobiographical material embedded in his writings. This book is based on the conviction that there is a good deal more of this material than has generally been recognised, and that it can be identified and used with a fair degree of confidence.

Defoe's one explicitly autobiographical work needs to be treated with considerable caution. *An Appeal to Honour and*

Justice (1715) was a desperate attempt to rehabilitate himself in the eyes of the Whigs, then newly restored to power, after he had to all appearances abandoned their cause for several years. It was a piece of special pleading, concerned only with his political record, highly selective even within those limits, and slanted to present his career in the best possible light. Yet it remains an important, and for some of his activities, the only source of information.

There is also much autobiographical material scattered throughout his other self-acknowledged writings. Though he usually wrote under the cloak of anonymity, the exceptions include one particularly valuable source — his *Review*, which he wrote single-handed several times a week from 1704 to 1713, and about whose authorship there was never any secret. Here he often illustrated or reinforced his arguments with autobiographical anecdotes which, though still subject to the vagaries of memory and the rationalising tendencies common to human nature, may well be more reliable than some autobiographical set-pieces. There are similar fragments in his anonymous or pseudonymous writings, though here his efforts to conceal his identity sometimes lead to deliberate distortions. The *Review* describes how he discomfited an Anglican who maintained that the sacrament should be received in a kneeling posture, by pointing to a picture in St George's Chapel, Windsor, showing the disciples seated at the Last Supper; but in his *Tour*, where he is supposedly an Anglican 'gentleman', it is a nonconformist friend who makes this point at his expense.[2] Sometimes, for various reasons, he attributes his own experiences to others, though seldom as obviously as in *The History of Apparitions*, where he carelessly transmutes 'some roguish London boys' into 'we'.[3] Similarly, when he gives vivid and detailed accounts of the dreams of 'acquaintances', there can be little doubt that they are really his own: for who, apart from psychiatrists, ever cared about other people's dreams?

The *Tour through the Whole Island of Great Britain* (1724—6) is a very useful source. Ostensibly an account of a series of 'circuits' begun in 1722, its real nature is more complex. Much of it is derived from various published sources; but when this material is eliminated, what remains is Defoe's own first-hand observations. Internal evidence or independent corroboration often make it possible to date these observations; and several of the journeys so revealed date from his earlier years. Similarly, exceptionally detailed treatment or obvious emotional involvement with certain areas is an invitation to search for evidence to confirm his special links with those areas. In the case of Dorking and its neighbourhood, this has led to important new evidence about Defoe's family connections and boyhood;[4] and his links with the Nene Valley to the west of Peterborough, with Ipswich and with Halifax, are also beginning to emerge, though not yet with complete clarity.[5]

In the less well-known *Atlas Maritimus & Commercialis* (1728), while disavowing any pretence that he had actually visited all the places described, he still claimed to have seen many of them; yet he could 'challenge the Reader to single out any of the Places he has thus seen or been at, by his Partiality in the Description'.[6] Defoe's challenge is difficult to resist. Though his sources have not yet been systematically investigated, he still sometimes gives himself away, if not by the 'partiality', at least by the immediacy of some of his observations, as well as by the disproportionate detail lavished on some quite obscure seaports. The *Atlas* thus helps to piece together his early trading voyages to European ports; while his lively and detailed accounts of some aspects of life in the Shetlands and Orkneys fits in with other evidence to throw light on how he spent the years immediately after his bankruptcy of 1692.[7]

Another important source is the *Journal of the Plague Year* (1722). The close correspondence of the supposed author, 'H.F.', to Defoe's uncle, Henry Foe, seems to require the identification of 'H.F.'s merchant brother with Defoe's father, James Foe; and this has led to other evidence calling for a revision of the accepted picture of his family background.[8] The *Journal* was well described by Sir Walter Scott as 'one of that peculiar class of writing which hovers between history and romance'; and even the *Tour* was in one sense a product of Defoe's imagination. This may embolden us to stray still further across the ill-defined frontier which divides Defoe's fiction from his other writings. When *Robinson Crusoe* (1719) was exposed to the world as an invention, Defoe was driven in acute embarrassment to justify its essential accuracy; it was to be read as an allegorical account of his own life; and in any case many of the incidents really had happened to him, though not necessarily exactly as described in the book.[9] Elements of his own real-life experience are certainly to be found embedded in his other pseudo-autobiographical fictions, if only they could be identified.

Creative writing, of course, can never be spun out of thin air, but must always be a transmutation of the author's real or vicarious experience. But Defoe had an exceptional respect, not indeed for the truth, but for facts. He often used his own experience in only a semi-digested state, so that when he can be compelled to disgorge a gobbet, it may still be recognisable. Thus the cave in which Crusoe found a dying goat was faithfully modelled on Poole's Hole in Derbyshire, which Defoe had probably visited in 1709, and which he described in his *Tour* (1726). Even where the details differ, it is with reference to the original, and for recognisable reasons.[10] Again, in one of the most quoted and admired incidents in the whole of Defoe's fiction, Moll Flanders robs a small child of a necklace in a narrow alley, but resists the temptation of the Devil to kill her to prevent her from crying out. Surely there can be nothing autobiographical in this! But Defoe gives two slightly differing versions of how a 'tradesman' of his acquaintance — presumably himself — *dreamed* that he robbed a small child of a necklace, but resisted the temptation of the Devil to kill it for his own safety.[11] So it may after all be a kind of reality that has given the incident the qualities that have struck so many critics. Yet, if every such item needs similar confirmation, we are clearly no nearer to being able to use his fiction as a source of biographical information.

However, there are common-sense criteria which may help to identify such autobiographical passages. Non-derivative elements embedded in borrowed material need to be looked at closely; so too do incidents irrelevant to the main theme, or awkwardly or gratuitously introduced; incidents recounted in excessive or irrelevant detail; those whose ingredients, essential or trivial, are repeated elsewhere in his writings; those in which he shows a high degree of emotional involvement; and those which fit into the established pattern of his life. Reconstructing Defoe's early life is like fitting together a giant jig-saw puzzle with many missing pieces, while many that we have may not really belong to the puzzle at all. Those which fit into the completed parts of the puzzle, or groups which merely fit together and can be placed in gaps in the picture, are those which are most likely to belong to it. As jig-saw addicts will know, an apparently 'meaningless' piece may suddenly acquire significance from its context; and when this happens the chances are increased that it really does belong in the picture.

Basically the method followed in preparing this book has been to scrutinise the available material more thoroughly, and to squeeze it a good deal harder than before, to extract biographical information from it. It may well be felt that the result is unduly speculative, and that the book ventures too confidently over insecure ground. It is seldom possible, without breaking the narrative flow, to discuss all the pros and cons of accepting a particular fragment of Defoe's writing as autobiographical, though an attempt is made to give some indications in passing. It may be objected, too, that what starts as a surmise sometimes ends up as a firm statement. Often the only alternative would be to overload the text and irritate the reader with qualifications. While it is too much to hope to attain complete objectivity and eliminate inaccuracies entirely, perhaps these are the inevitable price of a picture which, while remaining substantially accurate, will be very much fuller than would otherwise be possible. It is not as though the comparatively small body of received facts about Defoe's early life is entirely reliable; for many of the statements passed on from biographer to biographer were based in the first place upon misinterpretation of evidence, or even sheer guesswork.

A further complication in the identification of autobiographical material is uncertainty as to exactly what Defoe wrote. Of the hundreds of titles attributed to him, only a handful actually appeared under his name, though others were acknowledged by him in some other way; but the great majority remained anonymous or pseudonymous, and owe their place in the canon either to tradition or to internal evidence. The process of adding new pieces to the list still continues, though not with the same impetus as in the lifetime of Professor John Robert Moore, who was not only responsible for many new attributions, but placed all students of Defoe under an immense obligation with his *Checklist of the Writings of Daniel Defoe* (1960). Yet there are still many attributions, both old and new, of very doubtful validity; and today the tendency is rather in the direction of striking titles out of the list. Any suggested new attributions, depending as they must upon internal evidence, will certainly be looked at very critically. Yet, if internal evidence was never to be accepted, we would have to reject most of the works on which Defoe's reputation rests.

If it was simply a matter of searching for autobiographical clues, it would be possible to play safe and avoid using material from dubious sources. But the issue cannot be so simply dodged. Of over 500 titles in Professor Moore's *Checklist*, only 59 fall within the 22 adult years covered by this book. Of these, I have doubts about six, but would add a further 25, as well as one or two relevant ones outside these years; and it is easy to imagine the eyebrows that may be raised at this figure. If a 'no risk' policy was followed, some of these could be ignored without making very much difference, except that, as I believe them to be by Defoe, I feel that they should be dealt with in their place. But others, and especially fifteen that fall within a period of little more than twelve months in 1700—2, are absolutely crucial to the argument. There seems to be no alternative but to grasp the nettle. The reader is clearly entitled to know when a new attribution is being suggested; but to attempt to justify each one in detail would destroy the continuity of the narrative. The method adopted has been to hint lightly in the main text at the grounds for the attribution, and to expand on this in Appendix B, which discusses the general criteria that have been applied as well as their application to each particular case.

If Defoe's writings, questioned searchingly enough, can be persuaded to throw a great deal of light on the story of his life, the reverse is also true: the more is known of his life, the better his writings can be understood. Literary critics are sometimes impatient of too minute an examination of the lives of authors, or of too detailed a dialogue between life and works. The words on the page, they feel, should be allowed to speak for themselves. How they got there, how they are related to the real-life experience from which they in some way ultimately derive, is, they feel, of secondary importance; and undue preoccupation with such problems may hamper a true appreciation of the finished work. But little if any of Defoe's work was intended for anything but a passing occasion; and it is just a happy chance that much of it still has something to say to later generations. The whole point of most of his writings lies in their context — often in a fluctuating political situation which changed from month to month, sometimes even from day to day, and to which Defoe's personal involvement and motivation are very relevant. In other words, much of his work cannot be judged at all by purely literary standards; for it often depends for assessment, and sometimes for bare comprehension, on a knowledge of just what he was attempting to achieve.

But Defoe's life is in any case well worth reconstructing for its own sake. In its variety and vicissitudes it touched on many different aspects of the life of the age; and for some of these he is an almost uniquely articulate witness. Not only do his writings contain fascinating vignettes illuminating social conditions, but his comments on the political struggles which tore the nation apart during his adolescence and early manhood, though admittedly for the most part retrospective, enable us to see the Whig interpretation of history taking shape before our eyes. Nor was he merely a passive observer of these struggles; he was an active participant in many of them, and as time went on his role became more considerable. His part in Monmouth's Rebellion must have been insignificant; but as propagandist and confidential adviser to William III during the last eighteen months of that monarch's life, he was not only near the nerve-centre of political decision making, but played a real part in shaping the history of his time.

1 Sober and Orderly People

Daniel Defoe, master of literary disguise and destined to die in hiding, sets a puzzle from the outset by leaving no firm evidence of when and where he was born, or what his family background was. Patient research has dispersed some of the mists which surround his origins; but much remains obscure, and many of the facts that have emerged are themselves baffling. One cannot do much more than set out the problems, indicate what evidence there is, suggest some tentative conclusions, and wish better luck to future investigators.

Even the year of his birth is uncertain. His tombstone, formerly in Bunhill Fields, states that he died on 24 April 1731, 'in his 70th year', suggesting that he was born in 1661 or early 1662.[1] His marriage particulars, giving his age in December 1683 as 'about 24', point to 1659, a date that can be ruled out as a sister was born in June of that year.[2] He himself declared in *The Protestant Monastery*, probably written shortly before publication on 19 November 1726, that he was then in his sixty-seventh year.[3] This would place his birth in the summer or early autumn of 1660, a few months after the restoration of King Charles II. Defoe always found great significance in anniversaries and coincidences of dates; and when he made Crusoe lay such stress on 30 September, the date of his fateful shipwreck, and 'the same day of the year I was born on', this may have been because it was his own birthday.[4] Curiously, the exact date of the shipwreck was 30 September 1659, which cannot have been Defoe's exact birthday; but perhaps he was a year out in his reckoning, as he was on other occasions in *Robinson Crusoe*.[5] This is not the place to discuss in what sense, if at all, his first great novel was intended as an allegory of his own life. With so many imponderables, it would be rash to be dogmatic; but for the sake of convenience it will be assumed, when referring to Defoe's age, that he was born on 30 September 1660.

Defoe's birthplace was probably the populous London parish of St Giles Cripplegate, lying just beyond the walls on the northern outskirts of the City. The systematically kept parish registers[6] contain the following entry, under the year 1657:

Mary daught' of James Foe Tallowchandler & of Ailce Not christened but borne November 13.

Under the year 1659 is a further entry:

Elizab' daugt' of James Foe tallowchand' & of Ailce not Christe: borne June 19.

By the time that Daniel was born, the parish clerks had reverted to the original practice of recording, not *births*, but *baptisms*; so that if, like his two sisters, he was not baptised in infancy, we should no longer expect to find his birth recorded. He may not even have been born in this parish; but the question of his exact place of birth is really an academic one. The next documentary evidence, a poll-tax assessment list, shows that by 1667 the Foes were living in Jones's Rents, off Swan Alley, in the parish of St Stephen Coleman Street, a little to the south within the City walls.[7] There is circumstantial evidence that they had moved there as early as 1665, and probably several years before that; and Defoe's earliest memories seem to have been of this parish.

There is similar uncertainty about the occupation and status of his father, James Foe, who was about thirty years old when his son was born.[8] He is still often described as a butcher, on the strength of his membership of the Butchers' Company; and biographers have sometimes been tempted to stress the more sordid features of the butchery trade, perhaps to enhance Defoe's achievement in rising above his humble origins. But membership of a Livery Company is a very uncertain clue to the actual trade followed — Defoe himself eventually became a member of the Butchers' Company — and it is unlikely that James Foe ever slaughtered a beast or dressed a carcase. The Cripplegate registers twice called him 'tallowchandler', which must have been the trade in which he had been trained. He had been apprenticed in 1644 to John Levitt, then serving his second term as Master of the Butchers' Company; but the latter, who lived on Tower

Hill in the parish of St Botolph Aldgate, was himself described
in the parish register, on his death in 1666, as 'tallowchandler'.
Levitt was clearly a man of some consequence, prominent in
the affairs of his own Livery Company, a lieutenant-colonel in
the City trained bands, and frequently in demand as auditor of
the annual accounts of the very large parish of St Botolph
Aldgate and of Portsoken Ward in which he lived.[9] James Foe
too in later life was called on to audit the accounts of the
Butchers' Company; while Defoe in his turn was to pride himself
on his skill in keeping accounts.[10]

James Foe, in fact, was not long content to sell tallow candles
in one of the seedier quarters of the City, but soon began to
diversify his business activities and to branch out into overseas
trade. He was never styled 'tallowchandler' after Defoe's birth;
and a reference to him in 1671 as 'generosus' — gentleman —
though technically inaccurate, suggests that he was a cut above
the average small tradesman.[11] Wills of 1671 and 1676 simply
call him 'Citizen of London'; but in a legal document of 1673
he is styled 'Merchant and Citizen of London'; and it was as
'James Foe of London merchant' that he made his own will
thirty years later.[12] The most interesting evidence comes from
Defoe's *Journal of the Plague Year*, which undoubtedly incor-
porates some real family history. Defoe's uncle Henry Foe
corresponds so closely to the supposed author, 'H.F.', that the
latter's merchant brother, who lived in Swan Alley, off Coleman
Street, must be intended for James Foe. This means that Defoe's
father must have turned merchant some years before 1665.
There is mention of 'the *Turks* and *Mahometans* in Asia and
other Places, where he had been', and of 'my brother's correspondents in Portugal and Italy, where he chiefly traded'; he
had 'not many Years before come over from *Portugal*', while,
more specifically, 'my Brother being a merchant, was a few
Years before . . . returned from abroad, coming last from
Lisbon'.[13] There were of course merchants and merchants. The
signs are that James Foe, though never achieving affluence, was
from Defoe's early childhood at least, a man of some substance
and modest prosperity.[14]

Efforts to trace Defoe's paternal ancestry have not got past
his grandfather, but it is at least possible to dismiss some
unfounded ideas that have gained currency.[15] There is no

evidence that James Foe or his ancestors ever used the prefix
'De' until it was adopted by Defoe himself about 1695.[16] Nor is
there any basis for the persistent belief that he was descended,
in the paternal line at least, from Protestant refugees from
Catholic persecution in the Netherlands.[17] There is a record of a
grant in 1529 by the Abbot of Peterborough of lands in Peakirk
(a few miles north of Peterborough) to Thomas Foe and Cicilie
his wife, on a lease of 81 years. This part of England, near the
western edge of the Fen country, was at that time still dominated
by the great Abbeys, doomed to be suppressed within a few
years. By Defoe's time Ramsey, Thorney, Crowland and others
were in ruins; but the Abbey Church of Peterborough still
stood, now transformed into a Cathedral. The newly established
Bishopric had been endowed with the lands of the suppressed
Abbey, and the Foes had found themselves tenants of the Dean
and Chapter of Peterborough. They flourished, spread themselves into neighbouring parishes, and in at least five cases sent
up younger sons to be apprenticed in London. The lease was
probably renewed when it lapsed in 1610, for Foes are found in
the parish of Peakirk for several more decades.

James Foe had in fact been born at Etton, a few miles from
Peakirk, in 1630, the youngest of four children of Daniel Foe,
yeoman, and Rose, his wife, who had moved there from Peakirk
some years before. But as Daniel Foe died in the following year —
leaving the useful sum of £230 to be divided among his children
— he can have been little more than a name to his descendants.
In due course his eldest son, another Daniel, married and apparently took over the family farm at Etton; but he too died, in
1647, and it is not known what became of his infant family
(Defoe's older first cousins).[18] James Foe had another brother,
Henry, who had also been apprenticed in London, and became a
saddler in High Street, Whitechapel — the 'H.F.' on whom Defoe
fathered his *Journal of the Plague Year*.[19] There was also a sister
who apparently married and settled in Lincolnshire, probably at
Stamford.[20] But there are no signs of any Foes surviving in the
immediate neighourhood of Etton during Defoe's lifetime. So
there were no paternal acres or ancestral farmhouse to arouse a
nostalgic interest in his own yeoman forebears, about whom he
may not have known very much more than we do; and when he
came to write his *Tour through the Whole Island of Great*

Britain, he passed right through this area, on his way from Peterborough to Market Deeping, without finding anything worth comment.

Yet he had a great deal to say about another area a few miles to the south — the Nene valley between Wansford and Peterborough.[21] He described how, on the Huntingdonshire side of the river,

> At Overton, now call'd Cherry Orton, a village near Gunwade Ferry, is an old mansion house, formerly belonging to a very antient and almost forgotten race or family of great men, call'd Lovetoft, which I nam'd for a particular reason. The estate is now in the heirs of the Duke of Newcastle, and the house lies neglected.

Cherry Orton was otherwise known as Orton Waterville, and the Lovetofts had indeed held property there several centuries before; but they had also held estates in the adjoining parish of Orton Longueville, and it was the latter manor which had passed into the hands of the heirs of the Duke of Newcastle.[22] The suspicion that Defoe had confused the two Ortons, probably through careless map-reading, is supported by evidence which links his family with Orton Longueville. His grandmother, Rose Foe, who had been widowed in 1631 and left with a family of four young children, was remarried two years later, to another Etton yeoman, Solomon Fall; and by this marriage she had two more children. When her second husband died in 1641 her six children were all still under age.[23] Within a few years (by 1647 at the latest) she had married for a third time, to Thomas King, 'of Overton Longuevile, in the parish of Bottlebridge, Hunts, gent', a widower with two children, one of whom was the Ellen King of 'Overton' who in 1643 had married Rose's eldest son Daniel. Thomas King too died, in 1658, leaving Defoe's grandmother a widow for the third time.[24]

At first sight it is tempting to equate Thomas King with the 'grandfather' who, Defoe tells us, had a huntsman and a pack of hounds named after the generals of the Civil War;[25] and to imagine his grandmother Rose living on after her third husband's death to be visited by her grandson at her 'mansion house' during his childhood. In the face of the evidence this scenario breaks down at almost every point. Though Thomas King is more than once described as 'gentleman',[26] he was a man of modest means, who left his widow only an annuity of £5. His own father had been an illiterate yeoman whose total estate had been valued at less than £12.[27] He himself had been in possession of the 'manor and farm' of Nansickles in Bottlebridge (a kind of twin parish of Orton Longueville); but its total extent can have been little more than fifty acres, while the farmhouse of not more than four hearths could not by any stretch of the imagination have been called a 'mansion house'; and in any case he had sold it before his death. The purchaser had been Lady Mary Armyne, who also held the manor of Orton Longueville, acting on behalf of her nephew, William Pierrepont, Esquire. The latter resided at Orton Hall, an imposing residence of 20 (later 35) hearths; and this was the only house in the combined parish that could have been called a 'mansion house'.[28] The 'particular reason' for Defoe's interest in this house is far from clear, unless perhaps his grandmother Rose held some position in Pierrepont's household. Lady Mary Armyne and her nephew both had strong Puritan sympathies, and the same must have been true of Rose as well.

In *Due Preparations for the Plague* Defoe created a character who may well be a reflection of his grandmother. Like Rose Foe, she had been 'newly married' in 1625; and by the time of the Plague Year of 1665, in addition to two merchant sons and a daughter, she had raised another family by a second marriage, but was then a widow. This 'pious and excellent mother' emerges as a formidable personality, still able to exert considerable moral pressure by way of 'monitory discourses' upon her two grown-up sons; and it is implied that it was thanks to her that they had been 'religiously educated, and were what we call sober and orderly people'.[29] As James Foe had lost his father before he was a year old, and his stepfather when he was eleven, and had acquired a second stepfather when he was in his teens, the dominant and stabilising influence in his upbringing must have been his mother. On a purely worldly level, it must have fallen to her to see that James Foe, like his elder brother Henry, was given a sound start in life by a good apprenticeship in London. More important, it must have been thanks to her that he grew up, not only 'sober and orderly', but also a man of firm Puritan convictions.

Anyone anxious to investigate Defoe's roots might be well

advised not to bother too much about the broken line of his Foe ancestors, from whom he took his name but little more, and concentrate instead upon his grandmother, who may well hold the key to his spiritual ancestry. We do not even know her family name. Defoe's writings do, however, provide an admittedly tenuous clue which might lead us in the right direction. Among the innumerable anecdotes he tells to illustrate his arguments, we would expect to find a few based, not on his own experience or on his wide reading, but on family tradition. Of all the events of the half century before his birth, the one to which he reacted most strongly had taken place in 1633, when 'Bishop *Laud* . . . prevail'd upon his Royal Master, to begin his own Ruin, in publishing the Book of Sports . . . the Declaration for allowing May poles, Dancing, cudgel-Playing on the Lord's Day', which like its predecessor of 1618, was to be read aloud in every parish church. On this Defoe laid the blame for much of the subsequent religious and political strife in England.[30] 'How many worthy *yet conforming* Divines', he asked, 'left their Pulpits rather than read that *Accurs'd Book*?' If his grandmother Rose was the daughter of such a minister, this might explain, not only how Defoe came to have a copy of the *Book of Sports* in his possession in later life, and the vehemence of his Sabbatarian feelings, but also how he himself originally came to be 'set aside', as he tells us, for the Christian ministry.[31]

Whatever the truth of this, Defoe certainly sprang from a strongly Puritan background. The Puritans or Dissenters, as they were usually called throughout his lifetime, did not however form a single homogeneous movement, but often clashed as stubbornly with each other as they did with the Church of England. The two largest groups, the Presbyterians and the Independents (later known as Congregationalists) differed mainly over church organisation. The former, although opposed to the Bishops through whom royal control of the Church had been exercised, still believed in a single firmly organised and disciplined, though self-governing, Church; the latter favoured a much looser system of autonomous congregations, the so-called 'gathered churches', each acknowledging only the superior authority of God. United in supporting the Parliamentary cause in the Civil War, they found themselves at loggerheads when it was over, the Presbyterians favouring the continuance of the monarchy, though with reduced powers, while Cromwell and the New Model Army on which his authority rested were supported by the Independents. There are many indications that Defoe's own background was Presbyterian. Years later he told his readers that 'the author of this wears a mourning ring on his finger, given at the funeral of Mr Christopher Love, a Presbyterian minister, beheaded *Anno* 1653, for the horrid fanatic plot for bringing in, as they then called him, Charles Stuart, and restoring the monarchy'.[32] Unfortunately he did not say how the ring had come into his possession.

After the Restoration, when the Church of England was firmly back in the saddle, and Presbyterian hopes of taking over the national Church had finally faded, the differences between them and the Independents became less significant. They often collaborated, and Defoe was to have many contacts with ministers of both persuasions. All the same, he always identified himself as a Presbyterian.[33] Samuel Annesley, minister of St Giles Cripplegate when Defoe was born, was ejected in 1662 and set up a meeting house at Little St Helens, Bishopsgate, becoming one of the most eminent Presbyterian divines of the age. In manhood Defoe not only attended Annesely's services, but became his personal friend and wrote a poem in his memory on his death in 1697; and it has naturally been assumed that this was simply the continuation of a family connection established by his father some forty years before.[34]

Against this there is one very puzzling fact. The usual Presbyterian practice, followed by Annesley himself in the case of his own family, was to baptise children in infancy; but James Foe's daughters, and presumably his son as well, were 'not christened'. It is difficult to picture the religious life of such an exceptionally large parish as St Giles Cripplegate, where nearly 8000 were buried in the Plague Year, and which must have had a total population when James Foe lived there of well over 20,000. The minister could not possibly have known all his parishioners; and the parish church could only have held a small proportion of them. No doubt many attended churches or meeting houses elsewhere, while many among the flotsam and jetsam on the fringes of the City would normally have attended neither. Yet even though there must have been some births which never came to the attention of the parish clerk, the total number of baptisms in the course of a year was in the neighbourhood of 600. In other words, many parents who did not normally attend services in the parish church still had their children baptised there, and very few other births appear in the register. Thus in November 1657, out of a total of 65 births, only one infant in addition to Mary Foe was entered as 'not christened'; and in June 1659, Elizabeth Foe was the only one out of 38. In such a religious household as the Foes, this cannot have been through negligence or indifference; and the almost inescapable conclusion is that they were temporarily under the influence of a sect which rejected the whole idea of infant baptism.

The Baptists themselves come to mind. But not only is there no evidence to link the Foes with any Baptist minister or congregation, there is also the fact that Defoe himself in later life showed little interest in the Baptists and the issues on which they separated themselves from other Christian churches. On the other hand he seems to have been fascinated by the Quakers, never indeed identifying himself with them, but writing of them often and with a kind of bantering affection; and two of the best developed characters in his novels were Quakers.[35] But again, there is no trace of the Foes in the early records of the Society of Friends; so that, if they were for a while influenced by Quaker ideas, they must soon have abandoned them and returned to orthodox Presbyterian beliefs.

The answer may lie in the most conspicuously missing piece of the puzzle, Defoe's mother, Alice, or 'Ailce' as the parish clerk of St Giles Cripplegate always spelled the name. Was she perhaps one of the many women carried away by the extraordinary fervour of the Quaker, James Nayler, on his arrival in London in 1655?[36] Is there any echo of her in Roxana's Quaker landlady, upon whom Defoe showered so many complimentary epithets? If so, though 'grave', 'sharp and penetrating', she was not only 'kind', 'honest' and 'good', but also 'merry', 'friendly' and 'tender-hearted'; in fact, 'a most pleasant and agreeable Lady; I must call her so, for tho' a QUAKER, she had a full Share of good Breeding, sufficient to her, if she had been a Dutchess'.[37] Presumably she was a daughter of Defoe's hunting grandfather; but her family name is not known. She was apparently related in some way to Lawrence Marsh Esquire, a leading Dorking Puritan and former member of Barebones Parliament; but an extensive genealogical search has failed to show the exact connection. By a process of elimination, it seems most likely that she was a blood relation of Marsh's mother-in-law, who is herself unidentified.[38] Another of Marsh's unidentified relatives was 'Cousen Hardwicke', who might turn out to be the Mr Joseph Hardwick, listed in 1668 and 1673 among the 'principal English merchants' at Lisbon; so that it was perhaps through his wife's relatives that James Foe became involved in overseas trade.[39] Defoe only once mentions his mother — in a childhood memory — and it is almost certain that she died when he was still a boy, probably about 1668.[40] James Foe had many sterling qualities, but nothing we know of him explains how he came to father such a remarkable son; and perhaps the latter owed the maverick qualities of his personality, either by heredity or through his early upbringing, to his mother.

2 God's Terrible Voice in the City

The neighbourhood of Defoe's childhood home in the parish of St Stephen Coleman Street was described by John Strype some fifty years later, when it had begun to fall into decay:

> *Swan-alley* also goes out of *Coleman-street*, and with a turning Passage, runs into *Bell-alley*, and with another turning Passage, falls into another Alley, also called *Swan-alley*, which is better built, with Gardens to the Houses. More Northward this Alley runs into a Place called *Jones's Rents*, which is a ruinous Place, the Houses ready to fall down. Out of this Place, with a little narrow Turning, the Way leads into *Cross-Keys-Court*, which is indifferent good: and out of this Court is a Passage to *London-wall*.[1]

Jones's Rents have long since fallen, and the northern part of Swan Alley has been built over; but as recently as 1960 it was possible to thread one's way between office blocks, from Coleman Street to London Wall by the route described by Strype, through the devious alleys, passage-ways and courts, still bearing the names that were old in Defoe's childhood.

His earliest memories will have been of the simple cleanlinesss and calm discipline of a Puritan merchant's home. He only once mentions his mother: '*If you vex me, I'll eat no dinner*, said I when I was a little boy, till my mother taught me to be wiser, by letting me stay till I was hungry'.[2] His father, a grave man of business in his thirties, but sometimes ready to unbend and talk of his experiences abroad; his elder sister Mary (Elizabeth had apparently died in infancy); no doubt a maidservant: these completed the family.[3] The Foes apparently lived as sub-tenants in part of a house occupied by a somewhat older couple — John Ellsworth, a Blackwell Hall factor dealing in woollen cloth, and his wife Anna, *née* Schapelinck, from Bruges in Flanders.[4] The taxation returns place them in Jones Court (or Jones's Rents); but Defoe tells us that his father's door was in Swan Alley. Perhaps this was a back or side door to a house at the south-west corner of the Court where the Alley ran into it. Their part of the house 'had a little court before it, and a brick wall and a gate in it'; and in the courtyard stood several 'warehouses' or sheds where James Foe stored his goods.[5] The atmosphere of this quiet residential backwater may perhaps best be evoked by the contemporary paintings by Pieter de Hooch of domestic interiors and back-yards in Holland, with which the English trading classes had so many links.

Beyond the brick wall and the gate with its spring-lock lay the sights, sounds and smells of a livelier, harsher, more squalid world. London was no place to let out a small child alone. But the neighbours were respectable enough; amongst humbler folk, there were several merchants, a notary and an 'insurancer'. When the boy was old enough to be allowed out to play in the long winding alley, too narrow for carts to use, he would find older companions who could point out to him the house in Swan Alley from which, a few years before, in January 1661, Thomas Venner and his band of Fifth-monarchy fanatics had burst upon the City with their war-cry: 'The King Jesus, and their heads upon the gates!'; and also the spot in Coleman Street facing the Alley entrance, where Venner and one of his followers had been hanged, drawn and quartered.[6] He later reported a detail about which he may well have been told by a sympathiser:

When the fifth Monarchy Men made a Ridiculous Essay here, with 25 Men to *fight the Lord against the Mighty*, and raised a Rebellion against King *Charles*, for the Restoring King *Jesus*, as they term'd it; as an Old Woman, who was a Private Friend to the Design, was talking with some People in the Street, the Morning after they were Defeated, everyone was crying out, it was a Senceless, Mad Action, unaccountable and preposterous: *Ay*, says the old Woman, *That's True*, but what should we have call'd it, if it had succeeded?[7]

When he went further afield, with his mother or a maidservant, there were the manifold snares of the devil to be avoided.

Perhaps it would be an itinerant astrologer, 'a grave Fellow in a Velvet Jacket, a Band, and a black Cloak', with an excited crowd around him, or 'the Jack-puddings, Merry-andrews, Puppet-shows, Rope-dancers, and such like doings', past which he was reluctantly dragged.[8]

Though the Foes had apparently welcomed the restoration of the monarchy, they were soon shaking their heads at the greater licence it had brought in its train. Stories were circulating of scandalous goings-on at Court, while 'plays and interludes . . . gaming tables, public-dancing rooms and music-houses' began to burgeon at the fashionable end of the town.[9] Then there were the new religious laws passed by an ungodly Parliament, which first by the Act of Uniformity in 1662 drove out, so it was said, '3000 ministers . . . silenc'd, and depos'd in the Kingdom of England in one Day';[10] and then by the Conventicle Act of 1664 imposed heavy penalties on those who attended the meetings of these ejected ministers. It is true, this Act was not always strictly enforced, for Puritanism had too strong a hold on the trading classes; and we know of no hardship it imposed on the Foes. But Puritanism, recently triumphant, was now on the defensive, its adherents an aggrieved and sometimes perse-cuted minority; while the differences which had bitterly divided the sects were coming to mean less than their common feeling of being a beleaguered garrison, united under the name of Dissenters or Nonconformists. The Foes, however, seem to have separated more in sorrow than in anger, and tried to live in Christian charity with those from whom they differed. Though much of the grave talk must have been above the young boy's head, he knew that when the bells of the hundred City churches rang out for common prayer, they were not ringing for him. James Foe seems to have had nothing to do with his parish church of St Stephen Coleman Street. There would of course have been family prayers, and readings from the Bible, while on the Sabbath the family would walk out, perhaps to the meeting house in Little St Helens, off Bishopsgate, where Samuel Annesley held his services after his ejection from St Giles Cripplegate.

At the corner of Cheapside and Bread Street, at the sign of the Castle, lived Michael Stancliffe, citizen and haberdasher, 'stocking seller by traid'.[11] Years later Defoe was to have exten-sive business dealings with his son Samuel. If James Foe had similar dealings with Michael Stancliffe, and sometimes took his young son with him when he called at the sign of the Castle, this might explain why the latter carried in his memory from early childhood, a 'picture of the City of London, on the south side of Cheapside before the Fire: the timber-built houses, projecting forward and towards one another, till in the narrow streets they were ready to touch one another at the top'.[12]

He must often have been taken to the east end of the City where his uncle Henry lived, 'without Aldgate, about midway between Aldgate Church and Whitechapel Bars, on the left hand or north side of the street'.[13] Just opposite was Harrow Alley, 'a populous Conjunction of Alleys, Courts and Passages . . . full of poor People, most of them belonging to the Butchers, or to other Employments depending on the Butchery'.[14] Henry Foe, now well established in his trade of saddler, occupied a house of six hearths, one of the few substantial ones in this poor quarter of the City.[15] He was unmarried, and his household consisted of 'an antient Woman that managed the House, a Maid-Servant, two Apprentices'.[16] His shop and warehouses were on the spot; but his business was mainly 'not by Shop or Chance Trade, but among the Merchants trading to the *English* Colonies in *America*'.[17] In the workshop, with its smell of new leather, young Daniel may have spent many happy hours; and there, when his uncle's customers called, his imagination may have been fired by talk of a brave new England across the sea.

From his uncle's house, it was only a short step down the Minories to visit his father's old master, John Levitt, in his shop on Tower Hill. Perhaps the old man, who had no grandsons of his own, sometimes took the little boy across to see, amongst other savage beasts, 'the lions in the tower, enraged and locked up'.[18] What did he make of the story of Daniel in the lions' den? Did he ever hear, when feeding time approached, the 'dreadful noises of barking, roaring and howling of wild creatures' coming across the open space of Tower Hill from the Lion Tower, and striking a chill of horror into his young soul that he could still evoke fifty years later, when Crusoe made his way along the western coast of Africa? And why should it always be 'by night' that Crusoe should hear these 'horrible Noises, and hideous Cryes and Howlings', unless Defoe was calling back some memory of his impressionable early years?[19]

Another disturbing experience occurred in broad daylight.

Not far to the north of the Foe home, a narrow passage ran eastwards from a place called Petty France to Bishopsgate churchyard. On the left-hand side lay a row of almshouses; on the right, behind a dwarf wall surmounted by a palisado, lay another churchyard, bounded on the far side by the City Wall.

In this narrow Passage stands a Man looking thro' the Palisadoe's into the Burying-Place, and as many People as the Narrowness of the Passage would admit to stop, without hindering the Passage of others; and he was talking mighty eagerly to them, and pointing now to one Place, then to another, and affirming, that he saw a Ghost walking upon such a Grave Stone there . . . I look'd earnestly every way, and at the very Moment, that this Man directed, but could not see the least Appearance of any thing; but so positive was this poor man, that he gave the People the Vapours in abundance, and sent them away trembling and frighted, till at length, few people that knew of it, car'd to go thro' that Passage; and hardly any Body by Night, on any Account whatever.[20]

The ghost was supposedly gesturing in a way that could be interpreted, in retrospect at least, as a warning of disasters to come; and so too with another strange encounter, with a man who ran about 'Naked, except for a pair of Drawers about his Waste, crying Day and Night . . . *"O! the Great and Dreadful God!"* and said no more, but repeated those Words continually, with a Voice and Countenance full of horror, a swift Pace, and no Body cou'd ever find him to stop, or rest, or take any Sustenance, at least that I cou'd ever hear of'. This was 'the famous Solomon *Eagle*', more correctly Eccles, an eccentric musician turned shoemaker and Quaker.[21]

The first of these disasters was one of the periodic outbreaks of bubonic plague which were then to be expected at least once in every generation, and which struck London a few months before Defoe's fifth birthday. If 1665 has remained in the public mind as *the* Plague Year, rather than, say, 1593 or 1625, this is not only because that year's visitation proved to be the last, as well as the most severe since the first one in the fourteenth century, but also because we have several vivid accounts of its horrors. Two of these, *Due Preparations for the Plague*, and the more famous *Journal of the Plague Year*, were to come from Defoe's own pen many years later, in 1722;[22] but they can contain few childish memories, for the Foe family was out of London throughout the plague.[23]

James Foe must already have had some experience of the plague, in the comparatively mild outbreak of 1648, when he had been an apprentice in London, and also perhaps in the Mediterranean ports in the early 1660s. Convinced that 'the best preparation for the Plague is to run away from it', he sent his family out of town while the outbreak was still confined to the western outskirts of the City, and before the first plague burial in his own parish on 29 June. Though he still had 'several Friends and Relations in *Northamptonshire*, whence our Family first came from; and particularly . . . an only Sister in *Lincolnshire*, very willing to receive and entertain' his family, he sent them instead 'into *Buckinghamshire*, or *Bedfordshire*, to a retreat he had found out there'.[24] The first place reached on passing out of Bedfordshire into Buckinghamshire on the great post road from London to Chester, was Little Brickhill, a place sufficiently in Defoe's mind, in the very year in which he wrote his Plague books, for him to make it the scene of one of the main incidents in *Moll Flanders*.[25] It may have been on this journey that he passed through a plague-stricken town with a bunch of rue in his mouth to preserve him from infection.[26] James Foe remained a little longer in London, no doubt for business reasons; and when his brother Henry refused to abandon his saddlery shop, he left the key of his own house with him. Before rejoining his family, he first 'went away to Dorking in *Surry*', to attend the funeral of Lawrence Marsh, buried there on 14 July, and then 'fetch'd a Round' to be reunited with his wife and children in their country retreat.[27]

Even forty miles from London the Foes could not escape from the shadow of the visitation, and Little Brickhill, a stage on the post road, would have been particularly sensitive to reports from the capital; the plague certainly reached St Alban's, the next stage on the road to London. Defoe recalled how many of the poorer folk wandered out of London on foot, and crept into sheds and barns, or built themselves huts in the woods and fields, depending on the charity of the country people, who would carry them food but set it at a distance. If they died, 'the Country People would go and dig a Hole at a Distance from them, and then with long Poles, and Hooks at the End of them, drag the Bodies into these Pits, and then throw Earth in from as far as they could cast it to cover them; taking notice how the Wind blew, and so coming to that Side which the Sea-men call *to-Wind-ward*, that the Scent of the Bodies might blow from them'. When Defoe wrote, 'I know of so many that perish'd thus, and so exactly where, that I believe I could go to the very Place and dig their Bones up still', he is clearly forgetful of the supposed author, 'A Citizen who continued all the while in London'; and here, if anywhere in his *Journal*, writes from his own direct experience.[28]

James Foe still had his living to get. He had left behind him in London a 'warehouse' full of high-crowned women's hats, intended for export;[29] and at Little Brickhill he would be well placed to deal with the straw-hat makers of Bedfordshire and Hertfordshire. He also had contacts in the Leicester area;[30] and perhaps, like his son twenty years later, was concerned in the export of hosiery. Though the plague soon brought London's trade to a halt, he could at first continue his business through the outports, until many of these also became infected. The strictures in the *Journal of the Plague Year* upon the 'rash and foolish conduct' of those who, as soon as the Plague began to abate, 'flocked to Town without Fear or Forecast', suggests that the Foes remained out of town until well into the following year.[31] On 2 February 1666, when old John Levitt lay dying in London, though not apparently of the plague, he appointed as executor, not his former apprentice, James Foe, but the latter's saddler brother. John Levitt of Tower Hill, 'tallowchandler', was buried at St Botolph Aldgate on 11 April; and probate of his will was granted to Henry Foe on 4 May.[32]

The Foes had not been back in London for many months before 'God's terrible voice in the City' delivered yet another dramatic judgment upon the manifold sins of the capital.[33] In the small hours of 2 September a fire broke out in a baker's shop in Pudding Lane. By morning it had spread to neighbouring property, and was already completely out of hand. Fanned by an easterly wind, it spread rapidly through the heart of the City and raged for three days before its appetite was sated. The Foe home, in the north-eastern part of the old walled City did not at first lie directly in the path of the flames. But young Daniel, not yet quite six years old, was never to forget what he saw.

I remember very well what I saw with a sad heart, though I was but young; I mean the Fire of London. That all endeavours having been fruitlessly used to abate the fire, the people gave it over, and despairing citizens looked on and saw the devastation of their dwellings with a kind of stupidity caused by amazement. If any people, still forward for the public good, made any attempts, the water they cast on it made it rage with the more fury and boil like a pot; till scorched with the flames from every side and tired with fruitless labour, they gave over, as others had done before them . . . and the whole City was laid in ashes.[34]

Defoe has preserved one more precise detail of these days. 'Did the Magistrates of London', he asked, 'complain of breaking down the Walls of Moorfields and of People's Trespass in carrying their goods thither, to save them from the Flames, when the City was on Fire?'[35] No doubt, as the Fire edged more slowly northwards toward the Foe home, James Foe removed his household goods and the contents of his 'warehouses' into Moorfields, which lay only a few hundred yards to the north beyond the City wall. The scene there was viewed by both Evelyn and Pepys, the latter finding the fields 'full of people, and poor wretches carrying their goods there, and everybody keeping his goods together by himself; (and a great blessing it is to them that it is fair weather for them to keep abroad night and day)'.[36] The Foes may have interpreted the fine weather as a divine providence; and still more providential must have seemed the preservation, both of Henry Foe's home, which was never seriously threatened, and of their own as well — rented though these houses were. Almost the whole of Coleman Street, including the parish church of St Stephen, was reduced to ashes; and so were most of the narrow alleyways which ran off it on the eastern side. The greater part of Swan Alley was destroyed, but the Fire stopped a few score yards from their door.[37]

Such general disasters as the Plague and the Fire cried out for interpretation. The latter could of course be laid at the doors of the Roman Catholics, the universal scapegoats of the age; and in retrospect Defoe was sometimes inclined to go along with this. But the Foes are more likely to have looked on both disasters as judgments of God for national sins. The same could be said of the panic and humiliation of June 1667, when

Londoners could hear the gunfire of Dutch ships which sailed up the Medway, sank or captured several English warships, and were allowed to sail away unmolested. But little time was wasted in morbid self-examination. The rebuilding of the City was undertaken with vigour; and Defoe later recalled how 'there was never known such a trade all over England for the time as was in the first seven years after the plague and the fire of London'.[38] James Foe must have shared in the national resilience and prosperity; and his son found an endless source of interest in the renewed bustle of the City.

'Two or three Years after the Plague was ceas'd', about 1668 or 1669, when building was in progress at the upper end of Hand Alley in Bishopsgate Street, the workmen digging the foundations stumbled on the site of a plague pit, some of the bodies 'remaining so plain to be seen, that the Womens Sculls were distinguish'd by their long Hair, and of others, the Flesh was not quite perished'.[39] This macabre spectacle made a profound impression on the mind of the young boy; and other plague pits, still recognisable by the mounds of earth which covered them, became objects of morbid fascination to him, so that he could remember their exact locations to the end of his life. One of these, within the churchyard of St Botolph Aldgate, contained the remains of many of his uncle Henry's neighbours. Diagonally opposite the church, on the corner of the Minories, stood the Pye Tavern; and his uncle once told him how during the plague year it had been frequented by 'a dreadful Set of Fellows' who met there every night and 'behaved with all the Revelling and roaring extravagances as is usual for such People to do at other Times', blasphemously deriding the worshippers going into the church and even the mourners who followed the dead-cart. But the tale had a typically Puritan moral; before the pit was filled up, every one of the jeerers had died of the plague and been thrown into it.[40] This and other stories told him by his uncle, of the grim happenings in the Minories, Houndsditch, Aldgate High Street, Harrow Alley or Moses and Aaron Yard, were to remain with him all his life. It was largely through his uncle's eyes that he came to picture the Plague; and when he came to write his *Journal of the Plague Year* it was natural for him to put it into his uncle's mouth, and to add the initials 'H.F.' at the end. The records do not show whether Henry Foe, like 'H.F.', actually served for three weeks as an 'examiner', responsible for shutting up infected houses; but they do show that he was of sufficient standing to serve a year or two later as a Collector for the Royal Aid.[41]

He heard other stories about the Plague in Swan Alley and the other narrow alleys round his own home from 'honest *John Hayward*', a member of the Merchant Taylors' Company who had fallen on hard times and become in some way 'dependent' on James Foe, who perhaps found him casual work. By this time he was sexton of the parish of St Stephen Coleman Street; but during the Plague he had been only under-sexton, his duties including those of grave-digger and bearer, while his wife Dorothy had served as a plague nurse, preserving herself from infection by washing her hair in vinegar, and being commended by the parish for her honesty. Hayward told young Daniel stories of how families, shut up because of the plague, had managed to escape the vigilance of the watchmen, and of how those who died of the plague in the narrow alleys to the east of Coleman Street had to be carried out by the bearers because the dead-carts could not pass. The western parts of these alleys, destroyed by the Fire, were now being rebuilt a good deal wider — so that even today the limits of the Fire can be traced by the sudden narrowing of the alleys. It was from Hayward too that he heard the story of the sleeping piper who had been given 'a little more Victuals than ordinary at a Public House in *Coleman-street*' and had then been 'laid all along upon the Top of a Bulk or Stall, and fast a sleep, at a Door in the Street near *London-Wall*, towards *Cripplegate*' alongside the body of a plague victim. He had been taken up for dead and thrown into the cart. When they arrived at the pit, the piper had awoken and terrified the bearers by sitting up and calling out, '*Hey! where am I?*' Hayward, recovering himself, said, '*Why, you are in the dead-cart, and we are a-going to Bury you*'. To which the piper replied, 'But I an't dead though, *am I?*'[42]

Another prominent figure in the *Journal of the Plague Year* is 'H.F.'s' friend Dr Heath, probably to be identified with Geoffrey Heath, barber-surgeon of Coleman Street, perhaps introduced into the story as the only medical man known to Defoe at this early period of his life.[43] He may have treated young Daniel for childish ailments, but perhaps also visited the Foe household in connection with his mother's failing health. The absence of any younger children points in this direction, unless Alice Foe was a good deal older than her husband. A visit to Bath to take the waters would explain his own statement (in 1724) that 'I have my self drank the waters of Bath above fifty years ago';[44] and he recalled an incident on the journey:

> I remember some Gentlemen Travailling in a Stage Coach to the *Bath* fell out so foolishly, and so Ungentlemanly, that they could not forbear laying Hands upon one another in the Coach — A Lady . . . interpos'd . . . if you struggle here, you will overturn the Coach . . . the thing was Rational, the Gentlemen made a Truce, and agreed till they came to their Inn, and then they fought it out.[45]

In manhood Defoe normally travelled on horseback; and it is difficult to imagine him leaving it to a lady to intervene in the quarrel. It sounds as though the would-be peacemaker was his mother, travelling with her two young children as she had done a few years before when fleeing from the plague.

Alice Foe was still alive in 1667, but almost certainly dead by 1671.[46] Some time before the last Dutch War of 1672, and most likely 'about the year 1668 (when I first knew the place)', Defoe spent much of one winter at Ipswich, on a visit possibly connected with his mother's last illness and death.[47] His early memories centred round the masters of the great collier ships which then played a big part in the Newcastle coal trade; and he probably left London by the tradesman's entrance, the River Thames, aboard one of those same collier ships on its way to be laid up for the winter. Slipping down the river on the ebb tide, through the reaches with which he was to become so familiar, they would pass Bugsby's Hole, Barking Creek, the Old Man's Head, Hope Point and Hole Haven, before reaching the open sea. With a favourable wind they would make land again within twenty-four hours, and enter Harwich harbour, formed by the confluence of the Stour and the Orwell, known to the seamen 'by no other names than Maningtre-Water and Ipswich Water'. Following the latter for twelve miles, they would reach Ipswich itself, 'upon the edge of the river, which taking a short turn to the west, the town forms, there, a kind of semi-circle, or half moon upon the bank of the river'.

During the winter months, the coal trade came virtually to a halt.

All this while, which was usually from Michaelmas to Lady Day, the masters liv'd calm and secure with their families in Ipswich; and enjoying plentifully what in the summer they got laboriously at sea, and this made the town of Ipswich very populous in winter; for as the masters, so most of the men, especially their mates, boatswains, carpenters, &c., were of the same place, and liv'd in their proportions just as the masters did.

In *Colonel Jack*, into which Defoe worked many of his early memories, there is an account of the robbing in Billingsgate of a collier master called *'Cullum*, or some such a Name'. This and other clues suggest that the family with which Defoe stayed was that of John Cullum, mariner and owner of shipping, who lived in a five-hearth house in the waterfront district of St Clements. His young family, the eldest of whom was about Defoe's age, consisted of a daughter and three sons, at least two of whom grew up to command ships of their own.[48]

Even in winter, when 'the ships are unrigged, the sails &c. carry'd ashore, the top-masts struck', it must still have been possible in this sheltered inland haven to spend a good deal of time on the water. Young Defoe found it 'a very agreeable sight to see, perhaps two hundred sail of ships, of all sizes . . . moor'd in the river, under the advantages and security of sound ground, a high woody shore, where they lie safe as in a wet dock'. With his new companions he could visit the shipbuilding yard at John's Ness; while further downstream there was Sir Samuel Barnardiston's decoy for wild ducks, and at Lavington Creek there were 'shoals, or hills rather', of mussels to be seen at low tide. Before long he must have come to 'smell of the tarr', and to have picked up for the first time the nautical jargon that came so readily to his pen in later life.

Next door to John Cullum in Wicks Bishop, in a smaller house of three hearths, lived his kinsman, Timothy Grimble, a mariner and a Quaker, whose house had at one time been used as a meeting place for the Friends.[49] Here may lie the origin of Defoe's interest in sea-going Quakers, shown in the 'old Quaking skipper' who appears in *The King of Pyrates*, and more fully developed in Friend William, Singleton's bosom companion, and one of the most highly individual of all his fictional characters.[50] It is tempting to speculate whether the Cullums and the Grimbles

were among his maternal relatives; but no evidence for this has
come to light. For whatever reason, Defoe showed a lifelong
involvement with the complexities of the colliery trade; and he
often revisited Ipswich, for which he showed a partiality and
affection greater than for any other provincial town.

Perhaps when Defoe returned from his first long visit to
Ipswich his mother was dead. The lack of a close mother-and-son
relationship for much of his childhood might explain the development of the self-sufficiency and initiative which were to be
such marked features of his personality, features that are
reflected and exaggerated in the upbringing of several of his
main fictional characters — Moll Flanders, Bob Singleton,
Colonel Jack — all brought up the hard way with no parental
affection or control at all. There seems to have been a time
when young Daniel ran loose a good deal on the streets with
boys of his own age. He recalled how 'Air will blow up a Bladder
and make it bound and dance, till all the Boys in the Street get
together to make a Foot ball of it, but with much footing and
tossing about, the sport grows dull, the Ball dirty and heavy,
and at last returns to its original nothing',[51] He learned how to
stand up for himself, and tells how, 'From a boxing English boy
I learnt this early piece of generosity, not to strike my enemy
when he is down'.[52] There may even be echoes of his early
pranks in *Colonel Jack* — scarcely petty crime, or sleeping
rough among the ashes of a glass-bottle house — but perhaps the
wild chases through the back lanes and alleys, and the meeting
place for the gang in the middle of Moorfields.

When Defoe was about ten years old his father moved to a
new home. In February 1669 he had still been living in Jones's
Rents; but by 1671 he was established in French Court, off the
north side of Threadneedle Street, in the parish of St Benet
Fink.[53] This was several hundred yards nearer the commercial
heart of the City, in an area newly rebuilt after the Fire. It
suggests too that James Foe's business was thriving; and it
probably also means that he had remarried, for he certainly had
a wife living there with him in 1678.[54] Defoe's relations with
his stepmother were probably far from cordial. 'There is not a
Name under the Sun', he tells us, 'that the very Heathen have
loaded with so many infamous Epithets as that of Stepmother.'[55]
His new domestic situation may have contributed to the secretive-

ness and duplicity which were to become such marked features of his complex personality. His father was to remain in French Court for a dozen years; but young Defoe may not have seen much of his new home, for he was to spend most of the next five years out of London.

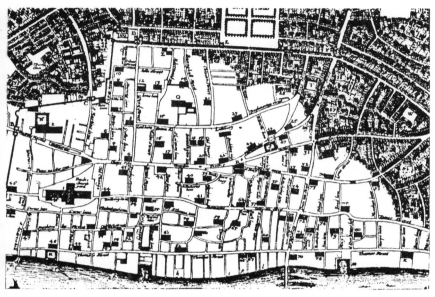

London after the Great Fire (*W. Hollar*)

3 A Boarding School for Boys

When James Foe 'went away to Dorking in Surry' to attend the funeral of Lawrence Marsh in July 1665, this was far from the end of his connection with the Marsh family or with Dorking.[1] Lawrence Marsh, only son of Roger Marsh, citizen and merchant tailor, descended from a prominent Wigan family, had settled in Dorking during the Commonwealth and Protectorate, acquiring, amongst other property, a large house of twelve hearths, later known as Shrub Hill, on the northern edge of the common of Cotmandene, on the eastern outskirts of the town. At that time he had been the leading figure in Dorking, and one of the two Surrey representatives in Barebones Parliament. A fellow member of this 'Parliament of Saints' had been Henry Colbron, a prosperous scrivener who, as 'Register of Crown Lands', had acted as estate agent when these were put up for sale. It must have been at the latter's house in Budge Row, in the London parish of St Antholin, that Marsh met Colbron's young kinswoman and established member of his household, Elizabeth Colbron. In 1655 she became his second wife and went to live with him at Dorking, where between 1656 and 1660 four sons were born. After surviving the Restoration apparently unscathed, Marsh died in 1665.

One of the bequests in his will was a gift of mourning rings to 'Cousen Foe and his wife'.[2] If James Foe himself had been related to the Marshes, so would have been his brother Henry; presumably then the actual blood relative was Alice Foe. The wills of Roger Marsh (1623, Lawrence's father), James Colbron (1647, Elizabeth's father) and Henry Colbron (1656) throw no light on the matter; but in his will of 1676 Henry Loxham, of Belgrave near Leicester, husband of one of Henry Colbron's sisters, left his watch to James Foe 'citizen of London'.[3] An echo of this relative occurs in *Colonel Jack*, whose supposed author accounts for his ill-gotten wealth by pretending that it was money saved while in the service of 'Sir Jonathan Loxham in Somersetshire'.[4] The family link was thus probably on the distaff side of the Marsh family; and if we could identify Elizabeth Marsh's mother, we might also be able to identify Alice Foe.

The widowed Elizabeth Marsh continued to live at Dorking with her four young sons until she too died in the autumn of 1671. Her will of 29 October named 'James Foe Citizen of London' as executor and guardian of her children.[5] Despite losses through bad debts, arrears of rent and the Fire of London, her estate was apparently worth some £3000. To administer an estate in these circumstances called for a man of substance, integrity and business acumen; and as recompense for his trouble James Foe was to have an annual allowance of £10 while his duties lasted, which would be for the next ten years. At a Court of the Manor of Dorking held on 14 November 1671, the youngest son, William Marsh, who by the local custom of Borough English inherited the customary lands, was admitted to them 'per Jacobum Foe gener(osum)'. The Steward of the Manor, Sir Edward Thurland, or his clerk, who thus incorrectly styled Defoe's father 'gentleman', must have been recording the impression he made on the Court.[6] His problems in administering the Marsh estate included involvement in a Chancery case in 1673, concerning a house in Chancery Lane on which Lawrence Marsh had ten years before advanced money on mortgage. More than once in the pleadings James Foe was referred to as 'citizen and merchant of London'.[7]

That Alice Foe was now dead seems likely from the fact that the four Marsh boys did not actually join the Foe household. Instead, their mother's will entrusted their 'keeping and governing . . . until such tyme as they are fitt to be put to some Trades or callings' to the wife of Mr John Alexander, merchant tailor, who lived in Budge Row next door to Henry Colbron's house where she had lived before her marriage. The eldest son, Lawrence, came of age in 1677, and soon afterwards returned to live quietly at Dorking, where he died, unmarried and intestate, in 1710. The second son, James, was apprenticed in the Fishmongers' Company in 1672, but then disappears from view. John Marsh, the third son, also apprenticed in the Fishmongers' Company, to Paul Pindar in 1674, eventually settled down as a tradesman in the London parish of St Lawrence Jewry, marrying in 1683 and raising a family. He kept in touch with James Foe, who left him £20 in his will made in 1706. William Marsh, the youngest son, and almost exactly of an age with Defoe, entered the Inner Temple and became a lawyer's clerk. When in 1692 they were joint defendants in a law suit, Defoe described him as 'an antient acquaintance and familiar friend' with whom he had often done business.[8]

The four Marsh boys, on their mother's death, probably continued at first as boarders at the same Dorking school as they had previously attended, that kept by the Rev. James Fisher, an elderly Independent minister, who had been ejected at the Restoration from the Rectory of Fetcham, a few miles to the north. He now lived in a house of six hearths just outside Dorking, probably to the north-east, on a six-acre holding called Nyecrofts, running down from Pixham Lane to the River Mole immediately opposite Box Hill, and itself part of the Marsh property now in James Foe's care.[9] Perhaps because he was not entirely welcome at home, Defoe too was sent there about this time to school.

Not a great deal is known about Fisher. Walker, in his *Sufferings of the Clergy*, referred to him, on the strength of an incident attributed to him thirty years before in his Fetcham days, as 'one Fisher, a man of very mean character'. Calamy, in his *Nonconformist Memorial*, warmly denied this and, appealing to the reputation he left behind him in Dorking, wrote of his 'humanity and tenderness'.[10] Of his abilities as a schoolmaster little can be said. He was no doubt a good scholar, having been educated at Emmanuel College, Cambridge, when it was famous as a nursery of Puritan divines; and when he died in Dorking in 1691 at the age of 86 he still had notes which he thought it worth while to bequeath, and books in Latin and Greek to divide among his grandchildren.[11] Defoe acquired at best a mere smattering of Greek; but he must have spent a good while in the study of Latin. He kept Latin books in his library throughout his life, for he often embellished his title pages with a suitable text, perhaps chosen from Virgil or Juvenal; and even when writing at large, he sprinkled Latin tags over his pages, often inaccurately and sometimes ungrammatically. He was too impulsive and indifferent to accuracy ever to have made a real scholar. Nor does Fisher seem to have made a strong personal impression on his young pupil, a fact to which the difference in their ages must have contributed, for Fisher was in his late sixties when Defoe went to his school. But James Foe must have been satisfied, for he kept his son there for some five years.

Although Defoe tells us nothing of his actual schooling at Dorking, the drudgery of parsing and construing passing soon enough into oblivion, he retained to the end of his life vivid memories of Dorking itself and its surrounding countryside, of the leading local families, and of his own youthful escapades. Fifty years after leaving Dorking he described one of these that took place soon after the death of Elizabeth Marsh, when he was eleven years old.

Not far off of the town of Dorking in Surry, the people . . . entertained a notion . . . that a ghost walked in such a place; that she (for it was an antient lady lately dead) was seen hovering about a mansion-house which was left uninhabited for some time, that she would be up and down in the house very often in the daytime, making a rumbling and clattering noise; and in the night-time she walked in the neighbouring fields with a candle in her hand, and that though the wind blew ever so hard, it would not blow the candle out; that sometimes she would appear in the open field, sometimes up in the trees, and particularly, there was a little heath near Dorking called Cottman Dean, where it was said she was frequently seen.

There was a boarding-school for boys in that town, where there was in particular some roguish London boys, who contrived all this walking from the beginning to the end:— First, they got a small rope, and tying one end of it to an old chair which stood in an upper room of the house (for they had found means to get in and out of the house at leisure) they brought the other end of the rope down on the outside of the house in a private place where it could not easily be seen and by this they pulled the old chair up, and then let it fall again, and made a great noise in the house, so as it might easily be heard by the neighbours; then others boys of the same gang took care to call out to the old women in the next houses, that now they might hear the old lady a playing her pranks; and accordingly they would all assemble in the court-yard, where they could plainly hear it, but not one would venture to go up stairs. If any offered to go up a little way, then all was quiet again; but as soon as ever they retired, the rumbling would begin again. This was for the day.

In the night, one of those unlucky boys had gotten a dark lanthorn, which was a thing the country people did not understand, and with this he walked all about the orchard, and two or three closes near the house, sometimes showing the light on this side, and then his companions calling all the old women about 'em to see it, on a sudden the light would go out, the boy closing the lanthorn; and then he would run swiftly across the whole field, and show his light again on the other side. Now he would be up in a tree, then in the road, then in the middle of the heath; so that the country people made no more question, but that the old lady walked with a candle in her hand, than that they saw the light of it; and in a word it passed for an apparition as certainly as we, on the other hand, knew what knavery agitated it all.[12]

It is clear that the 'antient lady lately dead' was Elizabeth Marsh, though in fact she had only been in her forties. Her house on the eastern outskirts of Dorking is known, from a survey made in 1649, to correspond in every detail to the 'mansion-house' mentioned by Defoe; for not only were there 'next houses', but the property itself included an orchard and several closes, while the whole was 'bounded on the south-east by the Common called Cotman dean'.[13] One of the duties laid on James Foe as executor had been, after setting aside various articles of household linen, to sell the remaining household goods as soon as possible, to raise money to meet the immediate needs of the orphaned Marsh boys. This done, the house would be standing empty — except it seems for an unsaleable old chair — awaiting a tenant, and would meanwhile be a happy hunting ground for those 'roguish London boys'. It is not difficult to guess who was the boy with the lantern, and the ringleader in these pranks, already showing some of the characteristics which were to mark his later career: initiative, enterprise and a delight in passing off fiction as reality. The incident symbolises almost too neatly the role he was so often to play in the future.

Less than half a mile away, at the southern end of Cotmandene, stood a much larger mansion house with eighteen hearths, Deepdene, the residence of the Hon. Charles Howard, brother of the Duke of Norfolk, and joint Lord of the Manor of Dorking. Deepdene was famous for its remarkable garden, several times visited by John Evelyn — though he never came to Dorking while Defoe was there — and celebrated by John Aubrey, who wrote ecstatically after visiting it in July 1673 that 'the pleasures of the garden &c. were so ravishing I can never expect any Enjoyment beyond it but the Kingdom of Heaven'.[14] Defoe was specially impressed by the situation:

> The garden is so naturally mounded with hills, that it makes a complete amphitheatre, being an oblong square, the area about eighty yards by forty, and the hills impassably steep, serve instead of walls, and are handsomely planted with trees, whose tops rising one above another gradually, as the hill rises at their roots, make a beautiful green wall, of perhaps fifty or sixty foot high.[15]

The encircling hill consisted of a soft greensand into which Howard had dug a number of caves, one of which he used as a chemical laboratory. Though Defoe makes no mention of these, he describes a similar enterprise, probably begun in 1673 and nearing completion in 1676. 'At the south end, the antient possessor Mr Howard, by what we call a perforation, caused a vault or cave to be made quite through the hill, which came out into a fine vineyard, which he planted the same year, on the south side, or slope of the hill.' This must be the remote original of Crusoe's cave, on which 'I work'd daily two or three Hours at enlarging . . . and by Degrees work'd it on towards one Side, till I came to the Out-side of the Hill, and made a Door or Way out'.[16] Another account of the Deepdene 'perforation' describes how, when it was nearly complete, 'for want of arch or support the earth fell in near one end, which put an end to the design. The miners were come out to breakfast, so that nothing but their tools were covered.' Crusoe was to have a similar experience when 'a great Quantity of Earth fell down from the Top and one Side . . . if I had been under it I had never wanted a Grave-Digger'.[17] As for a vineyard, Crusoe had no need to plant one, for he found wild grapes in abundance.

Beyond Deepdene to the south lay the Homewood, 'a vale chiefly grown with furze', where there was 'neither town nor village for many miles . . . much less any gentlemen's houses, but vast quantities of geese and poultry'. These the cottagers brought on Thursdays to Dorking market; and in the early summer, 'whole horse-loads of strawberries' as well. Beyond this lay the Weald, or as Defoe called it, the Wild, 'in antient times so unpassable a wild, or overgrown waste, the woods so thick, and the extent so large . . . that it was the retreat for many ages of the native Britons, who the Romans cou'd never drive out'; and though most of the woods had been cut down, the country was 'wild still, and perhaps having the same countenance now in many places, as it had above a thousand years ago'.[18] Perhaps the London boy sometimes led a group of his companions through this wild country, as Bob Singleton was to do through darkest Africa; or wandered off alone, to gain his first feeling for the trackless wilderness, which was to bring Crusoe to his deserted island.

But the area which Defoe knew best was nearer at hand. When he came to write his *Tour through the Whole Island of Great Britain* fifty years later, he found less to say about some entire counties than about a five-mile stretch of the River Mole near Dorking.[19] About a mile upstream, to the east, lay Betchworth Castle, the medieval seat of Sir Adam Browne, joint Lord of the Manor of Dorking and Knight of the Shire for Surrey, a strong royalist described a few years later as 'vassal to the Duke of York'. Perhaps it was from Betchworth Castle that the latter used to hunt in the Homewood, according to Defoe, 'some of the largest stags to be seen in England'. Below here the Mole passed the Marsh property of Nyecrofts where Fisher's house and school most probably stood; and then took into it the Pippbrook from Dorking, with a large corn mill just above the confluence. Next, swinging north, it entered 'a kind of vale, as if parted to admit the river to pass' as it cut its way through the chalk of the North Downs. Here were the famous 'swallows', where some of the water made its way underground through the chalk. Defoe tells us of the 'many curious people', of whom John Aubrey in 1673 seems to have been one, who visited the spot, 'not doubting but they should see some wonderful gulph, in which a whole river should be at once as it were bury'd alive'. But Defoe knew better. As the river passed the Stomacher, the precipitous western face of Box Hill, 'the waters sink insensibly away, and in some places are to be seen (and I have seen them) little chanels which go out on the sides of the river, where the water in a stream not so big as would fill a pipe a quarter of an inch in diameter, trills away out of the river, and sinks insensibly into the ground'. At Burford, where the river 'runs cross the road which leads from Dorking to Leatherhead . . . it runs very sharp and broad, nor did I ever know it dry in the dryest summer in that place, tho' I liv'd in the neighbourhood several years. On the contrary, I have known it so deep, that waggons and carriages have not dared to go through.' Farther on, however, after losing still more water, 'so much has sunk away, that in a very dry summer the chanel, tho full of water in pits and holes, cannot be perceiv'd to run; but this must be, I say, in a very dry season, and still there is the chanel visible where it runs at other times fiercely enough'. We can follow the fourteen-year-old Defoe along the river bed in the exceptionally dry summer of 1675,[20] past Mickleham, where 'the river fetches a circuit round a park . . . belonging to Sir Richard Studdolph'. This was Norbury Park, where the Stidolphs had been established for several generations. Then as the river approached Leatherhead the waters began to return; and here they passed by Thorncroft, the estate of Sir Thomas Bludworth, a wealthy city merchant who had been Lord Mayor at the time of the Great Fire, and who had never been able to live down his supposed remark at the beginning of the outbreak, that 'it was nothing and they might piss it out'.

Of all the local gentry it was Charles Howard of Deepdene who interested Defoe most. A brother of the Duke of Norfolk, he was a Roman Catholic, an adherent of a faith whose doctrines and ceremonies Defoe had been taught to look on as absurd, and whose political influence was generally regarded as sinister. Roman Catholicism in the abstract represented the unknown threat to the fabric of society; and since the Gunpowder Plot, no villainy, from the Fire of London downwards, was too extravagant to lay at its door. Yet Howard was palpably an 'honourable and antient gentleman' — though not quite as ancient as Defoe imagined — who lived quietly and inoffensively, like the young Cromwell in Marvell's poem:

> In his private garden
> Reservèd and austere
> As if his highest plot
> To plant the bergamot.

There were two other Catholic gentlemen in Dorking, Augustine Belson, father and son, whose chief claim to notoriety was that both of them, according to Defoe, were over seven feet tall. Reduced thus to human terms, Popery seemed less menacing; and it may have been here in Dorking that Defoe's ambivalent attitude, if not to Roman Catholicism, at least to Roman Catholics, had its origin.[21]

It was estimated that in 1676 the parish of Dorking contained 1000 who conformed to the Church of England, 200 Protestant Nonconformists, and 18 Papists.[22] In this and other ways, it was a microcosm of England, a stable community in which it must have been easier to grasp the elements of English society than in the anonymous fluctuating throng of London. Although it contained fewer than 2000 souls, all four of the recognised denominations of Dissenters were represented, and there were meetings in the town for at least three of these. Figures for 1669, which must also have included many who came from outside the parish, show that 100 Independents attended for worship at the house of Defoe's schoolmaster, James Fisher; at Westcott, at the other end of the town, no fewer than 300 Presbyterians worshipped under the Rev. John Wood, 'a grave, solid and judicious divine, who brought forth fruit in his old age'; 50 Baptists met at the house of John Barnard, a miller; and there was also an unspecified number of Quakers.[23]

It was not only worshippers who came from a distance; for under the heading of 'heads and teachers' there was listed as an assistant at Fisher's services, 'that frantick prophet' Christopher Feake, who travelled a dozen miles from his home at Chipstead. A younger contemporary of Fisher at Emmanuel College, he had emerged during the Commonwealth and Protectorate as a leader of the Fifth Monarchy Men, who interpreted the political convulsions of the age as heralding the second coming of Christ to reign with his Saints on earth: Feake's eloquence had won him the fanatical devotion of his followers; but he had always managed not to get involved in any actual acts of violence. Since the Restoration he had lived at Chipstead, but had also built up a personal following in Dorking. After spending six months in the Gatehouse Prison in 1664 he had avoided further clashes with the authorities.[24] As he grew older his earlier hopes may have faded, but his was an unquiet spirit that could not rest; and no doubt young Defoe heard from him much fiery and heady stuff, reflected fifty years later in the peroration of *The Serious Reflections of Robinson Crusoe*, where he wrote of the age when 'Heaven beats the drum itself and the glorious legions from above come down on purpose to propagate the work, and reduce the whole world to the obedience of King Jesus — a time which some tell us is not far off, but of which I have heard nothing in all my travels and illuminations, no, not one word'.[25]

The present was a time for obedience to King Charles, though not an uncritical one. It would be wrong to imagine Defoe growing up in a kind of rural paradise, remote from the tensions of national life. In London during his holidays, and at Dorking too — only a short day's ride from the City — he must have heard many anxious discussions about the issues, then beginning to emerge, which closely affected the mercantile class, and which were to dominate the political scene for most of his life. It is clear that even before he was in his teens Defoe had begun to take a precocious interest in politics; and from his later writings it is possible to piece together an almost continuous retrospective running commentary, from the beginning of the year 1672 onwards, on public events as seen through the eyes of the Dissenters.

On 2 January there took place the famous stop on the Exchequer, when the assets of the goldsmith-bankers of Lombard Street were suddenly frozen. In Defoe's words:

> On a sudden, like a clap of thunder, K. Charles shut up the Exchequer, which was the common centre of the over-plus cash these great bankers had in their hands. What was the consequence? Not only Lombard-street stood still as if they had been thunderstruck. The very report of having money in the Exchequer brought a run upon the goldsmiths that had no money there, as well as those that had; and not only Sir Robert Vyner, Alderman Backewell, Farringdon, Forth and others broke and failed, but several were ruined who had not a penny of money in the Exchequer, and only sunk under the rumour of it; that rumour bringing a run upon the whole street, and giving a check to the paper-credit that was run up to such an exorbitant heighth before.[26]

The seeds of distrust between City and Court had been sown. Defoe wrote that 'the Court envy'd the city's greatness, and the citizens were ever jealous of the Court's designs'; and no doubt echoing the talk he had heard as a boy, he counted the stop on the Exchequer among the 'fatal steps the Court took to humble the City'. Though he misjudged the King's motives, he was right in saying that the move 'turn'd to the discredit of the Court party'; for, 'after this, who would have lent King Charles II fifty pounds on the credit of his word and bond?'. Sir Robert Viner, the King's banker, who had advanced nearly a third of the £1,300,000 frozen in the Exchequer, still thought it worth while to court the royal favour, and went ahead with his plan to erect at his own expense in the Stocks Market, near the new Foe home, an equestrian statue of Charles II trampling Cromwell. It was formally unveiled on 29 May, and Defoe may have seen it for the first time when he returned from Dorking for his summer holidays.[27] Soon afterwards, when the King's mistress, Louise de Keroualle (later Duchess of Portsmouth) gave birth to a son on 29 July, Defoe tells us that a pillion appeared behind the figure of the King, with a note attached: 'Gone for a midwife.'[28]

Meanwhile Charles had made a bid for the support of the Dissenters. On 15 March he had issued his Declaration of Indulgence, dispensing with the penalties laid down in the Conventicle Act, in the case of dissenting ministers who were granted licences to conduct their own services. Both the leading Dorking Nonconformists obtained licences: Wood, the Presbyterian, on 11 April, and Fisher, the Independent, on 1 May.[29] Before long however many of the Dissenters were growing uneasy. Two days after issuing the Declaration of Indulgence, Charles had declared war on the Dutch; and for the third time in less than a quarter of a century the two Protestant maritime powers were fighting to assert their mastery of the waters that lay between them. On 28 May de Ruyter attacked the English fleet in Southwold Bay where, in Defoe's words, 'not to be too partial to ourselves, the English fleet was worsted'.[30] But this time England was fighting in alliance with France; and on land the French troops carried all before them. Though Defoe in later years was often inaccurate about the dates of historical events within his own memory, he never made any mistake about this campaign. 'Whoever looks back to the Year 1672' was a characteristically confident introduction to a comment on how the French troops, advancing down the Rhine, had by the end of the summer occupied, wholly or in part, five of the seven Dutch provinces.[31] The achievements of Louis XIV were beginning to dazzle the whole of Europe; and Defoe later recalled how, 'in a Medal struck in the Year 1672, the King is represented in a Chariot of the Sun, running his race round the World'.[32] In August an enraged mob at the Hague brutally murdered John de Witt, the Grand Pensionary who had conducted their affairs for so long, and his brother Cornelis. But a new national hero was emerging, the young William of Orange, whose name Defoe must now have heard for the first time. Appointed first Captain-General and then Stadholder, he breathed new life and courage into the Dutch forces, by breaching the dykes to create a water-line to protect the vital coastal provinces of Zeeland and Holland. An irresistible swing of public opinion was soon under way in England, and many began to feel that we were fighting on the wrong side. Charles's association with the Sun-King was looked on with increasing suspicion. Though the Treaty of Dover by which he agreed to declare himself a Roman Catholic remained a secret, sensitive political nostrils were beginning to scent a whiff of incense in the air. The King's brother, James, Duke of York, the heir to the throne, was now openly attending mass. Was the Declaration of Indulgence perhaps simply the first step towards not merely the toleration of Roman Catholicism, but its establishment and the destruction of parliamentary liberties? The equation of 'popery and slavery' was becoming a commonplace. When the King recalled Parliament in February 1673 to obtain further supplies for the war, the Commons insisted on dealing first with the Declaration of Indulgence.

Defoe referred more than once to the part played in this matter by 'that truly English Roman, Mr Alderman Love, Member of Parliament for many years, and generally chosen with the most unanimous Consent of Voices that ever was known for the City of London'. He was, Defoe tells us, 'the first Man in the House (tho' a Dissenter) who mov'd against it', saying, 'I hope the Dissenters understand their Liberty as English Men better than to accept of it in an Illegal Manner'.[33] Love was in fact a family connection of the Foes; for his sister had married Nicholas Wildbore, a London citizen who came from the same corner of rural England as the Foes, and whose father, Randall Wildbore of Glinton, had been a 'beloved friend' and probably a relative of Defoe's uncle Daniel Foe.[34] Though there is no evidence of any direct contact between James Foe and the more eminent William Love, the latter was obviously greatly admired in the Foe household.

Those who suspected the Court of favouring Roman Catholicism now passed to the counter-attack. Not content with the withdrawal of the Indulgence, they introduced in March a Bill 'for preventing dangers which may happen from Popish recusants', by imposing a sacramental test on all civil and military office holders, to be backed up by a declaration against transsubstantiation. This was to become famous as the Test Act. Defoe gave a long account of how the Court tried to persuade Love to oppose the Bill on behalf of the Dissenters; but he refused, on the understanding that the promoters would introduce another Bill to exempt Dissenters from the penalties of the Act.[35] After one such Bill had been stifled in the Lords, another was introduced in February 1674; but by this time Love was becoming suspicious of the good faith of some of those he had helped in the previous year:

> *For what, says he, is this Test made? To convert us you cannot pretend, the Papists are the Pretence: But that is Expos'd, by refusing to Confine it to such; and if it be against the Dissenters, 'tis to Exclude them from their Birthright, and Rob the Government of their Service.*[36]

Whether this measure would have fared any better than its predecessor we cannot tell, for it was foiled by a prorogation, and never revived.

Another interesting comment on public affairs concerns an incident a year or two later when, on 29 December 1675, the King, anxious about the growth of hostile public opinion, issued an abortive proclamation suppressing coffee-houses; 'upon which', wrote Defoe, 'Dr Wild made his famous Verses which ended thus:

> Then Charles thine Edict against Coffee recall,
> There's ten times more Treason in Brandy and Ale'.[37]

These lines are the last of eight, said to have been added as an afterthought to Andrew Marvell's *Dialogue between two Horses*, which began to circulate at the end of the previous November.[38]

Defoe's attribution to 'Dr Wild', whether correct or not, is intriguing. He must have meant the fat, gouty and witty Robert Wilde, who had been ejected in 1662 after serving for sixteen years as minister at Aynhoe, the Northamptonshire village from which William Love had originally come. Even more curiously, one of Wilde's poems had been 'The Tragedy of Christopher Love', the Presbyterian minister executed for his part in a royalist plot, one of whose mourning rings was to come into Defoe's possession. There is however no indication that Christopher and William Love were related.[39]

Of Defoe's family life during his school days, and of his personal experiences when away from Dorking, next to nothing is known. At some time during the Dutch War he saw at Harwich '100 sail of men of war and their attendants, and between three and four hundred sail of collier ships, all in this harbour at a time';[40] and this suggests another visit to Ipswich by sea. The sight of the graves in that town of some of the 600 seamen killed in the sea battle off Southwold must have helped to bring home the realities of war to him;[41] but he probably felt more keenly the loss of Timothy Grimble, the sea-going Quaker, 'drowned in the East Land' in October 1674.[42] The biggest shadow over his schooldays may have been the illness and death of his uncle, Henry Foe, the saddler, who was buried at St Botolph Aldgate on 28 February 1675. Though only in his middle forties, he must have lain physically helpless, perhaps after a stroke, for the best part of a year. He left no written will; but the probate court accepted instead a memorandum to the effect that about 19 April 1674, when 'sick of the sickness whereof he died', he had by word of mouth appointed his brother James Foe as his executor and sole heir.[43] This inheritance, whatever it may have amounted to, does not seem to have been enough to induce Defoe's father to alter his way of life, for he continued to live and trade quietly in French Court.

It was probably during the summer of 1676 that Defoe, still at Fisher's school near Dorking, became involved in a remarkable incident. A few miles to the north-east across the Downs lay the pleasant village of Epsom, whose medicinal wells, discovered a few decades before, were now becoming a centre of attraction for the more rakish elements of Charles II's Court. Defoe describes how it had become the custom for the gentry to travel on Sunday afternoons from Epsom to Box Hill, to 'divert or debauch' in the box-woods. At the very top of the hill, within sight of Fisher's school and barely half a mile away across the river, stood a Great Beech, beneath which a little cave had been fitted out by a Dorking vintner as a place of entertainment for these Sunday visitors. Soon the place became like a little fair, and 'it was very offensive, especially to the best governed people'. After this had gone on for two or three years, and complaints 'alledging the revelling, and indecent mirth that was among them, and on the Sabbath day too', had failed to secure any redress from the local justices, 'a certain set of young men, of the town of Dorking, and perhaps prompted by some others', blew up the whole place with gunpowder one Saturday night; and so secret was it kept, that upon the utmost enquiry, it cou'd never be heard or found out who were the persons that did it'.[44] Where else in Dorking, except among the Dissenters, could a 'set of young men' be found so full of moral indignation? And who can the 'others' have been who 'prompted' this miniature gunpowder plot, unless it was their ministers, and especially the fiery Feake, whose Sabbath route between Chipstead and Dorking took him through the midst of all the sacriligious revelling? And can we believe that young Defoe was sleeping quietly in his bed while all this was going on? In later life he showed a particular interest in such explosions, culminating in a really spectacular one in *Captain Singleton*, involving not only a cave beneath a hollow tree, but considerable bloodshed as well.[45]

One final local incident recalled by Defoe took place when a 'sudden hasty land flood' caused the River Mole to overflow, and Sir Adam Browne's son Ambrose recruited 'a little troop of the young fellows and boys of the town' to improvise a fish-trap. They built up the bank between the river and a depression which lay near it in the fields, probably just upstream from Burford, and then camped nearby for two nights till the flood drained away through the porous soil, leaving vast numbers of fish stranded, having no way to swim back into the river. The venture, which was profitable as well as enjoyable, was perhaps the start of Defoe's lifelong interest in the commercial possibilities of the fisheries. He places the incident in the year 1676, 'in the month of October or thereabouts'; and there were in fact exceptionally heavy rains in that month, Ralph Josselin recording on the 8th: 'Some places preacht not, it was so wett, I inter-

mitted not.'[46] The accuracy of Defoe's memory suggests that
the date may have had some special significance for him; and it
was probably at this time that he left Fisher's school to enter
on 'a new scene of life'. His father had been apprenticed at
fourteen, and two of the Marsh boys at fifteen. The fact that
Defoe had now reached sixteen without any such formal entry
into trade confirms that he had been 'set aside' for the 'sacred
employ' of the Christian ministry. From what can be gleaned of
his activities, it seems doubtful whether he ever really had a
vocation; but he must in some ways have been an outstanding
student, penetrating, original, and with an insatiable intellectual
curiosity. It was time for him to move on to something more
than Fisher could provide.

4 A Young Gentleman of Prompt Parts

The Universities of Oxford and Cambridge were closed to Dissenters; but the latter, anxious to ensure the continuity of their ministry, had already begun to improvise their own establishments for higher education. By the middle 1670s there were no fewer than four within a few miles of London; and it was to one of these, that kept by Charles Morton at Newington Green, that Defoe was sent towards the end of 1676, soon after his sixteenth birthday.[1] Morton had been a scholar of Wadham College, Oxford, where he had shown a special aptitude for mathematics, coming under the influence of John Wilkins, later Bishop of Chester, best known for his part in the foundation of the Royal Society. Morton too was interested in the development of science, though his only known contributions to scientific knowledge are a paper which he communicated to the Royal Society, on the use of sea sand in Cornwall to improve the soil, and a small book to expound his theory that swallows winter on the moon. Ejected from his living of Blisland in Cornwall in 1662, he eventually settled near London, and in 1672 had been licensed to preach at his own house at Kennington in Surrey. He can hardly have established his Academy at Newington Green before 1673, some three years before Defoe went there.[2]

We have two valuable witnesses to the methods used at what was perhaps the most remarkable educational establishment in England: Defoe himself, who was probably there from 1676 to 1679 or early 1680;[3] and Samuel Wesley, who attended from 1680 or 1681 until 1683, before conforming to the Church of England, removing to Oxford University, and eventually becoming Rector of Epworth in Lincolnshire and father of the more famous John and Charles Wesley.[4] In Wesley's time there were some 40 or 50 students, lodged in two houses, 'having annexed a fine Garden, Bowling Green, Fish-pond, and within a Laboratory, and some not inconsiderable Rarities, with Air Pumps, Thermometers, and all sorts of Mathematical Instruments'. Although the chief purpose of the Academies was to train up a succession of ministers, Morton clearly aimed at giving a general rather than a narrowly theological education. His establishment attracted a number of sons of wealthy men, even a few scions of the nobility, 'sent thither to avoid the Debaucheries of the Universities', though there were still one or two who were 'sufficiently remarkable' in that respect. Though there can have been only limited opportunities for riotous living in Newington Green itself, the students no doubt joined in the social life of London, less than three miles away, according to their tastes. Wesley's account mentions only boarders, but the location of the Academy suggests an effort also to attract Londoners who would live at home. Whether Defoe travelled daily from French Court or boarded at Newington Green is really immaterial, for Morton clearly had little control over the movements of his pupils in their spare time; for, to quote Wesley again, 'Tutors having no power, cou'd use but little discipline'. Whether for this reason, or because his political thinking was ahead of its time, Morton's students enjoyed 'a sort of democratical government', with 'laws carry'd by the Balet', and the power to impose 'pains and mulcts' on those who broke them.[5]

The organisation of the curriculum presented an equally difficult problem. Defoe implies that the normal course lasted three years, though those actually intending to enter the ministry spent longer on their studies; while Wesley's comment on 'a Distinction of the Faculties . . . whether Law, Divinity, Physick, or what Else' implies a variety of courses to meet the individual needs and abilities of the students.[6] Yet Morton seems to have run the place single-handed; for when forced to abscond for a while in 1683 to escape an ecclesiastical writ, Wesley wrote of his 'absenting himself from us, and leaving the *Senior* Pupils to instruct the *Junior*'.[7] Master of many disciplines though he was, he could only have found time to meet the varied needs of his students by leaving them to spend most of their time in directed private study and mutual education. Once again, Morton seems to have turned administrative difficulties to educational advantage.

Another handicap which the Academies suffered, in comparison with the ancient Universities, was the lack of adequate libraries.[8] Yet this did not stop Defoe from developing into a voracious reader; and it was probably at this stage of his life that he acquired the habit of buying books for himself. It is striking how often he shows himself familiar with newly published works; and the extensive library he built up throughout his life was for use rather than for show. His interests were wide. Books of travel in the remote and still little known parts of the world opened up new vistas to him, while history added a new dimension to his vicarious experience. He once wrote of reading an historical work with 'exceeding Delight', and even claimed to have read every history that had ever appeared in the English language, as well as many in French.[9] He found heroes in earlier generations, notably Raleigh and Gustavus Adolphus; he read avidly of the history of the Turks or of ancient Rome, or of anything which would help to fill the gap between the world's earliest ages, as portrayed in the Bible, and the very different world in which he was growing up. The influence of such reading upon his own later writings is plain. Puritan devotional literature must also have figured prominently in his reading; and recent research has traced his debt to spiritual autobiographies and conduct manuals.[10] Yet he cannot be fitted convincingly into any literary tradition. Though few writers knew the Bible as well as he did, its language finds remarkably few echoes in his work; and the same can be said of *Pilgrim's Progress*, for which he expressed great admiration, and no doubt read as soon as it was published in 1678. As a writer, as in other respects, he was to be largely a self-made man.

He himself gave the main credit to his tutor; for Morton was a pioneer in the stress which he laid on the use of the English language at a time when the Universities still looked on Latin as the indispensible key to all knowledge. As well as giving his own lectures in English, he also supplied his pupils with English 'drafts' of contemporary works published in Latin. Here again, Morton may have been responding to the shortage of books, or to the limitations of his pupils' grasp of Latin; but his policy had a more positive side:

> He had a class for eloquence, and his pupils declaim'd weekly in the English tongue, made orations, and wrot epistles twice every week upon such subjects as he prescrib'd for them or

upon such as they themselves chose to write upon. Sometimes they were ambassadors or agents abroad at foreign courts, and wrote accounts of their negotiations and recepcion in foreign Courts directed to the Secretary of State and sometimes to the sovereign himself.

Some times they were Ministers of State, Secretaries and Commissioners at home, and wrote orders and instructions to the ministers abroad, as by order of the King in Council and the like. Thus he taught his pupils to write a masculine and manly stile, to write the most polite English, and at the same time to kno' how to suit their manner as well to the subject they were to write upon as to the persons or degrees of persons they were to write to; and all equally free and plain, without foolish flourishes and ridiculous flights of jingling bombast in stile, or dull meanness of expression below the dignity of the subject or the character of the writer. In a word, his pupils came out of his hands finish'd orators, fitted to speak in the highest presence, to the greatest assem[b]lies, and even in Parliaments, Courts of Justice, or any where; and severall of them came afterward to speak in all those places and capascityes with great applause.[11]

Here Defoe slips so naturally from the discussion of spoken, to that of written English, and back again, that he scarcely distinguishes between them. In later life he seldom if ever had occasion to practise formal oratory; but his conversation must have been lively and persuasive, although unfortunately he had no Boswell to preserve it. His written English was apparently an exception to the saying that 'easy reading means damned hard writing'. Words always flowed effortlessly from his pen; and the cavils of purists at his grammatical inaccuracies are beside the point. Morton's training must have contributed greatly to Defoe's achievement of 'that Easie, Free Plainness which is the Glory of the *English* Tongue',[12] and to his mastery of a flexible and persuasive style, skilfully varied to suit his audience and his purpose, and never far removed from the natural rhythms of speech.

In his early fifties, when listing some of the scholars produced by Morton's Academy, Defoe rather surprisingly classed himself, together with Samuel Wesley, as a poet.[13] His poetic interests lay mainly among those who were his contemporaries, or nearly so, in his youth. To Chaucer, Spenser and Shakespeare he paid only lip service; while the verse of Jonson, Donne, Herbert and Herrick seems to have been unknown territory to him. He does show some knowledge of the work of three poets who had died in his childhood, George Withers, Sir John Denham and Abraham Cowley, and modelled some of his own verse on the latter's work in the manner of the so-called Pindaric Ode.[14] John Milton, too, had been dead for two years when Defoe moved to Newington Green. *Paradise Lost* certainly impressed him profoundly, but rather for the grandeur of its cosmology than for its poetic qualities.[15] But when in later life he quoted a line or two of verse, often inaccurately and presumably from memory, it was more often than not something that had appeared between 1675 and 1685. One of his heroes was 'old Andrew Marvel', the public-spirited MP for Hull who died in 1678, just too soon ever to be called a Whig; and it was his later satirical verse, directed against the Court, that Defoe knew, not the still unpublished metaphysical poetry on which his modern reputation rests.[16] But he could also appreciate 'the incomparable *Hudibras*', the last volume of which appeared in 1678, even though it was a satire on the Puritans; and a mention of 'Butler's garret' shows some knowledge of the poet's circumstances in the last years before his death in 1680.[17] His greatest admiration was for the Earl of Rochester, whose poetry he knew well and often quoted despite the vein of bawdy in it which he deplored, and despite his scandalous personal life — comparing him to Pan, 'half Man, half Goat'; and he more than once referred to his famous deathbed conversion in 1680.[18]

Defoe seems to have claimed personal friendship with one of the rising generation of poets; for he was probably the author of a tract which referred to 'the Sentiments of the Ingenious Mr. *John Oldham* (my particular friend) who says to this purpose

> *We have a good King, and he deserves laughter*
> *Who troubles himself with who shall come after.*'[19]

Oldham, some seven years older than Defoe, was employed from 1678 to 1681 as tutor to the grandson of Sir Edward Thurland, a retired judge living near Reigate in Surrey. The latter held the stewardship of a number of Surrey manors, including that of Dorking; and James Foe, as executor of Elizabeth Marsh and guardian of her four sons, must have had business with him until the youngest son came of age in 1681. Perhaps Oldham, whose tutorial duties were light, was occasionally used by Thurland in connection with routine legal business in London, or perhaps Defoe was sent down to Reigate on his father's behalf. In 1681 Oldham moved to become tutor to the son of Sir William Hickes at his residence at Ruckholt, near Leyton in Essex, a few miles from London, a large old house which Defoe found worth a mention in his *Tour*.[20] By that time Oldham had been taken up by the fashionable wits and poets of the day, but died of smallpox at Holme Pierrepont near Nottingham in December 1683 at the age of thirty.

Of Defoe's own early efforts as a poet, little can be said. His *Meditations*, dated 1681, which have survived in manuscript, show nothing of the influence of the poets whom he most admired—Butler, Marvel, Rochester; but these were probably far from typical, and may have differed as much from his adolescent efforts as they do from his first published poem, which did not appear until 1691.[21] It is unlikely that the world has lost any masterpieces, for he lacked the qualities of a true poet. Aesthetically he was limited. Though he claimed to have been 'no despicable performer on the viol and lute', he nowhere shows any knowledge of music or any feeling for it.[22] 'I had some pretension to judgment in pictures too', he tells us; yet his criteria seem to have been entirely representational. When he praised a picture, it was for the vivid portrayal of emotion by facial expression, or for its verisimilitude — 'I was perfectly deceived' was his highest compliment.[23] He seldom mentions a colour, and we are not even told whether Moll Flanders was fair or dark. Nor does he show any appreciation of formal values. He lived in an age of great architecture; yet though he was readily impressed by imposing buildings, he never discussed them with real understanding or discrimination. And he had so little to say about the innumerable fields where design is influenced by taste as well as function that his attitude is clearly philistine. He never attempted literary criticism. What he admired in contemporary poets was the sudden thrust of wit, encapsulated in a brief quotation; but he seems to have been deaf to the cumulative effect of a long passage, and insensitive to the architectural qualities of a whole poem. So in his own writing, he could produce the occasional happy flash or telling couplet, but could seldom sustain the effect: the longer the poem went on, the more its cutting edge was blunted; and his longest and most ambitious poem, *Jure Divino*, is almost unreadably tedious. 'One would think he rhymed in his sleep', John Dunton was to write of him;[24] and writing verse, of a kind, came almost too easily to him. But he never understood his own limitations as a poet.

It is unlikely that Defoe's youthful interest in poetry was directly stimulated by his tutor, for apart from producing some doggerel verses to assist his pupils' memory as part of his course in physics, Morton is not known to have taken any interest in poetry. In fact, it is curious how much of Defoe's intellectual development was independent of the formal instruction provided by the Academy. Languages are not mentioned among the options available; yet Defoe was later to claim that as a young man he had been 'pretty well master of five languages', apparently in addition to English. Latin he had learned as a boy. Of Italian, Spanish and apparently Dutch he probably picked up a smattering during his early travels.[25] But he was always anxious to air his knowledge of French; and it seems that he must at some time or other have had formal lessons, perhaps from Guy Miege, a Swiss Protestant from Lausanne, who had set up as a teacher of French and geography in Panton Street, Leicester Fields. At all events, in later years they were friends and collaborators, and this may have been what first brought them together.[26]

To what extent was Defoe influenced by Morton's special interest in mathematics and science? As far as the former is concerned, it would seem, not at all. His interest in mathematics was confined to commercial arithmetic, which he probably acquired from his father. 'I went some length in Physicks, or Natural Philosophy', he declared;[27] but he was never really a scientist. He must have been unusual, it is true, in having a barometer in his house in later years,[28] but he nowhere shows any understanding of or interest in scientific method. On the other hand his imagination was powerfully fired by the prevailing scientific view of the world. Perhaps stimulated by Morton's theory that swallows winter on the moon, he was fascinated by the phenomenon of migration — whether of the swallow (whose movements he came to know better than his master), the gannet,

the flying ant, the silkworm or, as he supposed, the herring.[29]
He ranged in his imagination to the moon, and beyond it into
the solar system and into inter-stellar space.[30] He was gripped
by the concept of the unity of nature, and of the physical
world as a 'great machine', controlled by the iron laws of 'cause
and consequence'. Throughout his life he was troubled by the
conflict, which he could never resolve, between this concept
and the ideas which he had absorbed from early childhood, of
direct divine control of the world, exercised by means of
providences and judgments. Sometimes he wrote as though
divine sovereignty lay in the initial creation and winding up of
the 'great machine', so that the whole course of nature and of
human history was simply the unrolling of a predetermined
divine purpose — though he seems to have been curiously little
troubled by predestination in the Calvinist sense, to salvation or
damnation. Sometimes it was simply that 'the age of miracles'
was past. Sometimes he held that the hand of God could still
make itself felt in the more recondite areas of nature — in the
remote regions where the winds were generated, or in the inner-
most recesses of the human soul, where God could speak through
dreams, premonitions or secret warnings.[31]

Among the courses Defoe followed at Morton's Academy was
one in logic.[32] Its influence is evident at a superficial level in
some of his favourite expressions — 'the nature of the thing',
'matters of fact', 'mathematical demonstrations' — from his
fondness for drawing a distinction between 'generals' and
'particulars' — and from his insistence on the unreasonableness
of being asked 'to prove a negative'. One practice common to
Morton and Defoe was to round off an argument by enumerating
and replying to possible objections. Defoe was not by nature a
systematic thinker; he tended to improvise, to digress and to
repeat himself. Yet he often attempted a formal analytical
approach to problems that was alien to his natural habit of
thought. Sometimes, for instance, he would begin by enumerating the points of his argument, but fail to maintain the pattern,
or even embark on another and conflicting series of numbered
points. On balance it is doubtful whether his training in logical
reasoning added to his powers as a polemicist by strengthening
the structure of his argument, or diminished them by imposing
a kind of strait-jacket upon the natural spontaneity of his ideas.

Another discipline covered at Morton's Academy was one

that it was dangerous for him to meddle with, but difficult to ignore, that of politics. The position of the Dissenters as a whole, and that of their academies in particular, was a delicate one. Their acquiescence in the withdrawal of the Indulgence and their support for the Test Act had left them legally exposed, though temporarily freed from the pressure of persecution, thanks to the moral obligation under which they had placed the Church of England. But this was a wasting asset. The memory of the execution of Charles I, and of Anglican clergy deprived of their livings, was still very much alive. Dissenting congregations could still be looked on as knots of potential rebels; and their academies were suspect, not only for invading the teaching monopoly of the ancient universities, but as hot-beds for the growth of republicanism and other dangerous political ideas. Morton understood very well the delicacy of his position. Even Wesley, when, as an Anglican convert, he wished to smear the academies, had to admit that Morton had set his face against seditious talk and scandalous libels against the government, 'telling us . . . That 'twas none of our business to Censure such as God had placed above us'.[33] It is true, he was the author of a book called *Eutaxia* — good government — which advocated a commonwealth in preference to a monarchy. But this remained in manuscript, now lost, and was shown only to his intimate friends. According to Samuel Palmer, in controversy with Wesley, it was 'a *Scheme* of Government drawn only for Diversion and Amusement in Imitation of Sir *Tho. Mores Utopia*', and 'does no more oppose the *English* Constitution, than a Game of *Chess* does most treasonably subvert and overturn the *King*, the *Queen*, and the *Bishops*'. For the use of his pupils he drew up a *System of Politicks*, which Palmer tell us,

. . . is exactly Correspondent with the *English Monarchy*. It secures the *Rights* and Honour of the Crown and the *Liberties* of the *Subject*. It requires from the Subject Love to the person of the King, a ready and cheerful Obedience to the Laws and a constant Assistance by dutiful Submission to Legal Taxes for the support of the *Crown*, and the *Laws*. It makes the Original of all Government to be the Institution of God, as indeed it is by our *Law*.[34]

Defoe, writing in 1704, was equally emphatic:

I have now by me the Manuscripts of Science the Exercise
and Actions of his School, and among the rest those of
Politicks in particular, and I must do that learned Gentleman's
memory the justice to affirm, that neither in his System of
Politicks Government and Discipline, or in any other the
Exercises of that School, was there any thing taught or
Encourag'd, that was Antimonarchical, or destructive to the
Government, or Constitution of *England*; and particularly
among the Performances of that School, I find a Declamation
relating to the benefit of a single Person in a Commonwealth,
wherein it is declar'd and Prov'd from History and Reason,
that Monarchy is the best government, and the best suited
to the Nature of Government, and the defence of Property
. . . [35]

Unfortunately neither Morton's *System of Politicks*, nor what
sounds very much like Defoe's own adolescent 'declamation',
has survived, so that it is difficult to tell exactly what influence
the political ideas of the master had upon his most famous
pupil. When Defoe began to expound his own political theories
in print from 1689 onwards, he maintained that, while government itself was of divine origin, since it was dictated by reason,
which had been implanted in men's minds by God, monarchy
itself was not divine, being only one among a number of possible
forms of government, though the one most suited to the genius
of the English people. Such cool approval of monarchy sounds
Hobbesian in origin; yet Defoe does not seem to have read
Leviathan, and does not include Hobbes among the impressive
battery of authorities quoted in his annotations to *Jure Divino*,
the most ambitious exposition of his political thought. Perhaps
he had absorbed some of Hobbes's ideas indirectly, filtered
through Morton's *System*, which he at least valued enough to
keep for a quarter of a century.

To Morton's students politics was no mere academic exercise,
but a matter of vital concern; and once again it is possible to
compile from Defoe's later writings a running commentary on
current political events as they appeared to the Dissenters.
Shortly after his eighteenth birthday rumours began to circulate
of a Popish Plot, inspired by the Jesuits, to murder the King.
The chief informant, Titus Oates, was known to have left a
copy of his deposition in the care of a London magistrate,

Sir Edmund Berry Godfrey. On 12 October 1678 Godfrey disappeared, and five days later his body was found near Primrose Hill, transfixed with a sword, and with signs of strangulation on his neck. This remains to this day an unsolved mystery, but at the time it was taken for granted that the murder was the work of 'the Papists'. Unreasoning panic swept the nation, and Oates and his associates were emboldened to embark on the wildest accusations, which were received with uncritical acceptance. Few doubted that there was a widespread and deep-laid plot, in which all the leading Catholics were involved, to overthrow the Protestant religion and the liberties of the nation. Defoe was no exception, for he declared:

> I firmly believe agreeable to the unanimous vote of the Parliament, in *November, I think it was* 1678. That there was a Horrid and Bloody Conspiracy set on Foot, and carried on by the Papists, for the Subversion of the Government in both Church and State, for the bringing in of Popery, and for the overthrow and Extirpation of the Protestant Religion.[36]

For a while it seemed that the very foundation of the Protestant faith, the Bible itself, the word of God freely available in English to every believer, was threatened. 'How many Honest, but over-Frighted People', he asked, 'set to work to copy the Bible into Short-Hand . . . ? At which work, I myself, then but a boy, work'd like a Horse, till I wrote out the whole Pentateuch, and was then so tyr'd that I was willing to run the Risque of the rest.'[37]

In reality the Roman Catholics were only a very small minority of the nation. Defoe later estimated that 'the Papists all over the Kingdom are not five to a hundred, in some Countries not one to a Hundred; within the City, hardly one to a Thousand'. But the civic authorities felt it necessary to look to the state of the City trained bands; and 'these Notions . . . made our City Blunderblusses to be all New burnish'd, Hatt and Feather, Shoulder-Belt, and all our Military Gewgaws come into Mode again',[38] Many Protestants believed themselves to be in personal danger, and among the weapons invented for self-defence was the 'Protestant flail', designed by the 'Protestant joiner', Stephen College. Defoe recalled how, 'for my part I have frequently walked with one about me in the old Popish days. I remember I saw an honest fellow . . . with one of these instruments exercise seven or eight ruffians in Fleet Street, and drive them all before him, quite from Fleet Street into Whitefriars.'[39] In retrospect, at least, Defoe was sceptical about some of the more extravagant rumours that circulated in London: 'tho' . . . I did firmly believe the reality of a Plot; yet when we run up that Plot to general Massacres, Fleets of Pilgrims, Bits and Bridles, Knives, Hand-Cuffs, and a thousand such things . . . I confess, tho' a Boy, I could not then, nor can now come up to them'.[40] He tells a long story of how a friend of his, whom he had arranged to meet in a public house, persuaded a credulous news-seeker, that on the previous night six Frenchmen had stolen the Monument — completed in the previous year, and itself commemorating a supposed Popish atrocity — 'and but that the watch stopp'd them as they were going over the Bridge, and made them carry it back again, they might for aught we know, have carry'd it over into France'.[41]

On 24 January 1679 Charles II, on the advice of his brother James and his chief minister Danby, dissolved the Parliament he had lived with since the beginning of his reign. Defoe describes the public reaction:

It was a most remarkable Time; the Nation was perfectly surprized at the King's dissolving that first Parliament; a universal Sorrow spread the face of the People, that had any sense of the publick Dangers upon them; and yet see the Shortness of Humane Understanding; the dissolving this parliament was the ruin of that very Party who designed it; and all their Attempts afterwards upon the Liberties of the People, met with a constant obstruction in that House, and the King could never come up to that Influence he had before amongst the Commons which, for that Reason, we Call'd *The Pension Parliament.*[42]

In February Defoe had his first chance to see what went on at a general election. Though he several times refers to a notoriously corrupt by-election fought at Winchelsea in the previous winter,[43] he seems to have made no specific comment about this general election, except perhaps for his remark about the 'unanimous Consent of Voices' given for Alderman Love in the City.[44] When the new Parliament proved even more hostile to the

Court than the old, Danby was made a scapegoat and sent to the Tower. There was now developing a determined campaign, managed by the Earl of Shaftesbury, to exclude the Duke of York from the succession, a campaign which might well have succeeded had there been a single generally acceptable substitute. But Shaftesbury's candidate, Charles's illegitimate son, the Duke of Monmouth, was as unwelcome to many of the peerage as he was to the King. However, an Exclusion Bill was introduced into the Commons; and when it became clear that the Commons would try to force the Bill through, Parliament was first prorogued and then dissolved. Another election in the summer produced results equally unwelcome to the Court, and successive prorogations delayed the meeting of Parliament for over a year. Party divisions were intensified, and new names appeared. 'Country' and 'Court' gave way briefly to 'Petitioners' and 'Abhorrers', only to be replaced by the abusive terms 'Whig' and 'Tory'.

Defoe claimed to speak with authority on the origins of both these pejorative labels. 'Whig', he tells us, was first the name of a liquor drunk in south-west Scotland, and was then applied to those who drank it. Some of these, rising in revolt, were defeated at Bothwell Brig in June 1679 by the Duke of Monmouth who, on his return to Court, was abused for being too merciful to the rebels:

> And D. *Lauderdale* told King *Charles* with an Oath, That the Duke had been so Civil to the *Whigs*, because he was a *Whig* himself in his Heart — This made it a Court Word, and in a little while all the Friends and Followers of the Duke, began to be call'd *Whigs*.[45]

This can only have been hearsay: but Defoe claimed to have been present in person at the baptism of the 'Tories', a name originally applied to Irish cut-throats and brigands:

> Their Godfather and who gave them the name, was Titus Oates, and the Occasion as follows: The Author of this happened to be present — There was a meeting of some Honest People in the City, upon the Discovery of some attempt to stifle the Evidence of the Witnesses, and tampering with Bedlow and Stephen Dugdale — and among the Discourse

Mr. Bedlow said he had Letters from Ireland, that there were some Tories to be brought over hither, who were privately to Murther Dr. Oats, and the said Bedlow. The Doctor, whose Zeal was very hot, could never hear any Man after this talk against the Plot or against the Witnesses, but he Thought he was one of those Tories, and call'd almost every Man a Tory that oppos'd him in Discourse; till at last, the word Tory became Popular, and stuck so close to the Party in all their Bloody Proceedings, that they own'd it . . . [46]

The *Domestick-Intelligence* of 26 December 1679 contains an account of what may well have been the very meeting mentioned by Defoe, held just a week earlier at the Three Tuns in Crutched Friars.[47]

While these events were taking place, Defoe was probably still a student at Morton's Academy, but he clearly did not take a cloistered view of the world. In fact he appears to have begun to move on the fringes of fashionable society and to have acquired tastes somewhat out of keeping with his intended career as a minister. He was no stranger to the taverns of the town — two of his stories about the Popish Plot were set in taverns — and a man who was to become an importer of wines and brandies, priding himself on his palate, can have had no scruples about strong drink. But he also prided himself on his moderation, and once offered £50 to anyone who could prove that he had ever been in the least disordered by drink.[48] His familiarity with the theatre, too, probably dated from this period of his life, though it would be rash to read too much into his fondness for such metaphors as 'the scene is changed' or 'hissed off the stage'. He had no objection to the stage in principle: 'nor am I so Narrow in my Opinion, as to think it an Unlawful Action, either in the Player's Acting, or the Person's *Seeing* a Play, if it could be Abstracted from all the Unhappy Circumstances that attend our Theaters'. And he illustrated his point with the gusto of a Hogarth or a Rowlandson:

. . . their Pitt and Boxes shine with Laughing Ladies, rallying Fops, Town Jilts, Country Cullies, young Citizens and old Sinners; the Galleries are throng'd with mask'd Beauties, and patch'd Ugliness, Pimps, Pickpockets, Whores &c in abundance. Here and there an honest Woman sits . . . Here and there a

Judge of Wit, Sence and Humour; Here and there one that can abstract the Wit from the Buffoonery, and like a Bee, gather the Honey, and leave the Poison; but alas of these, how few and how seldom to be seen.[49]

Many of the pastimes of men about town, such as cardplaying or similar forms of gambling, held no attraction for him; and the same is true of most country pleasures. He was temperamentally unsuited to angling, wildfowling was not to his taste, and he could see no pleasure in foxhunting.[50] But he always liked to give the impression of being knowledgeable about horses.[51] He could certainly ride better than John Gilpin, and in his lifetime was to travel many thousands of miles on horseback. His lifelong interest in horse-racing dates from his early years. He recalled seeing the Duke of Monmouth ride his own horses and win on several occasions, one of which was at Quainton, near Aylesbury on 6 September 1682.[52] His comments on a much later Newmarket meeting might equally well have applied to those which he attended during Charles II's reign. He found

. . . a great concourse of the nobility and gentry . . . so busy upon the sharping part of the sport . . . that to me they seem'd just as so many horse-coursers in Smithfield, descending (the greatest of them) from their dignity, to picking one another's pockets . . .

I was so sick of the jockeying part, that I left the crowd at the posts, and pleas'd myself with observing the horses . . .

Here I fansy'd myself in the Circus Maximus at Rome, seeing the antient games, and the racings of the chariots and horse-men; and in this warmth of my imagination I pleased and diverted myself more and in a more noble manner, than I could possibly do in the crowds of gentlemen at the weighing and starting posts, and at their coming in; or at their meetings at the coffee-houses and gaming tables after the races were over, where there was little or nothing to be seen, but what was the subject of just reproach to them, and reproof to every wise man that look'd upon them.[53]

Even as Defoe began to move about in the world, adopting the role of a detached, critical and often amused observer of the foibles of society, he must have become increasingly aware that he was an outsider. He was not a gentleman. His scorn of 'idolators who worship escutcheons and trophyes, and rate men by the *blazonry* of their houses' contained an element of sour grapes.[54] Although the time was passing when gentility could be determined by the College of Heralds on the sole criterion of an ancestral right to a coat of arms, the subtle barrier which excluded him was losing none of its force. He defined a gentleman as 'A Person BORN (for there lies the Essence of Quality) of some known or ancient Family; whose Ancestors have at least for some time been Rais'd above the class of mechanicks'.[55] He put his finger on one of his distinguishing marks: 'Heaven has given him his money, and he has enough; 'tis below him to get money, his business is to spend it.'[56] More important even than birth or inherited wealth was the social self-assurance and effortless air of authority which sprang from an upbringing in an environment of deference. Along with this went what Defoe called 'gallantry of spirit, greatness of soul, and . . . generous principles', an ideal of human personality which he found immensely attractive, even though it had little in common with that of industry and godliness to which he had been brought up. In practice, however, he found that many of the gentry fell far short of this ideal.

> I must entreat the gentlemen who are to Value themselves chiefly upon that advantage, that they will *stoop so low* as to admit that vertue, learning, a liberal education, and a degree of natural and acquir'd knowledge, are necessary to finish the born gentleman.[57]

And he declared, 'To me an untaught, unpolish'd gentleman is one of the most deplorable objects in the world.'[58] Nor was it merely lack of polish that he deplored. The characteristic vices of the gentry of Restoration England — drunkenness, whoring and swearing — seemed to him, not so much sinful, as contemptible and below the dignity of man. His feelings of social inferiority were at odds with his conviction of his own intellectual and moral superiority; here were the roots of his lifelong love-hate affair with the idea of gentility.[59]

To add to this turmoil of conflicting feelings he had also to contend with what he called 'legions of strong lusts within'.[60] We may smile at his later account of his awakening sexuality,

discreetly transferred to 'a Person, who the Devil so haunted
with women, fine beautiful ladies in bed with him, and ladies
of his acquaintance too, offering their favours to him, and all in
his sleep'. He tells us that 'the very first attack the Devil made
upon him, was with a very beautiful lady of his acquaintance,
who he had been something freer than ordinary with in their
common conversation'; and 'being a man of virtuous life and
good morals, it was the greatest surprise to him imaginable'.
The Devil continued to haunt him in this way 'frequently, and
that for many years together', so that 'he seldom slept without
some such entertainment'.[61] In his *Meditations* of 1681 he was
to write of

> Fatall and Accurst Desyres,
> That burst from Thence with too Uncertain Fires[62]

but for a while at least he seems to have had the fires well under
control.

It is obvious however that Defoe was becoming unsettled in
his intention of entering the Christian ministry — if indeed it
had ever really been his own intention, and not just his father's.
What finally snapped the thread was probably his intellectual
arrogance. In his *Meditations*, seeking in chastened mood to
find his way back to a faith from which he had strayed, he
wrote of fleeing

> From a false Confidence
> And all the Aery joy that Flows from Thence
> From all my Brain begotten Faith
> From all my Doubt
> And all my Foolish Thoughts about
> What Heaven Sayeth,
> From all my Growth in Morralls Schoole,
> With which I mock't my Maker, & my Soule.[63]

He did not specify the errors into which he had fallen; but
nearly forty years later he gave a sketch, ostensibly of a student
at a university, which may well be a deliberately distorted
account of himself at Morton's Academy. This student was 'a
young gentleman . . . eminent for learning and virtue, of prompt
parts and great proficiency, insomuch that he was taken great

notice of . . . and everyone promised fair in their thoughts for
him, that he would be a great man'; but, 'whether from his
earnest desire of more knowledge, or the opinion of his own
great capacity . . . this gentleman, falling upon the study of
divinity, grew so opinionative, so very positive and dogmatic in
his notice of religious things . . . that his tutor saw plainly that
he had little more than notions in all his religious pretensions to
knowledge, and concluded that he would either grow enthusiastic
or obstinately profane and atheistic'. So it was that he and
others who fell under his influence 'really reasoned themselves
out of all religion whatsoever . . . pretending that those things
really were not, of which they could not define how and what
they were, they proceeded to deny the existence of their Maker,
the certainty of a future state, a resurrection, a judgment, a
heaven, or a hell'. Indeed he 'gave out that he could frame a
new gospel, and a much better system of religion than that
which they called Christian; and that if he would trouble himself
to go about it, he would not fail to draw in as great a part of the
world to run after him as had after any other'.[64] Defoe's
Meditations, it is true, make no mention of atheism. Yet the
very strength of his horror of it in later years may be significant;
and so too may some of his assumptions about atheists — that
they always flaunt their atheism, that they make a jest of religion,
and that they do all this against their own inner convictions:

> The Atheist feels this trifle in his breast,
> And, while he trifles, trembles at the Jest.
> The secret Trepedation racks his Soul,
> And when he says, *No God*; replies, *Thou Fool.*[65]

Whatever the exact truth about this, there must have been some
kind of crisis of faith, as a result of which he finally abandoned
the idea of becoming a dissenting minister. He later wryly
observed:

> . . . the pulpit is none of my office. It was my disaster first to
> be set apart for, and then to be set apart from, the honour of
> that sacred employ.[66]

So, some time during the winter of 1679–80, after three years
or so at Newington Green, his formal education came to an end.

5 Some Strife in My Thoughts

If Defoe was not to become a minister, what was he to do with his life? For him, as for Crusoe at a similar age, it was now 'too late . . . to go apprentice to a trade, or clerk to an attorney'; and in any case he can have been no readier than Crusoe to settle down to the humdrum routine of such a life.[1] Crusoe's 'meer wandring disposition' led him to run away to sea; but even before his ship could reach London from Hull two storms had signified divine displeasure at his action.[2] But why *two* storms? Crusoe's explanation, that 'Providence . . . resolved to leave me entirely without excuse', is not altogether convincing.[3] Perhaps the answer lies in Defoe's own experience; for there are strong hints that he himself met with two storms on what must have been a very early voyage — before he was a fully fledged merchant — in his case from London to Oporto. He described the latter as 'a Barr'd Port, and dangerous enough, so that if the Sea goes high there is no venturing in, and the Ships are oblig'd to go away to Villa da Conde and sometimes to Viana, till the weather abates'. But even then, though the River Douro is deep enough to provide a good harbour at Oporto, 'when the Freshes or Land-Floods come down the River, in which case the Stream here is very violent, the Ships are obliged to lie close to the Walls, and so are fastened ashore, for no Anchors will hold them in the Stream'.[4] To the seamen, Defoe's first storm at sea may have been, like Crusoe's first, 'but a cap full of wind';[5] but his second nearly brought disaster. He must have had the return voyage in mind when he described how a merchant ship 'homeward bound from Oporto to London, laden with wines', came by night into Portland Road in a heavy storm, 'firing guns for help'. She came to an anchor and struck her top-masts; but, as 'she had been in bad weather, and lost an anchor and cable before' — presumably now lying at the bottom of the Douro — and with only a single anchor and a weak cable to rely on, 'they expected every hour to go on shore, and split to pieces'. Two Weymouth boats ventured out to investigate, returning within three hours with a spare anchor and cable, for which however the master had to draw a bill for £12 on his London owners; but, as this saved the ship and cargo, Defoe decided that 'it was not as extravagant as at first I thought it to be'.[6] Despite obvious differences, there are several parallels with Crusoe's second storm, in Yarmouth Roads. His ship also struck her top-masts, relying first on one anchor, and then on two, and firing guns for help; while he and his ship-mates owed their survival to the efforts of a boat's crew, 'rowing very heartily, and venturing their lives to save ours'.[7]

If Defoe made his voyage at the same age as Crusoe, a few weeks before his nineteenth birthday, it was probably while he was still at Morton's Academy, perhaps during a vacation; and, like Crusoe's, it was probably made upon impulse, 'without any consideration of circumstances or consequences', and without his father's approval.[8] But if he drew the same moral as Crusoe from the two storms to which he had been subjected, he too soon won 'as compleat a victory over conscience as any young fellow . . . could desire'.[9] Obedient instead to the 'secret over-ruling decree that hurries us on to be the instruments of our own destruction', he again allowed his 'foolish inclination of wandering abroad' to gain the upper hand.[10] If the places in Europe of which he appears to show a first-hand knowledge are plotted on a map, there emerges the unmistakable trace of a Grand Tour. Such a foot-loose journey seems far more likely in his early days before he had settled down to earn his living by trade; and several hints combine to suggest that this is how he spent most of the year 1680.[11] James Foe, who had intended his son for the ministry, would hardly have been willing to meet the expenses of a Grand Tour, even if he had been able to; and his attitude must surely have been that of Crusoe's father, who strongly resisted his son's desire to travel, and prophetically hinted at the disasters which would flow from his stubborn rejection of paternal advice.[12]

Some light on how Defoe may have been financed is shed by his *Memoirs of a Cavalier*, whose hero thought 'a gentleman ought always to see something of the world, before he confines himself to any particular part of it', and took with him a college friend, 'who had instilled into me the first desire of going abroad, and who I knew passionately longed to travel, but had not sufficient allowance to defray his expenses as a gentleman'.[13] Defoe may well have travelled as companion to the son of some Whiggish landed or mercantile family, whom he had known at Morton's Academy. Many years later he recalled a friend, whose father 'had gotten a great estate by Merchandise':

> I knew a private Gentleman, whose father had sett him up worth 20000 *l.* and bid him set up for a Gentleman . . . Once I saw a Calculation made from his estate in his own Presence; for I had so far an Intimacy with his Affairs, by which it appear'd, that in twenty five years more, had he liv'd so long, he must have been worth two Millions Sterling.[14]

Perhaps this was the man in whose company and at whose expense Defoe made his Grand Tour.

Defoe's route through Europe appears to form a rough figure-of-eight; and there are clearly more ways than one that such a course can have been traced. The Cavalier and his companion, like most Englishmen making the Grand Tour, headed first for Paris; but it is easier to make sense of Defoe's travels if we suppose that he visited the French capital on his way home. His scornful comment on a writer who made a topographical blunder — 'I suppose this Gentleman never went up the *Rhine* in *Germany*' — may give a hint of his route.[15] He knew how Cologne 'stretches itself in length along the shore' of the Rhine.[16] He casually mentions the Hunsruck, the mountain range which overshadows the western bank of the river between Coblenz and Bingen, though he carelessly applies the name to a more southerly range of mountains.[17] Next, following a tributary, the Nahe, he would come to Kreutznach, perhaps the source of the original name of Crusoe's family — Kreutznaer;[18] while the nearby village of Wintzenheim may likewise have been the original of 'Wintselsheim', from which Roxana took her title of Countess.[19] He would now be entering 'one of the Pleasantest Countries in all Germany', the Palatinate, whose devastation by the French a few years later was to rouse his indignation.[20] On the other side of the Rhine, at Heidelberg on the Neckar, he saw the 'vast Tun of Wine', with its pair of winding stairs resembling those leading up to a pulpit.[21] Further up the Rhine was a region falling under the growing shadow of French power. Although Strasbourg did not fall to the French until the following year, a line of French fortresses already dominated the whole course of the river from the borders of the Palatinate to those of Switzerland. A quarter of a century later he could still confidently recall 'Fort Khiel at the Bridge of Strasbourg, Fort Louis in an island in the Rhine' and 'the terrible Fort of Hunnighen within Canon-Shot of the City of Basel'.[22] Travellers passing this way in 1680 would see the latter still under construction by the great military engineer, Vauban.

Defoe would now be approaching the lakes and mountains of Switzerland. Here, after he had 'gone under so many of the most frightful passes in the country of the Grisons',[23] he may have descended the upper Rhone Valley to Lake Geneva where, 'upon any sudden Thaw and Melting of the Snows upon the Mountains, or upon any hasty Rains swelling the River . . . you may see the Motion in the Lake to be more furious where the channel of the River particularly lies, than in other Places'.[24] And so to the City of Geneva itself, a more fitting place than Rome for a Protestant pilgrimage — 'not a Person to be seen without Employment, and few or none ignorant and unconcern'd in his religion . . . the most formidable place, of so small a Tract of Ground, and so little number of Men, that is in the Universe'.[25] Next he apparently entered France, for mention of 'Pont a Voisin' in error for Pont de Beauvoisin, on the frontier near Chambery, suggests a faulty memory rather than careless map-reading.[26] He more than once mentions 'the *Pertuis Rostan* . . . a wonderful Passage cut through a Mountain near *Briancon*, on the frontiers of Dauphine . . . said to be the work of the Devil; only because the People have no History recording the Time and Manner of its making, or by who'.[27] He may have meant the Pertuis de la Traversette, cut two centuries before by Ludovico II, Marquis of Saluzzo, to link the valleys of the Durance and the Po. Defoe does not claim that he actually passed through this Alpine tunnel; and his route into Italy was probably that taken by Roxana — from Grenoble, through Briançon and Susa, to Turin.[28] Even here, though he was at last 'beyond those Snowy Mountains', he was not beyond the influence of France.[29] All the talk of Turin in 1680 was of the proposed marriage between Victor Amadeus II, the young Duke of Savoy, 'then fourteen years old', and the still younger Infanta of Portugal. Defoe writes knowledgeably of this scheme, 'in some things mysterious, yet in others . . . not so', engineered by France with the aim of removing the Duke to Portugal so that his French mother could continue to rule in Turin; and he tells how 'the *Savoyard* and Piedmontese Nobility were highly enrag'd' at what they took to be 'a Design to expose their Country to France'.[30]

As he moved through Italy, the scent of his route, though plentiful enough, becomes broken and confused. Though he writes with seeming confidence of the Duchy of Milan, 'full of Towns and Trade' and of 'great Rivers . . . join'd together by *Naviglio*'s, as they call 'em, or Canals', he gives no convincing evidence of familiarity with Milan itself or with any of the other cities in its neighbourhood.[31] He probably turned south from Turin into Genoese territory, getting his first glimpse of the Mediterranean some thirty miles west of Genoa:

> . . . the Shore . . . especially from *Savona* to *Genoa* is the most delightful of its kind in all Italy, full of Villages, Gentlemen's Seats and Towers; for all the Great Houses near the Shore are built like Castles that they may not be liable to Surprize, in case the Rover Turks, or in time of War Privateers, should land upon them.[32]

His Cavalier, travelling in Italy before turning soldier, took ship at Genoa for Leghorn; but Defoe may have continued along the coast. When he writes of convicts who 'labour with Chains and Clogs upon them . . . among the marble Quarries in Italy; and in the *Appenin* Mountains of *Genoa*' he probably means the marble quarries round Carrara some seventy miles along the coast.[33] Passing Lucca, 'a little but very rich republic', and Pisa, 'the Picture of a Great Body, sick of a Consumption, and drawing near its End', he would come to Leghorn, where 'the Body of the *English* Merchants . . . is the most considerable thing in the Place', and where perhaps his companion could draw fresh supplies of ready money by means of a letter of credit.[34]

We next pick up his tracks in Rome itself. As might be expected in a young man with a Protestant upbringing and a highly developed historical sense, his reactions were very mixed. Even his unscholarly Cavalier was stirred by the relics of ancient

Rome: 'It was pleasant indeed . . . to say, here stood the Capital; there the colossus of Nero; here the amphitheatre of Titus; there the acqueduct; here the forum; there the catacombs; here the Temple of Venus; there of Jupiter; here the Pantheon, &c.' But he found that the modern Romans 'were degenerated from the ancient glorious inhabitants, who were generous, brave, and the most valiant of all nations, to a vicious cowardly baseness of soul, barbarous, treacherous, jealous, and revengeful; lewd and cowardly; intolerably proud and haughty; bigoted to blind, incoherent devotion, and the grossest idolatry'.[35] Roxana, living in Rome with her Prince, was equally critical:

> I did not like it at-all; the swarms of Ecclesiastics of all Kinds, on one side, and the scoundrel-rabbles of the Common People, on the other, make *Rome* the unpleasantest Place in the World, to live in . . . when I was there, the Footmen made such a Broil between two Great Families in *Rome*, about which of their Coaches (the Ladies being in the Coaches on either side) shou'd give Way to t'other; that there was above thirty People wounded on both sides; four or six kill'd out-right; and both Ladies frighted almost to Death.[36]

Scornful though he was of much that he saw in Rome, Defoe could not withhold his admiration from St Peter's, 'the most finished piece in the world'; and he praised 'the magnificence of its inside work, the painting, the altars, the oratories, and the variety of its imagery'.[37] Even so, both here and in the churches throughout Italy, he 'found the face of religion, and no more'; and he quoted with approval a remark that 'Italy was a theatre, where religion was the grand opera, and the Popish clergy were the stage players'.[38]

His reactions to Naples were similarly ambivalent. It had 'without exception the best Harbour in *Italy*', and more fine public buildings than '*London, Paris, Amsterdam* and *Seville*, put all together', while the 'Prospect of the Sea, and of the Harbour, from the Streets and Houses adds to the Beauty of the Place, and in a word, it is without comparison the finest City in the World'.[39] But he was less enthusiastic about the Neapolitans than about their city. He found it dangerous to walk in the streets; and he was critical of their rigid social restrictions — 'the Limitations of their Dress, Habits, Liveries and Equipages', and 'the custom of Women going veil'd about the Streets and to Churches'.[40]

Perhaps at Naples he became involved in a new experience, which he attributed to his Cavalier:

> At a certain Town in *Italy* . . . I was prevailed upon rather than tempted, *a la Courtezan*. If I should describe the Woman I must give a very mean Character of my own Virtue to say I was allured by any but a Woman of an extraordinary Figure; her Face, Shape, Mein, and Dress, I may, without Vanity, say, were the finest that I ever saw. When I had Admittance into her Apartments, the Riches and Magnificence of them astonished me, the Cupboard or Cabinet of Plate, the Jewels, the Tapestry, and every Thing in Proportion, made me question whether I was not in the Chamber of some Lady of the best Quality . . . her Conversation . . . was . . . exceeding agreeable; she sung to her Lute, and danced as fine as ever I saw, and thus diverted me two Hours before any Thing else was discoursed of; — but when the vicious Part came on the Stage, I blush to relate the Confusion I was in, and when she made a certain Motion by which I understand she might be made use of, either as a Lady, or as — I was quite Thunder-struck, all the vicious Part of my Thoughts vanished, the Place filled me with Horror, and I was all over Disorder and Distraction.
>
> . . . though she easily saw the Disorder I was in, she turned it off with admirable Dexterity, began to talk again *a la Gallant*, received me as a Visitant, offered me Sweetmeats and some Wine . . .
>
> When I offered to go, and at parting presented her five Pistoles, I could not prevail with her to take them, when she spoke some *Italian* Proverb which I could not readily under-stand, but by my Guess it seemed to imply, that *she would not take the Pay, having not obliged me otherwise*: At last I laid the Pieces on her Toilet, and would not receive them again; upon which she obliged me to pass my Word to visit her again, else she would by no Means accept my Present.[41]

The impact of this encounter upon Defoe seems clear from the fact that he used it again, as the nucleus round which he con-structed his later novel, *Roxana*, whose central incident — already foreshadowed in the opening pages of the book — is that in which Roxana acquires her name by dancing before Charles II and his courtiers in a Turkish dress which she had brought from Italy. There are several hints that he originally intended Roxana, like the Italian courtesan, to sing as well, though she did not actually do so. Although the scene is transposed from Italy to London, and greatly elaborated, many of the same details reappear – the apartments, the jewels, the sweetmeats and wine, and even the cupboard of plate, quite gratuitously introduced.[42]

There was a sequel to the Cavalier's visit to the courtesan:

> I confess I had a strong Inclination to visit her again, and besides thought my self obliged to it in Honour to my Parole; but after some Strife in my Thoughts about it, I resolved to break my Word with her, when going at Vespers one Evening to see their Devotions, I happened to meet this Lady very devoutly going to her Prayers.
>
> At her coming out of the Church I spoke to her, and she paid me her Respects with a *Seignior Inglese*, and some Words she said in *Spanish* smiling, which I did not understand; I cannot say here so clearly as I would be glad I might, that I broke my Word with her; but if I saw her any more I saw nothing of what gave me so much Offence before.
>
> The End of my relating this Story is answered in describing the Manner of their Address, without bringing my self to Confession; if I did any Thing I have some Reason to be ashamed of, it may be a less Crime to conceal it than expose it.[43]

What the Cavalier called 'some Strife in my Thoughts' is matched by the obvious conflict in Defoe's own mind, forty years later, between frankness and reticence, which can leave little doubt that it was his own experience that he was recounting. His attitude was probably confused from the start. In the following year, when he was not more than twenty-one, he could write:

> The Last result of Satisfy'd Desire
> Fancy can Think no More nor wish no higher
> The Soul wrapt in the Encircling Arms of Peace
> And Envy stiffl'd in the Dear Embrace
> Desire Finish'd Hope and Fear Laid by
> And all's Fruition Joy and Extasye.[44]

Defoe seldom comes so near to true poetic feeling. Yet a later and sourer comment may have been more characteristic: 'As to the Vice, he protests to contemn it: and the Trifle call'd Pleasure in it, to be not worth the Repentance.'[45] This certainly chimes in well with the Cavalier's final comment on his adventure: 'The Particulars related . . . may lead the Reader . . . to a View of what gave me a particular Disgust at this pleasant Part of the World, as they pretend to call it, and made me quit the Place sooner than Travellers use to do that come thither to satisfy their Curiosity.'[46]

From Naples, the limit of his travels in Italy, he seems to have crossed the Appenines to the Adriatic coast, perhaps travelling by mule or donkey — 'poor *Boricco* as the Italians call him'.[47] Though this must have been a rough journey, he could still admire the 'walks of trees . . . orange, limon and citron' in 'the Abruzzo, and other southern parts of Italy' through which he passed.[48] Moving northwards, he would enter Papal territory, where 'it may be seen by the Misery of the People, as well in the great towns as in the small, the Sea Coasts as well as the Inland Country, that the Taxes and other Severities are so heavy, and the People so oppress'd by the Clergy, that none but the Priests and Churches have any show of Wealth among them'.[49] One place that had not merely a 'show of Wealth', but an 'Immense Treasure' was 'the Holy Casket of Miraculous Idolatry', the Santa Casa at Loreto: 'The City is enlarged merely by the Confluence of Strangers; and the chief Trade here is in Beads, sanctified Medals, bless'd *Agnus Dei*'s and Crosses; with all other Kinds of Popish Trumpery. The principal Houses serve to entertain the Pilgrims, of whom sometimes there are so many the Place cannot receive them.'[50]

He apparently took ship, perhaps from Ancona, for Venice; 'by Sea you see it half over the Gulph, for at the distance of 17 or 18 Leagues you see the Tower of St Mark on the one Hand, and the Hill of *Caldero* upon the Coast of *Dalmatia* on the other'. His stay in Venice may have been brief, for most of his account, contributed many years later to the *Atlas Maritimus*, is derivative. He did however recall it as

> . . . the Perfection of Order and Regularity, the Channels of Water cleans'd and deepen'd, the four Shores wharfed up with Stone and Timber; the Wharfs every where furnished

with Ranges of Buildings; here large Ware-houses for the
Merchants; there vast Store-houses for the Publick; here
Granaries for Corn, and there Magazines for the State; here
noble Houses of Merchants, there magnificent Palaces of the
Nobility.[51]

A clue to Defoe's route out of Italy may be found in *Colonel
Jack*, whose hero, after taking part in military campaigns in
northern Italy, stayed for eight months in the house of a
'burgher' in Trent, and then travelled 'through Tyrol, into
Bavaria, and so through Suabia, and the Black Forest, into
Alsace, from thence I came into Lorraine, and so to Paris'.[52]
We can certainly pick up Defoe's trail at various points along
this route. He remarked that 'all Men know' that at Trent 'the
River *Adige* is but a small one there at best, not bigger than the
River Lea at *Bow-Bridge*, or *Hackney-Marsh*';[53] he claimed
familiarity with the passes of the Tyrol;[54] and the Bavarian
capital was the setting for a clearly visualised little incident:

> An *English* Gentleman was Viewing the Duke of *Bavaria*'s
> Chamber of Rarities at Munich; as fast as ever the Person that
> show'd him anything, had opened it, and began to tell him
> what it was, instead of expressing himself pleas'd at what he
> saw, he continually Answer'd, *Encore, Encore*, again, or
> what's next. At last he show'd him an extraordinary pair of
> Globes, and began to read him a lecture in Geography; but
> still the *English* man was interrupting him, *Eh bien Monsieur,
> Encore*, i.e. Very well Sir, what next; the Man seem'd a little
> concern'd as if he banter'd him, and return'd, *Icy le Monde,
> apre le Diable: Here's all the World, and after that to the
> Devil.*[55]

It sounds as though Defoe's travelling companion could not
match his own stamina and appetite for new cultural experience.
   Forty miles to the west lay Augsburg; and Defoe referred
scornfully to a writer who slightly misplaced it, 'when all the
World, that knows anything of it, knows it is not in *Bavaria* at
all, but stands on the outer edge of *Suabia*, next to it, as Southwark stands upon the edge of *Surry*, next to *Middlesex*'.[56] He
was now treading in the footsteps of his hero, the Protestant
champion, Gustavus Adolphus, as he had done before at Kreutznach and Heidelberg. Gustavus's passage of the Lech, a few miles

north of Augsburg, was to provide a famous incident in the
Memoirs of a Cavalier, an incident whose impact may owe
something to Defoe's personal knowledge of the site;[57] and
he could quote 'the People of Donawert' for the statement
that the fortress of Schellenberg, above Donauworth on the
Danube, had been thirteen times attacked, but never taken till
it fell to Gustavus's forces.[58] Moving westwards he must have
crossed his previous route, probably at Strasbourg, before
travelling along one of the 'two famous High-Ways made about
the Year 1676, thro' the whole Country of *Lorrain*' to maintain
French military communications with Alsace and the Middle
Rhine, highways 'always kept in repair, and . . . broad enough
for the Horse to march a full Squadron in front'.[59]

And so to Paris, where he stayed long enough to familiarise
himself with the City and its surroundings. He knew the Tuiller-
ies, the Louvre, les Invalides, the Pont Neuf, the Conciergerie,
the Gallery of the Luxembourg.[60] He mentions the great
meander of the Seine below the City,[61] and claimed to have
seen many of the seats of the nobility which made 'the country
for twenty miles around Paris . . . a kind of Prodigy'.[62] Years
later he gave a lively account of a gathering at the great Protestant Church at Charenton, 'by my Calculations . . . about the
Year 1681, or thereabouts'; 'The Train of Nobility and Persons
of the first rank, the Appearance of the Coaches and Retinue
was such as seem incredible'; and here he heard 'the truly famous
Monsieur *Cloud*' preach, prophesying the fate of the French
Protestants, but promising them a happy issue out of their
afflictions.[63] At the newly built Palace of Versailles, then almost
ready for occupation, he could see how 'the king of France, in
the decoration of the Gardens . . . had oaks removed, which by
their dimensions, must have been above an hundred years old'.[64]
A detail in *Roxana* may reflect an occasion when Defoe himself
was 'at the fine Palace of Meudun, where the Dauphin then
was . . . While I was there, the KING happen'd to come hither,
from *Versailles* . . . After we had seen the KING, who did not
stay long in the Gardens, we walk'd up the Broad Terrass . . .
crossing the Hall, towards the Great Stair-Case.'[65] It would have
been fitting for Defoe to catch a glimpse of the Sun-King,
whose power was threatening to scorch the whole of Europe,
and whose politics he would in due time play no small part in
confounding.

Paris was the setting of another incident portrayed by Defoe in such convincing detail as to suggest a basis in his own experience. The hero of his first pseudo-autobiographical novel, *The Memoirs of Majr. Alexander Ramkins*, like Defoe's Cavalier, makes a fool of himself over a woman, though in a different way. At the age of nineteen, he began to pay court to a Spanish lady, giving her, among other presents, a snuff-box, and 'now and then a serenade according to the *Spanish* custom'. On one of these occasions his jealousy was aroused by the sight of a periwig reflected in her casement window. Soon afterwards he saw in the Chocolate House 'a young Gentleman . . . giving himself Airs with a Snuff-box' similar to the one he had given to the young lady, and wearing a periwig like the one he had seen in her chamber window, '*vid*. a flat Top, neither rais'd nor parted in the Middle, which spoke it a piece of *English* Furniture'.

> The Sight of the snuff-box drew all my Blood into my Heart, and left my pale Cheeks to account for the Consternation, wherefore not able to contain myself had I kept my ground, I flung out of the Chocolate House . . . However, at three Steps I was got again into the Chocolate House, and with a galliard Air, addressing my self to the Gentleman with the Snuff box, *Sir*, said I, *I confirm the Gift, and may all sniffling Fools that are in Love be serv'd like me.* I allow'd no time for a Reply, but bolting again into the Street, it came into my Head that perhaps two Snuff-boxes might be so much alike, as not to observe the difference without confronting 'em. This Thought gave me the curiosity to step into a Toyshop, where I desired to have a Sight of the newest fashion'd Snuff-boxes, and when among others, I saw above half a dozen exactly like that I had made the Lady a Present of, a Secret Confusion spread itself over my Soul to have given way to such a Suspicion.[66]

Defoe quickly brought Ramkins' love affair to an end by removing the young lady to Spain; but the original of the incident may have had a very different outcome. It was probably just outside Paris, and in the latter part of the year 1680, that Defoe, then himself barely twenty, underwent a traumatic experience that was to burden him for the rest of his life. A

number of clues lead us to a cupboard door, and though we still
lack the key to unlock it, we may strongly suspect that behind
it lies a skeleton — that of a young Frenchman killed in a duel.

Defoe certainly fought a duel at some time in his life. Years
later, he called himself 'an Enemy to Duelling as it is a Sin
against God — and therefore never speak of it, but I desire to
declare my own Penitence upon that Subject'.[67] And again,

> . . . *take that from one that will go to the grave with the*
> *Regret of that kind of Folly, and contemning the Reputation*
> *of Courage, I gain'd by it, thinks himself bound on all occa-*
> *sions to acknowledge it,* Cursed be that Kind of Wrath, *for it*
> *is fierce,* and all that Kind of Anger is *cruel.* — It has nothing
> in it but the Fury of Passion cover'd over with the Mask of
> Courage, and miscall'd *Honour.*

Commenting on a report that a duellist had spent the previous
night in prayer, he asserted, from his '*own unhappy Experience*',
that

> . . . such times are taken up, in the unrolling of the Passions,
> the boyling of the Blood, the furious agitation of the Animal
> Spirits, moved by the violence of the Provocation; if Con-
> science presumes to give a pinch in the Dark, or put in a
> Word, *the inflamed Organ answers,* come what will, I cannot
> go back, I cannot live, I had better be run a thousand times
> through the Body, I can dye but once, but to bear this is to
> be stabb'd every Day, to be insulted at the Corner of every
> Street, to be Posted, Caned, and the Devil; I cannot bear it, I
> cannot help it — [68]

Defoe never brought himself explicitly to 'descend to particulars'
and describe in his own person the duel he had fought; but
when, in his late fifties, he turned his hand to writing fiction, he
gave circumstantial accounts of no fewer than three — in *The
Memoirs of Majr. Alexander Ramkins* (1718), *The Memoirs of a
Cavalier* (1720), and *Colonel Jack* (1722) — and all three were
fought, without seconds, in or near Paris. It would be strange if
nothing of his own experience had found its way into these
accounts, and particularly into the first. This duel was fought,
not by Ramkins himself, but by his elder brother — perhaps a

device to distance himself from events from which he wished to dissociate himself, even while indulging his desire to recount and share them.

Some two years before the affair credited to the young Ramkins, his elder brother had been in Paris, in the year 1690, raising forces to join James II in Ireland. His attentions to a young lady in the same lodgings came to the ears of a relative of hers, an officer in the Regiment of Navarre, newly arrived in Paris, who put the worst interpretation upon what he heard. The elder Ramkins received one evening by post a note which was 'a double Surprize to him, first a bold and daring Challenge, and again, he neither knew whom he was to meet nor upon what Account, only the Time and Place were mentioned'. After discussing the matter with his friends, some of whom advised him to treat it as a joke, he decided to present himself at the appointed place. After spending the rest of the night in a tavern, 'a fitter preparation than praying for the Work he was about', he set off at five the next morning, with 'half a dozen of his Acquaintance following him at a convenient distance'.

When he came to the Place appointed, he saw a young Gentleman walking and musing under a Hedge with his Arms a Kimbo, whom he rightly judg'd to be his Man . . . my Brother's Antagonist . . . whips off his Cloaths into his Shirt, and open'd his Breast to show his Adversary he scorn'd to take any ungenerous Advantage. My Brother was also honourable upon the same score; for although he wore a short Buff Waistcoat according to the Fashions of those Times, and which might have deadened a Push, yet he threw it off and put himself upon a level with his Adversary in all respects, so to it they went. My Brother found himself much superior in Strength and Vigour, and that in all probability he could Command his Adversary's Sword, paried with him a considerable Time, and put by several Pushes without attempting the Gentleman's Life, but finding him Resolute, and that one of them must fall, he made a home Thrust, and drove his Sword quite through his Adversary's Body, falling upon him at the same time; and thus fell this unfortunate young Gentleman, a victim to his ungovernable Passion . . .

. . . My Brother being convinc'd his Adversary was incapable to Rally, made haste to gather up his Cloaths, exchanging the

Evangelical Advice of *burying* the dead, to that natural
Precept of *Self-Preservation*, and I must leave him pursuing
his Journey towards *Brest*.[69]

Some of these details must have been invented — there was, for
instance, no internal postal service in Paris at any time during
Defoe's lifetime — but others may well have been drawn from
his 'Own Unhappy Experience'. His Cavalier, who became
accidentally involved in a duel with a complete stranger in Paris,
also ran his sword 'quite through his body';[70] while Colonel
Jack quarreled with a Marquis whom he thought too familiar
with his wife, fought with him on the way from Paris to Charenton, 'under a row of trees adjoining to Monsieur ——'s garden
wall' and inflicted with his sword-point what he believed to be
a mortal wound in his body.[71]

All three of Defoe's fictional duellists fled from Paris; the
elder Ramkins to Ireland by way of Brest; the Cavalier to Italy,
by way of Orleans and Lyons; and Colonel Jack to England by
way of the Rhineland.[72] We can only guess at Defoe's route;
but there are tenuous hints that he may have visited Dublin
during Charles II's reign, and he specifically stated that he first
saw Liverpool 'about the year 1680'.[73] Only one of his fictional
duellists was actually pursued, and even then in the wrong
direction; but fear of pursuit would have given his own flight,
by whatever route, a nightmare quality, in which shock and
remorse at killing a man mingled with a desperate fear for his
own life. For, as he was later to remind readers of his *Review*,
Louis XIV had made it 'death without mercy' even to issue or
accept a challenge.[74] He declared this to have been one of Louis's
first actions on taking over the administration of France; yet
when he subsequently published a full translation of the French
King's edict on the subject, it was one that had been registered
in the Parlement as recently as 1 September 1679.[75] Perhaps he
had this in mind in his enigmatic reference, soon after his return
to England, to

> . . . all the Terrors of the Law
> That Kept my Soul in Slavish Awe.

These lines are to be found in Defoe's earliest surviving poem,
the first of seven which he carefully copied into a notebook

about the year 1681.[76] These *Meditations*, as he called them, reveal a man struggling to emerge from a severe spiritual crisis. The longest and most agitated is the first, entitled 'fleeing For Refuge to the hope Sett before us'. Its opening lines, the first words we have from Defoe's pen, are significant:

> In Misadvertant Slaughters we are Told
> Cittyes of Refuge Were Prepar'd of Old

— and he goes on to develop the theme to be found in Numbers 35, Deuteronomy 19, and Joshua 20, where God ordained cities of refuge for the Jews, where a 'manslayer' who had not been guilty of malice aforethought would be safe from the 'avenger of blood'.[77] Defoe seems to identify himself as such a man — 'a Nocent Innocent', bearing only 'a guilt Mishap did (Not Designe) Creat'. Yet he must have realised that the Old Testament distinguished only between premeditated murder and accidental mankilling. Could the latter really include death in a duel, however reluctantly inflicted? Was this why, throughout his life, Defoe so strenuously maintained the right of self-defence?

> *The Laws of God*, as I can understand,
> Do never Laws of Nature countermand;
> Nature Commands, and 'tis Prescrib'd to Sense,
> For all Men to adhere to *Self-Defence*:
> *Self-Preservation* is the only Law
> That does involuntary Duty Draw;
> It serves for Reason and Authority,
> And they'll defend themselves, *that know not why*.[78]

Yet, however Defoe might attempt to justify himself rationally, blood-guilt was not so easily argued away. His Meditation returns repeatedly to the theme of pursuit, a pursuit which still obsessed him even after he was physically safe:

> For he'll Oretake that does Persue to Slay

As the poem progresses, it becomes clear that the City of Refuge is really an emblem of Christ:

> To Thee I Flye
> For Refuge Lord, for the Avengers Nigh

But who then is the Avenger? Defoe himself asks, and tries to answer, this question:

> Let Me Not Go, But Flee,
> My God! To Hide my burthened Soul wth Thee
> Swift be my Steps, & Swifter my Desyre,
>   To such a Refuge to Retyre.
>   Teach me From what, and whom,
>   With Eager hast it is I come.
>   From Sin,
> And Legions of Strong Lusts within;
>   From a base heart
>   That Eagerly with Hell Takes Part,
>   From Fatall, and Accurst Desyres,
> That Burst from Thence wth Too Uncertain fires;
>   From all my Pride,
> And all the Lusts that have my Soul Betraid;
>   From an Alluring World,
> And all the Gawdy Vapour There Appeares:
>   From all my Former hopes & Feares,
>   That my Tosst soul has hurl'd;
>   From all my Care
> From my Presumcon, & From My Despair.

Yet although Defoe here implies that it is from his own sins that he is fleeing — Dr Jekyll in flight from Mr Hyde — it is clear that he also conceives of the Avenger as someone external to him who is pursuing him *on account of* his sins. Is he perhaps the figure, more readily identifiable by a psychologist than by a theologian, who appears in Crusoe's vivid and terrifying dream?

> I saw a Man descend from a great black Cloud, in a bright Flame of Fire, and light upon the Ground: He was all over as bright as a Flame, so that I could but just bear to look towards him; his Countenance was most inexpressibly dreadful, impossible for Words to describe; when he stepp'd upon

the Ground with his Feet, I thought the Earth trembl'd . . .
and all the Air look'd, to my Apprehension, as if it had been
fill'd with Flashes of Fire.

He was no sooner landed upon the Earth, but he moved
forward towards me, with a long Spear or Weapon in his
Hand, to kill me; and when he came to a rising Ground, at
some Distance, he spoke to me, or I heard a Voice so terrible,
that it is impossible to describe the Terror of it; all that I can
say I understood, was this, *Seeing all these Things have not
brought thee to Repentance, now thou shalt die*: At which
Words, I thought he lifted up the Spear that was in his Hand,
to kill me.

No one, that shall ever read this Account will expect that
I should be able to describe the Horrors of my Soul at this
terrible Vision, I mean, that even while it was a Dream, I
even Dreamed of those Horrors; nor is it possible to describe
the Impression that remained upon my Mind when I awak'd
and found it was but a Dream.[79]

Crusoe's dream ushered in a spiritual crisis, which Defoe
clearly meant to be a turning point in his story. For the first
time Crusoe acknowledged the sins for which God was punishing
him; yet he could not at first achieve repentance. Inspired by a
biblical text, he cried aloud: 'Jesus, thou son of David, thou
exalted Prince and Saviour, give me repentance!'; but even then
he could only say that 'from this time . . . I began to have
hopes that God would hear me'. The late Canon Lloyd, in what
he called 'The Riddle of Defoe', described these pages of
Robinson Crusoe as 'the best account in the Language of the
tortured state of mind to which the evangelical assurance is the
only answer'; and he saw in Defoe

> . . . a man who seems to know almost as much as St Augustine
> himself about the hidden torments of the sinful soul, and
> fully as much about its sense of despairing helplessness.
> Moreover, he could unerringly diagnose the disease as the
> urge to repent without the power actually to do it. He knew
> what some moral theologians seem to forget, that repentance
> is a problem first, and only afterwards a release; that it is
> more a free gift of God than a willed and deliberate expia-
> tion.[80]

Canon Lloyd's 'riddle' was to explain how such insight could have been gained by a man in whose life he could find 'not a single hint of any repentance of his own, nor any recognition that it might be as necessary for him as for his own Crusoe'. Yet if he had been familiar with Defoe's *Meditations*, he would have found that the second of these — 'come unto Me all ye That are Weary &c' — deals explicitly with the very dilemma he describes. After first deploring the 'Universal Impotence' which paralyses the human will in its efforts to meet God's demands, Defoe asks:

> But what Must I
> That Can do Nothing Do
> Why tho' you can Not Go yet go
> And trye
> Say Lord I can Not Come yet Here am I

The Meditation concludes:

> We Can do Nothing of o^r selvs but he
>   Has told us he'l Assisting be
> Who Knows But if Endeavours are Set on
> That help That is Sufficient May come Down.

If the *Meditations* and the events which gave rise to them provide an answer to Canon Lloyd's riddle, it is far from a complete answer. How did a young man suffering such spiritual agonies develop, within a comparatively few years, the self-righteousness and religious complacency so often shown by the mature Defoe, so that, of the many facets of his complex personality, that of the Christian is one of the least attractive? Though we have no direct evidence of his religious evolution during the next few years, the *Meditations* themselves offer a few clues. When these were being composed in 1681, the struggle was still in progress. The third Meditation — 'Thou hast Made us & Not We' — asks:

> How is it Then That I
> So much Aversion to My Duty Find
>   That Tho' I Own it Due
> And in a Sort performe it To
> Yet Lord! How Little does my Act Explain My Mind

The seventh and final Meditation — 'The Seige Raised' — adopts
military imagery:

> In all ye Conflicts of Our Souls
> reason wou'd be too hard for Sin
> Wou'd Inclinacon But Stand Neuter There
>   And Not betray Within
> But how Can We this Garrison Defend?
> When all our Troops are Out of Our Command
>   Basely Decline ye Noble Fight
> And Parley wth ye Adversary in Our Sight
>
>   Tis all in Vain
> The Thoughts of Victory to Entertain
> When the will the Captain-Genrall of ye Mind
>   To Mutiny's Enclin'd
> And troops of the Affeccons wavring Stand
> Apt to revolt from reasons just Command
>   And ye Corrupted rabble of Desires
>   Deep in ye black Confederacy of Sin
>   Raises Their Mob of Doubts and Feares
> And Boldly Lets ye Feirce Invader in.

Defoe was fighting his war on two fronts. Not only had he to
contend with his own unregenerate nature, but, even while
yearning 'To be New Made', and begging

> That all my Sins may be Passt by
> That Black Account may be Wip'd out

— he still had to struggle with 'Doubts' and 'half Conviccons'. It
is significant that the forces he was deploying against 'Sin' were
those of 'Reason'; and just as he had 'reasoned' himself out of
his faith in the first place, so now he was in the process of
reasoning himself back again. Even after his faith was fully
restored, he found the most conclusive argument against
atheism to be the purely prudential one: 'What if there should
be a God!'[81] His first Meditation had begged God to reveal
Himself to him — 'Some Glances of Thy Face, tis I Implore' —
but there are no signs that he ever received them. For him the
existence of God was to remain, not a matter of experience, but
of inference; and he clutched at evidence of the direct inter-

vention of God in the affairs of the world, stressing the intimations of the divine will in dreams, premonitions, coincidences, or in the apparent blind play of chance. His belief in the control of God over the details of life, exercised in advance by providences, or retrospectively by judgments, clashed with his belief in the iron chain of cause and consequence, which had room for God only as the original maker and clock-winder of the universe. Though aware of this conflict, he shrank from a direct confrontation — less, one imagines, through any lack of confidence in his ability to resolve it, than from a reluctance to be forced into a theological position which he was determined not to adopt.

However far the young Defoe may have ranged into theological space, he had never escaped from the gravitational pull of the Calvinist faith in which he had been brought up; and he made his re-entry at his point of departure. There are no signs that he ever contemplated embracing any other version of the Christian faith. In other matters he prided himself on his originality; and he even took a perverse delight in the belief that he alone was right and the rest of mankind wrong. He was never reluctant to cross swords with his fellow Dissenters over their private conduct or political tactics; but he was obviously determined never again to challenge Calvinist orthodoxy. Exactly when and how he finally stifled his doubts, we do not know; nor when he convinced himself, as he certainly seems to have done, that his sins had indeed been forgiven. The passage of time, his remoteness from the scene of his duel, the fact that his victim was apparently a stranger, would all help to make the whole hideous business increasingly unreal. Certain features of his own personality must have helped to heal his 'wounded conscience' — his unquenchable self-esteem; his natural resilience, the amazing energy with which he threw himself into new activities — even though one may wonder how much of this energy was neurotic in character. Throughout his life much of this energy was directed into religious channels; and perhaps, like Crusoe, he set himself a regular programme of Bible reading and drove himself to the punctilious performance of religious duties, in an effort to create for himself the religious faith which was really lacking. His facility in quoting from the Scriptures shows his lifelong familiarity. He was widely read, too, in contemporary devotional literature; and the sermons he heard during his life must have run into thousands. The series of sermons by the Rev. John

Collins which he attended throughout the year 1681, and carefully transcribed into the same notebook which contained his *Meditations*, may have been part of a self-imposed programme designed to assist in his spiritual recovery.[82] Yet despite all the time and thought that Defoe devoted to religion, he never succeeded in making it the driving force of his life. Religious duties lay in a separate compartment of their own, and might even conflict with the real business of life; for a 'man may say his prayers so long and unseasonably 'til he is undone, and not a creditor he has . . . will use him any the better'.[83] In most of the activities of his very varied life, Defoe's religious belief was simply irrelevant. Some people have felt that Crusoe's conversion left him fundamentally the same man as before, and we may be tempted to feel that it was the same with the author who created him. After Defoe's spiritual crisis he certainly set out on a new course in life; yet though his faith may at times have been the ballast that steadied his ship, it was never the wind that filled his sails.

Defoe was not, in fact, a truly religious man at all;[84] and one symptom of this is his inability to sympathise with alien beliefs, which he dismissed as based on superstition, ignorance and folly. It is not surprising that he made no contribution to theological or devotional literature, or that he has no place among the nation's hymn-writers. Some of his later books were certainly on ostensibly religious themes, and others contain lengthy religious passages. Yet to the modern ear these consist of little more than unctuous and sanctimonious religiosity, and form the least attractive part of all his writings. There were not lacking contemporaries and later critics to label him a hypocrite; and in his *Meditations*, at least, he confessed to the charge. But if he did profess a faith which was really lacking, he was also making prodigious efforts to deceive himself. In all this he must have been far from unique. There must have been many others who shared his dilemma, but who struggled in silence. Unfortunately for his reputation in this respect, Defoe was all too articulate.

6 A Wit, Turn'd Tradesmen

Even when his spiritual crisis had been resolved to his own satisfaction, it would have been out of the question for Defoe to return to his original intention of entering the Christian ministry. That was something from which he had been irrevocably 'set apart'.[1] Nor was he qualified for any other learned profession; and James Foe must have felt that the money spent on his education had been wasted. Defoe's decision to return to the way of life to which he been 'bred', that of a merchant,[2] though perhaps inevitable, may have helped towards a reconciliation between father and son.

James Foe, a merchant with correspondents in Portugal and Italy, and something of an expert in book-keeping, was now during the years 1679—84 holding various responsible positions in the Butchers' Company.[3] In 1680 the new post of Renter Warden was specially created to enable him to relieve that year's Master of his financial responsibilities, and in 1683 he was appointed auditor of the previous year's accounts. But he then dropped abruptly out of the active life of the Company, and never became Master. This may have been connected with some change in his family circumstances, perhaps the death of his second wife, Defoe's stepmother; for he now left French Court, where he had lived since 1671, and reappeared in 1683 as a lodger with 'Widow Scopelong' in the same house in Jones's Rents, Swan Alley, off Coleman Street, where Defoe had spent much of his early childhood.[4] He survived for more than twenty years, marrying yet again, and retaining his interest in trade to the end; for his will mentions a 'parcel of goods' entrusted to a relative to sell.[5] As the son of a London citizen, Defoe was, by 'the ancient and laudable custom of the City of London', legally entitled to a share of his father's personal estate. As James Foe's specific bequests were all to his grandchildren or family friends, Defoe must already have had his share, probably in the form of 'stocking money' to set him up in trade. There may be a hint of how much this was in his account of a young man beginning the world with £1000, but using credit to stock his warehouse with double that value in goods.[6]

Defoe's formal commitment to a mercantile career must date from about 1681, but he may have dabbled in trade even during his adolescence; for he was certainly alive to many developments in the nation's economic life during those years. He knew how Paternoster Row was rebuilt after the Fire to suit the convenience of the mercers.[7] He gave a brief history of 'black crapes' — introduced by French refugees, and used first for ladies' dresses, then for servants, and finally for men's wear:

> It serv'd the Gentlemen for Wastcoats, all Men for Linings, and the Clergy for Gowns; till an unhappy Author, writing a Book, call'd *Speculum Crapegownorum* . . . a Banter upon Sir Roger L'Estrange's Guide to the Inferior Clergy . . . these Gentlemen took the Hint, and immediately took a Pique at the Crape-Gown, as a Type of Inferior Clergyman, to the Irreparable Damage of the Innocent Manufacture which never recover'd its Reputation.[8]

The offending book appeared in 1682, But Defoe's knowledge clearly went back many years before that. He described how some French ribbon-weavers of Spitalfields contrived to foist on the Court the fashion of beribboned pantaloons, supposedly the latest French mode, but based on nothing more than a Harlequin's costume, seen among some strolling players in Paris.[9] He several times mentions a riot he had seen in Spitalfields 'in 1679 or 1680, if I remember right, when the weavers mutinied, upon some occasion of setting up Engine-Looms, as they call'd them, in which one Man might do as much work as 6 or 8, or more'.[10]

His early familiarity with the textile manufacture was not confined to London; and once again his main interest was in the various groups of Protestant refugees, who had settled mainly in the Eastern Counties. He told how the persecutions of Alva in the Netherlands

> . . . brought over a vast multitude of Flemings, Wallons, and Dutch, who with their whole families settled at Norwich, at Ipswich, Colchester, Canterbury, Exeter, and the like. From these came the Walloon Church at Canterbury, and the Dutch Churches at Norwich, Colchester, and Yarmouth; and from

hence came the true-born English families at those places with foreign names; as the DeVinks at Norwich, the Rebows at Colchester, the Papilons &c. at Canterbury — families to whom this nation are much in debt for the first planting those manufactures, from which we have since raised the greatest trade in the world.[11]

Among many such families with whom Defoe himself had contacts was one whose name he was to immortalise, that of Cruso. It has been assumed that he took the name from Timothy Cruso, Dissenting minister and former pupil of Morton's Academy; but they can have spent little time together there, for Cruso was at least three years older than Defoe, and there is no known contact between them in later life.[12] The London merchant family to which Timothy Cruso belonged was a junior branch of one which had migrated from Hondschoote in Flanders towards the end of Elizabeth's reign, and established itself in Norwich. Here for four successive generations they were described as 'hosiers', or stocking manufacturers; and a descendant of this family, born shortly after Defoe's death, was to be named Robinson Cruso.[13]

Defoe's early knowledge of Norwich appeared when he wrote: 'let any Man who knew the City about 25 Years before, compare its Condition to what it was reduc'd in the Year 1699';[14] and he stressed the contrast between the prosperous years at the end of Charles II's reign, when Norfolk stockings were sold in London, Holland and France to the value of '5000s. per week', and the collapse caused by the introduction in London 'about 1684' of the worsted knitting frame, 'which performs that in a day which would otherwise employ a poor woman eight or ten days'.[15]

In later years Defoe's enemies derided him as a hosier, a description which he warmly rejected. In the sense in which it was intended he was correct: he never kept a shop or sold stockings across the counter. The taxation lists however show him as a 'wholesale hosier',[16] though he simply described himself as an exporter of unspecified woollen goods.[17] He probably dealt at first with the master manufacturers of Norwich and the surrounding area — perhaps including the Crusos — buying hosiery in bulk and selling it overseas; and then from about 1684, dealing directly with the master weavers in Spitalfields, becoming familiar with the stocking-frame as something 'to be seen in every stocking weaver's garret'.[18]

He preferred to stress the other mainstay of his business, the import of wines and brandies; and to this too he seems to have been 'bred'. He gives a lively account of the changes over many years in the drinking habits of the London poor; and in particular how, after the Dutch War of 1672–4, beer and ale began to give way to spirits distilled from spoiled wines, and sold, 'to the personal knowledge of the Writer', in chandlers' and barbers' shops.[19] Perhaps his early familiarity with the seedier corners of the liquor trade means that his father had allowed him to gain some commercial experience and make a little youthful pocket money by selling to the 'Strong-Water-Shops' wines which proved unfit to drink. No doubt too the wine-ship in which he made his eventful voyage to Oporto had been trading on his father's account. But before long he was involved in this trade on his own account, referring to 'an Importation of 40000 Pipes a Year, as it was when I was concern'd in the Portugal Wine-Trade',[20] and declaring that 'I have for my own share, imported 700 Pipes of Oporto Wines in a Year, and sold them to advantage too', at a time when they paid £6 or £7 more duty a tun than the French wines.[21] Defoe also dealt in the latter: 'I have sold many a Tun of as good French *Claret* as is in the World, or perhaps ever will be, at 6 *l*. 10*s*. to 7 or 8 *l*. a Hogshead';[22] and offering years later to buy claret for his patron, Harley, he declared, 'This Trade being my Old business, I perswade my Self my Palat can Not be deceived in what will please him.'[23] By 1686 too he had 'frequently bought and imported Brandies in England, and had some judgment in them'.[24]

A contemporary newsletter may help to pin down one of his early trading ventures, when it describes how the *Biscay Merchant*, outward bound, 'laden with piece-goods, and very rich' was driven ashore in Sandwich Bay by a violent storm in the small hours of 29 December 1682; 'At the coming away of our letter she was not broken in pieces, and there were hopes, if the wind ceased, to save her.'[25] Defoe seems to provide the sequel when he recounted, many years later, an incident which he placed near the neighbouring town of Deal, about which

. . . I can tell you of my own knowledge, and not a little to my loss. When a ship came ashore in the night, and in distress, and coming gently ashore has sat upright, and the storm abating, the cargo might have been saved, and perhaps the ship got off again; when those mountain thieves have not rifled the loading only, but torn the very ship herself to pieces before help could be had . . . And in smaller time than one would think possible, a whole ship has been plundered and gutted, and the goods carried up country and irretrievably lost.[26]

No doubt Defoe had made all haste to the scene, but not in time to save his share of the cargo; and his only belated compensation may have been an idea or two on the plundering of a stranded ship, to use in *Robinson Crusoe*.[27]

Despite such setbacks, Defoe threw himself into his new career with characteristic enthusiasm, and probably soon convinced himself that he had chosen 'the most Noble way of Life':

A True-Bred Merchant . . . Understands Languages without Books, Geography without Maps, his Journals and Trading-Voyages delineate the World; his Foreign Exchanges, Protests and Procurations, speak all Tongues; He sits in his Counting-House, and Converses with all Nations, and keeps the most exquisite and extensive part of Human Society in Universal Correspondence.[28]

In fact, however, he was far from content with such vicarious experience as he could acquire while sitting in his counting-house; and another lengthy absence from home is implied when he writes of the time 'when I liv'd in Spain'.[29] Evidence of his presence in England on various dates leaves three possible periods for this: the first eight months of 1682, the first six months of 1683, and most of the year 1684. The last of these seems unlikely, as he was then newly married and established in a new home and business premises; and since he was presumably acting in a subordinate capacity for a principal or partner who remained in England, the earliest date is the most probable.

Defoe's contacts were with the far south of Spain. He knew Seville, with its fine bridge of boats, spacious 'Key' and noble customs house, as well as its Contraction House whose register reputedly contained the names of 'six Millions of People who are gone over from Europe to New *Spain*'.[30] He also knew

Cadiz, through which other European nations could trade, though only indirectly, with Spanish America.[31] A less distant Spanish possession to which these restrictions did not apply was the Canary Islands. Defoe's apparent familiarity with the Pico of Teneriffe might be dismissed as derived from some illustration in a travel book;[32] yet his knowledge of how the islanders obtained their pipe staves, as well as cheap beef and pork, from New England, and his contemptuous reference to ignorant projectors who 'have never been at, or traded to those Islands', suggest that he may have visited them himself.[33] In these dangerous waters 'not a sailor goes to Sea in a Merchant Ship . . . but he has a secret Dread upon his Soul . . . that it may one time or another be his lot to be taken by the *Moors*', a fate which befell Robinson Crusoe, captured near the Canaries and taken into Sallee.[34] Further south, he knew, lay 'that country which, lying between the Emperor of Morocco's and the negro's, lies wast and uninhabited', but filled in his imagination with 'prodigious numbers of tygers, lyons, leopards, and other furious creatures';[35] while beyond that again lay 'the Golden Shores of *Africk*, where they Barter Glass for *Gold*, and *Bawbles* for the *Souls of Men*'.[36]

There can be little doubt, at least, that Defoe sailed through what he called the 'Strait's Mouth' into the Mediterranean, discerning to the north 'a Ridge of Mountains which produce those rich wines we call *Mountain Malaga*'s' and which 'are seen at a great Distance as you sail by the Coast', and passing in sight of Malaga, which 'makes a noble Prospect, as Ships sail by in view of it'. His destination appears to have been Velez-Malaga, a little further east, set 'in a most delightful Country; wonderfully fertile . . . planted like a Garden, the Vales with woods of Olive Trees, and with Lemons, Citrons and Figs; and the sides of the Mountains . . . cover'd with Vines'. Though itself 'a small city within the Land', it had at Torre del Mar, 'a port for lading Fruit, as Raisins and Lemons. The Road is good, for Ships of any Burden, and several Ships do load here, especially *English* . . . generally by Orders from the . . . Merchants at *Malaga*.'[37]

It was most likely in this part of Spain that Defoe stayed long enough to pick up a smattering of the language, to learn several Spanish proverbs,[38] and to observe something of the Spanish way of life. He knew how '*Spaniards* walk, with their Hands on

their Swords';[39] how 'the *Spanish* Beggars . . . strut about in
their Cloak and Bilboes at their Sides'; how 'wine mingled with
Water is the ordinary Beverage';[40] how their fashions in dress
'are National, known, constant, and without or with but small
Variation';[41] and how seldom a true-bred Spaniard will 'pretend
to any line or genealogy farther back than the fifteenth or
sixteenth century' — since 'not a man will own himself descended
from a Moor', though 'most have undergone the mixture, and
have it not only in their language, their colour, their temper,
their names, but even . . . in their very faces'.[42]

Defoe was scornful of the commercial sloth of the Spaniards,
for not only allowing the Dutch and English to control their
foreign trade, 'but employing our Ships in their own Affairs
from Port to Port'.[43] Perhaps it was some such voyage that took
him further into the Mediterranean; for though he shows no
particular knowledge of most of the large ports along the
coast, he several times mentions Alicante, 'where the Raisins
of the Sun are cured', and two much smaller ports, Xevia (Javea)
and Denia, where the same fruit could be loaded.[44]

Whether he continued on the same north-easterly course to
Marseilles, or visited it on some other journey, Defoe was
certainly familiar with that seaport, admiring the great 'Key',
and noting the new churches and squares built to the order of
Louis XIV, and the country seats in the surrounding hills.[45] He
described how 'the fine *Lucca* Olives' were 'generally sent to
Marseilles, and thence to *Narbonne* in *France*, and brought
through the new Royal Canal . . . to *Thoulouse*, and so by the
Garonne to *Bourdeaux*, and thence by Sea to *London*'.[46]
Perhaps he followed this route himself, for he several times
mentioned what he called 'le Nouveaux Canal pour le joindra
les deux Mers' — the Canal du Midi, officially opened in 1681.
Though there was still 'very little to do' upon it in the way of
trade, he greatly admired it as a feat of engineering, and years
later proposed similar canals to link the Clyde with the Forth,
and the North Sea with the Baltic.[47] After passing 'for many
miles' through the vineyards which lined the banks of the
Garonne, he came to Bordeaux. 'The River making a small bay
just at the Town, the City is built most agreeably on the Circle
of it; and the Ships lying before it . . . it makes a most pleasant
View.'[48] Though puzzled by the local 'Gascogne' patoiś, despite
his familiarity with the 'politer French',[49] he felt very much at

home in other ways; for Bordeaux, once under English rule, still retained many English characteristics.[50] And with 'four or five hundred Ships in the River . . . loading Wines for *England*', a passage home can have presented no problems.[51]

Defoe may have been acting in Spain and France on behalf of his father or of some other business associate. Among those with whom he is known to have had dealings were Samuel and James Stancliffe, both descended from a family long established in the woollen manufacturing town of Halifax in the West Riding of Yorkshire, but also for half a century concerned in the retail trade in hosiery in London. Samuel was the son of Michael Stancliffe, who had been in business at the sign of the Castle, at the corner of Bread Street and Cheapside, for some twenty years before the Fire, and later returned to carry on his trade in the rebuilt premises. A member of the Haberdashers' Company, he was, according to the parish register of All Hallows, Bread Street, a 'stocking seller by traid'; and on his death in 1680 he left 'the counters presses and other things belonging to my trade' to his son Samuel, at that time a young married man about thirty years old. The latter was joined by his kinsman, James Stancliffe, about six years his junior, and son of John Stancliffe of Hagstocks, Halifax: and they continued together at the sign of the Castle, though apparently diversifying their business.[52] A dozen years later Samuel Stancliffe declared that he 'for several years past had an acquaintance and considerable dealings in the way of trade and otherwise with Daniel Foe', while the latter declared that he had at one time been in partnership with them.[53] It must have been from this friendship that Defoe developed a special interest in their native town of Halifax, visiting it several times in later life, and once spending some weeks there.[54] Like so many of Defoe's circle, the Stancliffes were Presbyterians; and the diary of the Rev. Oliver Heywood, the Presbyterian dissenting minister at Halifax, shows him as a close personal friend of James Stancliffe's parents, who confided to him the contents of their son's letters when, as an apprentice in London in 1675, he had passed through a severe spiritual crisis.[55] One of their kinsmen, another Samuel Stancliffe, was himself an ejected minister who ran a meeting in Jamaica Row, Rotherhithe.[56]

Two other clerical exiles from the same part of Yorkshire were well known to Defoe. One was the celebrated Dr John

Tillotson, born at Sowerby near Halifax, who despite his Presbyterian sympathies had conformed to the established Church, and was in fact destined to become Archbishop of Canterbury.[57] At this time he was best known for his sermons, whose spirit appealed more to the Dissenters than to his fellow Anglicans, and whose language was taken as a model by the prose writers of the coming age. The other Yorkshireman, who 'had the Honour to be Tutor to the Learned and most Excellent Dr. Tillotson', was the Rev. David Clarkson, originally from Bradford in the West Riding, but now an ejected minister living at Mortlake in Surrey.[58] Defoe greatly admired two of his books, *No Scripture Evidence for Diocesan Bishops*, and his posthumously published *A Discourse of Liturgies*, dealing with the two main issues on which the Dissenters felt themselves obliged to separate from the Church of England. But when he wrote that 'Mr. Clarkson was a Man of that Learning and Reading, so much a Gentleman, so much a Scholar, and particularly so modest and so humble, that even some of the best men in the Church of England admir'd him; and as I had the Honour to be acquainted with him . . . ', he was referring not only to a respected minister and theologian, but to a family friend.[59]

To explore the ramifications of Clarkson's family, in which the service of God and Mammon are inextricably intertwined, is constantly to encounter people with whom Defoe had dealings. Clarkson's second marriage, conducted by Tillotson in 1664, had been to Elizabeth (Kenrick), widow of Walrave Lodwick, citizen and fishmonger. The Lodwicks had come from 'Bell', presumably Bailleul, in Flanders during the reign of James I, and for more than a century were pillars of the Dutch Church, Austin Friars. On his death in 1662 Walrave Lodwick had left his widow a large house at Upper Tooting in Surrey, and a young family to bring up;[60] and there were several more children by her marriage to David Clarkson. One of the latter's step-children was Charles Lodwick, Defoe's personal friend, who at the end of 1683 alleged the particulars for his marriage licence.[61] A merchant, about three years older than Defoe, he went off to New York in 1685, fighting a few years later against the French in Canada, rising to the rank of Lieutenant-Colonel and becoming part-author of an account of the campaign. He headed one of the factions on the New York Council, serving as Mayor in 1694—5, and corresponded frequently with the Lords of Trade and Plantations, who clearly valued his advice. He returned to England about 1700, resumed his connection with the Dutch Church, Austin Friars, and eventually died at his house in Camberwell, Surrey in 1723; but apparently he had lost contact with Defoe long before that.[62] His half-brother, Matthew Clarkson, who had accompanied him to New York, apparently acted for a while as Defoe's factor there. He returned to England after his father's death, but in November 1689 was petitioning for the post of Secretary for New York. He supported his petition with a certificate to testify to his character as a factor; and one of the eight who signed it was Daniel Foe. Two others, James Moyer and Robert Knight probably had connections with Defoe. The remaining five were all close relatives of the petitioner — his brother David Clarkson; his half-brother Thomas Lodwick; his cousins, David King and John Rowett; and Gerard van Heythusen, who was either his uncle, now in his seventies, or more probably the latter's nephew of the same names. It seems likely that all the eight merchants who signed the certificate had dealings, not only with Matthew Clarkson, but also with each other. Despite the fact that his support came from such a narrow circle, Clarkson eventually succeeded in his aim, and settled and flourished in New York.[63]

Thomas Lodwick and the younger Gerard van Heythusen also found their way eventually to New York; and who better than Anglicised Netherlanders to flourish in a colony which until a couple of decades before had been known as New Amsterdam? It was probably through this family that Defoe himself became involved in trade with the English colonies in North America; but like so many dissenting mercantile families, the Foes must have had multiple links with New England. The Colbron family, from which Elizabeth Marsh had come, had contributed some of the earliest settlers in Massachusetts;[64] Henry Foe's saddlery business had been mainly with merchants trading to the American colonies;[65] John Abbott, of St Saviours Southwark, gentleman, who mentioned 'cousin James Foe' in his will of 1693, had a son, Josiah Abbott, living in Boston, Massachusetts.[66] The earliest datable link between Defoe himself and America was in December 1684; for he was present when Richard Wharton submitted to the Lords of Trade and Plantations 'proposals for the regulation of New England', which included the incorporation of a Company to develop the colony's resources, especially minerals. It appears that Wharton and his associates had 'discovered Mines of Copper and Lead and Blossomes of Royall Mines in New England'.[67] Defoe mentions the scene more than once:

> I know, it has always been a Court Maxim in *England*, while the Courts were afraid of the Peoples Greatness, to keep the Colonies under, and the Notions of their setting up for an Independency have been started to amuse the World, and justifie the Maxim, I speak of . . .
>
> This was the mighty frightful *Chimera*, that prevented *England* encouraging the proposal of a *Copper Mine* in *New England*, and I had many years ago the Pleasure to see, *and laugh at the Folly of* . . . a famous states-man making a long Oration full of nothing at the Council Board in King *Charles*'s Time . . . 'tis in meer Compassion to the Reputation of that Noble Lord, that I do not name him.[68]

And Defoe went on to demonstrate with irrefutable logic that it could never be in the interests of the American colonists to seek independence. The first clear evidence that he was trading with the American colonies on his own account dates from 1688, but that is unlikely to have been his first transatlantic venture. His outward freight was probably a mixed one: 'When Merchants send adventures to our *British* colonies, 'tis usual for them to make up to each factor what they call a *sortable cargoe*; that is to say something of everything that may furnish trades-men there with parcels to fill their shops and invite customers.'[69] The only return cargo we know of was tobacco, obtained in 1688 through his Maryland factor, Samuel Sandford; but he also had an unnamed agent in New York — possibly Charles Lodwick at that time, since Matthew Clarkson was in England — as well as correspondents in Boston, co-partners Joseph Beaton and John Sharp.[70] The latter may have been yet another member of the Lodwick–Clarkson connection, for David Clarkson's sister had married a man of those names more than fifty years before.[71] Another of Defoe's special interests was shipbuilding. His only surviving sister, Mary, had in 1679 married Francis Barham, junior, a shipwright of the parish of St Mary Whitechapel, who probably assisted his father, also Francis Barham, in a shipyard

which he owned near Execution Dock.[72] Samuel Pepys described
the elder Barham in 1686 as 'above three score years old . . . a
man of no spirit or method, and a Phanatick';[73] but the latter's
will of 1694 at least shows him as a man of some individuality,
specifying the timber and constructional methods to be used for
his coffin, apparently anxious for a seaworthy vessel to carry
him into the ocean of eternity. His will shows that he owned a
thirty-second part of an Ipswich ship, *The Friends Goodwill*,
whose commander Thomas Cullum was probably Defoe's
boyhood friend; and his daughter had married another Ipswich
master-mariner, Thomas Wright, who was probably related to
the Cullums. His will also shows that by that time the younger
Francis Barham was dead, leaving Defoe's sister with two children, and that she had remarried to another shipwright, Robert
Davis.[74] The latter was a man of enterprise and ingenuity who
was to remain for many years one of Defoe's closest and most
trusted friends; but his background and early activities remain a
mystery. He may have been the Robert Davis who witnessed
David Clarkson's will in 1686;[75] some hints suggest that he may
have had Dutch connections;[76] it may have been through him
that Defoe was to become exceptionally well informed about
the layout and organisation of the Royal Dockyards at Chatham
and Portsmouth.[77] But there are other possibilities — for
instance, through David Clarkson's nephew, Abraham Sharp, a
mathematician and assistant to Flamsteed, the Astronomer
Royal, who at various times used his influence to find him posts
in both these dockyards.[78]

After so many elusive figures half glimpsed in the mist, it is a
relief to turn to a scene sharply outlined in winter sunshine. On
1 January 1684, in the middle of the coldest spell of weather in
living memory, with the Thames above London Bridge frozen
solid for weeks on end, Defoe, then a young merchant of
twenty-three, stood in the parish church of St Botolph Aldgate.
A few hundred yards away in Whitechapel High Street his uncle
Henry had once run his saddlery business. Just outside the
churchyard was the site of the plague pit which had so powerfully affected his youthful imagination; and diagonally across
the road stood the Pye Tavern, whose blasphemous revellers —
or rather their lime-bleached bones — had lain in that pit for
nearly twenty years. But such morbid thoughts were probably
far from the mind of the young merchant who now stood on

the threshold of a 'new scene of life'. It was his wedding day. His young bride, about twenty years of age, was Mary, the only daughter of John Tuffley, Citizen and Cooper of London, and of Joan (Rawlins) his wife.[79] Mary Foe remains a shadowy figure. Defoe has left us no portrait of her, but we do at least know what qualities he considered desirable in a wife; so that, if she measured up to them,

> . . . she was a very honest, modest, sober and religious young woman; had a very good share of sense, was agreeable enough in her person, spoke very handsomely and to the purpose, always with decency and good manners, and not backward to speak when anything required it, or impertinently forward when it was not her business; very handy and housewifely in anything that was before her; an excellent manager . . . She knew very well how to behave to all kinds of folks she had about her, and to better, if she . . . found any.[80]

There can be little doubt that the husband whom she promised to 'love, honour and obey', and who once called her his 'faithful steward',[81] remained the dominant partner throughout the forty-seven years of their married life. During the next twenty years she was to bear him at least eight children, of whom she reared six, and proved a 'Vertuous and Excellent Mother'.[82] When she made her marriage vows, 'for richer, for poorer, for better or for worse', she can have had little inkling of what this would mean for her; but it would fall to her to hold her family together, not only through the extraordinary vicissitudes of her husband's career, but also his frequent absences, often prolonged, and often in very distressing circumstances. Yet theirs remained a stable marriage, based on mutual respect and loyalty.

How Defoe came to meet his wife we do not know. If the Tuffleys were an offshoot of the prolific yeoman family of that name which still flourished at Birstall near Leicester, this may indicate yet another link between the Foes and the Leicester area.[83] Possibly Defoe had dealings with John Tuffley in connection with the importation of wines and brandies; but we know nothing of his father-in-law's business affairs, except that he was able to give his daughter the very substantial dowry of £3700.[84] When he died a few years later he made no further bequest to her, leaving the bulk of his property to his widow and to his only son, Samuel.[85] As the latter's inheritance included some landed property in the Surrey parishes of Nutfield and Bletchingley, it may be that the dowry which Mary Tuffley brought her husband also included some real estate; and this might explain how Defoe came to have a tenant, a butcher, in Westminster, and might be the basis of his proud claim to be an English freeholder.[86] Samuel Tuffley remained a bachelor, and most, if not all, of the Tuffley property, amounting to at least £12,000, was destined to pass to Mary Foe, though not for some forty years.[87] Most likely, however, Defoe and his family received further financial support from his wife's relatives long before that. All we know of Mary Tuffley's more distant relatives is that she had an aunt named Mary Robinson, the only known claimant to be the original of Crusoe's first name.

Where Defoe had lived and done business as a bachelor is not known; but on marriage he set himself up in Freeman's Yard, a small court on the north side of Cornhill, in the parish of St Michael Cornhill, and within a stone's throw of the Royal Exchange. He first appears in the records of Cornhill Ward as a very junior member of the Petty Jury for 1684, being so little known that when the list was drawn up at the end of the previous year he appeared simply as '—— Foe'.[88] The area was much sought after. The premises had been rebuilt after the Fire, rents were high and frontages narrow. On the ground floor was his warehouse, with direct access from Freeman's Yard. In 1711, long after Defoe had gone, it was used by a gown wholesaler, Henry Bright, who identified his 'Gown-House' in press advertisements:

> This was the Ware-House of Mr. Daniel Defoe . . . My Customers may go in and out, without going through any House, or Coffee House.[89]

Above the warehouse would be his counting house where his business was conducted; and above that again, several storeys where he lived with his family. Beneath the warehouse was probably the vault where he stored his wines — perhaps the very one mentioned in an advertisement which appeared in his *Review* on 27 December 1711:

> *Brook* and *Hellier* give Notice, That there is a convenient

Place, newly fitted up, adjoining to their *Old Vault* in *Freeman's Yard*, Cornhill; for the Reception and Accomodation of Gentlemen, as well in respect of eating as Drinking, where their Wines are Sold at the same prices within Doors as Without.[90]

It may be that Brook and Hellier were old business associates of his, since for several months previously Defoe had been giving favourable publicity to their efforts to break into the retail trade in Portuguese wines in the face of the hostility of the vintners. A fortnight later he was looking back nostalgically to the surroundings of his early business premises, and sarcastically deploring the changes in the neighbourhood:

There's the fine and famous Street of *Cornhill*, since I remember, fill'd with Wholesale-Men, and Rich Shopkeepers, if I mistake not now you may see there, two or three most famous Perriwig-makers, five or six spacious Coffee-Houses, three or four Illustrious Cake-Shops and Pastry-Men, one or two Brandy-Shops, and the like; and these not in the small Shops, or meaner parts of it, but in the Capital Houses, of great Rents and large Fronts, in the very Prime of the Street: The Alleys, where the smaller places were full of Notary Publicks, Offices of Assurance, and such People who managed the necessary Appendices of Trade, now they are crouded with Stock-Jobbing Brokers, buying and selling of Bearskins, and Tricking and Sharping to get Estates.[91]

Perhaps the rot had already set in in his own time; for the taxation lists show that while his neighbours included other hosiers, linen-drapers and 'haberdashers of hatts', his own premises lay between a coffee house kept by Lawrence Lythe, and the establishment of William Hughes and Thomas Eaglesfield, dancing masters.[92]

It would be interesting to know just what his neighbours made of the young merchant who had never been through the mill as an apprentice, and who must have brought to his business the weaknesses as well as the strengths of an enthusiastic amateur. Nor had he abandoned all his old interests. He later indulged in a fanciful self-caricature:

A wit, turn'd Tradesman! what an incongruous Part of Nature is there brought together, consisting of direct Contraries? No Apron Strings will hold him; 'tis in vain to lock him in behind the Compter, he's gone in a Moment; instead of Journal and Ledger, he runs away to his *Virgil* and *Horace*; his Journal Entries are Pindaricks, and his Ledger is all Heroicks; he is truly dramatick from one End to the other, through the whole Scene of his Trade; and as the first Part is all Comedy, so the last Acts are always made up of Tragedy; a Statute of Bankrupt is his *Exeunt Omnes*, and he generally speaks the Epilogue in the *Fleet Prison* or the *Mint*.[93]

But the tragi-comedy had still a long while to run. If Francis Lodwick, uncle of his friend Charles Lodwick, could combine a merchant's life with the invention of a Universal Language and membership of the Royal Society, why should not Defoe still be able to pursue his own literary interests?[94] As it happens, nothing of his has survived from his early years as a merchant, apart from his *Meditations*; but there once existed in manuscript form a compilation, corrected for the press with a dedication, entitled *Historical Collections : or Memoirs of Passages collected from several Authors. 1682.*[95] Nor is any copy known of his first published piece, a pamphlet against the Turks which he tells us appeared in 1683.[96] He continued to read verse. In addition to Dryden, whose *Absalom and Achitophel* (1681) was to influence some of his own later verse,[97] he also shows familiarity with the work of lesser poets of the age. Among the poems he quotes are Charles Cotton's *The Wonders of the Peak* (1681),[98] Samuel Colvill's *The Whig Supplication* (1681),[99] Thomas Creech's translation of Lucretius, *De Rerum Natura* (1682),[100] and Samuel Wesley's *Gigantomachia* (1682), which he quotes twice — once apparently from memory, once from the book.[101]

A further hint that he continued to look on himself as a man of letters appears in his *Essay upon Projects* (1697), where, after discussing how the role of the French Academy had been 'to Refine and Correct their own Language', he continued:

I once had the Honour to be a Member of a small Society, who seem'd to offer at this Noble Design in *England*. But the greatness of the Work, and the Modesty of the Gentlemen concern'd, prevail'd with them to desist an Enterprise which appear'd too great for Private Hands . . . The *English* Tongue is a Subject not at all less worthy of the Labour of such a Society than the *French*, and capable of a much greater Perfection . . . And as my Lord *Roscommon*, who is allow'd to be a good Judge of the *English*, because he wrote it as exactly as any ever did, expresses what I mean; in these lines,

"*For who did ever in* French *Authors see*
"*The Comprehensive* English *Energy?*
"*The weighty* Bullion *of one* Sterling *Line*,
"*Drawn to* French Wire *wou'd through whole Pages shine*".[102]

In quoting from Roscommon's *Essay on Translated Verse*, published in 1684, Defoe gives a clue to the identity of the 'small Society' of which he 'once had the Honour to be a Member'. For although the idea of such an Academy had several times been canvassed, the only known attempt to put it into practice had been made by Roscommon himself during the last three years of Charles II's reign. In his manuscript biography of Roscommon, his friend Knightly Chetwood describes how he 'set himself to form a sort of Academy' whose main purpose was 'refining our Language without abating the force of it'.[103] Among those who shared in its labours, which can only have been fitful and were soon abandoned, were the Marquis of Halifax, Lord Maitland, the Earl of Dorset, Lord Cavendish, Colonel Finch, Sir Charles Scarborough and 'some few others of less note and abilities'. Defoe seems to have identified himself as one of these anonymous fellow toilers. How he can have gained entry to such a circle can only be guessed at; but Dorset was well known for his generous patronage of young talent, and Defoe's friend Oldham was one of those whom he encouraged.

A key figure in this group was 'the never enough to be praised' George Savile, Marquis of Halifax, at that time Lord Privy Seal and leader of the moderate faction at Court, described by Defoe as 'a noble Author who was an eminent Tory, though a friend of the constitution and of the Protestant interest (for such are consistent)'.[104] It is not impossible that Defoe may have acquired directly from Halifax, the Great Trimmer, that respect for balance and moderation which were increasingly to temper the rather crude Whiggery of his own early political attitudes. He never acquired any knowledge 'within doors', as he called it, of the politics of those times; but it may have been through Halifax that he was able for the first time to peep through the keyhole at Court society. He certainly gained access somehow to a surprisingly rich vein of anecdotes about Charles II and his Court. He recounted a catty remark by the Duchess of Portsmouth about Nell Gwynne,[105] as well as the equally catty remark, already quoted, by Lauderdale about Monmouth, from which he claimed that the Whig party got its name.[106] He described Charles's reaction to a line in *The Merry Beggars*, which had been produced about December 1683.[107] He quoted a derogatory remark he had passed about one of the City Companies,[108] and also his jest that if ever there was 'a visible church on earth' it was that of Harrow-on-the-Hill.[109] He described Charles's appreciation of satires aimed against himself, provided they were witty, and quoted the very lines from *The Dialogue of the Two Horses* which he most delighted to repeat;[110] he quoted his comment about the Whig journalist, Harry Care — 'Hang him, it is a witty Rogue, 'tis pitty he should be ruin'd';[111] and also his reply when urged to set up closer control of the press — '*No*, said the King, *let them alone, I can punish them for Printing, but if they are stop'd from Printing, they will write all the Wicked things in the World and there's no finding them.*'[112] Is it too fanciful to detect here the urbane accents of Halifax, entertaining his friends with amusing but harmless Court gossip, though discreetly avoiding any real political revelations, while on the outskirts of the group the young Defoe hung upon every word? The latter certainly achieved a shrewdly balanced assessment of Charles, whom he called 'a Prince who was neither a sound *Papist*, nor a zealous *Protestant*. Admired for his great Sagacity, beloved for his Clemency, and the fittest Prince in the World to Reign, had not his over-Indulgence to Ease and Pleasures made him averse from Business.'[113]

This retrospective judgment was more generous than he would have given at the time. Defoe's early years in trade were passed against a background of political reaction, with the Court and its Tory allies emerging unscathed from the crisis of the Popish Plot and the Exclusion Bill, and passing to the counterattack. Late in March 1681, Charles summarily dismissed his Oxford Parliament, and thanks to the subsidies of Louis

XIV, never needed to summon another. A fortnight later Harry Care's *Packet of Advice from Rome* was countered by the first issue of a Tory paper, the *Observator* of Sir Roger L'Estrange, whose vigorous journalism Defoe reluctantly admired, even while detesting his politics. In November the same current of opinion found another outlet in Dryden's *Absalom and Achitophel.* Defoe tells a tale (perhaps also relayed by Halifax?) of how

> . . . Mr. Dryden had describ'd the Duke of *Buckingham* with a great deal of Wit, but in one Line had given him ill Names, as *Fiddler* and *Buffoon*; . . . his Grace, finds him at a *Coffee-House*, and charging him with want of Decency, as no true part of Satyr, can'd him very smartly; *there, Sir*, said the Duke, *is for your ill Manners; and here sir*, says he, *is for your Wit*, and threw him a purse of Thirty Guineas at the same time.[114]

The counter-attack against the Whigs had already passed from words to deeds. In August 1681 Stephen College, the 'protestant joiner', had been tried at Oxford for treasonable words and executed. But a bigger fish escaped through a hole in the net. The leader of the exclusionist faction, the Earl of Shaftesbury, was brought to trial in November, only for the Grand Jury, nominated by the Whig sheriffs, to find no true bill against him.[115] This underlined the role of the City of London as a defiant stronghold of the Whig cause; and the Court now launched an attack on the City Charter by the long-drawn-out *Quo Warranto* proceedings, started in December. Luckily for the Court, there happened, through a split Whig vote, to be a Tory Lord Mayor at the time, Sir John Moore. He was persuaded to revive an obsolete custom which by courtesy allowed the Lord Mayor to nominate one of the Sheriffs, which he did at the Bridge-house feast on 18 May 1682, by drinking to another Tory, Dudley North. The Whigs challenged the legal validity of this, and in the following month chose two of their own party, Papillon and Dubois. The Lord Mayor insisted that this election was invalid, since there was only one vacancy, for which the Tories chose Sir Edmund Rich. Nearly thirty years later Defoe recalled how

> . . . When Sir *John Moor*, who was the first that made that

Experiment, *of Drinking a Sherriff into the Chair*, imposed upon the City in the Case of Mr. *Papilion* and *Dubois*, many that are still alive, and can remember it, aided and assisted in that great Assembly, (perhaps the greatest that ever was before or since) to cry NO CONFIRMATION, NO CONFIRMATION, no *Lord-Mayor Tyranny* &c.: so far did Right prevail, and the Zeal of the Citizens for their Legal well-known Privileges appear, that Sir *John Moor*, assisted and supported by the *Court-Tyranny* of those Days, was forc'd to carry on his new-invented Imposition by setting a Guard of Soldiers at the Hall Door, and suffering none to go in but their own Party.[116]

Ironically, the military force which enabled the Tory Lord Mayor to ride roughshod over the Whig majority among the liverymen was none other than the City Trained Bands which forty years before had turned out to resist the advance of Charles I upon the capital, and which had been revitalised a few years before at the time of the Popish Plot. But now,

. . . the City Trained Bands began to be Rampant . . . they began to Ride upon their Masters and Trampled under Foot the Liberty of that very City they were rais'd to Defend; were made the Engines of Oppression and Disorder; Disturb'd Meeting Houses, Possest *Guildhall*, chose Sheriffs, Captain Quiney for that; got Drunk upon the Guard, Abused the Citizens upon the Rounds, and their Prodigal Drunken Centinels Murther'd several People, upon Pretence that they would not stand at their Command.[117]

'Captain' Quiney was in fact Lieutenant-Colonel Quiney who, on 28 September, when the rival sheriffs presented themselves to be sworn in, was given the task of excluding those hostile to the Lord Mayor;[118] 'and by this Force the Antient Livery-men were shut out, and several of them thrown down, and insolently used, and the Sheriffs thrust away from the Hustings'.[119] Though not yet a liveryman himself, no doubt Defoe was there to watch the struggle.

The Whigs were reluctant to admit defeat, but a touch of desperation began to appear in their actions. Shortly before this Monmouth had made a quasi-royal tour into Cheshire, hoping to repeat the success he had achieved two years before on a journey to the south-west. His first day took him to Quainton Races, near Aylesbury, where on 6 September, among 'a mighty confluence of nobleman and gentlemen', there was also a young merchant, Defoe, probably travelling upon his own business.[120] He does not seem to have followed the Protestant Duke into the Midlands and Cheshire, where his presumption led to his arrest. He was soon released, but his ally Shaftesbury, now in failing health, was forced to flee to Holland, where he died in the following January. A handful of desperate men now planned to ambush and capture the King and his brother at Rye House, near Hoddesdon, as they returned from the April meeting at Newmarket. The scheme miscarried as a result of a serious fire at Newmarket which led the royal party to return sooner than expected; and it was not until the latter part of June that any inkling of the Plot leaked out. Then orders were given for the arrest, not only of the actual conspirators, but also of Whig leaders who had not been directly involved. Monmouth went into hiding, and eventually fled to Holland; but among those arrested were two men whom Defoe was to revere as martyrs to the cause of political freedom. Lord William Russell, executed on 21 July 1683, was in Defoe's words, 'barbarously and unjustly put to death by the straining of Circumstances, and calling that Treason, which in the utmost had been Misprision of Treason, and without any Evidence sufficient to prove that either'.[121] Algernon Sidney's offence was that he had committed to paper a reply to Sir Robert Filmer's *Patriarcha*, in which the theory of divine right had been expounded, a reply which he had made no effort to publish; yet he was brought to trial in November and executed on 7 December. In Defoe's words, 'the Manuscript being seized, and the Subject examin'd, it was thought fit, instead of answering him with the Pen, to answer him with the Axe, and to conquer his Argument by the extent of the very Power he exploded'.[122] The Tory jurymen who convicted these men were long remembered by their opponents in the City as judicial murderers.[123]

The theory of divine right, and its logical corollary, non-resistance to the power of the monarch, was enthusiastically taken up by the Anglican clergy. Defoe declared: 'I have heard it publickly Preach'd, that if the King Commanded my Head, and sent his Messengers to fetch it, I was bound to submit, and stand still while it was cut off.'[124] In such a climate of opinion the Dissenters were vulnerable. Ten years before they had helped to pass the Test Act, 'For Preventing Dangers which may happen from Popish Recusants', on the understanding that it would not be turned against themselves. According to Defoe,

> . . . this Part of the Law was not much insisted on till about the Year 82 and 83, when the *Popish* Plot being turn'd to Ridicule, and several Plots trumped upon the Dissenters . . . Then this Law was turned full-but upon the *Dissenters* . . . and with all imaginable Eagerness insisted upon, even so much as to Common-Council Men of the City of *London*; nay they began to talk, or to offer at, allowing no Citizens to Vote for the Common-Council Men or Aldermen, but such as had taken the Sacrament.[125]

He even recalled talk of applying the sacramental test to keepers of alehouses and taverns.[126]

It was not merely discrimination but active persecution that the Dissenters had once again to fear. Defoe's old tutor, Charles Morton, went into hiding early in 1683 to avoid arrest; but many were less lucky, and Defoe referred to 'near 8000 Protestant Dissenters that perish'd in Prison, in the Days of that merciful Prince King *Charles* the Second'.[127] The case that roused his greatest indignation was that of Thomas Delaune, who took it on himself to answer a challenge issued by Benjamin Calamy in a published sermon, entitled *A Scrupulous Conscience*. Delaune's reply, *A Plea for the Nonconformists*, was taken to be a seditious libel, for which he was arrested in November 1683 and brought to trial on 17 January 1684.[128] When he later quoted 'words, which one that knew me took in Short-hand, though without my knowledge' at the trial,[129] he was probably referring to Defoe, who certainly knew shorthand, and seems to have been present, praising 'the greatness of Mind he discover'd at his Tryal', and stating that the court only remitted him the pillory in deference to his learning.[130] Unable to pay his fine of 100 marks, he was forced to return, with his wife and two children, to Newgate, where they were dependent for bare subsistence on the charity of friends. After seeing all three die, Delaune himself, after fifteen months confinement, died there too. Defoe was scornful of the Dissenters who neglected to raise the money which would have freed their self-appointed spokesman, though it is not clear how much he himself did to help him. Another victim mentioned by Defoe was Delaune's fellow-prisoner, William Jenkyn, committed to Newgate in September 1684 for refusing the Oxford oath, to endeavour no changes in church or state. His petition for release on account of failing health was ignored, and he too died in Newgate in the following January. A hundred and fifty coaches brought mourners to the funeral in Bunhill Fields, and his daughter gave mourning rings inscribed: 'William Jenkyn: Murdered in Newgate'.[131]

Defoe himself does not seem to have suffered personally as a Dissenter, and certainly never considered conforming to the established Church, even though he looked on the latter as a true Protestant Church from which he was only justified in separating himself because of conscientious scruples on matters of church ceremony and organisation. He several times mentions the dispute about the 'posture of receiving' — whether Holy Communion should be taken seated, as was the practice among the Dissenters, or kneeling, as the Anglicans insisted. Great was his delight to see on one occasion in St George's Chapel, Windsor, an altar-piece depicting the Last Supper, with the disciples of course seated, while Christ himself ministered to them.[132]

Like Defoe, most Dissenters suffered more in apprehension than in reality. With the outlook of a beleaguered garrison, they looked anxiously at the encroaching forces of Popery. In France, Louis XIV was persecuting the Protestants with increased savagery; and with the failure of efforts to exclude the Duke of York from the succession, many feared that it would only be a matter of time before attacks would be made upon Protestantism in this country too. This was why, when the Turks were besieging Vienna from July to September 1683, many Dissenters welcomed them as a relieving army, which they fondly imagined would help the Protestant Hungarians against the Catholic House of Habsburg. 'O that Cursed house of *Austria! was the Word then*', Defoe recalled,[133] and 'many a hard Word had I from you' for characteristically setting himself against the prevailing opinion of his associates:

> *The first Time* I had the Misfortune to differ from my Friends, was about the Year 1683, when the Turks were besieging *Vienna*, and the *Whigs* in *England*, generally speaking, were for the *Turks* taking it; which I having read the History of the

Cruelty and perfidious Dealings of the *Turks* in their Wars, and how they rooted out the Name of the Christian Religion in above Threescore and Ten Kingdoms, could by no means agree with; and tho' but a young man, and a younger Author, I opposed it, and wrote against it; which was taken very unkindly indeed.[134]

But sooner than he realised, his personal response to the Catholic danger at home was to be put to the test.

7 A Person Who Had No Right to Rule

On 6 February 1685 Charles II the crypto-Catholic died, and his brother the Duke of York, whom the Whigs had tried so strenuously to exclude from the throne, quietly succeeded as James II. 'He came in like a *Lamb*', Defoe tells us, perhaps sharing in the brief period of optimism, when 'so great on a sudden were the hopes of this King, that *Edward* III and *Henry* V, the most glorious Monarchs of *England*, were like on his Account to be hissed out of our *English* Chronicles'.[1] But by the end of April, 'ill Omens at his Coronation' could be interpreted as signs of divine displeasure;[2] and Defoe soon convinced himself that James had no right to the throne:

> For my part, I thank God, that when he was King, I never owned him, never swore to him, never prayed for him (as King) never paid any act of homage to him, never so much as drank his health, but looked on him as a person who, being Popish, had no right to rule.[3]

The latter view had no possible justification in law, outside the court scene in *Alice in Wonderland*. The attempt to exclude James by Act of Parliament had failed; and the only legally tenable ground for rejecting his right to rule lay in maintaining the legitimacy of the Duke of Monmouth. As James's diplomacy began to harass the exiled Duke, he was stung into a desperate attempt to make good his claim; and on 11 June he landed with a small party at Lyme Regis in Dorset.

Defoe's claim that he had been 'in arms under the Duke of Monmouth',[4] has sometimes been doubted, but is confirmed by a pardon granted to him nearly two years later.[5] But this still leaves many problems unsolved. How was it possible for him to live openly in Freeman's Yard for part at least of the intervening two years? Why did his political enemies never taunt him with his part in the rising? If he was at Sedgemoor, why is there no trace of such a traumatic experience in his later fictions? Why was his name not included in the list of those 'absent from their homes' in Cornhill Ward during the rising?[6] And why was he so knowledgeable about what was happening in London during those fateful weeks? His recollection of how 'Hundreds of the honestest and most innocent Men in the Nation having but the general character of *Whigs*, or being only *Dissenters*, were taken up and kept under Guard in the Halls and publick places in the City', may suggest only that he remained in London for a few days after the Duke's landing became known.[7] More puzzling is his accurate recollection, nearly forty years later, of a sequence of events in London, which began twelve days before the landing, but which did not end until nine days after the Duke's execution. He described how

> . . . one Dangerfield . . . convicted of Perjury . . . after a long Tryal, was sentenc'd to be publicly whipt. After he had suffer'd the Law, he was struck in the Eye with a small Cane, by an officious Wretch, as the Officers of Justice were bringing him back to Newgate; of which wound he died in a few Days . . . The Murderer was immediately apprehended, and being condemn'd, no Intercession could prevail with the King to pardon him; but he was hang'd, as he deserv'd, all Men abhorring the barbarous Action.[8]

Dangerfield's trial began on 30 May; Monmouth landed on 11 June; Dangerfield was sentenced on 29 June, and the incident of the cane was on 4 July; Sedgemoor was on 5 July, Monmouth was captured on 8 July and executed on 15 July; Dangerfield's assailant, Robert Francis, was sentenced on 16 July and executed on 24 July.

Before trying to reconcile Defoe's apparent first-hand knowledge of the Dangerfield affair with his undoubted participation in Monmouth's Rebellion, there is another witness to be called. Although none of Defoe's fictional heroes played any part in that rising, one of them was involved in the Jacobite Rebellion of 1715. Colonel Jack was living in Lancashire with his wife Moggy, when he heard of the rising under Lord Derwentwater.

I was all on Fire on that Side, and was just going away with Horse and Arms, to join the Lord *Derwentwater*, but *Moggy* begg'd me off, *as I may call it*, and hung about me so, with her Tears and Importunities that I sat still and look'd on, for which I had Reason to be thankful . . . She sav'd my Life to be sure, because I had then publickly espoused the Rebellion, and been known to have been among them, which might have been as fatal to me afterwards, tho' I had not been taken in the Action, as if I had.[9]

But later, when the rebels came nearer, Colonel Jack slipped away after all and joined them at Preston. However, 'I was not so publick here, as to be very well known, at least by any one that had Knowledge of me in the Country where I liv'd; and this indeed was my safety afterward'. After staying with the rebels for only three days, the Colonel took a dislike to their military measures, 'and from that Moment I gave them all up as lost, and meditated nothing but how to escape from them'. He managed to get away by swimming his horse across the River Ribble, riding hard all day until, nearing home in the evening, he concealed himself in a wood, shot his horse and buried it in a gravel pit, and finally reached home at two in the morning, arriving so secretly that 'I was not known by any Body in the Country to have been among them'.[10]

Many of these details cannot be applied to Defoe's own case; but it would have been possible for him to have joined Monmouth's forces belatedly and briefly, slipping back home before his absence was generally known or could begin to appear sinister. If he had left home on 20 June, a week after Monmouth's landing was known in London, he could have reached the rebel army, then in north Somerset, by 23 June. In that case he would have seen something of the skirmish at Keynsham, on the Avon between Bath and Bristol, on 24 June, and may have been drawing on his own experience when he described how 'the Duke of Monmouth, finding himself defeated in his expectation of the city of Bristol, and repuls'd at the city of Bath, and press'd by the approach of the king's troops who endeavour'd to surround him, made his retreat'.[11] Monmouth in fact first turned south from Bath, hoping to pick up mounted reinforcements at Warminster. A few miles south of Bath, at Norton St Philip, 'was a fight between the forces of King James II and the

Duke of Monmouth, in which the latter plainly had the better; and had they push'd their advantage, might have made it an entire victory'.[12] Monmouth, however, continued south to Frome. Here he actually thought of abandoning his followers, but followed instead the equally defeatist plan of turning back west. On that day, 28 June, many of his army, discouraged and wearied by long marches up hill and down dale in pouring rain, began to desert. Though royalist forces lay to the north and east, the route to the south-east, through Warminster and then across Salisbury Plain, still lay open. Defoe could have been back in London before the end of the month, four days before the fatal assault upon Dangerfield, and five days before Sedgemoor.

If this chronology is correct, although Defoe played no part in the bloody night battle which finally ruined Monmouth's cause, he was with the rebel army on two occasions when they were in action — at Keynsham on 24 June and at Norton St Philip on 27 June. Monmouth's forces did not impress him: 'his men were raw, a mere Militia';[13] and for his own part he admitted, 'I am no soldier, nor never was'.[14] When he came to concoct his *Memoirs of a Cavalier* he gave that doughty soldier a very inauspicious start to his career. Visiting the French army in northern Italy, he was involved in two actions in quick succession. The first time, we are told,

> . . . I was but a raw Soldier, and did not like the Sport at all . . . I ran away very fairly one of the first, and my Companion with me, and by the Goodness of our Horses got out of the Fray, and not being much known in the Army, we came into the Camp an hour or two after, as if we had only been riding abroad for the Air.

The Cavalier gave no better account of himself in another engagement five days later, escaping from the fighting by dismounting and forcing his way into the thick undergrowth of a wood, where he was joined by twenty or thirty more runaways.

> One Kindness it did me, that I began to consider what I had to do here, and as I could give a very slender Account of my self for what it was I run all these Risques, so I resolved they should fight it among themselves, for I would come among them no more.[15]

One can only guess how far the Cavalier's highly uncharacteristic conduct during these two actions reflects Defoe's own 'little Experience . . . in a Military Station'.[16]

Whatever the exact truth about Defoe's share in Monmouth's rising, he certainly continued to live quite openly in Freeman's Yard for another six or eight months. It must have been with mixed feelings that he heard of the total destruction of Monmouth's forces at Sedgemoor, and of the capture of the Duke a few days later in a Hampshire ditch; and he is unlikely to have been present at Tower Hill on 15 July when Jack Ketch so brutally bungled the execution of the Protestant hero. As official anxiety gave way to relief, Defoe had the mortification of hearing the rebellion 'sung about the Streets as a senseless ridiculous Attempt; that those, who were concern'd in, Merit little but our Pity as Lunaticks'.[17] During the following weeks news reached him of the capture and trial during Jeffreys' 'Western Campaign' of men he knew, including three former pupils of Morton's Academy. When listing the distinguished men produced by that establishment, he mentioned the *'Western Martyrs . . . Kitt. Battersby, Young Jenkins, Hewlin'*.[18] By *'Kitt. Battersby'* he must have meant Christopher Battiscombe, son and heir of a Dorset country gentleman;[19] *'Hewlin'* was Benjamin Hewling, grandson of the wealthy City Baptist, William Kiffin; while 'Young Jenkins' was William Jenkyn, son of the dissenting minister, whose death in Newgate a few months before had made him too a martyr in the eyes of his fellow Dissenters.[20] All three had played a prominent part in the rising, and all three were executed, the last two dying together at Taunton on 30 September, on what may have been Defoe's twenty-fifth birthday. It is curious that Crusoe, commenting on his providential deliverance in being thrown ashore on his island, should refer to ' a strange Concurrence of Days, in the various Providences which befel me', for 'The same Day of the Year I was born on, (*viz.*) the 30*th September*, that same Day I had my Life so miraculously saved 26 Year after.'[21]

On 23 October there died Alderman Cornish, belatedly condemned for alleged complicity in an earlier conspiracy, indignantly protesting his innocence; and to the Whigs this was another case of judicial murder. In Defoe's words, he was 'butcher'd by the Barbarity of those Times'. Twenty years later he recalled how 'it rain'd hard and thundred and lightned that night . . . in such a manner as it never has done since . . . a Token that God Almighty did not like the Work'.[22]

The same month came news that Louis XIV had formally revoked the Edict of Nantes, which had guaranteed the rights of the Protestants in France, though as they had been under heavy persecution for several years, this was an action of mainly symbolic significance. But it must have added in Defoe's mind to the sense of impending doom, and the conviction that the reign of 'popery and slavery' was coming. James, now in an over-confident mood, seemed to be moving in the same direction, and the favour he was showing to the Roman Catholics was beginning to strain the loyalty even of his Church of England supporters. Defoe later recalled how 'that very House of Commons who but a little while before was so highly cajol'd and caress'd by the King, went away with a repulse to their honest address against Papists bearing Offices without legal Qualifications; and in a few days he prorogued them, and never met them more'.[23] The Commons' address was on 16 November, the King's 'repulse' on 18 November, and the prorogation on 20 November; the accuracy of Defoe's recollections confirms that he was still on the spot. His inclusion once again on the Petty Jury of Cornhill Ward shows that he was still living in Freeman's Yard at the end of December, the time when he himself tells us that ward and parish officers were chosen;[24] and the burial on 11 January 1686 of Jane Fenn, 'servant to Mr. Foe' at St Michaels Cornhill, tells the same story.[25] So too does his recollection of the trial of Lord Delamere in the same month, for assisting the rising in the west; 'the latter was acquitted', he recalls, 'in open Court, *the King present*, after all the Endeavours the Court-Party had made to entrap him, and yet for a Fact, which it was well enough known, his Lordship was concern'd enough in'.[26] The first anniversary of James's accession fell on 5 February; and if we can take literally Defoe's statement that he had 'had the honour' to see a calculation about the balance of trade made before the Privy Council in the second year of King James, he was still in London after that date.[27]

On 10 March, James, his thirst for vengeance at last slaked, issued a general pardon to all those who had taken part in the Rebellion, except for those who had actually sailed with Monmouth, or had served as officers under him, or were included in a list of some 170 names.[28] For whatever reason, far from having

his mind set at rest, Defoe began about this time, like Colonel
Jack after his safe return from Preston, to grow 'not thoroughly
easy'.[29] The colonel thought it safer to flee to America. Defoe
chose the natural refuge of Whig exiles, Holland.

He may well have visited that country before, but this must
have been his longest stay, of more than a year; and he probably
took his wife with him, leaving his business in London in the
care of a partner or his father. Many intimate glimpses of Dutch
life show his familiarity: how 'the Dutch have an infinite
Number of small Craft, such as Galliots, Hoys, Busses and
Bylanders or Hoys for their River Navigation';[30] how 'the very
ditches are navigable, and people pass from town to town in
Boats';[31] how 'no beggars are to be seen in the streets',[32] and
how a Dutch labouring man with the equivalent of nine shillings
a week 'will live tolerably well, keep the wolf from the door,
and have everything handsome about him';[33] how, 'when a
young tradesman in Holland or Germany goes courting, I am
told, the first question the young woman asks him, or perhaps
her friends for her, is *Are you able to pay the charges?*'[34] His
fictional Captain Singleton declared that goat-flesh in Madagascar 'looked red and eat hard and firm, as dried beef in Holland'.[35]
And he more than once referred to the way 'the Sign-Painters in
Holland' write 'over every piece they draw, — "This is a Hog!
This is a Bear! This is a Bull!" and the like'.[36] Familiarity with
the country in several seasons is implicit in his account of how

> . . . there is a kind of emulation in Holland, between the
> fishermen that go to sea in pinks and line-boats, winter and
> summer, and those fishermen that go in the busses, and do
> call them Koe-milkens, or Cow-milkers; for indeed most part
> of them be men of occupations in winter, or else countrymen,
> and do milk the cows themselves, and make all the Holland
> cheese, when they be at home.[37]

He must have been there in the autumn to see the vast quantities
of corn stored 'in the corn chambers and magazines in Holland,
when the fleets come in from Dantzick and England';[38] and he
knew enough of winter conditions to describe how 'in Holland
and Germany . . . the ice is often strong enough to bear a piece
of Cannon upon it . . . and . . . the Skate-riders use it to go upon

their ordinary Business, to markets and Fairs, and on Journies and the like'.[39]

He certainly knew Amsterdam, 'so surrounded with Water, every now and then within two inches of being swallow'd up, and yet seldom, if ever, receiving any considerable Damage';[40] and he drew a moral from 'the pump-house . . . where they put offenders in for petty matters . . . it is nothing but *pump* or *drown*, they may chuse which they like best'.[41] He gave a detailed and lively account of the fitting out of the whaling fleet between Amsterdam and 'Sourdam', and of how after they have taken 'Pilots over the *Pompus*, and through the *Zuider-Sea to the Texel*, where the Ships come to an Anchor a second time', the owners follow them to give them final clearance for their voyage.[42] He thought that though there were 'more vessels in less room' at Amsterdam than at London, there were fewer altogether.[43] Similarly, though at 'Sourdam' (more accurately Saardam or Zaandam) near Amsterdam, there were more vessels built than on the Thames, yet 'almost all the ships the Dutch have, are built there, whereas, not one fifth part of our shipping is built on the Thames', while 'the English build for themselves only, the Dutch for all the world'.[44]

In making this comparison many years later Defoe, by a quirk of memory or slip of the pen, twice wrote 'Schedam' instead of 'Sourdam'. Schiedam was in fact the Scottish quarter of the other great Dutch port of Rotterdam, which he also knew well. When seventeen years later, Defoe made a vain request to three leading ministers to pray with him in Newgate, they may all have been old acquaintances from his exile in Holland. John Spademan was minister of the English Church in Rotterdam; Robert Fleming was the son, and later successor, of the minister of the Scottish Church there; while the third, John Howe, was himself in exile in Utrecht.[45] William Carstares, in later life Defoe's intimate friend, was at this time minister of the Scottish Church at Leyden, not many miles distant; and his brother, Alexander Carstares, and cousin, James Dunlop, were both successful merchants at Rotterdam.[46] The leading figure among the Scottish merchants was Andrew Russell, for many years the Scottish factor there;[47] and long afterwards Defoe's brother-in-law, Robert Davis, who may himself have had Dutch connections, was to marry Russell's niece as his second wife, and then his daughter as his third.[48] It was probably among the

Scottish community at Rotterdam that Defoe met one of the
men who had assassinated Archbishop Sharp at St Andrews in
1679. He gives a circumstantial account of this killing, 'which I
had from the mouth of one of the actors' — probably Russell of
Kingskettle or Balfour of Kinloch, both of whom fled to
Rotterdam after the defeat of the Covenanters at Bothwell
Brig.[49] A very different kind of exile known to Defoe was the
visionary French Protestant, Pierre Jurien, who lived near the
Walloon Church at Rotterdam of which he was second pastor.
By a slip similar to that which had transferred Schiedam from
Rotterdam to Amsterdam, Defoe wrote that 'it was said of
Mons. *Jurien* at Amsterdam, that he us'd to *lose himself in him-
self*'.[50] Though the evidence is, as usual, tantalisingly incon-
clusive, it seems likely that Defoe spent part of his own exile at
Rotterdam, and that he established contacts there among the
Scottish community which may have been the basis for his later
strong links with Scotland itself.

He tells a long story, probably set either in Amsterdam or
Rotterdam:

> When I liv'd abroad, I once had a commission sent me from a
> merchant in *London* to buy a large parcel of Brandy: The
> goods were something out of my way, having never bought
> any in that country before. However, it happen'd that I had
> frequently bought and imported Brandies in *England*, and
> had some judgment in them, so much that I ventur'd to buy
> without taking a Cooper with me, which was not usual in
> that place. The first parcel of Brandy I saw was very good,
> and I bought freely to the value of about 600 *l.* and ship'd
> them for *England*, where they gave very good satisfaction to
> my employer.

When he tried to buy more, to the value of £460, to complete
his commission, the merchant tried to take advantage of his
inexperience, by mixing malt spirits with the brandy after Defoe
had tasted and touched the casks with the marking-iron, but
before the bargain had been struck. 'But young as I was, I was
too old for that too'; he insisted on tasting the brandy again,
and refused to buy.[51] He does not say where this took place,
but mixing malt spirits with brandy was a malpractice he
attributes elsewhere to the Dutch.[52]

One of his early trading memories was of how he 'had an adventure in a ship' captured by Algerian pirates 'within sight of Harwich'.[53] It has been supposed that Defoe himself must have been taken prisoner, however briefly; but he probably used the word 'adventure' in the sense employed by Crusoe when he declared that he 'carried an adventure of £40' with him on one of his voyages.[54] Bold as the Algerine Corsairs were, they only ventured into such restricted northern waters in the summers of 1686 and 1687, when with the connivance of the French and English governments, they confined their attentions to Dutch ships. What sounds like the very pirate ship Defoe had in mind actually put into Harwich in September 1686, to the acute embarrassment of James II's government which was then in treaty relations with the Algerines.[55] Louis XIV was less squeamish; for Defoe recalled, from the Dutch viewpoint, how 'the *Algerine* pirates came into the Channel, took prizes even in the Mouth of the *Thames*, and were admitted to carry them into the Ports of *France*, as they did three Ships bound from *London* to *Amsterdam* at one time . . . King *James* then reigning in England'. He went on to describe a medal, struck in Brussels:

Four Princes were plac'd at a Council-Table, consulting together for their united Interests, *Soliman* III the *Turkish* Sultan. *Mezomorto* Dey of *Algiers*. *Louis* XIV, King of *France*. And *James* II King of *England*. And on the Reverse, the Devil, with this Motto,

IN FOEDERE QUINTUS
The Fifth in the Confederacy.[56]

What Defoe's fate might have been if he himself, and not merely some of his goods, had fallen into the hands of the Algerines, can be guessed from a slightly later incident. On 7 June 1687 a ship carrying French Protestants from England to Rotterdam was seized within sight of the Dutch coast; and within forty days the wretched passengers were in slavery in Algiers. One of them, Isaac Brassard, wrote letters begging for help; and it was Pierre Jurien in Rotterdam who was largely responsible for securing their release. This was not until the end of 1688; and a few months earlier, the French, falling out with their former ally, had bombarded Algiers, while some of the captives, in retaliation, had been blown from cannons.[57] Long before this however Defoe's exile had come to an end.

For a clue as to how this may have happened, we have Colonel Jack's account of how his wife planned to obtain a pardon for him, when he too was in exile for treasonable activities:

> She would write to a particular Friend at *London*, who she could depend upon, to try to get a pardon for a Person on Account of the late Rebellion, with all the Circumstances which my Case was attended with, *viz.* of having acted nothing among them but being three Days in the Place . . . if he saw the way clear, and that he was sure to obtain it, he should go thorough Stitch with it, if within the Expence of two, or three, or four Hundred Pounds, and that upon the advice of its being practicable, he should have Bills payable by such and such a Person on Delivery of the Warrant for the thing.
>
> To fortifie this I enclos'd in her Packet a Letter to one of my Correspondents, who I could more particularly Trust, with a Credit for the Money, on such and such Conditions . . .[58]

This interest in the procedure by which Colonel Jack could obtain from overseas a pardon, which in his case proved unnecessary, may well reflect the action taken by Defoe himself in 1687. The stress on the trustworthiness of the correspondent, and the insistence that nothing should be done unless the pardon was certain, suggests that the authorities still knew nothing of his apparently minimal complicity in the rebellion, and that exile and pardon alike were really only precautionary. At all events, on 31 May 1687 a warrant was issued from Windsor to the Justices of Assize and Gaol Delivery for the Western Circuit, naming thirty-three persons, 'who were engaged in the late rebellion', and to whom the King had 'extended his grace and mercy', 'for causing the said persons to be inserted in the next General Pardon, without any condition of Transportation'. Thirtieth in the list appeared the name of Daniel Foe.[59]

Allowing a month or so for red tape, and for Defoe to wind up his affairs in Holland, he is unlikely to have returned to England before the late summer. His return journey may have taken him through Flanders, which he certainly visited at some time;[60] and perhaps he crossed to Dover from Nieuport, which he still thought of nearly forty years later, as the terminus of the packet-boat service, though it had in fact long been switched to Ostend.[61] During his absence there had been sad changes in his circle of friends. Charles Morton, who had been forced to close his Academy in 1685, had in 1686 sailed for New England. His friend Charles Lodwick had already gone to New York in the previous year; and in the late summer the latter's step-father, the Rev. David Clarkson, had died.[62] A few months later Defoe's own father-in-law, John Tuffley, had also died.[63]

Public affairs were in an unhappy state. James II was increasingly at loggerheads with some of the most loyal of his former supporters, the Tories of the Church of England, who had staunchly resisted the attempt to exclude him from the throne. The most bitter issue was his determination to force a Catholic President upon Magdalen College, Oxford. Defoe refers so often to this controversy, which came to a head in September and October 1687, that it seems likely that he was back in England by that time.[64] James had now embarked on a new policy of 'caressing' or 'wheedling' the Dissenters; and on 4 April 1687 he had issued his first Declaration of Indulgence, restoring their freedom of worship. There followed an inspired and organised series of addresses of thanks from dissenting congregations, which continued to flow in for several months. The Anglican clergy, who had been active a few years before in urging the persecution of the Dissenters, now began to change their tune. Defoe later urged them to 'remember the Years 1687 and 88, when all their Sermons and Pamphlets were fill'd with Invitations to the *Dissenters* to love and mutual Forbearance one of another, joyning Hands for general Safety, and standing together against popery and slavery'.[65] In this tug-of-war for the affections of the Dissenters, Defoe had no doubt where he stood. Perhaps remembering the stand taken by William Love when Charles II had issued a similar Declaration fifteen years before, he went on record, though whether in print is uncertain, to denounce James's move as a trick to usher in 'popery and slavery'. In this he went against the consensus of opinion among the Dissenters, and gave offence to 'honest blinded men'. 'I had their reproaches when I blamed their credulity and confidence in the flatteries and caresses of popery under King James, and when I protested openly against the addresses of thanks to him, for his illegal liberty of conscience founded upon the dispensing power.'[66] Apparently the pardon he had been granted a few months before had not left him with any sense of obligation to James's government; nor was he overawed by his escape.

Exactly how he had kept the London end of his business going while he had been in Holland is uncertain. His name, which had been dropped from the Petty Jury list of Cornhill Ward in December 1686, reappeared in the following year, confirming that he was again living in Freeman's Yard.[67] On 12 January 1688 he was admitted to the Butchers' Company by virtue of his father's freedom, paying a fine of £10 15s. to be discharged from all offices.[68] No doubt he had paid his money to become a Citizen of London, a formality which followed on 26 January.[69] He could now vote at the elections for the Lord Mayor and for Members of Parliament to represent the City; and he was entitled to various trading privileges in other cities, both at home and abroad. Perhaps his immediate concern was to be admitted to the Merchant Adventurers (Hamburg) Company, for there are hints that he spent the spring of 1688 in that city.

A few weeks earlier, on 23 December 1687, King James had announced the pregnancy of his Queen, the Catholic Mary of Modena. To the Catholics this was a near miracle which might produce a Catholic heir to supplant James's Protestant daughters in the succession, the elder of whom, Mary, was married to the Protestant champion William of Orange; and in anti-Catholic circles James's announcement was looked on with suspicion. Defoe's comment that 'the intended fraud was the Discourse of Europe' certainly suggests that he spent some of the early months of 1688 in a Protestant country abroad; while a taxation list for 1688, in which James Foe's name appears in the place where we would expect to find Defoe's own, confirms that he he was again absent for a while from Freeman's Yard.[70] About this time, too, he was selling goods on commission for Joseph Braban, a merchant from King's Lynn, a port whose eastern outlook may be significant.[71] Although another visit to Holland is possible, Defoe certainly came to know Hamburg well, and on balance it makes most sense to place him there in the spring of 1688.

No details are known of his trading activities at Hamburg, but he later recalled that English stockings were exported there to an annual value of £20,000. He was impressed by the prominent role played in the City by the 'English Hans' as they called the Hamburg Company, which enjoyed special privileges, with jurisdiction over its own members, its own Court, and its own church and minister. He also admired Hamburg's management of its poor — no beggars in the streets, but the deserving poor supported from a fund raised by voluntary contributions, including some from sailors' wages, brought to the church after every voyage in a locked iron box.[72] But Lutheran worship did not impress him: 'It was Popery and no Popery . . . The service differed indeed from the mass, but the difference seemed to be made up very much with the trumpets, kettle-drums, fiddles, hautboys, &c. and all the merry part of the Popish devotion . . . and as for the pious part, I saw very little of it.'[73] Calvinists could only worship by going further down the Elbe to Altona, in Danish territory, which also served as a refuge for debtors. The close proximity of the Danes was a constant threat to the security of Hamburg, which only a year before had had to face an invasion; but other close neighbours, the Swedes, Prussians and 'Lunenburghers', reluctant to see the city fall into Danish hands, had come to the rescue, providing Defoe with an early lesson in the balance of power.[74]

By early summer Defoe was back in England; and some inkling of the scale and variety of his business dealings can be gleaned from details revealed in subsequent litigation.[75] On 18 June he made an agreement with Humphrey Ayles, junior, master and part-owner of the *Batchelor* of London, by which the latter would sail to Boston, New York and Maryland with merchandise and passengers provided by Defoe, and return with goods provided by the latter's factors in America. On 26 July he came to an account with the King's Lynn merchant, Joseph Braban, by which it appeared that Defoe owed him £396 7s. 1d., being debts which he had not yet collected from his customers; shortly afterwards he agreed to collect the money and pay Braban in monthly instalments, entering into a penal bond to complete the payments within nine months. On 13 August he 'sold' a ship, the *Desire* of London, to a mariner, Robert Harrison, for £260. According to a later legal deposition Harrison raised only three-quarters of the purchase price, leaving Defoe the reluctant owner of a quarter of the ship. The reality of the transaction seems to be that Defoe entrusted to Harrison, the master, the task of finding other part-owners, a common method at that time of spreading the risk.

But Defoe still looked on himself as a 'wit' as well as a 'tradesman'. In the course of the summer his friend Guy Miege, from whom he may have learned his French, produced an *English Grammar*, to which Defoe contributed, anonymously, a foreword and 'A Prefatory DISCOURSE, concerning the Original, and Excellency of the English Tongue'.[76] In the former he urged that young people should be well grounded in their own language before being introduced to Latin; while the 'Prefatory Discourse' echoes both the enthusiasm of his former tutor, Charles Morton, for the flexibility of the English language, and also the concern of Roscommon's abortive Academy for 'refining our language without abating the force of it'.

The *Copiousness* I need not use much Art to demonstrate. For besides the Treasures of the ancient *Dutch* which the *English* retain in the Saxon Monosyllables, the choicer Wits of this Nation have fetcht hither the very Quintessence of some forein Languages; who, like Bees, have gathered the best, and left the worst. By which means they have so happily improved their Mother Tongue, that those amongst Forreiners who understand the Genius of it are in a Maze to see this Language so far outdo their own, and to find many of their Words transplanted here, thrive better in *England* than in their proper and natural Soil . . . Thus, when Substance combined with Delight, Plenty with Delicacy, Beauty with Majesty, and Expedition with Gravity, what can want to the Perfection of such a Language? Certainly such is the Mixture of the *English*, that one may frame his Speech Majestical, pleasant, delicate or manly according to the Subject. Of all which advantages inherent to the *English* Tongue Forreiners are at last become sensible . . . As for its *Mutability*, 'tis at least as groundless an Objection. For 'tis well known, that Languages, as states, have their Infancy and Age, their Wax and Wane.

But now the *English* is come to so great Perfection, now 'tis grown so very Copious and Significant, by the Accession of the Quintessence and Life of other Tongues, 'twere to be wished that a stop were put to this unbounded Way of Naturalizing foreign Words, and that none hereafter should be admitted but with Judgment and Authority. Were this Nation contented to improve what Gain they have already, without Over-stocking themselves from other Parts, and putting their Language on a perpetual Motion, it would be much for the Credit of it. And the truth is, there is as much as is needful, and as much as the *English* Soil is well able to bear.

When Defoe again gave literary help to Miege some three years later, he showed his satisfaction with the 'Prefatory Discourse' by borrowing it almost *verbatim*; and in his *Essay upon Projects* (1697) he expressed very similar ideas.[77] It seems apt that his first identifiable published piece of writing should be in praise of the language he was to use with such distinction.

The summer of 1688 was not a happy time for Defoe. On 7 September his infant daughter Mary, probably his only surviving child at that time, was buried in the lower vault of his parish church of St Michael Cornhill;[78] and his personal grief was matched by anxiety about public affairs so intense that 'we were almost in despair, sadly thinking with our selves to what strange countries we should repair to avoid the impending storm'.[79] On 10 June the Queen had given birth to a son, James Edward, in circumstances which made it easy for the King's enemies to persuade themselves that it was all a 'pious fraud'. This could not alter the fact that there was now a Catholic heir to the throne; but the fireworks which celebrated the royal birth brought no joy to most of the nation. Two days after James Edward's birth, seven Bishops of the Church of England were committed to the Tower for signing a petition against James's second Declaration of Indulgence. It is true that on 30 June they were, in Defoe's words, 'rescued by an honest Jury';[80] but even though the troops on Hounslow Heath cheered the news of the Bishops' acquittal, they were still a standing army capable, under the command of Catholic or servile officers, of endangering the liberties of the nation. When on 24 August James decided to summon another Parliament, this was not as a concession to his opponents, but in the belief that he could control the elections and obtain a tractable House of Commons. The aim was to win parliamentary consent for the removal of anti-Catholic laws; and for this purpose James expected the support of the Dissenters, who now had considerable influence on many remodelled corporations.

Once again, Defoe ran counter to the prevailing feeling among the Dissenters. This time he appeared in print, with his earliest surviving political tract. His *Letter to a Dissenter from his Friend at the Hague*, supposedly issued by a non-existent Dutch printer, Hans Verdraeght, went straight to the point; 'Sir, I suppose you are very busie about the Choice of *Parliament-Men*, and all hands are at work to Elect such Members as may comply with the great Design to Repeal the *Penal Laws* and the *Test*.' He argued that the Dissenters' liberty of conscience was already safe under the Declaration of Indulgence, and that no one could now enforce the penal laws. In this he was being both inconsistent and disingenuous, since he had previously condemned a toleration based on the disputed dispensing power. But his motives were clear:

> You may go to *Conventicles*, and the *Papists* may go to Mass without any disturbance though the Test be never repealed: and therefore the *only design* of repealing that must be to give a legal Qualification to Papists to possess all places of *Honour, Profit* and *Trust* in the Nation, which is to put our Lives and Liberties into *their* hands; which I confess is a great Complement to a Roman Catholick Prince; but a Complement may sometimes be overstrained.[81]

The authorship, though secret, must have been known to many of the Dissenters; for he recalled that he 'had the discouragement to be told by some grave, but weak men, that I was a young man and did not understand the dissenters' interest'.[82]

At this dark hour, a glimmer of light now began to appear in the east.

> And thus the new erected Fabrick throve
> And Freedom long with dying Pangs had strove,
> Till Fate disclos'd its Restoration nigh
> The Mighty Sound dispirits Tyranny
> So darkest Clouds the Morning Brightness fly.[83]

Even before the end of August reports reached London of extensive military and naval preparations in the United Provinces, and rumours began to spread of an intended invasion of England. At first these were received with some scepticism, not only by the purblind James, but also by the coffee-house strategists, who asked whether William would dare to leave his country exposed while Louis XIV had large forces on the borders of the Netherlands. Then came news that the French army had been moved eastwards towards the middle Rhine, a blunder which Defoe could only explain by the direct intervention of the Almighty:

> How the King of *France* came to be so infatuated, to send away his Forces up to the Empire, and fool away their Time at the Seige of *Phillipsburgh*, as if he had on purpose given the Dutch an Opportunity to send over the P. of O. to assist the People of *Britain*, we must ask him that takes away the Judgment of the Wise.
> *Quos Jupiter vult perdere prius dementat.*[84]

By the end of September even James could see his danger, and the need to conciliate his subjects. Reluctantly he began to dismantle much of the 'new erected Fabrick' he had been constructing over the past two years. The parliamentary writs were withdrawn; the restoration of the City Charter was promised; the Court of High Commission was abolished; even the ejected Fellows of Magdalen College seemed likely to return.

> Thus having been Exercised to the Right and to the Left, Backward and Forward, we found ourselves at last much *As we were* at first. And, had there been any rational Hopes of continuing thus, without any further Breach, these gentle Methods (tho upon a forced Put) would perhaps have gone a great way to turn the Stream, and to quiet the People. But, what Assurance could be had of having these our Rights continued to us any longer than would serve our Enemies Turn?[85]

The month of October, while a Papist wind from the west kept William's fleet in harbour, was a time of suspense and frustration, of declarations on the one hand and proclamations on the other, of rumours and troop movements. For several months James had been introducing Irish troops into England, and the fears and prejudices to which this had given rise were

cleverly played upon in the ballad *Lillibulero*, whose catchy
tune soon swept through the nation. But these Roman Catholic
troops did not form the bulk of James's forces.

> The King had a gallant Army, but most of them were Protest-
> ants, and not a few true English Men, readier to draw the
> Sword for the Defence of the Protestant Religion and the
> Liberty of *England*, than the maintenance of those two
> Inseparable Monsters, Popery and Slavery. The People gener-
> ally waited for the Princes Coming with great Impatience,
> and could not conceal the Joy which the Expectation of him
> had diffus'd all over the Kingdom. So that, if this were an
> Invasion, one could every where read Treason in their Faces,
> and a Man could scarce turn about him but he met a Traytor.
> They that knew not the North from the South, or the East
> from the West, fell to learning the Compass, to find out how
> the Wind sat, whilst they longed for that Wind which must
> bring over the Prince. So mindful were the People of the late
> Attempts upon their Religion, Laws and Liberties, that they
> look'd upon him as their *Saviour*, whom the Court Party
> called *Invader*.[86]

Enlarging in bantering style on how Rumour had 'turn'd *Whig*'
in this crisis, Defoe described how

> . . . she serv'd King *James* another base Trick, she made him
> believe the *Dutch* Fleet was scatter'd by a great Storm,
> Abundance of Men drowned, their Horses lost, the Design
> ruin'd, and that it was impossible they could be in a Condition
> to do the Business that Year — Upon this the honest *Papists*
> discover'd themselves again, began to repent their Repentance,
> put a stop to the Restitutions they were making . . . but the
> next Post let us know, that this was nothing but a Trick of
> that false Jade RUMOUR, and all return'd to its former
> Condition.[87]

William's fleet had in fact sailed on 19 October, and had almost
at once been dispersed by a violent storm. Yet all the ships
returned safely to harbour, and William refused even to disem-
bark.

At last on the first of November the weathercocks showed a

stiff breeze from the east. The first reports indicated that the Dutch fleet had set a course to the north-west, and a landing somewhere in the north was anticipated. By 4 November it was known in London that the fleet had changed course, and about noon on the previous day had passed through the Straits of Dover. Defoe later described, perhaps from a mixture of hearsay and imagination, what he can hardly have seen for himself:

> In this great Splendour and Order the whole Fleet sailed with a Kind of Bravado betwixt *England* and *France*, Drums beating, Colours flying, the trumpets sounding, and the Hoboys playing, for the space of three hours. Great was the Concourse of Spectators on both Shores, at 20 miles distance from each other, to see this glorious Sight, worthy of the greatest Monarch to behold.[88]

The progress of the Protestant Armada could be followed that night from Beachy Head: 'And when Night came upon them, all the Ships set out their Lights, which made a most glorious Shew upon the Sea. . . All which at a distance appeared like so many Stars, moving upon the Water.'[89] The same wind which carried William's fleet briskly down the Channel, kept James's ships weatherbound in the mouth of the Thames. An attack on Portsmouth was expected, but did not materialise; and several days were to pass before it became known in London that William's forces had been successfully landed at Brixham in Torbay on the morning of 5 November. The wind, as if anxious to make amends for its contrariness in the previous month, had even shifted suddenly at the last moment, enabling William's pilot to correct an error of navigation which would have carried the fleet past the intended landing point.

In London the news of William's landing brought excitement to fever heat, and on Sunday 11 November the mob was out on the streets, ready to attack and loot the strongholds of popery. Defoe himself saw them assault a Catholic seminary at Berkeley House, near St John Street. Unable to force the gates, some of them ran off to borrow a smith's sledge-hammers, and then conscientiously returned them, together with part of the gate in payment.[90] For a while London could only wait, and eagerly swallow the news that came in from the provinces. Delamere in Cheshire, Danby in Yorkshire, Devonshire in Derbyshire, raised the standard of revolt. William himself waited at Exeter for events to play into his hands. James had ordered his forces to concentrate on Salisbury Plain to bar the way to London, and belatedly rode west to join them. But no news came of any great battle; instead, that of defections among the King's military leaders — Churchill and Kirke both decided to put their loyalty to the Protestant faith before their loyalty to the crown. An even more dramatic desertion took place on the night of 25 November, when James's second daughter, Anne, slipped away from Whitehall with an escort headed by Henry Compton, Bishop of London, to join the northern insurgents.

> I cannot but remember the Consternation among the People, when it was first Nois'd abroad, that the Princess was Missing; and as at first, it was warm among the People, that they had murther'd her, or made her away. I want words to Express the Confusion that appear'd in the Countenances of the People; . . . the very Soldiers talk'd of setting *Whitehall* on Fire, and cutting the Throats of all the *Papists* about the Court; the People ran Raving up and down, and confused Crowds Throng'd in the Apartments at *Whitehall*, Enquiring of every one they met, if they had heard of the Princess.
>
> Had it not presently been made Publick, that the Princess was withdrawn, nay had not the Letters left behind, been made Publick, some fatal Disturbance had been seen in the Pallace, and that within a very few Hours.[91]

James returned to London that same evening (26 November) and remained there for a fortnight. Ostensibly he was prepared to make further concessions, summon a Parliament, and negotiate with the slowly advancing William. In reality he was seeking only to gain time to arrange for the safe escape of his family and himself to France.

Perhaps remembering his narrow escape at the time of Monmouth's rising, Defoe this time was in no hurry to commit himself. On 11 December the news was all round the town that James had slipped away from Whitehall in the night, and was no doubt well on his way to France. William, cautiously advancing, was now in Berkshire, and James's army was disintegrating. Defoe now went west, and on the night of 12 December was at Windsor. Here he was aroused by messengers in a panic, 'dark, and rainy, and midnight as it was', with a report that Irish dragoons had burned Colnbrook and Staines, and were on their way to do the same elsewhere.

> I rode the next morning to Maidenhead: at Slough they told me, Maidenhead was burnt, and Uxbridge and Reading, and I know not how many more, were destroy'd; and when I came to Reading, they told me, Maidenhead and Okingham were burnt, and the like. From there I went to Henley, where the Prince of Orange, with the second line of his army, entered that very afternoon, and there they had the same account, with the news of King James's flight.[92]

It soon became known, however, that James's ship had been boarded by 'some sturdy Fellows then Jesuite-hunting', who brought him into Faversham;[93] and he was eventually escorted back to Whitehall, arriving on the evening of Sunday, 16 December, to a surprisingly enthusiastic reception. Defoe, now also back in London, commented on the fickleness of the mob:

> Did we not see them one Day holloo, and set one another on, to tear *Popery* to pieces, make Bonfires of all the Mass Houses, or at least of their inside Furniture, and run to meet the Prince of *Orange* by Hundreds and by Thousands; and, within but three Days after, when King James came back from *Faversham*, halloo him back again, and toss up their caps as high as before.[94]

But James soon found his position untenable; on 18 December he was allowed to slip down the river once more; and 'the same Rabble . . . huzza'd with Ten-fold Acclamations the Prince that depos'd him', when William at last entered the City a few hours later.[95] James spent four days in Rochester Castle, and then, with William's connivance, finally made his getaway to France on 22 December.

Perhaps driven by the instincts of a news-hound, Defoe was also soon on his way down the Thames. He passed through Gravesend, the scene of one of the few incidents of bloodshed in the 'bloodless revolution'. His version ran:

> Of all the Priests and Jesuits who were taken at *Gravesend*,

where I myself then was, not one was injur'd in his Person; as for their Effects indeed they thought it no crime to take from them what they, contrary to Law, had robb'd the Nation of. There were indeed One or Two Irish Soldiers kill'd, but it was in their own Defence, on their firing on the Townsmen, to force them to send them a Pilot to get off an *East India* Ship, which they had seized to carry off, and had run aground. Yet spight of this Provocation, they did no Injury to Captain Newgent, or the other Soldiers who were taken in that *Tiltboat*, but confine them and dress their Wounds.[96]

The shooting, involving Irish troops turned out of Tilbury Fort after James's first flight, had taken place on 13 December. Defoe cannot have been an actual eye-witness, but Captain Nugent no doubt still lay wounded in the town, before being removed to Maidstone Gaol where, after several months with a charge of murder hanging over his head, he was eventually pardoned and released.

Defoe moved on to Faversham, where he 'immediately enquir'd' about the recent dramatic events. His informant was probably the landlord of the inn in whose upper room James had taken refuge from the hostile mob, until rescued by 'Persons of Quality', who removed him to the Mayor's house. Defoe later gave several slightly different versions of a conversation between a well-known local clergyman and the King, who complained, 'Sir, 'tis Men of your Cloth have reduc'd me to this Condition', and asked for his help to quieten the mob; but 'The Gentleman's Answer was cold and insignificant; and going down to the People, return'd no more to the King'. James also invited in a man who had been inciting the mob, and asked his assistance. 'What the fellow answer'd to the King I know not; but as I immediately enquir'd they told me he did not say much but this, What can I do with *them? and what would you have me do with them?*' and 'when Persons of Quality in those Parts tender'd him their best Service, his constant Answer was, *the most acceptable service you can do me, is to facilitate my departure; and to procure means for my going beyond sea*'. Yet several of the gentry and clergy of the district who had 'formerly Preach'd and Talk'd up this mad Doctrine' of passive obedience, 'never offered the King their Assistance in that Distress; which as a Man, whether Prince or no, any Man would have done'.[97] Defoe himself, whatever he may have thought of James as a King, now pitied him as a man. 'I am heartily sorry for his fate', he wrote, 'but it is better so than see three kingdoms perish.'[98]

8 Projects and Undertakings Beyond My Reach

The final withdrawal of James was followed by heart-searching throughout the nation, with anxious negotiations within doors and vehement discussion without. Few doubted that effective power must pass into William's hands, but on what terms? The constitutional crisis forced men to examine the basic principles of their political beliefs. The Tory theory of divine right by inheritance left no room for a political vacuum. Either James was still king, or else he could be considered to have abdicated. In that case, his infant son was king, unless, as it suited many Tories to believe, he was really a changeling. If that was so, then James's elder daughter Mary reigned *jure divino*. In all this there was room for William only as Regent or Consort, roles he was most unlikely to accept. The Whig contractual theory of the state avoided all these difficulties; and Defoe for one had no hesitation in interpreting the situation as a return to the state of nature which had existed before civil government had come into being.

> Let any Man but put the Case to January, 1688 [i.e. 1689], the King was gone, there was no Representative Power in being, nor any Power which had any Legal Authority to call a Representative, the whole Machine of Government was unhing'd, and the Substance dissolv'd, all Delegated Power ceased, all Commissions determin'd, and none could grant more; there was no Officer nor Magistrate could act, or any power to make new ones. Authority was at an End; all Men had an Equality of Power, Laws indeed were in being, but no Man had any just Authority to put them in Execution . . . all retreated to the great Original Power of the People.[1]

Although no Parliament was in being, and none could legally be summoned, at William's invitation elections were held in the early weeks of January for a quasi-Parliament, to be styled a Convention. Among the countless pamphlets offering advice to this body when it met on 22 January was one which was apparently Defoe's first published contribution to political thought: *Some Short Considerations relating to the Settling of the Government; humbly offer'd to the Lords and Commons now Assembled at Westminster.*[2] It is unlike most of his later tracts in its brevity, and in the taut formality of its argument, which is developed in eleven numbered steps, some with sub-divisions, and even sub-sub-divisions. Its gist was that 'the King has forfeited his Power Several ways'; that 'the Supreme Power Real remains in the Community; and they may act by their Original Power'; that the nation is at liberty to order its affairs as it sees fit; but that 'the Original Constitution is the best, justest and most desirable'. He recommended, not the joint monarchy which eventually found favour, but that William should be made king for life, with remainder to Mary, and that provision should be made for the succession.

The theological underpinning of the argument was characteristic. He pointed out that 'tho *Saul* and *David* had a Divine Designation, yet the People assembled; and in a General Assembly, by their Votes, freely chose them; which proves, that there can be no orderly or lasting government without the consent of the People tacit or express'd; and God himself would not put them under a Governor without their Consent'. He returned to this theme for his peroration, when for the only time he gave a loose to his pen:

And it is worthy of Observation, That before the Theocracy of the Jews ceas'd, the manner of the Divine Designation of their Judges was by God's giving the People some Deliverance by the hand of the Person, to whose Government they ought to submit, and this even in the time of extraordinary Revelations . . . And I challenge the best Historians to give an Instance (since that Theocracy ceas'd) of a Designation of any Person to any Government, more visibly divine than that which we now admire. If the hand of Providence (miraculously and timely disposing natural Things in every Circumstance to the best advantage) should have any influence upon men's Minds, most certainly we ought not here to be insensible; if the *Voice of the People be the Voice of God*, it never spoke louder. If a nation of various Opinions, Interests and Factions, from a turbulent and fluctuating state falls suddenly into serene and quiet Calm, and mens Minds are strangely united of a sudden; it shews from whence they are influenc'd. In a word, if the hand of God is to be seen in human Affairs, and his Voice to be heard upon Earth; we cannot any where (since the ceasing of Miracles) find a clearer and more remarkable Instance, than is to be observ'd in the present Revolution.

So pleased was Defoe with this ingenious argument, which turned the theory of divine right upon its head, that three years later he repeated it with only minor changes of phraseology;[3] and he once explicitly claimed that 'if *Vox Populi* be *Vox Dei*, here is plain Divine Right'.[4]

However, at this stage the outcome still hung in the balance. On 28 January the Commons passed a resolution to the effect that, James having broken his contract with the people and having abdicated, the throne stood vacant. Defoe was actually present on the following day when this resolution was debated by the Lords, and when they were interrupted by the arrival from the Commons of a second resolution. He wrote of 'that Famous Vote of the Convention, *which I have often quoted, and which with Inexpressible Joy*, I heard deliver'd at the Bar of the Lords House, in a message from the Commons, by Mr. *Hambden* of *Buckinghamshire*'. The actual wording ran:

> That it hath been found by experience to be inconsistent with the safety and welfare of this Protestant kingdom to be governed by a popish prince.

Defoe's memory was to give a significant twist to these words, of which he gives several slightly differing versions.[5] The earliest runs:

> That it is inconsistent with the Laws and Liberties of this Protestant Nation to be govern'd by a popish prince.

Thus he could persuade himself that 'This is not a new Law . . . but a Declaration of that which was Law before'. The actual words could not bear this construction; but Defoe's distortion of them neatly illustrates the conservative instincts of those who supported the Revolution. When at last, though not with the 'Unanimity and Dispatch' which Defoe had called for in his tract, William and Mary were invited to occupy the vacant throne, he could still feel that 'our Deliverance was like a Dream to us', and had no doubt that 'The Lord was our Deliverer'.[6]

In the early months of 1689 Defoe found time to work on what was to be for some years his most ambitious piece, licensed for publication on 7 April, and entitled *Reflections upon the Late Great Revolution.*[7] He aimed to prove from the Scriptures that monarchy was not originally divinely ordained; that even after it was established among the Jews, the people appointed their own kings; and that even those who *were* divinely chosen remained limited monarchs. After tracing the history of the Jewish kings in some detail, Defoe concluded that the actual powers of monarchs could not be deduced from the Scriptures. Even Christ, he declared, 'does not pretend to tell us what is *Cesar*'s due, because no general Rule could be given in that Case, the Rights of Kings and People varying almost in every Country. Therefore 'tis from the Statute-Book, not the Bible, that we must judge the Power our Kings are invested withal, and also of our Obligations and the measures of our Subjection.' From this base he launched into a panegyric of our own limited monarchy, 'the happiest Constitution under the Heavens'.

> For I think I may challenge the whole World to shew so equal and so happy a Constitution of Government as is this day in *England*, which is so exactly and harmoniously composed, that I know of nothing to compare it to but itself; for as Vertue does commonly lie in the mean, so our Legislators have wisely pickt out all the good that was in all sorts of Government, but shunn'd the Extreams that any one might have betray'd us to; For here the Populace have Liberty without a Democratical Confusion and Fury; the Nobility have all the Priviledges to which the Aristocracy it self could entitle them, without the necessity of running into Factions and Cabals for it; the King's Power so equally ballanced between the Two other, that his Power can hardly ever degenerate into Tyranny, nor, on the other side, while he governs by Law, can he ever want Authority, either to protect or correct his Subjects.

Having dismissed the theory of divine right, he took the contractual origin of royal power almost for granted: 'So that 'tis
evident, that the power of the People is not only antecedent to
that of Kings, but also that the Kings did receive and derive
their Authority at first from the People.' Finally, he tried to
show that in various ways James had forfeited that authority.

This tract is the earliest fully developed expression of Defoe's
political theory, which he did not materially alter or develop in
later years. Though the classical justification of the Revolution —
Locke's *Treatise on Civil Government* — was not published until
the following year, the idea of a contract between king and
people was already in the air; Lords and Commons had already
agreed 'That King James II, having endeavoured to subvert the
constitution of his kingdom by breaking the original contract
between king and people', had thereby forfeited his throne. The
exact route by which these ideas entered Defoe's thought is
uncertain, but it is natural to suppose that they had been
absorbed by him a decade earlier at Morton's Academy. The
Reflections, as well as expressing Defoe's own sincere convictions, had also a tactical purpose. It was an attempt to dispel
the misgivings, especially strong among the Anglican clergy, at
the settlement in which the Tories had sacrificed their principles
to political necessity. An attack on the principles of divine right
and passive obedience, however reasoned and moderate in tone,
would scarcely have found its way into the studies of country
rectories if it had appeared under the name of a known Dissenter.
So he attributed it to a 'lay hand in the country', and went out
of his way to pretend to be a member of the Church of England.
Thus, among his efforts to allay the guilty pangs that were
troubling sensitive Anglican consciences, he wrote:

> And truly, the Causes and Occasions of those two great
> Revolutions in 48 and 88, were not more distant than their
> Designs and Ends were; the *first* intending the Subversion,
> and the latter the Establishment of the best and purest
> Religion in the World.[8]

Defoe had already set his foot on the slippery path that would
lead him to *The Shortest Way with the Dissenters*, to Newgate
and the pillory.

Three months later, in *The Advantages of the Present Settle-*

ment (licensed on 4 July), he was playing on a different string.[9]
Still maintaining anonymity and the pretence of being a member
of the Church of England, he now spent no time on political
theory or constitutional niceties, but simply invited his supposed
fellow-Anglicans to look back twelve months. He enlarged on
James's ingratitude to the Church of England and his plan to
bring in popery at the expense of the nation's liberties; he
pointed out that the ex-king could only be restored with the
help of the Irish and the French, and that he would only be a
puppet of Louis XIV. Though neither of these tracts made any
great stir, Defoe could feel that he had contributed his mite to
driving a wedge between the Anglican Tories and the Jacobite
cause.

Alongside his literary activities, Defoe continued to be
involved in the political and commercial life of the City. He had
now acquired enough seniority in Cornhill Ward to be chosen to
serve as Butler at the Wardmote Inquest for the year 1689,
apparently an intermediate stage between service on the Petty
and Grand Juries of the Ward.[10] In the early summer he had
enrolled in the newly formed Royal Regiment of Volunteer
Horse, consisting of 400 leading citizens, mostly Dissenters, 'to
be maintained at their own charges'.[11] The King himself con-
sented to be their colonel, and they were commanded by the
Earl of Monmouth, later to win fame in Spain as the Earl of
Peterborough. Of the six captains, all eminent City knights,
Defoe probably served under Sir William Ashurst, for he was
certainly familiar with the 'very beautiful house' which Ashurst
had built at Highgate, 'at the very summit of the hill, and with a
view from the very lowest windows over the whole vale, that
they see the very ships passing up and down the river for 12 or
15 miles below London'.[12] We can picture the young merchant
at Ashurst's house on some business in connection with the
Royal Regiment, but with half his mind on his own affairs,
perhaps wondering whether among the ships slowly winding
their way up the river on the flowing tide, was one of his own,
overdue but now at last come home.

The Royal Regiment certainly provided a means for the City
Whigs to demonstrate their support for the new regime; but
from the first it was little more than a gesture, and never carried
out more than ceremonial functions. Defoe told how he 'had
the honour to attend her majesty', Queen Mary, when in the

late summer she paid her first visit to the gardens of Kensington Palace, recently purchased from the Earl of Nottingham, to give orders for their enlargement;[13] and this may well have been as one of an escort provided by the Royal Regiment. Their most spectacular appearance, however, came on 29 October, when the new Lord Mayor was installed. The Regiment, 'gallantly mounted and richly accoutred', and led by the Earl of Monmouth, escorted William and Mary from Whitehall to Cheapside, where they watched the show from a balcony. 'Amongst the troopers', records Oldmixon, 'was *Daniel Foe*, at that time a hosier in Freeman's yard, Cornhill.'[14]

This same autumn Defoe became involved in the first of a number of legal wrangles which were to extend over several years.[15] Despite the considerable number of lawsuits in which he was concerned, he does not seem to have been particularly litigious; he was nearly always the defendant in the original suit in each dispute. Nor was there at first anything discreditable to him in these cases, which at the worst suggest that he was liable to get out of his commercial depth. The glimpses they offer of trading ventures gone astray ought probably to be balanced by bold strokes which succeeded, and so never ended in the courts.

He had still not succeeded in collecting all the debts due to Joseph Braban, the King's Lynn merchant, from his customers, although the nine months allowed him were long since past. Although Defoe claimed to have paid more than he had received, Braban was suing for payment on certain promissory notes, and was threatening to sue on the £600 penal bond. On 4 November Defoe began a Chancery suit to oblige Braban to come to a just account. He probably had this dispute in mind when he wrote some years later:

> I my self have heard very famous Lawyers make sorry Work of a Cause between the Merchant and his Factor; and when they came to argue about *Exchanges, Discounts, Demorages, Charter-Parties, Fraights, Port-Charges, Assurances, Barratries, Bottomries, Accounts Currant, Accounts in Commission,* and *Accounts in Company,* and the like, the Sollicitor has not been able to draw a Brief, nor the Council to understand it . . .
> . . . And I remember a pretty History of a particular Case, by way of Instance, When two Merchants contending about a long Factorage-Account, that had all the Niceties of Merchan-

dizing in it, and labouring on both sides to instruct their Council, and to put them in when they were out, at last found them make such ridiculous stuff of it, that they both threw up the Cause, and agreed to a Reference; which Reference in one Week, without any Charge, ended all the Dispute, which they had spent a great deal of Money in before to no purpose.[16]

Another dispute was in progress between Defoe and Humphrey Ayles, master of the *Batchelor*, although it did not come to court until the following summer. If all had gone smoothly, Ayles should have discharged cargoes and passengers for Defoe at Boston, New York and Maryland, and taken aboard more merchandise to be provided by Defoe's factors. Ayles complained that when he had arrived in Maryland on 3 December 1688 there had been only seven hogsheads of tobacco available, and that though he had 'rid and travailed several hundred miles . . . in frost and snow', he had failed to obtain any more; and after spending 64 days in all on demurrage, he had been forced to take cargoes for other merchants. He claimed that Defoe owed him £424 0s. 7d. for demurrage and other expenses. Defoe, however, claimed that the delay was entirely Ayles's fault, alleging that he had wasted twenty-six days in New England on his own business, and that by the time he arrived in Maryland his correspondent there, Mr Samuel Sandford, had been obliged to make other arrangements for shipping his tobacco. The case dragged on for years, but the final outcome is not known.

Meanwhile Defoe had run into various difficulties with his own ship, the *Desire*. He complained that he had been made the victim of a piece of sharp practice, by which ship's fitters, with the connivance of the masters, put in inflated bills for their services, taking half in money, and the other half in a share in the ship, which thus really cost them nothing, while also ensuring business for themselves in the future; and so 'the poor Merchants and Owners become Milch-Cows to the Tradesmen'.

If the Gentlemen of *Wapping* and *Redriff* think themselves injur'd in this, I undertake to Name them a Man, who refitted a Ship that receiv'd some small Damage, and by the Assistance of the Master, whom he made merry over a Bowl of Punch, got his Hand to a Bill of ninety eight Pounds, in which it

appear'd, and he confess'd afterward, he clear'd 50 *l*. of the
Money — and the Fool thus impos'd upon, was no body but
myself.[17]

Defoe seems to have met this bill, for in the course of subsequent litigation with the master, Robert Harrison, it was
stated that Defoe had paid £97 10*s*. out of £160 10*s*. 1½*d*. due
for his share of fitting out the ship. On 20 March 1689 Harrison
sailed for France, apparently with a cargo of Defoe's; for the
latter complained that he had not been told when the ship
sailed, though 'masters usually took leave of their owners'.
Perhaps he hoped to dispose of his cargo and pick up a return
freight of French wines before the outbreak of war, which was
actually declared on 4 May. But things went wrong: 'I had the
Honour, Disaster, or what else you will please to call it, of losing
the first Ship that was taken upon the Breach of the last war,
and before it was declared.'[18] By the autumn Harrison was back
in England, apparently through an exchange of prisoners, and
was suing Defoe. The evidence as to what happened to the *Desire*
is so conflicting that it is almost impossible to guess at the truth.
Harrison's story was that, because of the war, he had gone to
Lisbon instead of France, but had been captured when homeward bound and taken into Brest. Defoe, for his part, declared
his belief that Harrison had gone to Nantes or Rochelle with
passes from French agents, but had been seized there. It may be
that Defoe was himself privy to some scheme for trading with
the enemy. He certainly saw no objection to this in principle,
arguing that such trade could never be prevented, but could
always be arranged through third parties who creamed off most
of the profits. He tells us, 'I had the Honour to defend this
Opinion, and give my Reasons for it, before both the House of
Commons, and before the Privy Council in the late Reigns.' This
was probably in July 1689 or December 1690, when bills to
prohibit trade with France were under discussion in the Lower
House.[19]

However unsuccessful these ventures may have been, Defoe
had other irons in the fire. In August 1689 he bought from
Robert Knight, junior, a lease of some 30 acres of marshland in
the parishes of Chadwell St Mary and Tilbury in Essex.[20] The
purchase price of these lands, which were let at a rental of £40
per annum, was £855. Defoe raised £555 of this himself, and

borrowed the remaining £300 from one Robert Stamper. In November 1690 he made a further purchase from Knight of the lease of another 38 acres adjoining. The annual rent was £50, and the purchase price £1000. This time Defoe raised only £400 himself, and borrowed £600 from John Ghisleyn and Peter Maresco, to whom, as in the case of Stamper, the property was conveyed on mortgage. It is unlikely that Defoe dealt directly with Stamper, Ghisleyn and Maresco; for such deals were normally arranged through a scrivener. When Roxana was seeking a safe investment for her money, she 'got a substantial safe Mortgage . . . by the Assistance of the famous Sir Robert *Clayton*', whom she described as 'a Man thorowly vers'd in the Arts of improving Money, but thorowly honest'. Clayton, quite often mentioned by Defoe, was the leading scrivener of the day, and was related by marriage to his Lodwick associates; perhaps it was through him that he borrowed the money to complete these purchases.[21]

It was quite usual for a prosperous merchant to invest some of his profits in land, often as a first step towards establishing a family of landed gentry. But as Defoe had to borrow nearly half the money he required he can hardly have been seeking an outlet for idle capital. Nor could he seriously have intended his family to take root and flourish in these unhealthy marshes, which were chiefly used for the winter grazing of sheep intended for Londoners' dinner-tables. Defoe remarks that 'the landlords let good penny-worths . . . for it being a place where everybody cannot live, those that venture it, will have encouragement, and indeed it is but reasonable that they should'.[22] Nor, on the face of it, was this a profitable investment; for he was borrowing at 6 per cent to buy lands which yielded less than 5 per cent in rents. The explanation must lie in the situation of the marshes, on the northern shore of the Thames, just upstream from Tilbury Fort, completed a few years earlier to protect shipping in the river after the devastating Dutch raid of 1667.[23] The outbreak of war with France was bound to loosen the nation's purse-strings; and Defoe presumably hoped to net a handsome profit from development of the area near the Fort. There were thoughts of establishing the central artillery arsenal at Tilbury; but, unfortunately for Defoe, second thoughts fixed upon Woolwich.[24] At a later date he wrote to the Admiralty offering to sell his lands at Tilbury for the construction of a naval dockyard. The situation, with protection already afforded by the Fort, was in many ways ideal. But, as he himself acknowledged later, while a Dutch War favoured development on the east coast, a French War was more propitious to the south coast; so the defences of Portsmouth were strengthened and a new yard established at Plymouth, while his own proposal was rejected.[25] Yet he had certainly shown a certain flair, even though two centuries were to pass before the commercial docks were constructed at Tilbury, within a stone's throw of the site he had suggested.

Meanwhile the reception of his political tracts which had appeared in the first half of 1689 must have been favourable enough for him to publish near the end of the year three more pieces, of a more general nature. On 23 August a licence was granted for a tract entitled: *A Discourse of the Necessity of Encouraging Mechanick Industry: Wherein it is plainly proved, That Luxury and the want of Artisans Labour, became the Ruin of the four grand Monarchies of the World, in the Former Age, and of Spain and other Countries, in This; and the Promoting of manual Trades the rise of the* Dutch, Germans, *&c. Parallel'd and compar'd with, and shewn to be practicable under the Present Constitution of* England.[26] Here he argued that, since the curse of Adam, felicity was only to be achieved by labour, which is part of the very order of nature:

> The very inanimate Creatures, the Sun, Moon and Stars, have in their kinds their proper and distinct Offices of Labour . . . The trees and Plants . . . discharge their several Functions, in concurrence with this grand Design. What Slavery and Toil is undergone by Sensitive Creatures . . . In the order of Creation, the next degree above these are Men . . . But to pass by them at present, if we look up to a higher Species or Rank of Creatures, the Angelical Beings, we shall find that those Blessed Spirits are continually busied and employ'd either in repeated Hallelujahs and Eucharistical Praises; or else are sent upon frequent Embassies and Negotiations into this lower World . . . Shall then Man be excepted who was made but a little lower than the Angels.

After praising the stress placed upon labour in Holland and Germany, he argued that more should be done in this direction at home. His real concern was with the sons of the lesser gentry who 'come abroad into the World like *Pharaoh*'s Frogs', the 'sharpers' who formed gangs in London and assaulted those who did not share their Jacobite sympathies. One remedy was to pass a law to forbid any child with an income of less than £300 per annum to remain at school beyond the age of fifteen; instead he should be put to a trade, despite the genteel prejudice against this. For those who already burdened society, he proposed a still more drastic remedy, 'to exchange them for honest Men, that were taken upon their lawful Employments at Sea by the Turks'.

On 24 October a licence was granted for a companion piece, *St. Paul the tent-maker; in a discourse shewing how religion has in all ages, been promoted by the industrious mechanick.*[27] He began by contradicting the prevailing view that men of business were too engrossed in worldly cares to follow a religious life. He pointed out that Christ was 'a Carpenter before he was a Preacher', and that his disciples were all 'mechanicks'. Since 'it is impossible for a Man to poize himself so equally in the World, as neither to do Good or Evil', he should guard against 'the Parent of all Sin, which is Idleness'.

> Men as really serve God in their Callings, as in their constant and immediate attendance upon Divine Worship.
>
> He that has commanded us to pray . . . has also bid us work with our Hands . . . this Extremity in Religion to the neglect of our proper and lawful Business, obstructs the Divine Favours, and will make all our Toil in Religion turn to no good account . . .
>
> . . . 'tis not a moderate, but an inordinate pursuit of worldly Business, which interferes with, or carrys any opposition to the Gospel.

He concluded with examples from Geneva, Holland and New England, to show that, wherever men were remarkable for their industry, Christianity flourished. Though these two tracts were published anonymously, and although he tried once again to pass himself off as an Anglican, despite the obviously Calvinist character of his thinking, Defoe for once seems to have had no ulterior political motive. He simply expands in a relaxed manner some of his thoughts on his main interests in life — trade and industry, society and religion — and tries to bring them into a related system.

The third tract, licensed on 11 November, and provocatively entitled *Taxes No Charge*, shows more political involvement.[28] After discussing, in lively but unsystematic style, the different forms of taxation levied in various parts of Europe, he argued that taxes, far from being a burden on society, act as a stimulus to trade. He claimed that a miser was a worse enemy to a community than a thief, suggesting 'a double imposition upon Mony lock'd up in chests, more than what is out at Usury, which being employ'd, is upon the Duty it was made for'; and he commented that 'there is no Mony, which circulates so fast, as that which comes into the hands of seamen and soldiers'. Though this tract was clearly related to the demands that would soon be made upon Parliament to meet the costs of the French War, Defoe does not seem to be writing from the point of view of any particular group, still less any statesman; he was still the public-spirited amateur, apparently more anxious to impress the reader with his paradoxical views than to exert any real influence on the course of events in Parliament. No doubt he hoped to profit personally from the increased public expenditure. This has already been suggested as the explanation of his dealings in Essex marshlands; and the same is true of another venture in which he became involved in the winter of 1689/90.

In the course of the year 1689 it had become clear that one of the main centres of the European struggle would be in Ireland. In March James II had landed there with French forces, and soon controlled three of the four provinces. Though Derry had been relieved in July, and Schomberg had landed with a small force in August, James still held the whole country outside Ulster. William decided to build up a much stronger force at Chester, and take it across himself in the following year. Meanwhile Schomberg's army lay under appalling conditions at Dundalk, while their commander wrote repeatedly to complain of lack of supplies. One palliative was an Order in Council removing all duties from various goods exported to Ireland, for a period of three months from 1 November.[29] Among the merchants who took advantage of this to send supplies of creature comforts to raise the morale of the Protestant forces there was a group consisting of five Huguenot traders, and one Englishman — Defoe. According to a later petition, the merchants and their cargoes were: Gabriell Guichard, described as a French Protestant perfumer, who sent brandy or English spirits, Hungary water and flour; Peter Boytoult, wines and hops; John Lambert, probably the future South Sea director and baronet, the son of a merchant from the Isle of Rhe, but educated at an English Protestant Academy, who sent brandy and other goods; James Decaux, felt hats; John Degrave, hops; and Daniel Foe, six pipes of Porto wine, six pipes of beer, four hogsheads and two barrels of tobacco — perhaps some of the cargo which Ayles had found so difficult to obtain during the previous winter — one barrel of tobacco pipes, two trunks of hoses and stuffs, 120 gallons of English spirits, and 100 lb of Spanish snuff.[30]

Just as Crusoe on his fateful voyage was acting as supercargo for a group of Brazilian planters,[31] so Defoe himself in the winter of 1689/90 apparently travelled with the ship to take care of their cargo for the Huguenot merchants. His absence from home is confirmed by the omission of his name from the Cornhill Wardmote lists when they were drawn up at the end of December;[32] and his ship had in fact dropped down the river on 14 December, bound for Belfast. They had almost seven weeks to reach Ireland before the customs moratorium expired; but Defoe was soon to learn that this was 'a terrible long, and sometimes dangerous voyage'.[33] It was a very wet and stormy winter, with almost continuous westerly winds. On Christmas Day a violent storm from the south-west cast away several vessels near Plymouth; but Defoe's ship, having already weathered Land's End but fearful of being driven ashore on the coast of South Wales, ran for the shelter of Hartland Point, 'lying . . . under the lee, as they call it of these rocks, for shelter from the S.W. . . . winds'. Here, probably at Clovelly, he saw seamen from the 'fisher-boats of Barnstaple, Bideford and other towns of the coast', engaged in the winter herring fishery, 'go on shore . . . and supply themselves with provisions' at Hartland, which he found to his surprise to be 'a market-town, though so remote, and of good resort too, the people coming to it out of Cornwall, as well as out of Devonshire'.[34] More trouble lay ahead, and the ship had to put into harbour several times more. It must have been on this voyage that he visited Whitehaven, establishing business relations with the Mr Gale who later acted as his agent there,[35] and being struck by the number of coal-ships in the harbour, awaiting a favourable wind; for he later recalled how ' 'tis frequent in time of war, or upon the ordinary occasion of cross-winds, to have two hundred sail of ships go at a time from this place for Dublin, loaden with coals'.[36]

Worse was to come. On the night of 11 January there was a storm of exceptional violence from the north-west.[37] They had again to take shelter, this time at Kirkudbright in south-west Scotland. Here, he found 'a fine river navigable for the greatest ships to the town key, a haven, deep as a well, safe as a mill-pond; 'tis a meer wet dock, for the little island of Ross lyes in the very entrance, and keeps off the west and north-west winds and breaks the surges of the sea; so that when it is rough without, 'tis always smooth within'. At Kirkubry, as Defoe preferred to spell it, he first met the Scots at home, and with very mixed feelings. On the one hand they were a 'sober, grave religious people', strict Sabbath-keepers; and 'if a mean boy, such as we call shoe-blackers or black-guard boys, should be heard to swear, the next gentleman in the street . . . would cane him and correct him'. On the other hand he was shocked both at their poverty and at the apathy with which they accepted it, when with initiative, hard work and a little imported capital they could build ships, make use of their fine harbour and of the fish which were asking to be caught, and prosper.[38]

They may have lain windbound at Kirkudbright for several weeks, while Defoe fretted at his enforced idleness; and there was to be yet another delay, this time at Port Patrick, 'the ordinary place for the ferry passage to Belfast'. They stayed here long enough for Defoe to go ashore on what must for once have been a fine day, and to climb a nearby hill, from which he 'could plainly see Ireland to the west, England (viz.) the coast of Cumberland to the south, and the Isle of Man to the south-west, and the Isle of Isla, and the Mull of Kyntire to the north-west'.[39] The inaccuracy of some of these directions suggests that his account, written many years later, was based on real memories, not simply read from a map. Defoe also mentions the packet-boat at Port Patrick, which had been established only in the previous August by William Fullerton, the Collector of Customs there, to speed communications with Schomberg's forces in Ireland.[40] Nearly thirty years later, Defoe's favourite brother-in-law, Robert Davis, was to marry as his fourth wife the daughter of a customs official of that name; and this was perhaps the outcome of a friendship struck up at this time.[41]

But there can have been little love lost between Defoe and the customs officers on the other side of the North Channel. His ship did not reach Belfast until 6 February, six days too late to benefit from the customs moratorium, and the authorities were not prepared to relax the letter of the law. Defoe was unable to pay the duties, said to be greater than the value of the cargo. How long he spent in Ireland, trying to get them to changes their minds, we do not know. Did he perhaps find time to visit the army, some fifty miles south at Dundalk? He certainly mentions it on several occasions, and in *Reformation of Manners* (1702) he devoted 28 lines to an account of the drunkenness and debauchery among the English there.[42] He must soon have realised that the customs officers were adamant; and rather than carry his cargo back home he decided to leave it in their possession. By 10 March Gabriell Guichard, presumably notified of the situation by post, had petitioned the Treasury for the cargo to be released; but, as usual, the outcome is not known.

Defoe himself was soon on his way home, this time by the most direct route, overland from Liverpool, which he mentions having seen in 1690, commenting on its rapid growth since his previous visit ten years before.[43] On his approach to the port he had seen, off Hoylake, how 'the men of war rode, as our ships do in the Downs', while waiting to escort the army across to Ireland. He knew how 6000 Danish mercenaries had marched from Hull in late February to join the army encamped at Chester; and a visit to the latter at this time is confirmed by his description of the breakdown of the system of water supply in the city, so that 'they had no water to supply their ordinary occasions, but what was carried from the River Dee upon horses, in great leather vessels, like a pair of bakers panyers'.[44] His way may have lain through Coventry where, on his first visit to the city, he witnessed election riots. The two parties passed each other in procession in the street, 'the kennel in the middle only parting them', and then turned on each other with clubs and staves along the whole length of the street, fighting 'with such obstinacy 'tis scarcely credible . . . Nor were these the scum and rabble of the town, but . . . the burgesses and chief inhabitants.'[45]

The occasion was a general election, then in full swing, following the unexpected dissolution of Parliament on the same day as Defoe had reached Belfast. William's experience of the past twelve months had given him a distaste for the Whigs, not least because of their assumption that as the only true friends of the Revolution they were entitled to a monopoly of royal favour and opportunities to pay off old scores. It had been a proposal to exclude from municipal office all those who had been concerned in the surrender of town charters that had prompted him to dissolve the old Parliament; and the electors now obliged with a predominantly Tory House of Commons. He began gradually replacing Whig ministers with Tories, though he had no intention of allowing either party a monopoly of office. When after a short parliamentary session he left London on 4 June to take command of his forces in Ireland, he left behind him a Council of five Tories and four Whigs to advise Mary at a critical time. Jacobite reaction to the Revolution seemed to be steadily gathering strength and cohesion. Many of the clergy had refused the oaths of allegiance to William and Mary; many more to save their livings, had brought themselves to take them only by drawing a jesuitical distinction between a king *de facto* and a king *de jure*. Leading conspirators were in touch, not only with James, who still held most of Ireland, but also with Louis XIV, who had assembled a powerful fleet in the Channel under Admiral Tourville. In the event of a French landing, no one knew how many crypto-Jacobites might come into the open, or whether William's government might not collapse in the same way as James's had done eighteen months before.

At the end of the month came disastrous news. On 30 June Tourville gained a complete victory over an Anglo-Dutch fleet in an engagement off Beachy Head, in which Admiral Torrington was almost universally accused of cowardice for leading the English fleet out of the action. But neither the French nor the Jacobites were ready to exploit their opportunity. Defoe later asked:

When the *French* Fleet was on the Coast, King *William* absent, no Troops at home, our Fleet over-power'd, and flying from the Enemy, if ever they would have shown themselves, it would have been then . . . Did a man of them Stir? . . . all they did, and all they have done ever since, is to stay at home, and drink for him, swear for him, rail and snarl at those they dare not oppose.[46]

This was perhaps retrospective confidence. For the moment all looked very black, until hard on the heels of the naval defeat came news of William's complete victory on 1 July at the Boyne.

> Just then when sinking Horror did surround,
> And present Fears our absent Hope confound;
> The wondrous Trump his Conquest sounded ore,
> So once his Aspect sav'd the Land before.
> Moments of time the vast occasion hit,
> To those surprizing, and to these compleat:
> Had the great deed exactly tim'd by Fate,
> One weighty juncture slipt, 't had come too late;
> Had he not fought, or had it not been then,
> Tho he had conquer'd, it had been in vain.
> So mighty *Nassau*, so did Heaven contrive,
> That thy great hand should twice the Nation save.[47]

At this critical juncture, when a French invasion was still daily expected, the City of London was torn by party strife.[48] Though the Whigs still held the major city offices, the Tories had gained control, not only of the City's parliamentary representation, but also of its armed forces. Their influence was still further strengthened when it was decided, early in July, to supplement the six militia regiments with six regiments of auxiliaries. The Queen ordered a review of all available forces to be held in Hyde Park on 21 July. But so strongly did party feelings run that the Whigs, and Defoe with them, felt that the Tories were rejoicing at the country's difficulties:

> View them in Arms when our Invaded Coast,
> Some glittering hopes propos'd that all was lost;[49]

In the belief that the Tory-controlled forces of the City represented a greater threat to the Whig interest than they did to the French, the Whigs looked on in silence, or laughed behind their hands at the incompetence of the Tory colonels.

> Meanwhile the Martial Terrors of the Field,
> The threatn'd Whiggs with just Disdain beheld.[50]

There was no part in this review for the Royal Regiment of

which Defoe had been a member; for it had already been suppressed, thanks to the influence of Henry Compton, Bishop of London, with Queen Mary;

> *When the Grave Prelate made with humble Tears*
> *To the Royal Petticoats his Christian Prayers;*
> *And for disbanding grace made his ORISONS*
> *Which like his Lordship's Sermons too were wise Ones.*[51]

Petticoat government came to an end with the return of William to England in September. Though the conquest of Ireland was still incomplete, he now felt strong enough to plan a campaign for next year in the Netherlands; and the parliamentary session which opened on 2 October was devoted mainly to obtaining the substantial supplies needed to continue the campaign in Ireland, to strengthen the Navy, and to establish an army of 70,000 men to fight on the continent. For the most part the proceedings were harmonious; but a discordant note was struck by a petition presented on 2 December from 117 members of the Common Council of the City of London, complaining that a number of City posts were still held illegally by the Whigs, despite an act of the previous May making void the Quo Warranto proceedings of 1683 and declaring vacant all appointments made during the period when the City had been without its charter. On the face of it, this was simply a move in the bitter political in-fighting which had been going on in the City for a decade. But the author of a pamphlet entitled *Reflections upon the late famous Petition of the Common Council of LONDON, and the Well Timing it, &c.* imputed a more sinister motive.

> His majesty wants a Supply to answer the Expectations of all *Europe*; and Lewis XIV can find no other way to obstruct their generous Proceedings, than an unseasonable Petition . . . bringing the petty Brabbles of Ward-motes before the Parliament, to interrupt the Grand Affairs of Christendom . . . they imagin'd they should find so much Work for the Parliament, that they should not be able to compleat the King's Supply before he went into Holland. . . . So that if we consider the Time, we shall find these Subscribers so punctual to King *Lewis*, that if they had been his Clock-makers, or his Band of

Violins, they could not have observ'd his measures more exactly.

Without actually accusing the petitioners of treasonable intentions, he suggested that they were being exploited by Jacobite conspirators: 'However, this is the Godly Protestant Design afoot, and the Petitioners are made Tools and Cullies to drive it on. Unhappy in this, that they who spur 'em forward get all the *Louisdores*, while they are forc'd to drudg for nothing; no, not so much as a Treat at the Tavern.'[52]

This tract, quite possibly by Defoe, is certainly parallel in thought to his satirical poem on the same manoeuvre, *A New Discovery of an Old Intreague.*[53] Here, however, the stress is much more upon City politics. Some of its comments on recent events have already been quoted, but Defoe also showed that he could not forget or forgive things which had happened years before. Two of the petitioners had been members of the jury which had convicted Russell in 1682.

> Some of the sort have Crimes are Capital,
> On whom their Brothers Blood do's Vengeance call;
> Tender of these, we say of *Rouse* and *Brough*,
> *Eternity is Punishment enough.*
> Take an Authentick Term for your Condition
> 'Twas *Murther* Styl'd by th'House you now Petition.[54]

The whole force of this poem came from its often obscure topical allusions, so that it means little to us today without a running commentary. Very different in content and style from his *Meditations* of 1681, it is significant as being the first he is known to have published, the forerunner of many other satires in similar vein in years to come; and the heroic couplet was to become his favourite verse form.

The greater part of another verse satire, though not published until 1704, was apparently written by Defoe about this time. *The Locusts: Or Chancery Painted to the Life, and the Laws of ENGLAND try'd in Forma Pauperis* appears from internal evidence to have been mainly written between May 1690 and November 1692.[55] This was a time when Defoe was still heavily involved in Chancery litigation. Though the Braban case had probably been settled out of court, the Harrison case was still in progress in October 1690, while the Ayles case dragged on throughout 1691. He was shocked by the professional morality of the lawyers:

> How wretched are such Men who can comply
> With ev'ry Villany to Forge and Lie;
> That change their Tongues to plead in ev'ry Cause,
> And, like *Stock-jobbing* Brokers, sell the Laws?[56]

He compared them with the astrologers:

> But both alike our Expectations cheat,
> *Astrologers* the Poor, *Lawyers* deceive the Great:
> No Difference then betwixt them we can find,
> For both, like *Fanes*, submit to ev'ry Wind;
> But of the Three, the Weather-Cocks most kind,
> These see themselves mistaken, it is blind.[57]

His special target, however, was the Court of Chancery:

> Oh! cou'd I but *Anathema's* Decree
> My heaviest Curses I'd bestow on thee,
> Thou worst of Ills, thou Hell, thou *Chancery*.[58]

Once again, the real sting of the satire was in a series of savage thumbnail sketches of the leading Chancery lawyers; and perhaps it was his continued personal involvement in Chancery suits that decided him not to risk publication at this time, even anonymously.

During the year 1691 he was again collaborating with his friend Guy Miege, for whose *English Grammar* he had written a 'Prefatory Discourse' three years earlier. Since 1669 Edward Chamberlayne had been publishing a kind of early equivalent to *Whitaker's Almanack* or *The Statesman's Yearbook*, under the title of *Angliae Notitia*, or *The Present State of England*. Miege now planned a rival compilation, free from the Tory bias of Chamberlayne's work, and to be called *The New State of England*. Internal evidence shows that it was being prepared for the press during the winter of 1690/1. Once again Miege leaned heavily on Defoe's superior literary talents.[59] An almost *verbatim* repetition of the latter's eulogy of the English language was introduced

1. Courtyard Scene, by Pieter de Hooch. See p. 19 – 'a little court . . . and a brick wall and a gate'.

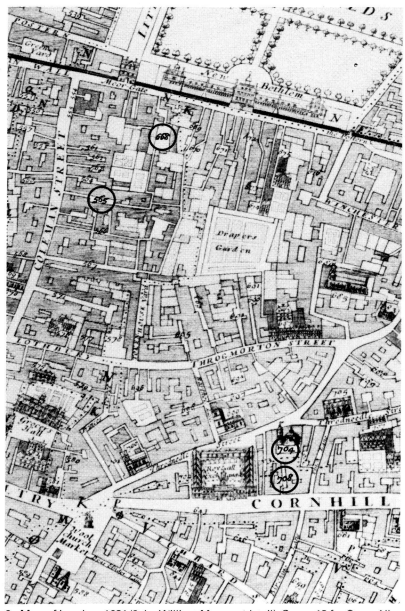

2. Map of London, 1681/2, by William Morgan (detail). See p. 18 for Swan Alley (565) and Jones's Rents (near 668); see p. 30 for French Court (unnumbered, opposite 704); see p. 101 for Freeman's Yard (708).

3. The London Scene
The Tower, by W. Hollar, 1647 (above); Stocks Market, with statue of Charles II trampling Cromwell (below).

Meditaçons

Fleeing for Refuge To The hope
sett before us   See Page. 125

In Misadvertant slaughter we are Told
Cittyes of Refuge were Prepar'd of Old;
Whither He fled who gave Unwilling fate,
A guilt Mishap did (Not Designe) create:
The Allmighty Legislator wisely knew
How Relative Affeccon would Persue,
So Made That Law (y Next of Kin Might be
Reveng'd of The Unhappy Tragedye,
And without Further Process Execute
The Errand of The Dreadfull Attribute:
Whose Fury Swift as Fate
With Eager Steps The Slayer Might Persue;
And If one Foot The Sacred fort could gaine,
His Fainting Mate Too Short, he Might be slain.
         No Less Th innocent Innocent Puts on
The Wings of Speed for The Securer Towne;
Feare gives New Life, & Fainting Spirits revive,
Ep'd w New hopes, and strong Desyres of Life;
Still when The Swift Persuer he Descrys,
Horrour Spurrs on, & where before he Ran he Flyes;
The Willing Gates w Eager Wishes Views,
And as his hopes revive his Speed Renews;
Till The long'd Ports Conceale his Picture fate,
And Vengance Stops at Not Pacifick gate.
The Eager Hebrews his Speed Commend,
His Fruitless Fury Spent, he's now a Friend,
Anger bould Ros w Law, and Still w Justice Ends

                                                  Thus

4. Defoe's First Meditation (1681). See p. 81 *et seq.*

5. Maritime Adventures
   Trading Vessels in a Rough Sea (above); Diving Operations (below).

6. Where Public Opinion was Made
   Merchants on the Royal Exchange (above); Coffee House Frequenters (below).

7. Defoe's Political Patrons
   William III – 'my dear and glorious master' (above); Charles Montagu, Lord
   Halifax (below left); Lord Somers (below right).

Laudatur et Alget
Juven . Sat . I.

8. Daniel Defoe: Portrait from _Jure Divino_ (1706).

with the words: 'As to the Excellency of it, I have little to add to what has been lately published by Mr. Miege in his Prefatory Discourse to his *English Grammar*.'[60] Defoe had overlooked the fact that he was supposedly writing *as* Miege; but in the second edition the slip was corrected, and the reference was to 'my *English Grammar*'.[61] Defoe was also responsible for other parts of the *New State*, notably Part II, Chapter XIII, 'Of their Present Majesties, King WILLIAM and Queen Mary, with a brief Account of their Accession to the Crown', a summary, from a Whig viewpoint, of the political struggle which had culminated in the Glorious Revolution. This chapter was further developed in a separate and more ambitious piece of work, which appeared towards the end of the year 1691: *A Compleat History of the Late Revolution from the First Rise of it to this present Time.*[62] This appeared anonymously; but Defoe later gave the credit for it to Miege, who was presumably responsible for collecting the considerable number of public documents relating to the Revolution which formed the bulk of the work. The linking material, however, is an expansion of Defoe's chapter in the *New State*, which is often followed *verbatim*, so that he was responsible for the narrative and commentary which give the work its interest. It found a ready market, for it was claimed that '1600 Books were sold in Six Weeks Time'; and today it still holds some interest as an early, if not the first, example of the Whig interpretation of the history of those times.[63]

Defoe's name has also been linked, though without any convincing evidence, with the *Athenian Mercury*, launched in 1691 by the original but eccentric bookseller, John Dunton, to answer readers' queries, real or concocted, on a wide range of scientific and ethical problems.[64] However, when Charles Gildon brought out *A History of the Athenian Society* in 1692 to boost Dunton's project, Defoe was among 'the Chief Wits of the Age' who contributed prefatory odes;[65] and he was to make use of its methods himself a dozen years later when he launched into periodical journalism on his own account. When Dunton called Defoe 'a man of good parts, and very clear sense' whose 'conversation is ingenious and brisk enough', he was writing from personal knowledge, for the two men certainly moved in the same circles.[66] Like Samuel Wesley, Dunton had married a daughter of the Rev. Samuel Annesley, whose meeting house at Little St Helens, Bishopgate, was attended by Defoe. It had

been in Annesley's parish of St Giles Cripplegate that the latter
had probably been born. Whether or not the Foes had been
regular members of his congregation ever since his ejection in
1662 — and one feels that Defoe at least would have felt the
need for more variety — Dunton testified that the latter was '*a
great Admirer and constant Hearer* of my Reverend Father in
Law Dr. *Annesley*'.[67]

A tradition, recorded years after Defoe's death, links his
name with another congregation:

> The Congregation of Protestant Dissenters at Lower Tooting
> in Surrey, Owes its original to the Celebrated Mr. Dan.[1] De
> Foe, who first endeavoured to form the Dissenters resident in
> this Neighbourhood into a Regular Society, they met for
> some time in a private House, & their first Pastor was Mr.
> (afterwards Dr.) Joshua Oldfield, Son of Mr. John Oldfield,
> an Ejected Minister of Great Eminence, both for his Piety,
> & Learning.[68]

Oldfield, who had been ordained early in 1687, had moved to
Oxford by 1691; and the Tooting meeting was probably set up
in the latter part of 1687, when such conventicles were permitted
by James II's first Declaration of Indulgence. A quarter of a
century before, the parents of Defoe's friend, Charles Lodwick,
had lived in a substantial nine-hearth house in Upper Tooting;[69]
and if the family still had an interest in it, Defoe may have been
in occupation as their tenant. In 1692 he certainly had a 'house
in the country', apparently in Surrey;[70] while the situation of
Tooting fits neatly with a story he tells, in the third person, but
almost certainly about himself, of 'a man, who being some
distance from London, not above six or seven miles, a friend
that came to visit him urged him to go to London'. When at
length he agreed, 'he found a letter, and messengers had been at
his house to seek him and to tell him of a particular business,
which was, first and last, worth above a thousand pounds to
him'.[71] Defoe had no hesitation in ascribing this to the direct
intervention of Providence.

In the comparatively small world of the dissenting congregations Defoe must have been widely acquainted, and some of
those he knew were men of considerable influence. Daniel
Williams, who had left his Presbyterian congregation in Dublin

and moved to London shortly before the Revolution, was a wealthy man who gave great help to later Protestant refugees from Ireland. King William, and in his absence Queen Mary, both made use of his 'extraordinary Knowledge of Persons, the Strength of Interests, Places and Parties' in that kingdom.[72] William Carstares, whom Defoe may have met in Holland, was now one of William's chaplains, and his most trusted adviser on Scottish affairs.[73] Defoe came to know both of these men well, although it is not certain that he knew them at this time. Another Royal chaplain whom he certainly knew was the famous John Tillotson, a former pupil of David Clarkson, but himself a Low Churchman who, to the disgust of the Tories, was Archbishop of Canterbury from 1691 until his death in 1694. Defoe quoted the 'testimony . . . I have had the Honour to hear him express' to the effect that King William 'was a very Devout Person, and a Constant Observer of Religious Duties, both in Publick and Private'.[74] A very different acquaintance was the veteran republican conspirator, Major John Wildman, who served William for a while as Postmaster-General as well as involving himself actively in City affairs; and Defoe later recalled 'having frequently discoursed the Affairs of the War with him'.[75] Perhaps too it was at this time that he was on familiar terms with Sir Richard Haddock, 'for many Years Commissioner for the Navy (from whose own Mouth I had a full Account . . .)' of the Battle of Southwold in 1672, in which he had been nearly drowned.[76]

If Defoe sometimes moved among those on the fringes of political power, it was without any deep personal involvement at this time; and though he still cherished literary ambitions, his dogged anonymity suggests that he was coy about exposing them. In the eyes of the world he was simply a merchant, though an unusual one. He was still living in Freeman's Yard, off Cornhill, near the commercial heart of the City. By December 1690 he had acquired enough seniority to be chosen a member of the Grand Jury for Cornhill Ward for the following year. His name also appears in a number of taxation lists. One of these, about August 1689, includes 'Daniell Foe & Partner', the latter tantalisingly unnamed.[77] A poll tax list of 1690 shows that his household then included his wife, one child, one manservant and one maidservant.[78] The child must have been Maria, presumably born after the death of Mary in 1688. That there was only

one surviving child after more than six years of marriage suggests
that there may have been other children who died young,
perhaps in Holland. A later poll tax list, dated 6 March 1691/2,
shows a considerably expanded household.[79] There was now a
second child, who must have been either the elder of his two
sons, Benjamin, or more probably his second daughter, Hannah.
Five servants were listed: Richard Addis, apparently a business
assistant, capable of keeping things going in Defoe's absence, for
he later appears as the householder and hosier in his own right;
Richard Vesey, Mary, Anne and 'Nourse'. The head of the
household was 'Daniel Foe, Whole Sale Hosier' — to which might
have been added, wine and tobacco importer, land speculator,
marine underwriter, not to mention political theorist and
pamphleteer, satirical poet and lay preacher.

Defoe never seems to have been unduly concerned with social
ostentation, but followed the usual pattern of rising young
merchants in having, not only a town house above his business
premises, but also a country house — probably, as we have seen,
at Tooting in Surrey. Here he must have had a coach-house and
stables, for he tells us that he had acquired that status symbol
of the age, a coach and horses.[80] A coach called for a coat of
arms to be painted upon the door panels. The Foes were not an
armigerous family, and there is no record of any grant of arms
to Defoe; but it may have been at this time that he adopted the
arms that were later, in the frontispiece of *Jure Divino*, to be
engraved beneath his portrait: *per chevron engrailed, gules and
or, three griffins passant countercharged.*[81] Substituting *sable
and argent* for *gules and or*, we have the arms borne by a family
named Knight of Westerham in Kent.[82] There is no known link
between them and the Foes, though it is interesting to find that
in 1672 the house of Michael Knight at Westerham was licensed
for nonconformist worship.[83] The name Robert Knight crops
up in several different contexts in connection with Defoe, but
the man, or men, have not been positively identified. Were
these Knights, or some of them, his maternal relatives, a variation of whose arms he now unofficially appropriated? At all
events we can imagine him and his family taking the air from
time to time in his coach, heraldically resplendent in red and
gold. Like others of his background, if his ambitions lay in that
direction, he might aspire to a fortune, a City knighthood,
perhaps even the Lord Mayor's chair and the founding of a

family of landed proprietors. But, like Crusoe on his Brazilian plantation,

> . . . increasing in business and wealth, my head began to be full of projects and undertakings beyond my reach; such as are indeed the ruin of the best heads in business . . . I must go and leave the happy view I had of being a rich and thriving man . . . only to pursue a rash and immoderate desire of rising faster than the nature of the thing admitted; and thus I cast myself down into the deepest gulph of human misery that ever man fell into, or perhaps could be consistent with life and a state of health in the world.

Indeed, he was already dangerously near the edge of that gulf.[84]

9 The Infinite Mazes of a Bankrupt

The *London Gazette* of 1–4 February 1692 contained the following laconic item:

> Plymouth, Jan. 31. Yesterday arrived here the *Desire* of *London*, with Wines from Lisbon.[1]

So unless there were two London ships called the *Desire*, and both engaged in the Portugal wine trade, Defoe's old ship, captured three years before, was once again sailing between Lisbon and London. He himself explains how this could happen. After discussing the heavy losses at the beginning of the war, including that of his own ship, he continues:

> Ships were so cheap in *France*, that they lay up by the Wall, as the Sailors call it, and perish'd for want of using; and our Merchants frequently rebought several Ships from them, for half their worth.[2]

However this unusual form of trading with the enemy was arranged, it seems that the *Desire* was once again in his ownership. He may even have sailed in her on that winter voyage, for his name is missing from the jury list of Cornhill Ward, made up in December 1691.[3] His *Essay upon Projects* (1697) contains a detailed and highly indignant account of what must have been his own last venture as a wine importer. He tells how 'a merchant' paid £475 in Lisbon for a hundred pipes of Spanish wines, to which freight and other charges added a further £165. The customs amounted to £700, a sum which the merchant could only raise by borrowing from a Lombard Street goldsmith, originally for two months only, making the wines over to him by bill of sale as security. The goldsmith held the key to the cellar where the wines were stored, and the merchant could not even take customers to see them, or his cooper to look after them, unless the goldsmith's man was present. Worse, because of 'a word or two spoken amiss to the goldsmith, *or which he was pleased to take so,* he wou'd have none sold but the whole parcel together'. After two months, when the wines remained unsold, the goldsmith demanded a further premium for extending the loan; and in fact the wines remained in the cellar for eighteen months. Though Defoe complained bitterly of 'the Extortion of this Banker', he may have been motivated as much by distrust of the merchant as by avarice.[4]

It is clear that by the early months of 1692 Defoe lacked the ready money to carry on his normal business transactions. How had this state of affairs arisen? When towards the end of his life, he recommended a steady and unremitting application to business, he was being wise after the event. Like Crusoe, he could seldom resist his 'foolish inclination of wandering abroad', and welcomed the chance to set off on a journey to somewhere new, when it would have been more prudent to have remained in Freeman's Yard keeping a close eye on the details of his business. As a 'Wit turn'd Tradesman' he spent time deep in books of history, travel or theology, that a more orthodox merchant would have spent poring over his day-book or ledger; or himself writing political tracts or satirical verse, instead of supervising his counting-house or warehouse. He had never been through the mill as an apprentice to master the humdrum details of the various trades he dabbled in; and the very fascination he found in the technicalities of commercial transactions also reveals him as something of a dilettante. He was so obviously different from the average merchant on the Exchange that he must sometimes have appeared as an innocent in trade, inviting the attention of the unscrupulous. He tells, for instance, of a man who bought goods from him on credit, and immediately carried them into the debtor's sanctuary of the Mint;[5] and we have already come across other attempts to defraud him, with varying success.[6] Defoe's own sanguine nature led him into bold projects, often unsuccessful, since he was prone to underestimate the difficulties and risks. His involvement in marine insurance, of which no details are known, must have played its part; for he was later able to persuade a Commons committee that his failure had been due to losses at the hands of French warships and privateers, among shipping which he had insured.[7] When he wrote of 'plain known inevitable causes which humane wisdom could not foresee or humane power prevent' he may have meant storms at sea, particularly one which he placed 'about the year 1692', when over 140 colliers were driven ashore on the Norfolk coast.[8] Varied and complex as the causes of his troubles seem to have been, his dealings in Essex marshlands may illustrate his basic mistake. He had sunk £1855, nearly half of it borrowed, in a project which *might* have yielded a big profit, but which had so far produced very indifferent returns. He later diagnosed his own weaknesses accurately enough: by 'grasping at too many undertakings at once' especially those 'out of the common road', a tradesman drains himself of his ready money which, 'like the blood let out of his veins', leads to the collapse first of his trade and finally his credit.[9]

Defoe's instinct when in difficulties was to gamble more deeply. Another London merchant in similar trouble, who reacted in the opposite way — by cutting his losses — was John Barksdale, who was offering for sale some seventy civet cats, whose musk-like secretion fetched high prices from the perfumers. He had a house in Newington specially 'fitted and made convenient and proper for the keeping and feeding' of these exotic creatures, with 'severall coopes with troughs and cisterns to feed them in and stoves for keeping fires in the severall rooms for the preservation of the said Catts'. On 21 April Defoe agreed to buy the cats and equipment for £852 15*s.*, a sum he certainly could not raise in ready money. However he managed to find £200 for a down payment, agreeing to pay a further £300 within a month, and the balance within six months. After giving notes for the £300 to some of Barksdale's creditors, he was allowed possession of the cats; but when the notes proved worthless, Barksdale refused to complete the legal transfer. Defoe, however, kept control of the cat-house, and at least made a show of raising the money needed to complete the purchase. In June Samuel Stancliffe, his close business associate, to whom he already owed £1100, lent him a further £400 for this purpose, though Defoe actually used the money to meet even more pressing demands.[10] Once again he had plunged himself still deeper into debt for the sake of hypothetical future profits.

By this time Defoe's situation was desperate. He later recalled

... the miserable, anxious, perplexed life, which the poor tradesman lives under before he breaks; the distresses and extremities of his declining state; how harass'd and tormented for money; what shifts he is driven to for supporting himself; how many little, mean, and even wicked things will even the most religious tradesman stoop to in his distress to deliver himself? even such things, as his very soul would abhor at another time; and for which he goes, perhaps, with a wounded conscience all his life after?[11]

One such dubious action arose out of a macabre incident which took place near the end of May. William Marsh, the youngest son of Lawrence Marsh of Dorking, and born within a few months of Defoe, who called him 'an Ancient Acquaintance and Familiar Friend', was at this time employed as a clerk by John Hoyle, a barrister of the Middle Temple. The latter, described by Whitelock Bulstrode as 'an Atheiste, a Sodomite professed, a corrupter of youth, and a blasphemer of Christ' had been an intimate friend of Aphra Behn, whom he had helped with her plays, and who often referred to him in her poems. In an incident which formed the subject of Sir Charles Sedley's *Ballad to the Tune of Bateman*, Hoyle, while drinking with friends in the Young Devil tavern in Fleet Street on the night of 26 May, expressed Whiggish views on the powers of kings. A young lawyer, George Pitt, son of 'a rich old usurer', a stranger to Hoyle and of Jacobite sympathies, picked a quarrel with him, followed him from the tavern at two in the morning, ran him through with his sword and killed him on the spot. A charge of murder against Pitt was eventually reduced to one of manslaughter on the grounds that Hoyle had raised his cane to defend himself.[12]

At the time of his death Hoyle had in his chambers a bill for £100 drawn by Richard Shaw of York, merchant, on George Styles of London, which had been sent to him by way of remittance by Thomas Nisbett of York, a wealthy Baltic merchant, and a near relative. While Hoyle still lay unburied in his chambers, Marsh took the bill to Defoe, who gave him £60 for it and endorsed it on 30 May to be paid to himself; and by a further endorsement on 20 June he ordered the contents to be paid to Thomas Williams, a Lombard Street goldsmith, a creditor who was pressing him for payment. When Nisbett's son searched Hoyle's chambers for the bill, Marsh admitted passing it on to

Defoe; and Nisbett senior, who was Hoyle's executor, lost little time in commencing a Chancery suit against Defoe on 7 July. In his reply three weeks later Defoe claimed that the transaction had been completely above board, but falsely asserted that it had taken place when Hoyle was still alive. He could not deny that he still owed £40 on the bill; he just did not have the money to pay it.[13]

While still desperately struggling to keep his head above water, Defoe had a remarkable dream, which he could still recall many years later, though characteristically attributing it to an acquaintance:

> I knew another, who, being a Tradesman, and in great distress for money in his business, dreamed that he was walking all alone in a great wood, and that he met a little child with a bag of gold in its hand, and a fine necklace of diamonds on its neck; upon the sight, his wants presently dictated to him to rob the child . . . and . . . accordingly, he . . . did so.
>
> But the Devil . . . hinted to him that perhaps the child might . . . single him out, . . . and therefore it would be better for him to kill the child . . . and that he need do no more but twist the neck of it a little, or crush it with his knee; he told me he stood debating with himself whether he should do so or not; but in that instant his heart struck him with the word murder, and he entertained a horror of it, refused to do it, and immediately waked.
>
> He told me that when he waked, he found himself in so violent a sweat as he had never known the like; that his pulse beat with that heat and rage, that it was like a palpitation of the heart to him, and the agitation of his spirits was such, that he was not fully composed in some hours; though the satisfaction and joy that attended him when he found it was but a dream, assisted much to return his spirits to their due temperament.[14]

This dream, of which he gives a slightly different version in another book, must have been the origin of the famous incident in which Moll Flanders steals a necklace from a child in a narrow alley, but resists the temptation to commit child murder.[15] It gains a sharper edge from an unlikely source — a poll-tax list for Broad Street Ward, drawn up a few months later. Defoe's father,

James Foe, then in his early sixties, was living in Throgmorton Street; and he had in his household not only a wife — probably his third, about whom all we know is that her name was Elizabeth — but also a child.[16] The life of this child, whoever it was, may well have stood between Defoe and the eventual inheritance of some property.

About this time Defoe became involved in yet another desperate attempt to restore his fortunes. Among the many projects which had burgeoned during the early years of William III's reign were several for raising treasure from sunken ships by means of diving engines. This mania had been triggered off by the phenomenal success of Sir William Phipps, who had returned to England in July 1687 with over £200,000 in gold and silver, salvaged from a Spanish vessel sunk off the Bahamas, and providing the adventurers with a profit on their investment of 10,000 per cent. Defoe commented:

> Witness Sir *William Phips*'s Voyage to the Wreck; 'twas a mere Project, a Lottery of a Hundred thousand to One odds; a hazard, which if it had failed, every one wou'd have been asham'd to have own'd themselves concern'd in; A Voyage that wou'd have been as much ridicul'd as *Don Quixote's Adventure upon the Windmill*: Bless us! that Folks should go Three thousand Miles to Angle in the open Sea for Pieces of Eight! why they wou'd have made Ballads of it, and the Merchants wou'd have said of every unlikely Adventure, 'twas like *Phips* his Wreck-Voyage: but he had Success, and who reflects upon the project?[17]

Among those eager to jump on the bandwagon was a Cornishman, Joseph Williams, who on 17 October 1691 had been granted a patent for a diving engine which he had invented. Williams was allotted 118 out of 400 shares, the rest going to three men who were presumably his backers: John and Nicholas Honychurch, and James Trefusis, of the influential family of that name at Mylor, near Falmouth. In the summer of 1692 Defoe bought ten shares from Williams for £200 and was appointed secretary and treasurer of the company.[18] About 16 June it was agreed to levy 10s. per share to raise working capital to buy a vessel with which to begin diving operations. Williams paid Defoe by means of bills to the value of £54, which the latter actually used to pay part of his debt to Thomas Williams, the Lombard Street goldsmith who was pressing him for payment; and when the Cornish inventor failed to honour these bills litigation followed between the two Williams.[19] It is curious that the total sum due to Defoe as treasurer of the company was exactly the same as he had supposedly paid for his shares. He could hardly have raised £200 at this time in cash; and since he was using the money raised on the shares to pay his personal debts, it is difficult to see how he can have obtained a ship, as apparently he did, without actually paying for it. Perhaps it was his own ship, the *Desire*, which he had 'sold' to the company of which he was treasurer; or in other words, he had traded in his ship for a share in the diving venture. £200 would seem a fair price for a small vessel valued four years before at £260.

Their objective was the Lizard where, among other wrecks, a Genoese vessel laden with silver coins had gone down on the Bumble Rock in 1667; while a few hundred yards further west a Spanish ship had been lost in Polpeor Cove in 1619 with silver ingots valued at £100,000.[20] Defoe's share of the latter would work out at £2500, less royalties of one-fifth to be paid to the Crown as well as a rake-off for Thomas Neale, the Groom Porter, who had acquired not long before a grant of all the wrecks on the south coast.[21] By mid-August they had reached Falmouth, which Defoe clearly visualised from a seaward approach.[22] But they found others before them at the Lizard, 'some with one sort of diving engine and some with another; some claiming such a wreck and some such and such others'.[23] In any case it was rather late in the summer to begin serious operations, for they would soon be overtaken by the autumnal gales. Even during what he called 'our short stay here' Defoe had a chance to see 'with what fury the sea comes sometimes against the shore here . . . How high the waves come rowling forward, storming on the neck of one another', and how, after a stormy night, 'the sands were cover'd with country people running too and fro' to see if the sea had cast up any thing of value' — 'going a shoring' as the seamen called it.[24] As far as Defoe's group was concerned this was probably only a reconnaissance, and they certainly achieved nothing worth while. Disputes soon followed, for by the following February the project had collapsed, and Joseph Williams the inventor was suing both Thomas Williams, the goldsmith, and Defoe. In retrospect the latter could take a detached view of the failure, declaring that he could 'give a diverting tale of an inventor whose cully was none other than myself',[25] and could refer almost jocularly to the rival projectors: 'However we left them as we found them, and far from being discouraged; and if half the golden mountains, or silver mountains either, which they promise themselves, should appear, they will be very well paid for their labours.'[26]

While still at the Lizard, on Sunday 21 August, he and his companions enjoyed for several hours a grandstand view of a spectacle calculated to take their minds off their financial problems:

> . . . it was with a mixture of pleasure and horror that we saw from the hills at the Lizard . . . an obstinate fight between three French-men of war, and two English, with a privateer, and three merchant ships in their company; the English had the misfortune, not only to be fewer ships of war in number, but of less force; so that while the two biggest French ships engaged the English, the third in the mean time took the two merchant-ships, and went off with them; as to the piccaroon, or privateer, she was able to do little in the matter, not daring to come so near the men of war, as to take a broadside, which her thin sides would not have been able to bear, but would have sent her to the bottom at once; so that the two English men of war had no assistance from her, nor could she prevent them taking the two merchant-ships; yet we observ'd that the English captains manag'd their fight so well, and their seamen behav'd so briskly, that in about three hours both the French-men stood off, and having been sufficiently bang'd, let us see that they had no more stomach to fight; after which the English having enough damage too no doubt, stood away to eastward, as we suppos'd to refit.[27]

The pride of the watchers on the shore at the gallant fight of their seamen against odds was somewhat misplaced; for other accounts show that the warships which had given such a good account of themselves were in fact Dutch, and that no English vessels were on the scene at all.[28]

After leaving the Lizard, Defoe did not immediately return to London, for he had other business in those parts, unconnected with the diving machine. Their ship followed the windings of the Fal estuary to the limit of tidal water at Truro, which Defoe found to be

> ... a very considerable town too; it stands up the water north and by east from Falmouth in the utmost extended branch of the haven, in the middle, between the conflux of two rivers, which though not of any long course, have a very good appearance for a port, and make a large wharf between them in front of the town; and the water here makes a good port for small ships, though it be at the influx, but not for ships of burden.[29]

He states that Truro was not suitable for vessels of more than 150 tons, the larger vessels all putting in at Falmouth, 'the trade of Truro being now chiefly if not only for shipping off block TINN and copper ore'.[30] It was probably with the former that they loaded, perhaps on behalf of the local man, Trefusis; for by this time Defoe certainly had neither cash nor credit for such a transaction.

Now at last they sailed for London, but only to take more cargo aboard; and soon they were slipping down the river again. Defoe gives a vivid account of how he was 'with some merchants in a large yatch, bound for France; they had a great quantity of block-tin on board, and other goods, which had not been entered at the custom-house'. At Gravesend they should have anchored to undergo a second customs clearance; but the master decided to take advantage of the misty morning to drift down with the tide. In fact,

> ... there was so thick a fog, that it was scarce possible to see from the mainmast to the bow-spirit ... When he came among the other ships and over against the town, his greatest danger was running foul of them, to prevent which he kept a man lying on his belly at the bowsprit end, to look out, and so, tho' not without some danger too, he went clear: As for Gravesend or Tilbury-Fort, they could see no more of us than they could of London-Bridge; and we drove in this fog undiscern'd by the forts of the custom-house men, as low as Hole-Haven, and went afterwards clear away to Caen in Normandy without being visited.[31]

Defoe may only have been putting into practice his belief in the propriety of trading with the enemy; but all the same, it was an illicit trade that he would hardly have risked at any other period of his trading career. And, as with his visit to Cornwall, it helped to keep him out of the way of his creditors.

By this time Defoe had at last given up the struggle to avoid bankruptcy.

If I were to run through the Infinite Mazes of a Bankrupt, before he comes to the *Crisis*; what Shifts, what Turnings, and Windings in Trade, to support his Dying Credit; what Borrowings of one, to raise Money to Pay another; What Discounting of Bills, Pledgings and Pawnings; what selling to Loss for present Supply; what Strange and unaccountable Methods to buoy up Sinking Credit . . . I appeal to those Gentlemen who have gone through the Labyrinths, and Entangled in the Toyl of failing Credit, have struggl'd themselves out of Breath, and at last like a Deer, hunted down, are driven to stand at bay with the World . . .

. . . Is he entrusted with the Orphans Estate, or the Widows small Remnant . . . he hopes to make it good again . . . and Ventures to take it . . . he Ventures to Buy, where he knows he cannot Pay; to promise where he knows he cannot perform; to stop one Man's mouth, with another Man's Goods; and innumerable Injuries he does, that in the very doing them, are like a Sword thrust into his Liver, and Wound him to the Soul . . .

. . . Accept a Cordial from one, whose Fatal Experience, entitles him to be a Doctor in this Case.

BREAK, GENTLEMEN . . . BREAK, while you still have something to Pay . . . something to tempt them to Refrain from a Statute of Bankrupt; to the Ruine both of your Family and their Debts.[32]

Defoe later gave what sounds like an idealised version of his own dealings with his creditors. He described how a tradesman, seeing that his failure is inevitable,

. . . resolves to call his creditors together in time, while there is still something to offer them, and so gets a friend to discourse them, and then draws up a state of his case to lay before them.

First, He assures them that he has not wasted his estate, either by vice and immorality, or by expensive and riotous living, luxury, extravagance, *and the like*.

Secondly, He makes it appear that he has met with great losses, such as he could not avoid, and yet such and so many, that he has not been able to support the weight of them.

Thirdly, THAT he could have stood it out longer, but that he was sensible if he did he should but diminish his stock, which, *considering his debts*, was properly not his own; and that he was resolved not to spend one part of their debts, as he had lost the other.

Fourthly, THAT he is willing to shew them his books, and give up every farthing into their hands, that they might see he acted the part of an honest man to them. And

Fifthly, that upon his doing so, they will find that there is in goods and good debts, sufficient to pay them fifteen shillings in the pound; after which . . . he hopes they may give him his liberty, that he may try to get his bread, and to maintain his family in the best manner he can; and if possible to pay the remainder of his debts.[33]

The friend who was negotiating on Defoe's behalf was his old business associate, Samuel Stancliffe, who was himself owed £1500, money which he had apparently advanced with his eyes open in an effort to stave off the bankruptcy. These negotiations must have been in progress while Defoe was out of the way in Cornwall, or running contraband tin to France, and it was not until mid-October that matters came to a head. On 15 October Stancliffe obtained a writ of seizure on Defoe's goods and chattels, which the Sheriffs of Middlesex and Surrey were ordered to execute.[34] Among the rest the Sheriff of Middlesex took possession of the cat-house at Newington and its occupants. A valuation was made, and with striking promptness they were purchased on 17 October by Defoe's mother-in-law, Joan Tuffley, at the valuation figure of £439 7s., little more than half the price at which Defoe had originally agreed to buy them. Since the latter had never actually completed the purchase or taken legal possession of the cats, this has been looked on as a hire-purchase fraud perpetrated by Defoe upon his mother-in-law. This is certainly too harsh an interpretation of an admittedly complex, and possibly dubious, transaction. It is difficult to see why Defoe should have tried to defraud, for his creditors' benefit rather than his own, the mother-in-law on whose goodwill and concern for her daughter and grandchildren he would have to depend for some time to come. Most likely this was a collusive transaction between Defoe, Stancliffe and Joan Tuffley, to preserve for Defoe and his family an asset in which he thought he had a legitimate interest, since he had already paid £200, as well as £300 in allegedly worthless bills; and it can hardly have been a coincidence that it was rushed through only a few days before his final payment of £352 15s., fell due on 21 October. Barksdale had in fact by this time deeded the cats to one of his own creditors, Sir Thomas Estcourt; and when next spring the latter's servants seized the cats, Joan Tuffley began a Chancery suit in which she alleged that she had been defrauded, not just by Defoe, but by a conspiracy which also included Stancliffe, Barksdale, Estcourt, a scrivener John Blunt, not to mention the Sheriff of Middlesex — for it was usual in Chancery cases to bring in Uncle Tom Cobley and all.

At the time when the civet cats had been first seized by the Sheriff and then bought by Joan Tuffley, Stancliffe had still been treating with Defoe's creditors. His total debts amounted to some £17,000; and it seems that an instrument was drawn up and offered to the creditors for signature, for a composition at the rate of 15 shillings in the pound, with time allowed for him to get in his estate. Of 140 creditors, almost all, with debts amounting to about £15,000, either signed the instrument or tacitly acquiesced in it. Four creditors only, with debts totalling less than £2000, refused composition, and thereby invalidated the agreement;[35] and these four soon showed their determination to get their pound of flesh.

Writs of seizure were granted at the instance of John Selby for a debt of £100, and of Edward Lambert for one of £60; and in discharge of these writs Defoe was brought before Sir John Powell, one of the justices of the King's Bench, and committed by him to the Fleet Prison on 29 October. A marginal endorsement in the prison records shows that he was removed the same day to the King's Bench Prison. On 4 November he was again committed to the Fleet by the same judge for a debt of £700 owed to Thomas Martin, and one of an unspecified amount to Henry Fairfax, Esquire. He was again immediately removed to the King's Bench Prison.[36] Nothing is known of Defoe's dealings with these four stubborn creditors. Lambert seems to have been a Lombard Street goldsmith; while Martin was a merchant of Love Lane, who had recently been involved in a project for manufacturing saltpetre — perhaps yet another scheme in which Defoe had been involved in the last few frantic months.[37] Defoe cannot have spent more than a few hours in the Fleet Prison. His stay in the King's Bench Prison may have been longer, long enough to hear from the turnkey a droll story of Frank, an old man who had been released by 'old *Farrington*, Marshal of the King's Bench' after spending eighteen years in prison for debt, and who had set up an apple-stall by the prison door, until finding trade bad, he indignantly demanded to be re-admitted.[38] Defoe's imprisonment was certainly far shorter than old Frank's, for he is known to have been at liberty in London in the following February; and he was probably bailed and set at liberty after a few days.

For the time being, however, it was unsafe for him to appear publicly in London, or to frequent any of his usual haunts; and he must have spent part of this winter in one of the legally tolerated sanctuaries for debtors, almost certainly the Mint.

> And were a man but to hear the Discourse among the Inhabitants of those Dens of Thieves when they first swarm about a New Comer, to comfort him; for they are not all harden'd to a like degree at Once . . . *Well*, says the first, *Come, don't be concern'd, you have got a good Parcel of Goods away, I promise you*; . . . *Damn the creditors*, says a Third, *Why, there's such and such a one, they have Creditors too, and they won't agree with them, and here they live like Gentlemen, and care not a farthing for them. Offer your Creditors Half a Crown in the Pound, and pay it them in Old Debts, and if they won't take it, let them alone, they'll come after you, never you fear* . . . [39]

He observed the 'bullying of Creditors . . . saying if you won't take this you shall have nothing, I'll lie here and spend it, help yourself how you can, *the antient Language of* Snow's *Coffee-House in the Mint*',[40] while Moll Flanders, forced for a while to take lodgings in the Mint, 'found that an agreeable Woman was exceedingly valuable among those Sons of Affliction there; and that those who wanted Money to pay Half a Crown in the

Pound to their Creditors, and run into Debt at the Sign of the *Bull* for their Dinners, would yet find Money for a Supper, if they lik'd the Woman'.[41] Certainly Defoe now had a chance to extend his knowledge of the seamy side of life. He observed with disapproval, though not without compassion, how men would drink and debauch away what little money they had left, in an effort to forget the wives and families they could no longer support.[42] He was shocked by the universal cynicism he found, quoting 'an Old Street Proverb . . . much us'd among the *Alsatia-Men*, viz, the Knight-Shelterers of the *Mint, Whitefryers* &c. . . . *the World's a Cheat, the Knaves carry it on, and he's a Fool that has no Hand in it*'.[43] Even in his extremity, and despite the 'little, mean and even wicked things' he had done, Defoe still prided himself on being a man of principle. He could say with Moll, 'I was not wicked enough for such Fellows as these', and he soon acquired 'a just Abhorrence of the Place and of the Company'.[44]

Defoe was now 'unhing'd from matters of trade'. He had to give up his premises in Freeman's Yard; but apparently the hosiery business continued under the control of Richard Addis, formerly his assistant; while the appearance in the same house a year or two later of James Moyer, linen draper, a business asssociate of Defoe, is another sign of continuity.[45] Defoe's wife and family were in no real danger of destitution; for his mother-in-law, Joan Tuffley, and her bachelor son Samuel had been left comfortably off. It was at their house at Kingsland, a mile or two north of the City, that Mary Foe and her children took refuge; and it was here too that Defoe came to live when it was safe for him to do so.[46] His own country house, his coach and horses, and all his remaining unmortgaged assets were forfeited. It was Samuel Stancliffe, as Defoe's trustee in bankruptcy, who was responsible for realising these assets, and using them to satisfy the creditors as far as possible; and after his death in 1695, his kinsman James Stancliffe took over the task.[47] Nothing is known of these transactions, nor of how the four obstinate creditors were sufficiently appeased, for a while at least, to make it possible for Defoe to appear again in the world.

Defoe's failure was of course a profound shock to his self-confidence and self-esteem. But though stripped of his worldly goods, there were some assets of which he could not be deprived: his knowledge, his skills, his energy, his courage and his resilience.

For the time being, it is true, the wind was out of his sails, and he was uncertain of his course for the future; and it would be some years before he regained a positive sense of direction. In the long run, it could be argued, Defoe's bankruptcy led him to earn his living with his pen, and for this posterity can be grateful. One by-product of his troubles was that he became an expert on the subject of bankruptcy, and he was to be influential in bringing about changes in the bankruptcy law. The problem, never entirely solved, was how to protect the trading public from fraudulent bankrupts, without making it possible for unreasonable creditors to ruin honest but unfortunate debtors, so that they were unable to recover and perhaps be able to pay off their debts. For his part, there is no reason to doubt him when he says that he was determined, eventually, to pay all his debts in full; and he made substantial progress towards this before further misfortunes overtook him. As it was, he never threw off the burden of debt. He had to go through life looking over his shoulder, in case some 'sleeping lion' — as he termed a dormant creditor — might be stirring.[48]

10 Publick Good and Private Advantage

Defoe, an early advocate of self-help, was never a man to wait passively for something to turn up. More enterprising than his fellow bankrupt, John Barksdale, who found a lowly niche in the customs services as a tide-waiter, he had several strings to his bow.[1] Perhaps it was about this time that he was offered an 'Annuall Summe' to translate the *Paris Gazette* into English, a project unfortunately 'Supprest by the Government'.[2] He declared, 'I could have set up for a Country Almanack Maker, as to my skill in Astronomy';[3] but he was never reduced to such an extremity. Although he now had no capital, his assets included a liberal education and an unusually varied commercial experience. He claimed that 'Matters of Accounts are my perticular Element, what I have Allways been Master of';[4] and he probably had himself in mind when he described how such expertise 'has recommended a tradesman so much to his creditors, that after the ruin of his business, some or other of them have taken him into business, as into partnership, or into employment, only because they knew him qualified for business, and for keeping books in particular'.[5]

The creditors in question appear to have been two Spanish merchants, James Dollyffe and Solomon Merritt;[6] and the enterprise whose books Defoe was to keep was one for catching, curing and marketing white fish, from a base to be set up in the Orkneys. He refers obliquely, perhaps with deliberate vagueness, to this venture in his *Tour*, when he makes out that at some unspecified place in northern Scotland 'we unexpectedly met here some *English Men* who were employ'd by Merchants in the S. (whether *London* or *Edinburgh* I do not now remember) to take and cure a large quantity of White Fish, and afterwards of Herrings, on account of Trade'.[7] In the *Atlas Maritimus* he was more specific, and in his account of the Orkneys mentions

'Attempts made by the *Merchants of England*, as well as of Scotland, to establish a Fishery in the Islands of the *Orkneys*, and of the *Hebrides* or *Western Isles*'.[8] The scheme seems to have been in operation in 1693 and 1694; and Defoe himself spent some of these years in Orkney and Shetland, although the exact chronology of the account which follows is inevitably somewhat speculative, and the events of those two summers may even have been transposed.

Defoe was still in London on 13 February 1693, when the goldsmith Thomas Williams met him in the street, the first time he had seen him for several months.[9] He was probably gone by the end of April; for when Joan Tuffley brought a Chancery suit on 20 April concerning the civet cats, he was the only defendant who failed to file an answer, and by 29 April subpoenas had been issued against him by the Sheriffs of London and Surrey.[10] He was on his way north by sea, acquiring familiarity with the landfalls and sailing distances along the eastern coasts of Britain, and on this or other voyages to or from Orkney visiting Scarborough, Dundee, Peterhead and John o' Groats — all places of which his knowledge is otherwise difficult to explain.[11]

He was as far north as Shetland in time to see how, from 'the beginning of *June*' the Dutch herring-busses 'come gradually on', and how the Dutch 'pitch Tents on Shore, and form a Kind of Camp', trading wines, brandy and spices for Scottish produce.[12] He was so impressed by what he saw of the herring fishery that when, a dozen years later, he wrote his poem *Caledonia* in praise of Scotland, it was to the herring and their supposed migration that he gave pride of place. He claimed that they were divinely directed to the shores of Scotland for the benefit of the inhabitants who, to their shame, played only a minor part in reaping this divine harvest:

> If thou reject the Bounties of the Sea,
> No more complain of Poverty.[13]

The herring fishery was dominated by the Dutch, thanks to their methods of salting, their care in attesting the quality of their fish, their organisation of mother-vessels so that the herring-busses did not, like the Scottish vessels have to return to harbour after each haul, and to the fact that in trading to the south

Baltic ports they returned laden with corn, thus saving freight charges.[14] Defoe, however, seems to have had no personal involvement in the herring fishery; and it was perhaps some business at the fishing fair that had taken him to Shetland.

Before the summer was over he was in the Orkneys, helping to establish a shore base for curing white fish, principally cod. He does not say just where this was, but the logical place would have been at the expanding port of Cairston, at the western end of Mainland;[15] for it was on this side of the Orkneys that the fishing grounds lay, Defoe himself reporting 'good fishing for cod on the west side, and among the Islands of the Leuze and other parts called the Western Islands of Scotland'.[16] In Ultima Thule Defoe was well out of reach of the most persistent creditor, and he now had a chance to regain some of the peace of mind lost during the desperate months of the previous summer. In the quiet remoteness of Orkney he may have first acquired his feeling for islands, with time for once to stand and stare:

> Nothing can be pleasanter of its Kind in the World, than to stand on the Shore and see the Sea in calm, fine Weather, in those narrow Sounds and Passages between the Islands; How the Tide runs like a Sluice, as well one Way as t'other, and a Boat runs with it like an Arrow out of a Bow; and as for going against it, 'tis like rowing thro' *London-Bridge* against a steep Fall.[17]

But even though this was one of his rare moments of relaxation, Defoe did not let the 'Tide . . . like a Sluice' run entirely to waste; twenty-five years later he found a use for it, to drive Crusoe's dug-out canoe, with 'a tide like the sluice of a mill', away from his 'Beloved island', apparently without hope of return.[18] But Crusoe was saved by what Defoe called an 'eddy', a reverse current 'returned by the repulse of the rocks'; and, though Defoe does not mention it, this is also a feature of the tidal currents among the Orkneys.[19]

In these northern latitudes Defoe found that 'in the month of June . . . you might see to read the smallest print, and to write distinctly, without the help of a candle . . . all night long'.[20] He became familiar too with the Northern Lights, 'seen continually every Summer in the Evening, and . . . not at all wondered at;

they call them the Dancers';[21] and he reported another spectacular phenomenon. In discussing the volcanic activity of Mount
Heckla in Iceland, he recalled

> ...that the Reflection of it in the Clouds in the Night I saw
> when I was at the *Orkneys*. I cannot positively affirm it was
> the Fire of *Heckla*, but the People there assur'd me it was,
> and that they had often seen the same; but this I affirm, that
> nothing else of a Natural Cause could produce such a Reflec-
> tion of Flame in that Part of the World, and that it was in the
> direct Situation of the Place.[22]

As Heckla lies some 600 miles to the north-west, Defoe's doubts
are understandable; yet when it is recalled that magnificent sun-
sets were seen all over the world for three years after the eruption of Krakatoa in 1883, perhaps what Defoe saw was connected
with Heckla after all. Clouds of volcanic dust at great altitude,
and the sun never far below the horizon might combine to
produce a sunset effect at any time during the night. For the
first time since 1636, Heckla was in violent eruption from May
until December 1693, confirming the date of Defoe's visit to
Orkney.[23]

By 31 October he was back in London, when he belatedly
answered a Chancery Bill brought against him in February by
the inventor, Joseph Williams.[24] About the same time he was
forced to agree to the sale of the wines which had lain for
eighteen months in a cellar whose key was kept by the goldsmith who had advanced him £700 to pay the customs; but
'Leakage Decay and other Accidents' had so reduced their value
that they fetched only £922, the whole transaction showing a
loss of over £600.[25] On 22 November a group of Merchant
Insurers, ruined by the heavy losses caused by the war and
blaming the inefficiency of the Fleet, petitioned the Commons
for relief; and on 9 December leave was given to bring in a Bill
whose effect would be to make any composition accepted by
two thirds of their creditors, in number and value, binding upon
the rest. On 9 February 1694, while a select committee was still
hearing creditors' objections, 'Daniel Foe, Merchant' petitioned
for his name to be added to the Bill. His case must have been
strong enough to convince the committee, for on 22 February

the Commons accepted an amendment to that effect. The Bill passed its third reading in the Commons on 27 February, only to founder on its second reading in the Lords on 9 March.[26] Defoe was apparently still in London on 16 March when he brought a Chancery suit to delay proceedings brought against him in another court by the younger Thomas Nisbett.[27] But another Chancery suit, brought against him by the mortgagees of his Essex marshlands on 28 April, went unanswered; and he was probably again on his travels.[28]

On 22 January 1694, on the petition of Solomon Merritt of London, merchant, leave had been granted by Order in Council for the *John*, a ship of 140 tons, with a crew of 14 men, to sail from London to Newcastle for coals, thence to Portugal for salt, and finally to Newfoundland to bring home a cargo of fish.[29] There is reason to suspect that this may have been Defoe's old ship, the *Desire*, now owned by his creditors, and renamed because there was already a *Desire* in the Newfoundland trade;[30] and he probably sailed once more in her, on her second leg to Portugal. He shows a first-hand knowledge of Setubal, or St Ubes, a port whose existence centred round its export of the finest salt in Europe, widely used for preserving fish, and doubly important to the English and Dutch since the war had deprived them of salt from the French Biscay shores. Defoe recalled it as 'a considerable Place. Some Geographers tell us the Inhabitants are 3000; I suppose them more than twice that Number.' He also recalled '2 or 300 Sail of *Dutch* Ships at St. *Ubes* at a time, loading Salt', while 'the *Dutch* Sailors, encourag'd by the Throng of People who come thither as to a kind of Fair, bring every Man their little Adventure of Goods'. Most of these, it seems, were smuggled ashore without paying customs, for 'the *Portuguese* deal with them not only on shore, but come in small Boats from other Towns upon the Coast'.[31]

He had probably visited Lisbon before, but it was most likely in the summer of 1694 that he found 'the Heats . . . so excessive, that they are almost insupportable, especially to Strangers'. He contrasted the beauty of the city as viewed from the river with the reality, at close quarters, of mean buildings without glass windows, and streets that were 'narrow, unpaved and most loathsomely filthy'.[32] Perhaps it was Defoe's own experience that enabled Crusoe to give a vivid description of an *auto-da-fé*:

They carried in procession all their criminals to the great church, where eight of them appeared first, dressed up in gowns and caps of canvas, upon which were painted all that men could devise of hell's torments, devils broiling and roasting human bodies, and a thousand such frightful things, with flames and devils besides in every part of the dress.

Those I found were eight poor creatures condemned to be burnt . . . for crimes against the Catholic faith . . . some were Jews, whose greatest crime . . . was that they were very rich; and some Christians . . . whose greatest misery was that they were very poor.[33]

He recalled another piece of Portuguese pageantry when he wrote of 'the Armies of the King of Portugal, with the great Wooden Image of St. *Anthonio de Padua*, Elevated in the Front, who is call'd their General, and as I am told, has his Pay accordingly, which the Priests that attend him Receive'. Perhaps he saw the procession on 13 June, the Saint's day; but in one respect he had been misinformed — St Anthony was only a captain, a rank to which he had been promoted in 1683 after many years of valuable service in the ranks.[34]

It is not clear whether Defoe paid a second visit to Orkney after his return from Portugal; but it is clear that the fishing venture was not flourishing. The merchants had got their sums wrong. On the one hand, there was 'the extraordinary Expence incurr'd in the Management, setting up Warehouses and Dwelling-houses for the people employ'd, building Fishing vessels and places to lay them up in, besides the Charge of refitting those vessels every Season, and other things'. On the other hand, 'not but there were great quantities of Cod, and the fish very sizable and good, but not so great a quantity as to make that dispatch in taking them, (as they are taken by hook and line) sufficient for loading ships or laying up a large quantity in a season'.[35] Elsewhere, in his most explicit reference to his own involvement in this scheme, he pointed out that despite the length of the voyage to the Newfoundland fishing grounds, ships could be loaded there 'in one fifth-part of the time, and consequently so much cheaper; and the author of this has found this to be so by experience'.[36] Presumably this was book-keeping experience; for though a transatlantic voyage in the *John* is chronologically possible, it would certainly have left traces in his later writings.

A final glimpse of the sinking venture comes from a document of 5 January 1695, which complains that the pink *Desire*, owned by Dollyffe and Merritt, had been 'unjustly' seized in the Orkneys by the Governor (perhaps on account of debts or customs unpaid?) and then sent by him on his own business to Carrickfergus in Ireland, under the name of the *John* of Orkney. By this time no doubt 'the Adventurers were discouraged and gave it over'.[37]

Dollyffe and Merritt were both engaged in the Spanish trade; and Defoe may have been referring to them when he wrote: 'Misfortunes in business having unhinged me from matters of trade, it was about the year 1694 that I was invited (by some merchants with whom I had corresponded abroad, and some also at home) to settle at Cadiz in Spain; and that with offers of very good commissions.'[38] Not only was Cadiz the port through which English merchants could share at second hand in the trade with Spanish America; it was also gaining a new importance as a result of the war. For the first time since the days of Admiral Blake, an English fleet, commanded by Sir Edward Russell, had been operating in the Mediterranean throughout the summer of 1694, and with such success that it was decided that it should winter at Cadiz. It may be that this opening for Defoe arose from the increased business which the presence of the fleet must have created for English merchants there. The problem of victualling the fleet proved so great that in the autumn the Admiralty persuaded one of the Victualling Commissioners to go out to Cadiz and take charge in person. This was Humphrey Ayles, father of the Humphrey Ayles whose unsuccessful trading voyage to America on Defoe's behalf some six years before had ended in litigation between them.[39] Whether this had any influence on his decision cannot be said; but 'Providence, which had other work for me to do, placed a secret aversion in my mind to quitting England upon any account, and made me refuse the best offers of that kind'.[40]

Defoe's tracks can next be picked up about the year 1695 in Sussex and Hampshire, visiting gentlemen's houses, apparently to investigate their reserves of oak-timber. As he never claimed to be expert in this commodity, he was probably accompanying someone who was; and the strongest candidate is the man who was to become his closest friend and confidant, Robert Davis, second husband of his sister Mary, and, like her first, a shipwright.[41] The latter may have been acting either directly for the Admiralty, or for one of the big timber merchants supplying the needs of the vast naval building programme undertaken because of the war.

In his *Essay upon Projects*, published at the beginning of 1697, it was this part of the country that he chose to illustrate the deplorable state of England's roads:

> I have narrowly observ'd all the Considerable Ways in that unpassable County of *Sussex* . . . I have seen in that horrible Countrey the Road 60 to 100 Yards broad lie from side to side all Poach'd with Cattel, the Land of no manner of Benefit, and yet no going with a Horse, but every step up to the Shoulders, full of Sloughs and Holes, and covered with standing-water.[42]

A quarter of a century later he could still recall how he had fatigued himself travelling through 'this deep and heavy part of the country', East Sussex:

> The timber I saw here was prodigious, as well in quantity as in bigness, and seem'd in some places to be suffer'd to grow, only because it was so far off of any navigation, that it was not worth cutting down and carrying away; in dry summers indeed, a great deal is carried away to Maidstone, and other places on the Medway; and sometimes I have seen one tree on a carriage, which they call a tug, drawn by two and twenty oxen, and even then, 'tis carry'd so little way, and then thrown down, and left for other tugs to take up and carry on, that sometimes 'tis two or three years before it gets to Chatham; for if once the rains come in, it stirs no more that year and sometimes a whole summer is not dry enough to make the roads passable . . . [43]

There is ample evidence in Defoe's *Tour* to place his travels in this area in the middle 1690s. Near Hastings he saw 'the bones of one of the Dutch men of war, which was burned and stranded by the French' after the battle of 1690 off Beachy Head.[44] At the rotten borough of Bramber, a 'vintner . . . boasted, that upon an election, just then over, he had made 300 *l.* of one pipe of canary'; and by a process of elimination this election must almost certainly have been that of October and November 1695.[45] When he visited Sir John Fagg at his 'noble antient seat' nearby at Steyning, he heard him refuse an offer by some London butchers of £26 a head for four prodigiously fat bullocks, beasts which did end up at Smithfield, however, with their equally portly owner, in the pages of *Colonel Jack*.[46] Defoe put this visit 'in the year 1697', but his dates were not always exact. Further west, his familiarity with Petworth during or soon after its rebuilding by the Duke of Somerset in the years 1688–96, tells the same story.[47] Uppark too appears as 'the seat of the late Earl of Tankerville', though the latter had died in 1701, over twenty years before Defoe wrote this part of his *Tour*.[48] A similar date seems likely for his visit to the Earl of Scarborough's house at Stansted,

> . . . a house seeming to be a retreat, being surrounded by thick woods, thro' which there are the most pleasant agreeable visto's cut, that are to be seen any where in England, particularly, because through the west opening, which is from the front of the house, they sit in the dining-room of the house, and see the town and harbour of Portsmouth, the ships at Spithead, and also at St. Helens; which when the royal navy happens to be there, as often happen'd during the late war, is a most glorious sight.[49]

His whole account of Sussex in the *Tour* is studded with references to the size and quantity of the timber, the routes by which it was taken to the builders' yards, and the uselessness of much of the timber that was remote from the water-carriage. Crusoe was to find the same, when he constructed his first dugout canoe, but could not drag it to the water.[50]

Defoe's comments on the country estates in southern Hampshire link them even more explicitly with the supply of timber for the shipbuilders' yards, stressing its quality and abundance, 'notwithstanding the very great consumption of timber in King William's reign, by building or rebuilding almost the whole navy'. At Hursely near Winchester, 'formerly belonging to Mr. Cromwell, grandson of Oliver Cromwell . . . they might have cut twenty thousand pounds worth of timber down, and yet have left the woods in a thriving condition'. He mentions 'Colonel Norton . . . whose seat at Southwick is within six miles of Portsmouth and within three miles of the water carriage; this gentleman they told me had an immense quantity of timber, some growing within sight of the very docks of Portsmouth'. Above Southampton,

> . . . the river on the west side of the town in particular comes by the edge of the great forest, call'd New-Forest; here we saw a prodigious quantity of timber, of an uncommon size, vastly large, lying on the shoar of the river, for above two miles in length, which they told us was brought thither from the forest, and left to be fetch'd by the builders at Portsmouth-Dock, as they had occasion for it . . . Farther west it is the like, and as I rode through the New-Forest, I cou'd see the antient oaks of many hundred years standing, perishing with their wither'd tops advanc'd up in the air, and grown white with age, and that could never yet get the favour to be cut down, and made serviceable to their country.[51]

Defoe referred specifically to one of the smaller yards which burgeoned during the war, that at Burseldon, on the Hamble between Portsmouth and Southampton, where he informs us, 'is a building yard for ships of war, and in King William's time, two eighty-gun ships were launched here'.[52] This was a new yard, where William Wyatt, and after his death his widow, actually built three such ships between 1692 and 1695.[53] It was to 'Busselton' that the hero of *Captain Singleton* was taken as a boy, assisting the carpenters who were building a ship for his master; and soon afterwards he was captured at sea, 'if my Account stands right . . . about the Year 1695'.[54] Defoe's main base in this area, however, seems to have been Portsmouth, whose defences he describes in detail, comparing them with those on the Thames at Tilbury; and he was familiar with the internal arrangements of the dockyard, and of the effect of the war in bringing prosperity to the town.[55] It was in all probability when he was at Portsmouth that his life took a new turn.

In *An Appeal to Honour and Justice*, after describing how he had rejected offers to settle in Cadiz, he went on: 'Some time after this I was, without the least application of mine, and being seventy miles from London, sent for to be accountant to the commissioners of the glass duty, in which service I continued until the determination of their commission.'[56] This was not, as has sometimes been supposed, the window tax, but 'the duties on glass wares, stone and earthen bottles, as by the Act of 6 and 7 William III c.18', one of many new taxes introduced to meet the soaring costs of the war. On 7 September 1695 three Surveyors were appointed to manage these duties, each at an annual salary of £200, to take effect from 29 September.[57] On 9 September William Lowndes, the Secretary of the Treasury, wrote to them, nominating their subordinate officials;[58] but they must have successfully resisted this attempt to dictate to them, for none of Lowndes's nominees actually served. A Treasury document giving the office expenses from 29 September to 28 December 1695 shows that the most highly paid servant in the office, at an annual salary of £100, and with two clerks under him, was 'Daniel de Foe, Accomptant'.[59] A dozen years later Defoe was *persona non grata* to Lowndes, and perhaps the feeling between them dates from this time.[60] He must have owed his appointment to one of the Surveyors, Dalby Thomas, a close personal friend of his, with interests in the African and West Indian trades, and concerned in a number of rather extravagant projects, for the public good as well as private advantage.[61] When Defoe wrote that he himself had been 'concerned with some eminent Persons at home in proposing ways and means to the government, for raising money to supply the occasions of the war', Dalby Thomas may have been one of those he had in mind; and perhaps both men had a share in devising the tax which they were helping to administer.[62] Defoe was to remain as accountant until the Glass Duty was removed in 1699. The chief importance of his new post to him may have been that he had his foot on the bottom rung of a ladder at the top of which was a very remarkable man, Charles Montagu, the Chancellor of the Exchequer, who was proving himself a financial wizard in dealing with some of the most intractable problems the nation had ever faced. Defoe was probably not even known to Montagu at this time; but it was to be through him, a couple of years later, that he was first to become involved with politics at the highest level. Meanwhile, though his salary of £100 a year was useful, it could make little impression on his load of debt. However, if the Glass Duty money actually passed through his hands — and he later declared that he had been entrusted with many thousand pounds of public money — the standards of the day allowed him to take some private advantage of this.[63] In any case he had several other irons in the fire.

Among Dalby Thomas's close associates was Thomas Neale, the Groom-Porter, in charge of gambling in the ante-room of the royal palace. Defoe had probably already had dealings with him in 1692 in connection with the wreck project. Whenever a scheme appeared for conjuring money out of thin air, Neale was likely to have a hand in it, in which a useful percentage of the takings would stick — not that he managed to accumulate riches, for he was a free spender, constantly in financial trouble.[64] He had launched the first lottery on the Venetian model into England, on 1 November 1693, 'in view of a vast multitude of spectators' in Freeman's Yard, Cornhill.[65] Though it is tempting to imagine that this was in Defoe's old premises, it was more probably in Lythe's coffee-house next door. However, when on 3 October 1695 he advertised another lottery in the *Post-Boy* — 'The Profitable Adventure for the Fortunate for 50000 *l.* at 20*s.* per Ticket', the thirteen 'Managers trustees' included 'Mr. D. De Foe', the earliest known use of the prefix to the name. This lottery was drawn on 20 November; and on 28 December yet another was advertised. Despite an even more imposing title — 'The Profitable and Golden Adventure for the Fortunate' — the scheme was now rather more modest, with 50,000 tickets at half a guinea each. Defoe was probably out of town, for his name was now missing; but when the lottery was re-advertised on 25 February he re-appeared, this time simply as 'Mr. D. Foe', without the prefix. A final advertisement on 17 March announced that the lottery *'will certainly be drawing in the Great Room at the Swan Tavern* in Exchange Alley, London, *on* Tuesday *the 24th of this instant March*, 1695' (i.e. 1696). This lottery had not gone too well, for it was announced that since many who had promised to buy tickets had not yet done so, the size of the prizes would depend on the number of tickets sold, while those who preferred it could have their money back.[66]

The main problem must have been the acute shortage of cash, then at its height, brought about by the difficult recoinage operation then in progress. There was also the competition of at least two other private lotteries, both advertised in the *Post-Boy*, as well as the much more ambitious Million Lottery established by Act of Parliament. This offered big prizes to those who lent money to the government on the security of the salt duties, the tickets costing as much as £10 and the draws being held in the Guildhall. The twenty-one 'Commissioners' for the Million Lottery were more eminent than the 'Managers Trustees' of Neale's private lotteries.[67] They included Neale himself, and Dalby Thomas played a prominent part in organising it; and the two men were joint authors about this time of a number of publications on the lotteries.[68] Despite Defoe's links with both men, there is no evidence to connect him in any way with the Million Lottery. In retrospect he was to dismiss the whole lottery mania as a 'mischief'; and he never mentioned his own part in it.[69]

We have seen that in October 1695 Defoe was first referred to as 'Mr. D. De Foe', and that a few months later he was again styled 'Daniel de Foe'. Was the prefix which now began to insinuate itself into the homely name of Daniel Foe a piece of social pretension, adopted at a time when he again felt himself to be rising in the world, and perhaps influenced by the name of the French diplomat and former ambassador in England, d'Avaux? Earlier in this same year there had appeared a new English translation of Camden's *Britannia*, where he could read of the pleasant seat in Warwickshire belonging, as he was later to write, to 'an antient Norman family of the name of De Beaufoe, whose posterity remain there, and in several other parts of the county, retaining the latter part of their sirname, but without the former to this day'.[70] Defoe may well have bought this book soon after its publication, for he mentions it in his *Essay upon Projects* (January 1697).[71] Yet it is difficult to believe that the future author of *The True-Born Englishman* would really wish to delude himself or others with illusions of Norman lineage.

> For Fame of Families is all a Cheat,
> *'Tis Personal Virtue only makes us great.*[72]

Most of the bearers of French names with whom he had dealings were humbler and more recent Protestant refugees from the religious persecution revived in France in his own lifetime. The author of *The True-Born Hugonot* (1703) assumed, apparently in all seriousness, that Defoe was actually a Huguenot; and the name Defo has in fact been found amongst the French Protestant weavers at Canterbury about this time.[73] Perhaps several of these hints combined to persuade Defoe that his family name had originally carried the prefix 'De'. It may have been a passing whim which happened to catch on, but neither he nor anyone else seems to have attached much importance to the matter. None of his political enemies in later life, always eager to find grounds on which to deride him, ever picked on this point. And the simple name Foe also continued to be used long after this, without arousing comment.

On 5 June 1696, for instance, 'Mr. Daniell Foe' contracted to supply bricks for the building of Greenwich Hospital; and during the next year or so he appears several times in the Hospital records under that name, though also occasionally as 'De Foe'.[74] This is the earliest evidence of yet another enterprise by which he hoped to recover his fortunes, and one which was presumably already well established. Among his assets at the time of his bankruptcy had been the leases of some 70 acres of marshland in Essex, just above Tilbury Fort. As £900 of the £1855 purchase money had been borrowed on mortgage, the actual title to the property had been conveyed to the three mortgagees, Marescoe, Stamper and Ghisleyn, with the result that the leases had been kept out of the hands of Defoe's business creditors when he failed in 1692. On 28 April 1694 Marescoe, Stamper and Ghisleyn had begun an action in Chancery to recover from Defoe the moneys advanced; but despite further efforts on their part in 1698 and 1699, it was not until 4 May 1699 that Defoe put in an answer. However, thanks to the principle known as the equity of redemption, the mortgagees could not foreclose until the debt, with its accumulated interest, reached the actual value of the property. Defoe admitted that he had made no interest payments, but stated that the mortgagees had been drawing the rents of part of the property, to the value of £72 a year, apparently ever since 1692. His total indebtedness in 1699 stood at about the same figure as it had done when he had completed the purchase in 1690, so that there was no immediate danger of foreclosure. At the same time he had been able to retain under his own control 20 acres immediately adjoining the Thames, with the use of a wharf and apparently a house. It was here that, probably about 1694, he began what was for several years to prove a flourishing business.[75]

This was the manufacture of bricks, and of the graceful Sshaped roofing tiles known as pantiles, which he declared had hitherto been 'a Manufacture always bought in Holland'.[76] When the railway to Tilbury was built during the last century, the site of the brickworks was discovered, just to the west of the station, on land then used as allotments by the railway workers. William Lee, one of Defoe's most enthusiastic biographers, visited the site, and found remains of clay pits, drying floors, and the foundations of kilns and other buildings. He was struck by the fine red colour, close texture and sonorous sound of the pantiles, the narrowness of the bricks and the unusual shape of the clay pipes that were found.[77] Defoe's concern was not with the day-to-day management of the workmen, but with the business side of the manufactory. The local demand for bricks must have been limited, and the success of the venture must have hinged on active sales promotion; but there is little firm evidence as to where he sold his bricks and tiles.

Though the records of Greenwich Hospital show payments to him totalling £98 16s. 0d. for 152,000 place bricks, he was soon supplanted by a Captain Nicholas Goodwin, who supplied bricks in much greater quantities.[78] One of the Commissioners for this foundation, Sir John Morden, was himself building in brick a little more than a mile away, on the edge of Blackheath. This was the charitable foundation known as Morden's College, a refuge for 'decay'd merchants', to be conducted on much the same semi-monastic lines as he had been familiar with in the English factory at Aleppo. Not only does Defoe show a remarkably detailed knowledge of its buildings and internal arrangements; he also discusses Morden's 'first design, as I had it from his own mouth the year before he began to build', about 1694.[79] Perhaps this provided Defoe with his first big order to establish his Tilbury brickworks. The architect of Morden's College, as of Greenwich Hospital, was Sir Christopher Wren; and it may have been in this connection that Defoe came into close enough contact with the latter to hear, 'from the mouth of the author', the great architect's comments on the restrictions which had hampered him in the rebuilding of St Paul's.[80] Some of Defoe's bricks may also have gone towards the construction of new streets of houses in the rapidly expanding capital; for the leading property developer of the age was a close associate of Thomas Neale — Dr Nicholas Barbon, a son of 'Praise-God Barebones', described by Defoe as 'better known as a Builder than a

Physician'.[81] There are records of an abortive attempt by Defoe
to become a property developer on his own account. Some time
before 15 May 1696 he drew up a project to pull down two old
timber-built houses adjoining Woolstaple Market in Westminster,
the property of Christ's Hospital, and replace them with twelve
brick-built houses, divided by a passage leading from the market
to the river-side; but the scheme came to nothing.[82] As for
pantiles, Defoe merely reports that they were much used for
'sheds and outhouses';[83] but the word 'pantile' was coming to
be particularly associated with the Dissenters, because so many
of their meeting houses which had sprung up since the Toleration
Act of 1689 were roofed with pantiles.[84] For several years
Defoe's Tilbury works seem to have been the only domestic
source of supply; so perhaps he had been able to profit by his
many contacts with dissenting ministers and congregations. A
very different market is suggested by his statement that all the
materials used for the African Company's forts, in which they
stored their English merchandise and also the human merchandise
awaiting the Middle Passage, were sent out from England, 'even
the very bricks and tiles'.[85] Defoe's interest in the Africa Company may have come from his friend Dalby Thomas, who later
went out to West Africa as Governor; and when he came to
prosper once more for a while he invested £800 in the Company's
shares, as well as becoming an active apologist for it in its disputes with the separate traders.[86] Nor would there have seemed
anything incongruous at this time for him to supply building
materials simultaneously for chapels and for slave prisons.

To the landsman, the site of Defoe's brickworks was a remote
and desolate spot. The nearest villages, West Tilbury and Chadwell St Mary, stood two miles inland, across marshes which
were 'rather rich in land, than inhabitants, occasioned chiefly
by the unhealthiness of the air',[87] and which Celia Fiennes, who
passed this way in 1697, described as 'a great flatt to the land
full of watry ditches'. Even today a public house near the spot
is called The World's End. But to those who occupied their
business in great waters this was a vital pressure point on the
world's greatest artery of trade. Half a mile away across the
river lay Gravesend, described by Celia Fiennes as 'a little snugg
town under a hill, the houses little and thick together, fitt only
for seamen and soldiers that are employ'd in the water or the
fort'.[88] Here was the customs house from whose officers every

outward bound ship had to obtain clearance — unless, like Defoe a few years before, they could glide past unseen. To persuade the reluctant to heave to, the customs men had the close support of the gunners of Tilbury Fort, on the Essex side of the river, described by Defoe as 'the key of the river Thames, and consequently the key of the city of London'.[89] When this had been built a quarter of a century before, the ferry house had been removed to a site immediately to the west of the Fort. Defoe himself mentions 'my House, which stood by the Rivers edge';[90] it was there that he had presumably installed his 'Clerk and superintendant', Castleton by name;[91] and there he must have stayed when he visited the place himself. As there is no evidence of any other house in the immediate neighbourhood, Defoe perhaps occupied part of the ferry house itself, on the site of the present World's End public house, and also shared their landing facilities. He once mentions 'two Servants rowing a small Boat over the River';[92] but about the ferry itself, controlled by the Commander of the Fort, he has nothing to say. He was, however, usually highly critical of the 'mean' or 'sorry' ferry boats available at other estuary crossings.[93]

From the number of tales he tells about Tilbury or the brick-making trade, it seems that over the years Defoe must have spent a good deal of time on the spot. He tells how the brick-makers around London, by mixing 'Sea-coal-ashes or Laystall-stuff' with their clay, could save eight chaldrons of coal out of the eleven they would otherwise need to burn 100,000 bricks.[94] He tells of an ignorant purchaser who rejected the grey but firm and well-baked bricks in favour of the half-baked 'Sammel' bricks whose pink colour he preferred.[95] He describes how he ran to part two of his brickmakers who had quarreled and *'fell to Boxing* . . . being to Fight Up and Down *as they call it'*.[96] It must have been from his experience here that he formed most of his opinions of the English working man: 'I once paid six or seven men together on a Saturday night, at least 10*s*. and some 30*s*. for work, and have seen them go with it directly to the alehouse, lie there until Monday, spend every penny and run into debt to boot, and not give a farthing of it to their families, though all of them had wives and children.'[97] Was Defoe's own house also perhaps serving as an alehouse? Several years later there was to be a lawsuit arising from a dispute about 'small and strong drink' supplied for his workmen, though it is not clear whether this was for resale.[98] Brickmaking was certainly thirsty work, and an alehouse on the spot would also have been very convenient for off duty soldiers from the Fort. Defoe declared that he 'Employ'd 100 Poor People' and that he 'generally made Six hundred pounds per Annum' from his manufactory.[99] This implies production on a considerable scale, to which he may not have built up until some years later.

Nor was his mind always on his business. He recalled seeing a remarkable flight of flying ants come across the marshes, 'Black like a cloud', and fall over an area of several square miles, two pecks falling into his boat, and 'my Hatful down the Funnel of two Chymnies in my House'.[100] But there was always plenty of interest to see. From the windows of his house, or from the wharf where his bricks were loaded, he could enjoy a splendid view of the shipping borne along the great artery by the 'draught and reflux of the mighty river'.[101] 'To put one's thumb to stop the tide at Gravesend' was an expression he often used to describe a ludicrously inadequate effort.[102] Perhaps, like Crusoe in his island look-out, he equipped himself with a perspective glass; and few were better able to interpret the changing scene. There were the Gravesend tiltboats used to ferry passengers, some fifty at a time, to and from London; for 'it is hardly credible what numbers of people pass here every tide, as well by night as by day'.[103] There were the 'large hoys, of fifty or sixty tons burthen', carrying Kentish pippins or cherries to the capital, or taking chalk rubble from the pits at Northfleet to sweeten the sour clays of Essex or East Anglia.[104] There were the Barking fishing-smacks, laden with mackerel from the Folkestone fishing-boats, flying 'up to market with them, with such a crowd of canvas, and up so high that one would wonder that their small boats cou'd bear it and should not overset'.[105] One of the most splendid sights of all was provided by the powerfully built colliers, when a 'fleet of five to seven hundred sail of ships, comes up the river at a time', deep laden with Newcastle coal for London hearths.[106] Other coasters brought grain from scores of small ports between the Solent and the Wash, or Cheshire cheese carried round by 'the long sea'. Merchant ships brought Oporto wines or Virginia tobacco, but no longer on Defoe's account. There were the huge East Indiamen laden with tea or calico. And in the riverside taverns in Gravesend he could meet sailors with tales of shanghai-ings and piracy, of slavery in

Algiers or Sallee, of cannibalism and strange customs in Lappland, Ceylon, Campeche or Madagascar. To the end of his life distant places maintained a powerful hold on his imagination; but he was not yet ready to turn all this to literary account.

In fact, the shock to Defoe's self-confidence brought about by his financial troubles had made his pen dry up; for it is unlikely that any of the handful of tracts tentatively assigned to him between 1692 and 1695 are his;[107] and the next that can be claimed for him with any confidence appeared early in 1696: *A Discourse about Raising Men*,[108] which anticipated an argument which he put forward, more briefly, in his *Review*, thirteen years later.[109] In each case a universal obligation to serve as a soldier is deduced from the contractual theory of the state, by which men part with some of their liberties for the common good; and in each case a parallel is drawn with the obligation to pay taxes. In each case, however, the application of this principle is to be tempered in practice by expediency. The parishes should choose for preference the 'idle and dissolute' (*Discourse*), or 'the most useless and unprofitable' (*Review*). The *Discourse* reads very much like something which has strayed out of a more ambitious work that Defoe was probably already preparing, his *Essay upon Projects*, and rushed into print because of the urgent recruiting problems of the winter of 1695/6 after heavy losses in the previous campaign.

An Essay upon Projects, published on 25 January 1697, was to remain for eight years Defoe's most ambitious work. It was one of the few books which he openly acknowledged, by adding the initials, D. F., to the preface which he addressed to his friend Dalby Thomas. In his introduction, in which he sought to outline the history of his subject, he began by going back to such Biblical projects as Noah's Ark and the Tower of Babel, but then leaped forward abruptly to 'about the year 1680', when 'began the Art and Mystery of Projecting to creep into the World'. The nearest he came to defining his subject was when he wrote of 'both the essential Ends of a Project . . . Publick Good and Private Advantage';[110] and since it would have been quixotic to expose to the world schemes offering much in the way of 'Private Advantage', his emphasis was naturally upon 'Publick Good'. His *Essay* was in fact a series of loosely linked essays on various matters of public interest, then actually under discussion, or suggested by his own experience.

He began by discussing Banks, a matter of bitter political controversy since the establishment of the Bank of England by Charles Montagu, with the backing of Whig financiers in the City, and its chief rival, the Royal Bank set up in 1696 with 'country' support, to advance money on the security of landed estates. He was scornfully critical of the latter; but he gave qualified approval to the Bank of England, which he considered 'a very good Fund . . . useful to the Government . . . and profitable to the Proprietors'. However he thought that it needed to increase its stock at least fivefold so that it could 'manage the whole Business of the Town; which it ought, tho' not to do, at least be Able to do'. The super-bank which he envisaged would have six distinct offices to deal with such varied transactions as advancing money to merchants to pay customs duties, mortgages on land, and even simple pawnbroking. Branches should be established in every county; or alternatively there should be a series of local banks, corresponding directly with each other or through their local cashiers.[111]

An equally topical, though less controversial, problem was the state of the highways. With the growth of population and trade, the old system by which each parish maintained its own highways was beginning to break down. The country was already feeling its way towards an alternative system, though the early turnpike schemes were managed, not by trustees, as eventually became the rule, but by the county magistrates. Defoe's proposals, worked out in detail for his own county of Middlesex, also involved county management. Men, horses and carriages would be pressed by the county authorities for the initial construction of the roads, and a permanent labour force for their maintenance would be provided by negro slaves and highwaymen reprieved from the gallows. Some public expenditure would be inevitable at first; but eventually the costs would be met from the rents of enclosures of hitherto useless land on either side of the highways which, when properly managed, would not need the immense width which they had developed as a result of efforts to avoid the sloughs and potholes.[112]

Defoe next discussed insurance of various kinds. Several fire insurance schemes had been started in the 1680s, and he himself had been involved in marine insurance. But he had a wider vision of what might be achieved by insurance, which 'seems a Project we are led to by the Divine Rule . . . Mankind might be secur'd from all the Miseries, Indigences, and Distresses that happen in the World . . . not a creature so Miserable, or so Poor, but should claim Subsistence as their Due, and not ask it of Charity'. He worked out in detail insurance schemes to compensate seamen for injuries, for widows, and against ill-health — the last to include free medical attention and medicines, as well as a pension for life if permanently disabled. Some at least of these schemes should be made compulsory, by denying alternative forms of relief to those who refused to join. Not content with foreshadowing the welfare state, Defoe casually threw off, without bothering to develop it, the idea of collective security: 'General Peace might be secur'd all over the World by it, if all Powers agreed to suppress him that Usurp'd or Encroach'd upon his Neighbour.'[113]

He also suggested the foundation of a number of Academies. First he proposed an English equivalent of the French Academy,

> . . . to polish and refine our *English* Tongue . . . to establish Purity and Propriety of Stile, and to purge it from all the Irregular Additions that Ignorance and Affectation have introduc'd; and all those Innovations in Speech, if I may call them such, which some Dogmatic Writers have the Confidence to foster upon their Native Language, as if their Authority were sufficient to make their own Fancy legitimate.[114]

When he himself had been a member of a group which had 'seemed to offer at this Noble Design' — presumably Roscommon's Academy — they had found the task 'too great for Private Hands'; and he now suggested that a new Academy should be founded by the King. It should consist of twelve noblemen, twelve gentlemen and twelve others chosen only for merit; clergymen, physicians and lawyers, whose pedantries had a harmful effect on the language, should be excluded, except 'upon very extraordinary Occasions'. They might start by setting an example against swearing — an example which might not be readily followed in his second proposed Academy.

This would be one for military studies, to provide professional training for army officers, but also open to volunteers. Once again, Defoe was thinking on a grand scale: 'I think such a House as *Chelsea-College*, only about four times as big, wou'd answer.' As for the site,

... the House must be built where they may have Ground to cast Bombs, to raise Regular Works, as Batteries, Bastions, Half-Moons, Redoubts, Horn-Works, Forts, and the like; with the convenience of Water to draw round such Works, to exercise the Engineers in all the necessary Experiments of Dreining and Mining under Ditches. There must be room to fire Great Shot at a distance, to Canonade a Camp, to throw all sorts of Fire-works and Machines, that are or shall be invented; to open Trenches, form Camps, &c.[115]

No doubt, if pressed, he could have suggested an ideal site, in the Essex marshes just upstream from Tilbury Fort, where an enterprising brickmaker already established on the spot could supply them with all the bricks they might need, and sell them some of his surplus land into the bargain.

Equally ahead of the time was his proposed Academy for Women: 'I cannot think that God Almighty ever made them so delicate, so glorious Creatures, and furnish'd them with such Charms, so Agreeable and so Delightful to Mankind, with Souls capable of the same Accomplishments as Men, and all to be only Stewards of our Houses, *Cooks and Slaves.*' His remedy was a kind of academic nunnery, within which women should be allowed great freedom, but from which men should be rigidly excluded.[116] His other proposals included a 'Fool-House', comparable to Bedlam, but for 'naturals' — 'persons born without the use of their Reason' — to be paid for by a tax on books or a charity lottery;[117] a reform of the bankruptcy law, to do equal justice to the honest debtor and the reasonable creditor, while restraining fraudulent debtors and vindictive creditors;[118] a Court Merchant, consisting of six merchants, to try with a minimum of formality the commercial cases of which the ordinary courts made such heavy weather;[119] and an ingenious scheme by which all seamen were to become 'the King's hir'd servants', to be paid 24 shillings a month when at sea and half pay when unemployed, ships' masters to finance the scheme by paying 28 shillings a month for each seaman they employed; and since this was well below the inflated figure of wartime wages, they could still afford to pay extra duties to the government, so that 'the King might be made the General Ensurer of all Foreign Trade'.[120]

Taken together, Defoe's projects read like the programme of

some late nineteenth-century progressive political party. How dedicated was he to their achievement? It must be admitted that, with the notable exception of the bankruptcy law, he showed in later life only a sporadic interest at best in most of these causes. Yet he was certainly more firmly rooted in reality than the political philosophers who put forward speculative Utopias. He attempted to cost many of his schemes, though his calculations usually appear over-sanguine, and he was too inclined to minimise practical difficulties. But throughout his life he continued to produce similar optimistic projects, few of which had any chance of realisation.[121] The fact is that the state of society and government in England did not favour such schemes. They were not money-spinners likely to appeal to wealthy projectors or the cupidity of the investing public; they were not the kind of material that could generate party political pressures; and they demanded more resources and authority than philanthropists could command. Defoe's projects needed for their fulfilment a stronger executive than England then possessed. If he had been in the service of some benevolent despot, he might have had a chance to put some of his ideas into practice. As it was, a whole age of *laissez-faire* was to intervene before they again became practical politics. The fact that he followed up so few of his ideas may stem in part from a realisation that the times were unpropitious, but also from the chance or, as he would have insisted, the providence, which set his life on a different course. Defoe had no unduly idealistic view of the perfectibility of man; but he did believe that the human lot could be made more tolerable by the amelioration of society. His eagerness to put his ideas before the public, and without the full cloak of anonymity, suggests that his self-confidence was now fully restored.

The same impression is created by his first poem to appear in print for some five years: *The Character of the late Dr. Samuel Annesley. By Way of Elegy.*[122] The veteran dissenting minister, of whom Defoe had been not only 'a great Admirer and constant Hearer',[123] but also a personal friend, had died early in January 1697. The poem reveals less about its subject than its author, who with characteristic perversity, refused to mourn his dead friend:

> *Sighs for departed Friends are senseless things*
> Which them no Help, nor us no Comfort brings.

Even while admitting ignorance about the next life —

> Whether he's inform'd of Things below,
> *Is needless as impossible to know*

— he contrives to sound dogmatic even about that. He is even prepared to lay down the law to God Almighty:

> 'Twas spoke from Heaven, the Best of Men must Die,
> *No Patent's seal'd for Immortality*:
> Not even God's own Favourites can Shun the Stroke
> Even God himself cannot the Law revoke:
> He can't unless he should at once repeal
> The Eternal Laws of Nature; Change his Will;
> Declare his Works imperfect, Life restore
> To all that's Dead, and be a God no more.

So, by the act of creation, God had voluntarily abdicated his absolute sovereignty, and was now only a limited monarch, without even the power of dispensation.

The winter of 1696/7, which saw the appearance of Defoe's *Essay upon Projects*, also saw him, for the first time for several years, taking an interest in parliamentary affairs. He was present in the Commons on 13 November 1696 when a notorious Jacobite conspirator and would-be assassin of William III was questioned. Nine years later he recalled 'of what mighty Consequence, how Earnest were the Debates in the Case of Sir *John Fenwick*, only upon that *to outward appearance*, most insignificant Ceremony, whether at the coming of Sir *John* into the House, the Mace should lie upon the Table or no'.[124] It was probably business rather than curiosity that had brought Defoe to the Commons that day. The length of the debates about Fenwick seem to have delayed until the following day a matter in which Defoe took a keen personal interest, the 'abuses of Prisons and other pretended privileged places'. The question was debated on 14 November, and a committee set up to look into it; and their labours eventually produced a Bill which received the royal assent on 17 April 1697. Defoe later boasted of his part in bringing this about, 'in a day when I could be heard', perhaps through a friend in the House, or by giving evidence before the committee. He described how the privileges 'were very much reduc'd, the

Fryers abandon'd, the *Rules* of Prisons restrain'd, and the *Mint* brought to a more regular Restraint'.[125] However, 'as this effectually took away the Screen from the honest Debtor' Parliament took steps to remedy the situation. This was the Act for the Relief of Creditors, which became law on 1 April 1697, and which extended to all insolvent debtors the benefits which the unsuccessful Bill of three years before would have bestowed only on certain specified merchant insurers — that a settlement made between a debtor and two thirds of his creditors, by number and value, should be binding upon the rest. Defoe did not claim any credit for this measure, and in his *Essay upon Projects* had proposed a much more radical reform of the bankruptcy law; but as the two Acts apparently formed a kind of package deal, it may be that he had some influence here too. He later admitted that there was 'one very unhappy Omission in this Act, *viz*. That it did not require the several Creditors to appear personally and prove their Debts', thus opening the way to fraudulent bankruptcies with the aid of spurious or collusive creditors.[126] For this reason the Act was repealed in the following year.

However, during the short time that it was in force Defoe was apparently able to benefit from it and gain at last a legal discharge from his own bankruptcy. He later gave a long and emotionally involved account of a scene of which he claimed to have been a witness, in which a debtor was granted such a discharge by one of the Barons of the Exchequer. Many of the details corresponded exactly with his own case: debts of £17,000; 15s. in the £ offered to the creditors in vain, since four of them, with debts of less than £2000 rejected the terms; prison, the Mint, and a subsequent government place. But other details certainly did not apply: twelve years imprisonment, a statute of bankrupt in force for fifteen years without paying a dividend, the creditors willing to discharge him in return for a bond for a purely nominal payment, since 'the poor man had nothing'.[127] Most of this extraneous material, no doubt introduced for effect or for disguise, was probably drawn from a scene which Defoe really did witness when seeking his own discharge. He told elsewhere how he saw a man led into a judge's chambers, 'between two of his Creditors, crying like a Child'. This same man he had formerly seen, in his prosperous days, clothed in embroideries and cloth-of-gold waistcoats, with a coach and six horses and footmen waiting for him at the Exchange gate, while his lady in her gilt chariot, her dress studded with diamonds, 'rivall'd the late Queen in the Mercers-Shops and China-Warehouses, and bought what she (that modester Mistress of true Glory) thought too dear for her self'. This man now came, with his creditors' consent, to be discharged under the Act, making 'composition for one Penny in the Pound . . . for ninety thousand Pounds debts; and as one of the creditors told me, they were to take his Bond for that Penny'.[128] He placed this scene in 'Baron Hatsell's Chamber in the Temple'; and it must have taken place between November 1697 when Hatsell was first appointed a Baron of the Exchequer, and April 1698 when Defoe left London for several months, not returning until after the repeal of the Act. Towards the end of his life he asserted in the course of legal pleadings that 'about the year 1695' he had made composition with his creditors 'for time only'; but the evidence suggests that it must have been during the winter of 1697/8 that he was granted his discharge, though it is not clear on what terms.[129] He sometimes implied that his creditors agreed to accept something less than their full debts, though he acknowledged a moral responsibility to pay in full as soon as he could. He certainly never succeeded in clearing all his obligations; but it seems that for several years to come he was free from the overwhelming pressures of the previous five or six years.

11 The Stream of Ignorance Running High

The winter of 1697/8, besides seeing Defoe's conditional discharge from bankruptcy, also marks a major turning point in his life, his first employment as government propagandist and confidential agent. It had already been possible for him to write during the previous winter of 'the French King, who now inclines to Peace, and owns it';[1] and though the war had dragged on for another rather half-hearted campaign, the real business of the summer had been the negotiations which finally led to the signing of the Treaty of Ryswick on 21 September. Louis XIV agreed, not only to give up some of the territories he had occupied during the previous twenty years, but also to recognise William III as King of England, and to give no countenance to any scheme to restore James II. As Defoe pointed out, only a few years before most people would have laughed at the very notion of such favourable terms;[2] and indeed Louis had made concessions not really justified by any successes in the field. This was partly because, despite acute financial difficulties, the English economy had proved more resilient than the French; and ' 'tis not he who has the longest Sword, so much as he who has the *longest Purse*, will hold the War out best'.[3] Equally powerful in the mind of Louis was the desire to have his hands free to deal with the urgent problem of the Spanish Succession. Yet the Treaty was a considerable success for William, and when he at last returned home on 16 November he was given a hero's welcome. That night there were bonfires and fireworks. The weather was fine, giving the rejoicing crowds a clear view of an eclipse of the moon. Defoe could not resist improving the occasion: 'I told them, I fear'd the Joy of that Peace would suffer some Eclypse.'[4]

It was on the domestic, rather than the international, front that peace was first eclipsed. Late in November appeared a powerful anonymous pamphlet, *An Argument shewing that a Standing Army is inconsistent with a Free Government*. Immediately, a political volcano that had been grumbling for some months was in violent eruption.[5] To William, the Treaty he had just signed was a truce rather than a lasting settlement. He believed that to hold Louis to his agreement and negotiate effectively in the future, it was necessary to maintain a force of at least 40,000 men. But public opinion of almost every shade was against him. The Jacobites had an obvious motive for wishing to see William's forces at the lowest possible level. The Tory squires, whose land tax had met the main cost of the war, were easily persuaded that it had really been quite unnecessary, fought in the interests of the Dutch and their continental allies. They believed that England should avoid continental entanglements, and rely for security upon the navy, and in the last resort the militia. This chimed in with a strong undercurrent of hostility to William personally and all that he stood for. Defoe had already noticed the strength of this feeling as early as the previous March, when a Bill for the general naturalisation of foreigners in this country had been defeated in the Commons — 'when the Stream of Ignorance running high, Wise men were content to embrace the general Folly, that they might be in the Mode: The Word *Foreigner* was a Shibboleth of a Party, who made it popular, that they might the better affront that great Foreigner . . . King *William*'.[6] With the end of the war, this strong undercurrent was free to surge to the surface. And these feelings ran equally high amongst the Whigs. The Grumbletonians, the malcontents who had been passed over for public office, were ready to believe any evil of the King's ministers; but there was also a long and honourable Whig tradition of suspicion towards a standing army as a potential instrument of tyranny, which might at some time be used to suppress the nation's parliamentary liberties. The *Argument* was in fact written by John Trenchard and Walter Moyle, two young Whig members of Parliament, and those who continued the debate were from the same stable. In fact the pamphlet war was to be continued on both sides by Whigs of different shades, while the Tories, the main beneficiaries of the struggle, remained silent. The *Argument*, as well as being a serious and well-argued contribution to an important constitutional debate, was also a shrewdly timed stroke in the cut and thrust of politics; for it appeared just as the members were assembling for the parliamentary session due to open on 3 December.

The main burden of the coming session would rest on William's Chancellor of the Exchequer, and manager of the government's business in the Commons, Charles Montagu. He had already to his credit three remarkable financial achievements: the establishment of the Bank of England, whose privileges had been granted in return for a loan of £2 million for the conduct of the war; recoinage without devaluation; and the introduction of Exchequer Bills to maintain trade during the shortage of currency caused by the recoinage operation. He had established links with powerful Whig financial interests in the City, whose support was invaluable to the government. Together with Somers, Orford and Wharton, Montagu made up the Junto, a group of Whig magnates who consistently pooled their political influence in an effort to make themselves indispensable to the King. This was resented by William who, while appreciating the services of Montagu and Somers, the Lord Chancellor, had no great enthusiasm for Orford and a strong aversion to Wharton, resisting all attempts by his allies to bring him into the administration. The Junto also roused resentment in parliamentary circles, a resentment concentrated mainly upon Montagu. The other great figure, Somers, cautious, well-balanced, courteous and smooth, made few enemies and gave fewer handles to his political opponents. Montagu, on the other hand, combined a taste for power with more than a touch of arrogance. He fancied himself as a patron of letters, but his demands for deference, and his appetite for fulsome dedications, incurred derision. Though a grandson of a Duke of Manchester, as the younger son of a younger son, he was looked on as an upstart. The very success of his financial measures infuriated his opponents, especially the Tory squires who believed that long-term government borrowing at high rates of interest had raised the cost of mortgages and reduced the value of their estates. In their eyes Montagu's City friends had enriched themselves at their expense. Inevitably they went on to impugn his financial integrity, nicknaming him Filcher; but the closest scrutiny failed to make good the charge, and attempts to incriminate him rebounded on his accusers. But he was now in a very unenviable position. On the one hand was William's desire to maintain an effective force to give some teeth to his diplomacy; on the other was the overwhelming current of public opinion against standing armies. Nor had William taken him fully into his confidence. He had never been willing to discuss foreign affairs with any Englishman, and Montagu was not fully briefed as to the reasons for the King's requirements. Indeed, the latter would not even name a figure for the number of troops he considered necessary. In the inevitable struggle between King and Commons, Montagu could hardly avoid being caught in the cross-fire.[7]

The *Argument* could not be allowed to go unanswered; and one of the promptest replies was Defoe's *Some Reflections on a Pamphlet lately published*, which certainly appeared before the Commons committed themselves on 11 December.[8] He may still have been writing as a public-minded citizen, characteristically running counter to the general consensus of public opinion; and his personal interest as Accountant for the Glass Duties pointed in the same direction. But there are indications that, for the first time, he may have been applying himself to an imposed task, albeit a congenial one. In some ways this was a perfunctory piece of work. He began simply by following the *Argument*, cavilling at each point as he came to it; then he concluded with some very general reasons for maintaining an army, and for his assertion that our liberties were in as much danger from the navy or the militia as from the army. He must have been writing to a deadline — 'Had I more time to consult History', he wrote in the Preface. He cannot have been writing directly for King William; for he showed no 'within doors' knowledge of the considerations of foreign policy which weighed most with the King, and nowhere hinted at a force of more than 20,000, just half of what William considered necessary. Perhaps Montagu, realising from the *Essay upon Projects* that he had an able writer in his department, had called on him for a quick reply to the *Argument*; but, since Defoe for once acknowledged the authorship of a political tract with his initials, this may have been a signal to attract Montagu's attention. At all events Defoe now embarked on a career as a government propagandist which was to prove his real metier, and which he never abandoned willingly or for long.

On 11 December the Commons approved a motion proposed by the renegade Whig, Robert Harley, calling for the disbandment of all forces raised since Michaelmas 1680. This, it was estimated, would leave a force of rather less than 10,000 men.

Since the *Argument* had denied the need for any army at all, this might be regarded as a modest success for Defoe and the other government pamphleteers, the most distinguished of whom had been Somers himself with his famous *Balancing Letter* — though it is at least possible that Defoe had a hand in that as well.[9] But William looked on such a force as next to useless; and he now called on his ministers to obtain a force of 15,000, a figure which, in the opinion of Gilbert Burnet, would have been agreed with little difficulty if it had been put forward in the first place.[10] So the debate continued. In the course of this Defoe again appeared in print, this time anonymously, with *An Argument shewing, that a Standing Army, with Consent of Parliament, is not Inconsistent with a Free Government, &c.*[11] In this lively and well-argued tract, described by one critic as 'one of Defoe's finest pieces of political rhetoric', he again concentrated on confuting the original *Argument*, that any army at all was a threat to our liberties; and he even made a show of accepting the decision of the Commons to reduce the army to its size in 1680, which he placed as low as 6000 men. He claimed that this decision itself implied Parliament's rejection of the *Argument*, and that the only issue was how large an army was both necessary and safe. On 8 January the Commons rejected a ministerial proposal to reopen the question, and eventually clinched the matter, as they believed, by voting only the sum of £350,000 necessary to maintain the force they had in mind. This however, was only the first round of the contest, which was to be renewed with even greater bitterness in the following winter.

The excitement of battle had set Defoe's adrenalin flowing, and stimulated an outburst of literary activity. The winter of 1697/8 saw, in addition to his tracts on the Standing Army question, four others on a variety of topics, as well as other writings which did not appear in print until later. The only one on a specifically political issue was the last, published on 7 April: *The Interests of the Several Princes and States of Europe Consider'd, with respect to the Succession of the Crown of Spain. And the Titles of the several Pretenders thereto, Examin'd.*[12] Here Defoe made his first sally into foreign policy, with a clear analysis of the complex diplomatic problem which was to tax the statesmen of Europe for the next three years, before plunging the continent into a dozen more years of war. Charles

II of Spain might die at any time without issue. His elder sister, Maria Theresa, who had married Louis XIV, would have been next in line, had she not renounced her claim, for herself and her heirs, at the time of her marriage. The right of succession thus passed through a younger sister to her grandson, Joseph Ferdinand, the Electoral Prince of Bavaria. It was feared, however, that Louis would now put forward legal pretexts to declare the renunciation void, and then to press the claims of the Dauphin, who would thus be heir not only to France, but also to Spain and to her vast possessions in Italy, the Netherlands and the New World. In this tract Defoe showed the disastrous effects this would have on the interests of all the other European states, but especially on the Empire, the United Provinces and England; and so 'it must be in the Interest of all the Princes of *Europe* to join their Forces with the utmost vigour, and endeavour to prevent it'.

If Defoe had any ulterior motive beyond that of analysing and expounding a matter of urgent national interest, it might have been to insinuate the folly of allowing the army to run down at such a critical juncture; but if so, he did not venture to make it explicit. Someone who could clearly see the connection was Count Tallard, who had recently arrived in England as Louis XIV's ambassador. Only four days before Defoe's tract appeared, he had written to his royal master, advising him to strengthen his bargaining position by avoiding any provocative action until the troops were disbanded.[13] In fact, Louis had at this time no real hopes of gaining the whole Spanish inheritance for his son, and had already taken the first steps towards an agreement with William III, to avoid a general war such as Defoe foresaw, by a partition of the Spanish Empire among those powers whose rulers had a claim to the inheritance; and William, perhaps because of the very diplomatic weakness to which Tallard had drawn the French King's attention, was for once prepared to depart from his usual policy of resolute opposition to Louis. The negotiations went on in the utmost secrecy. William's only confidants were Portland and Heinsius, both Dutchmen, and none of the English ministers had any idea of what was afoot. As for Defoe, the whole tenor of his tract shows that the possibility of a deal between William and Louis had not crossed his mind. He was not yet in William's confidence.

About the same time there appeared another tract, almost

certainly by Defoe: *A Modest Vindication of Oliver Cromwell From the Unjust Accusations of Lieutenant-General Ludlow in his Memoirs.*[14] This was in fact only a half-hearted defence of Cromwell's usurpation, but rather an attack upon Ludlow and the republican cause he had supported; 'for that restor'd the Monarchy, though not the Person; but the other would have pull'd down the very Fabrick and Constitution of the English Government'. The oblique political message behind the tract was the suggestion that the posthumous publication of the *Memoirs* was really part of a campaign to denigrate King William. He expressed surprise that those responsible for the publication did not 'consult the Honour of the Author, to let such an Antimonarchist as *Ludlow* to appear in *England*, with his *Helvetian* Commonwealth Meditations, barefac'd and in all his Republican Colours, at a Time when the Monarchy had recover'd her Ancient Splendor in the Kingdom'.

A few months earlier he had published a tract on what must at the time have seemed quite a trivial matter. In the previous November the Lord Mayor, Sir Humphrey Edwin, had aroused controversy by twice attending an Independent meeting house in state accompanied by his sword-bearer. Originally the dispute had been simply about whether the sword-bearer should have been obliged to attend the conventicle. But at the end of 1697 or early in 1698 Defoe had broadened the issue in his tract, *An Enquiry into the Occasional Conformity of Dissenters, in Case of Preferment. With a Preface to the Lord Mayor, occasioned by his carrying the Sword to a Conventicle.*[15] Under the Corporation and Test Acts no one might hold any office in either municipal or national government without first qualifying by taking the sacrament according to the form used in the Church of England. With the passage of time and the blunting of much of the animosity between Anglicans and Dissenters, the practice had arisen by which some of the latter qualified for public office by taking the sacramental test on a single occasion, while continuing regular attendance at dissenting meetings. It was this practice of occasional conformity which Defoe now attacked, arguing that if a man could conscientiously conform to the Church of England, he ought to do so at all times; if his conscience would not let him conform regularly, it could not be right to do so for the sake of office. 'This', Defoe declared, 'is *playing Bo-peep* with God Almighty.' There was perhaps something perversely self-righteous in his attack on a practice which most of his fellow Dissenters considered harmless; and he admitted many years later that he had 'had the misfortune to make many honest men angry'.[16] It is not clear how widely he was known as the author until he went out of his way to draw attention to the fact two years later, when he still seemed unaware that he had constructed a time-bomb that could blow up in his face.[17]

The laxity of principle which Defoe was attacking was only a pale reflection of a more serious malaise which had afflicted society for a generation; and now voices began to be raised in protest. William's first speech to Parliament after the war had urged that measures be taken to curb profanity and immorality; and on 24 February a proclamation on the subject had been issued by the King, the first since Charles I who could have done so without provoking ribald laughter. Defoe now set down his thoughts on 'Immorality of Conversation' with a view to publication, although they did not actually reach print until, more than twenty years later, he incorporated them into his *Serious Reflections of Robinson Crusoe.*[18] Developing an idea from this still unpublished tract — 'The deficiency of our laws is chiefly the want of laws to reform the law-makers' — Defoe published on 31 March a characteristically provocative piece: *The Poor Man's Plea. In Relation to all the Proclamations, Declarations, Acts of Parliament, &c. Which have been, or shall be made, or Published, for Reformation of Manners, and suppressing Immorality in the Nation.*[19] Here he denounced all the laws by which a magistrate could set a poor man in the stocks for immorality, because in practice they were never applied to the nobility or gentry: 'These are but cobweb laws, in which small flies are catched, and great ones break through.' Tracing the spread of vice, by which he meant drunkenness, swearing and whoring — but chiefly the first of these — he found that it had spread from the Court to the nobility and gentry, and thence to the whole nation. Sometimes the very magistrates who sentenced men to the stocks were worse offenders themselves. Since the spread of vice had been due to the example, or even the active encouragement, of the gentry, the latter should either reform themselves, find means to punish offenders among their own number, or leave the poor alone. This tract made enough impact to go into a second edition; but Defoe was probably even more pleased when 'an Honest, Learned and

Judicious Clergyman' infuriated 'the leading Men of the Parish of St. J——, not far from the City of *London*', by taking his tract into the pulpit and basing his sermon upon it.[20]

The campaign against vice took a new turn with the publication on 21 April of Jeremy Collier's *A Short View of the Immorality and Prophaneness of the English Stage.*[21] This raised a considerable stir, and the authorities took the hint. On 10 May Narcissus Luttrell recorded: 'The justices of Middlesex did not only present the playhouse, but also Mr. Congreve, for writing the Double Dealer, Durfey, for Don Quixote; and Tonson and Briscoe, booksellers, for printing them; and that women frequenting the playhouses in masks tended much to debauchery and immorality.'[22] A brisk controversy developed, and by the middle of July replies to Collier had come from Gildon, Filmer, Dennis, Vanbrugh, Motteux, Durfey and Congreve himself. Defoe, for his part, strongly disapproved of Collier as a non-juring minister who had granted absolution without repentance on the scaffold to would-be assassins of William III;[23] but he completely shared his views of the stage.[24] Although not considering dramatic productions to be necessarily objectionable in themselves, he believed that they were conducive to vice in practice; and years later he actually proposed a scheme to close the theatres by taking bonds from the actors never to appear on the stage again, in return for financial compensation to be paid out of money raised by public subscription.[25] His silence on this occasion, on a matter on which he felt so strongly, may seem surprising; and it supports other strong hints that in April 1698 he had set out on his first journey by land to Scotland.

His way north took him through Newmarket, where he observed the unusually large gathering at the spring meeting attended by William III from 5 to 16 April.[26] He passed by the new house then being completed for the Earl of Nottingham at Burley on the Hill in Rutlandshire, and wrote a poem in its praise.[27] His route probably lay through Gainsborough, where by 1706 he had an agent, 'Mr. Coates, merchant', through whom he distributed political tracts; and through Newcastle, where his agent was Joseph Button, a printer and bookseller with a shop on the Bridge.[28] This journey was made during an exceptionally severe spring, so that as late as the first week in May Evelyn was recording in his diary: 'Extraordinary great

Snow, & frost"[29] Defoe was thus probably recalling his own
first entry into Scotland on horseback, when he described in
his *Tour* how, after crossing the Tweed, they mounted a steep
hill in the face of 'a Scots gale of wind' which forced them to
dismount — 'a wind so exceeding keen and cold . . . it pierc'd
our very eyes, that we could scarcely bear to hold them open'.[30]

He would certainly need to keep his eyes open when he
finally reached Edinburgh.[31] When he again went there in 1706,
ostensibly on his own affairs, but really on Harley's behalf,
Montagu (by that time Baron Halifax, and no longer in government office) immediately got in touch with him to ask for
reports on the state of public opinion there.[32] In the spring and
summer of 1698 Montagu would have much stronger motives
for seeking information. The main topic of conversation in
Edinburgh was the affairs of 'The Company of Scotland Trading
to Africa and the Indies', which had been established by an Act
of the Scottish Parliament in 1695. In origin this had been at
least in part an attempt by a number of London merchants to
break through the monopoly of the East India Company; but
vested interests had been strong enough to scare off the English
supporters of the scheme. The Dutch East India Company had
likewise foiled efforts to raise capital in Amsterdam, while
William III had pulled diplomatic strings to achieve the same
result at Hamburg. The venture thus became an entirely Scottish
one, and for this reason the object of defiant national pride.
£400,000 had been subscribed, and although only £150,000
had actually been called in and paid up, this in itself was a severe
strain on the financial resources of a small and poor country.
The Directors had by now adopted the ideas of William Paterson
of founding a Scottish colony at Darien on the isthmus of
Panama. The exact objective was a closely guarded secret, but
no secret was made of their 'intended Expedition to settle a
colony in the Indies'. Twelve hundred prospective settlers were
enrolled; cargoes and provisions were collected; ships were
bought — the *St Andrew* and the *Caledonia* at Hamburg, the
Unicorn at Amsterdam; these with the two tenders, the *Enterprise* and the *Dolphin*, made up the little fleet which assembled
in the Firth of Forth late in 1697. During the spring of 1698
the ships were being loaded at Bruntisland over on the Fife side.
Early in March the Company announced the impending departure of the expedition; at the beginning of June notices appeared

on the walls of the coffee-houses in Edinburgh and Glasgow calling on the settlers to be ready for sailing; and finally on 14 July the ill-fated little fleet, carrying the hopes of a whole nation, slipped quietly out of the Forth.

The Scots as a whole had little appreciation of the wider repercussions of their scheme, but there must have been many people in London who would have given a good deal to know the exact destination of the expedition. In the delicate state of international relations which centred on the question of the Spanish Succession, William would be obliged, for instance, to repudiate any attempt to establish a colony on territory claimed by Spain. A Scottish trading station in West Africa might threaten the interests of the Africa Company; and there must have been many who were concerned at the possible effects of the Company's operations on the English East India interests, which in this very summer were passing through a major crisis. The old East India Company whose monopoly rights were based on a royal charter had been a stronghold of Toryism in the City; and the interlopers who had defied their monopoly were now, with the support of the Whigs, about to supplant them. Montagu, as Chancellor of the Exchequer, was devoting the last part of the parliamentary session of 1697/8 to carrying through yet another major financial operation in favour of William's government and the Whig interest. In return for a loan of £2 million, a new East India Company was to be established on the ruins of the old, and a new Whig stronghold set up in the City. It must have been of great concern to Montagu and his backers in the City to know the intentions of the Scottish Company. Only two days before the expedition sailed, Narcissus Luttrell, who picked up most of his information from the gossip of the Exchange, thought that their destination was India.[33] In government circles it had been at least suspected for as much as twelve months that it was Darien. In fact, the government probably knew of the destination but pretended not to. Even so, it needed confirmation, as well as up to the minute reports on the progress of the preparations.

It is unlikely that Defoe had any personal financial interest in the Darien scheme, however indirect; and his acquaintanceship with two of the Directors, Lord Belhaven and William Paterson (who had in fact ceased to be a Director, though he sailed with the expedition) probably dates from some years later. Most likely he was provided with some plausible commercial business which would enable him to insinuate himself into the trading community, to listen to and sift the gossip of the Edinburgh coffee-houses and the waterfront at Leith, and report back to Montagu. If so, Defoe, who a few months before had become a government propagandist, was now anticipating the role he was to play nine years later for Harley at the time of the Union, that of a government spy. It is a pity, but scarcely surprising, that he has left no record of his impressions of the intense excitement and rumours of that summer in Edinburgh. His comments on the Darien affair in his later writings are few, brief, usually non-committal, and sometimes contradictory. It has to be remembered that he later became the chief middleman between public opinion in England and in Scotland, and was always aware of the effect that his words might have north of the Tweed. The Darien scheme was the sorest and most delicate topic that could be raised before Scottish readers; and Defoe may have felt that the less he said about it the better. And if it had ever leaked out that he had been acting as a government spy in 1698 his credit with the Scots would have been utterly destroyed.

Once the expedition had left the Forth in mid-July there was nothing to detain Defoe in Edinburgh; and almost at once he was on his way south, by a route which can still be traced in part. His comparison of the fruitfulness of the lands between Edinburgh and Berwick with those between Berwick and Newcastle implies knowledge of conditions in summer.[34] He saw an ox which Sir Edward Blacket of Newby Hall, near Ripon, caused to be 'led about for a sight, and shewed as far as Newcastle, and even to Scotland, for the biggest bullock in England'.[35] At Tadcaster, where 'the antient famous bridge . . . was just pull'd down, and the foundation of a new bridge was laid', he had to ferry across the Wharfe; for 'altho' I passed this place in the middle of summer, we found water enough in the river'.[36] The weather was unseasonably stormy and the rivers were in spate. He saw the damage done earlier in the year by the Don at Sheffield;[37] and then, after crossing a 'waste and houling wilderness', he suddenly looked down on 'the most delightful valley, with the most pleasant garden, and the most beautiful palace in the world' — his first sight of Chatsworth.[38] Yet as he passed south towards Derby he could still hear the Derwent, roaring 'like the breaches of the sea'.[39] His way lay through Coventry; and it may be that the election riots which he described so vividly took place, not in 1690, but in 1698;[40] for Parliament had been dissolved on 5 July, and throughout the rest of that month and August the elections were in full swing.

Not long after Defoe's return from Scotland there was advertised, on 13 September, a tract entitled: *Lex Talionis: Or, An Enquiry Into the Most Proper Ways to Prevent The Persecution of the Protestants in France.*[41] In several ways this is rather a puzzling work. It was included in the pirated *Collection* of his works which appeared in 1703, but omitted from his own *True Collection* later in the same year. This may mean that he really did not write it; but it certainly seems very characteristic of him — at least in its style. Internal evidence suggests that it may have been written shortly after the Treaty of Ryswick had brought the war to an end, nearly a year before, and at a time when many in England were concerned that the Treaty offered no protection to the Protestants still remaining in France. The author argued that it would not have been proper to seek to interfere in the internal affairs of France, and that the best way to protect the French Protestants was by retaliatory expulsion of Catholics from England. Such reprisals would bring pressure to bear on Louis XIV, or at worst make room for a further wave of Huguenot refugees. This tract falls far short of Defoe's usual standards of moderation and humanity; and this may be why he omitted it from his *True Collection* at a time when he was desperately anxious to show that his writings had always tended to heal the divisions within the nation. Though apparently written in all seriousness, *Lex Talionis* seems little more than a political doodle, an academic exercise remote from the really urgent issues of the day.

In the autumn of 1698 the previous winter's political crisis, over the standing army, was coming to the boil for a second time. William, reluctant to admit defeat on so vital an issue, was doing his best to evade the intention of Parliament. Taking advantage of the fact that the Commons, instead of specifying the precise numbers of the establishment they were prepared to accept, had tried to restrict the army by voting only the money needed for 10,000 men, he had delayed carrying out the full disbandment, a procedure which inevitably meant allowing pay to fall into arrears. His hope was that the nation would have second thoughts, and that the newly elected Parliament would prove more amenable and be ready to make good the deficien‐ cies. But his attitude had served only to inflame feeling still more; and Montagu, who would have to bear the brunt of it in the Commons, looked on the coming session with dread. On 25 November, a fortnight before the new Parliament was due to assemble, appeared another telling pamphlet, *A Short History of Standing Armies*, by John Trenchard, one of the co-authors of the *Argument* which had caused the government so much trouble almost exactly a year before.

Once again the chief government spokesman, though under the cloak of anonymity, was Defoe. The first reply, not pre‐ viously claimed for him, but almost certainly his work, was *An Argument, Proving, That a small Number of Regulated Forces Established during the Pleasure of Parliament, cannot damage our Present Happy Establishment.*[42] All the indications are that most of this tract was written before the *Short History* appeared, probably left over from the previous year's controversy. It starts as an attack, upon familiar lines, upon the original *Argu‐ ment* which had started the whole debate. Only in the last few pages is the attack switched, in an obviously hurried and scrappy manner, to the recently published *Short History* — 'Because I want to have done, I will read on at a venture'; and he is content to pick out and cavil at a few points without developing any continuous argument. This omission was repaired in *A Brief Reply to the History of Standing Armies.*[43] Here he concentrated less on the legality of a standing army with consent of Parlia‐ ment than on its expediency. The dangers of such an army, he argued, were far less than those of having no army at all. How‐ ever efficient the fleet and the militia might be — and he expressed doubts about whether the latter could ever be made efficient — they could do nothing to protect Flanders, which was vital to any attempt to hold Louis XIV in check; and now that warfare had become so technical, hastily improvised armies were no longer adequate. Finally the motives and characters of the author and his friends were attacked. They were the 'Socinians and Commonwealthsmen' who, by obstructing supply, had prolonged the late war by two years: 'They bid defiance to the Son of God on one hand, and to the King and Government on the other.' He complained too that both the *Short History* and the previous year's *Argument* had been 'tim'd to appear just at the opening of the Parliament'. Despite this, the government was not caught entirely on the wrong foot, for the *Brief Reply* went into a second edition on 8 December, within a fortnight of the appearance of the *Short History*, and the day before the new Parliament assembled. Defoe may also have been responsible for two further tracts: *The Case of a Standing Army Fairly Stated, and Reflections on the Short History of Standing Armies in England.*[44] Though dated 1699, the latter must have appeared earlier, for one of its avowed objects was to influence the choice of Speaker.

The Court in fact succeeded in securing the election of its nominee for the Speakership, Sir Thomas Littleton; but this was its last success. The few voices raised in defence of William's policy of maintaining a substantial army were simply lost in the violent gale of public opinion. A few weeks later the French ambassador, Tallard, wrote to Louis XIV:

> I cannot express to your Majesty with what fury the House of Commons urges the reduction of the troops. This is not an affair conducted merely by those who are opposed to the Court: the whole nation concurs in it. This has been brewing the whole summer: all the great men are agreed. In short it is a kind of general conspiracy on this point.[45]

On 14 December the Commons stopped a motion for supply until they had gone into committee to consider the whole question of the army. On 16 December the Earl of Ranelagh laid before the House estimates which showed that, instead of the 10,000 troops which the previous Parliament had intended, nearly 15,000 still remained on the English establishment. Next day they carried without a division a motion proposed by Robert Harley to disband all forces in excess of 7000; and to this was added an amendment, proposed by Jack Howe and also carried without a division, stipulating that these should be none but 'natural-born Subjects of England'. On 20 December William wrote in despair to Heinsius in Holland, 'I am so chagrined at what passes in the lower house with regard to the troops, that I can scarce turn my thoughts to any other matter.'[46] By the end of the year he had so far lost his usual self-control that he retired to Windsor to write a speech of abdication, which he intended to deliver to both houses when they re-assembled on 4 January after the Christmas recess. Second thoughts, and the persuasive tongue of Somers, led him to reverse this decision. He would soldier on, and submit with grim-faced stoicism to any further rebuffs or even insults he might receive from the Commons. The latter now showed their determination to prevent any further evasion of their wishes, by incorporating them in a Bill. They approved the third reading on 19 January; and before the end of the month it had passed through all its stages in the Lords and received the royal assent.

William could not even take comfort in the thought that the secret Partition Treaty he had made with Louis XIV at the end of the previous summer had reduced the risk of war over the Spanish Succession; for at the end of January came the news of the unexpected death of the young Electoral Prince of Bavaria to whom Spain itself had been assigned in that treaty. The negotiations would have to begin all over again, at a moment when William's bargaining power had been reduced to its lowest level. Nor was there anything in the new situation to produce a change of heart in the Commons, for they neither understood nor cared about William's diplomatic problems — a fact for which he was himself partly to blame. He did however expose himself to one further humiliation, in an effort to save the apple of his eye, his Dutch Guards. On 17 March, just nine days before the Disbanding Act came into force, he sent a message to the Commons, informing them that ships were ready to transport the Guards back to Holland, but adding that he would take it kindly if the House would allow them to stay. His request was promptly rejected, and William had no option but to comply.

For the ministers, and especially for Montagu, the whole session was one long martyrdom. As early as 24 December the Whig Secretary of State, James Vernon, had written to Shrewsbury: 'While this controversy lasts, the ministers and managers have no very good time of it, who are represented in the country as the supporters of an army, and perhaps are looked on at Court as having very much contributed to reduce it below what was necessary.'[47] Somers too wrote to Shrewsbury on 29 December to much the same effect: 'The King is dissatisfied to the highest degree . . . He blames the ministers for their easy giving way to it';[48] and Tallard's diagnosis was similar 'Even the ministers have abandoned the King.'[49] A symptom of this is that, though the opening of the new Parliament had been heralded by a flurry of pamphlets in defence of a standing army, once the Commons had committed themselves in mid-December no attempt was made to continue the pamphlet war, by Defoe or by any other government propagandist.

It must have been shortly before the end of the session on 4 May that Defoe at last gave vent to his feelings by firing a salvo in verse at the departing House of Commons. Entitled *An Encomium upon a Parliament*, it consisted of nineteen stanzas, with two more for a chorus, in the ballad metre known as 'Cherrie-and-the-Slae', a verse form used in Northumbrian and Scottish border ballads, with which Defoe may have grown familiar on his journey to Scotland in the previous year.[50] Two stanzas, on the treatment of William's Dutch Guards, are typical:

> Faile not our Freedom to Secure
> And all our Friends disband
> And send those Men to t'other Shore
> Who were such fools as to come o'er
> To help this grateful land
>
> And may the next that hear us pray
> And in distresse releive us
> Go home like those without their Pay
> And with contempt be sent away
> For having once beleived us.

Next to the disbanding of the army, his main complaint was the failure of Parliament to honour the nation's debts, shown by repealing taxes before the loans which had been advanced on their credit had been repaid. One of these was the Glass Duty, in whose continuance Defoe had, of course, a personal interest. He was to repeat this kind of valedictory ballad at the end of several future parliamentary sessions.

He was not quite alone in his attacks on the unco-operative attitude of Parliament towards William and his ministers. Soon afterwards his *Ecomium* was quoted with approval by Richard Kingston, in his *Cursory Remarks upon some late Disloyal Proceedings;*[51] but this was really the last salvo from a sinking ship. Even before Parliament had met, Charles Montagu had betrayed his lack of confidence by securing for his brother Christopher the lucrative post, then vacant, of Auditor of the

Exchequer, a life appointment which was being kept warm for
him should he need it for himself. In June he resigned the
Chancellorship of the Exchequer; and finally, in November, he
laid down his post as First Lord of the Treasury. His ally
Somers continued as Lord Chancellor until William reluctantly
dismissed him in April 1700. No doubt he was made of sterner
stuff than Montagu, but he did not have to face the House of
Commons.

The political eclipse of Montagu must also have been a
financial setback for Defoe, though there is no evidence of what
rewards he had received for his services. In other ways too his
affairs were taking a downward turn. During his absence in
Scotland, the Act for the Relief of Creditors had been repealed;
but since he had apparently succeeded in making composition
with his creditors, this may not have mattered to him. Thomas
Neale and Dalby Thomas had both been in trouble with the
Commons, being accused of embezzlement in connection with
the Million Lottery — no doubt a politically biased charge, since
both seem to have been exonerated.[52] A new private lottery
advertised by Neale in November 1698 had apparently been
abandoned;[53] and a bill making such lotteries illegal became law
on the last day of the session.[54] Even before this Neale had
been expelled from the Commons, early in 1699, for bribery at
the previous election; in July he was reported seriously ill, and
in December he died.[55] Dalby Thomas was also in hot water in
February 1699, being ordered into the custody of the Serjeant-
at-Arms for making unsubstantiated charges of bribery in
connection with a distilling Bill then before the House.[56] The
Glass Duty, too, was on its way out. It had already been halved
in 1698, and had been under further attack in the session of
1698/9. The Commons called for the accounts, and a report
survives, signed Daniel de Foe, Accomptant, and dated 17 April
1699, showing that between 1 August 1698 and 4 February
1699 the duty had brought in £5124 at a cost of £727.[57] On
the last day of the session royal assent was given to a Bill
entirely abolishing the Glass Duty, with effect from 1 August
following. On that date Defoe's salary of £100 *per annum* came
to an end, and with it his formal connection with the government.

One result of the collapse of the political cause to which
Defoe had committed himself was the drying up of his pen.

During the eighteen months from the early summer of 1699 to November 1700 there were no further political tracts; nor did he grind any of his own personal axes. The only known piece of his published during these months was his poem, *The Pacificator*, which appeared on 20 February 1700.[58] This was a light-hearted contribution to a literary squabble which seemed more important at the time than it does in retrospect — between the 'men of sense' and the 'men of wit' — which managed to embrace, not only the controversy about stage plays, but also an apparently irrelevant dispute about a dispensary for the sick poor, alleged to infringe the rights of the apothecaries. Defoe adopted a detached and bantering tone of moderation:

> *United: Wit* and *Sense*, makes Science Thrive,
> *Divided*: neither *Wit* nor *Sense* can live:
>
>   *   *   *   *   *   *   *   *
>
> Let either side abate of their Demands,
> And both submit to Reason's high Commands.
>
> To their own Province let him all confine,
> Doctors to Heal, to Preaching the Divine;
> D[ryde]n to Tragedy, let C[reec]h Translate,
> D[urfe]y make Ballads, Psalms and Hymns for T[at]e:
> Let P[rio]r flatter Kings in Panegyrick,
> R[atcli]ff Burlesque, and W[esle]y be Lyrick:
> Let C[ongrev]e write the Comic, F[o]e Lampoon,
> W[ycherl]y the Banter, M[ilbour]n the Buffoon,
> And let the Transgressing Muse receive the Fate,
> Of Contumacy, Excommunicate.

It was the kind of thing that Defoe could have thrown off in a few winter evenings. How did he spend the rest of these eighteen months? As it happens, the publication of *The Pacificator* is the only firm date in the whole of this period; and there is a dearth of information, even of an indirect kind, about his activities — perhaps the most striking hiatus in his whole life.

No doubt much of this time was spent in supervising his brick-and-tile works near Tilbury, which he later told Harley 'began to pay me very well. I generally made Six hundred pound profit per Annum.' But he also had heavy outgoings:

'I began to live, Took a Good House, bought me a Coach and horses a Second Time. I paid large Debts gradually, small Ones wholly, and Many a Creditor after composition whom I found poor and Decay'd I sent for and Paid the Remainder to tho' Actually Discharged.'[59] It may be that the burden of living up to his re-established position in society made him ill able to afford the loss of his subsidiary sources of income, and set him thinking once more of sunken treasure off the Lizard.

About this time his ingenious shipwright brother-in-law, Robert Davis, invented a diving machine, no doubt at Defoe's instigation,[60] and they probably went down together to Cornwall to try their luck. There are clear hints in his *Tour* of an otherwise unrecorded journey through the coastal areas of Dorset and Devonshire; and the picture which emerges is one of relaxed and leisurely travel in early summer. The gap in the chronological record invites us to assign it conjecturally to the year 1700. It was probably on this journey that he passed through Christchurch, 'a very inconsiderable poor place, scarce worth seeing', to Wimborne with its imposing church, and then 'over a sandy wild and barren country to Poole'.[61] Beyond Wareham, probably at East Lulworth, he and his companions were viewing a newly constructed decoy when they saw an eagle caught in a trap.[62] They 'rode in view of the Sea' to Weymouth, and then ferried across 'with boat and a rope' to the Isle of Portland where, 'tho' seemingly miserable, and thinly inhabited, yet the inhabitants being almost all stone-cutters, we found there was no very poor people among them'.[63] Passing the famous swannery at Abbotsbury, they continued along the coast towards Bridport, observing the fishermen seining for mackerel, which that year were so plentiful that the country folk came with carts to buy fish to manure their fields.[64] It may have been on this journey that he saw at Totnes on the Dart salmon peal caught in a tidal mill with the aid of a dog;[65] and at Dartmouth, going out with a local merchant to view the castle at the harbour entrance, he was the first to spot a school of pilchards, with porpoises in pursuit, driving up the river.[66] When he next came to Devonshire, in 1705, he already had friends, not only at Exeter, but also at Bideford on the north coast; but perhaps the latter lay on his homeward route.[67] At the Lizard, according to a certificate signed in 1704 by a number of inhabitants of the Lizard parish, Robert Davis had 'some years before' gone down in his machine in Polpeor Cove and there, several fathoms under water, had sung the hundredth psalm. Encouraged by this he had several times gone down to the silver wreck off the Bumble Rock, 'where were taken up several bars or pigs of silver'.[68] Why this venture should have come to nothing after such a promising start is not clear, but not apparently through any defect in Davis's machine.

Defoe was now approaching forty. Had he been content to concentrate on his brick-and-tile works he had a reasonable prospect of living in comfort and slowly paying off his debts. But this did not give enough scope for his restless energy; and his head must have been teeming with every kind of new project. During the eighteen months in which he remained 'unhinged' from political pamphleteering he must have had ample leisure to reflect upon the state of the nation, and upon his own perform-ance as a government propagandist. In the debate upon standing armies, he must have felt that he had more than matched his opponents, not only in volume of output, but also in strength of argument. No doubt an impartial judge, adjudicating from an Olympian height, or at a distance of several centuries, would have found in his favour; yet the jury on the spot, the Parlia-ment of England, had decided otherwise. He must have asked himself how it was that he had had the better of the argument and still lost his case. When he turned again to political pam-phleteering he was to employ far more sophisticated tactics than before. He seldom argued simply for victory — to get the better of an opponent and win the applause of his own sym-pathisers — for he seems to have realised that this produced no worth-while results. His future tracts were nearly always designed to influence some clearly envisaged section of the public, by first gaining their confidence by a show of agreement with their prejudices, and then imperceptibly leading them in the desired direction. He was in fact to become the master of the tract directed, not *against* his political opponents, but *towards* them.

His aim was to become the manager of public opinion — but in whose interest? Montagu was now out of office, and although Somers had clung to office for some months longer, William had virtually abandoned any attempt to influence what passed in Parliament. The humiliation he had suffered over the army was redoubled in the session of 1699/1700, when the Commons, now dominated by Robert Harley, could spare time for little else but forcing the King to revoke the grants he had made of forfeited Irish estates — grants which were contrary to a promise he had made to consult with Parliament about the disposal of these lands, and many of which had gone to foreign favourites who by no stretch of the imagination could be said to have contributed to the conquest of Ireland. William was more vulnerable on this than on any other issue, but his position was made worse by the lack of any effective voice raised in his defence. Although he could not yet bring himself to take the inevitable step of giving office to the Tories who dominated the Commons, the comparative nonentities who filled the major offices of state enjoyed little of his confidence. In Parliament and outside, the King's case went by default. On 11 April, he abruptly prorogued Parliament without even making a speech, after what he described to Heinsius as 'the most dismal session I have ever had'.[69] With public affairs in this deplorable state, Defoe seems to have come to the characteristically daring conclusion that what was needed was a spokesman for William and his policies, and that he himself was the man for the task. When he later wrote of 'Providence, which had other work for me to do', it must have been this that he had in mind.[70]

12 The Closet of a King

The mists which obscure so many of Defoe's activities are never more frustrating than in the later months of the year 1700; for this was the crucial period of his life when he entered the service of King William III. In *An Appeal to Honour and Justice*, written in 1715 to justify his past political conduct, he has left an obviously elliptical account of these events:

> During this time, there came out a vile abhor'd Pamphlet, in very ill Verse, written by one Mr. Tutchin, and call'd THE FOREIGNERS: In which the Author, *who he was I then knew not*, fell personally upon the King himself, and then upon the *Dutch* Nation: and after having reproach'd his Majesty with Crimes, that his worst Enemy could not think of without Horror, he summs up all in the odious Name of FOREIGNER.
>
> This fill'd me with a kind of Rage against the Book, and gave birth to a Trifle which I could not hope should have met with so general Acceptation as it did, I mean *The True-Born Englishman*. How this poem was the Occasion of my being known to his Majesty; how I was afterwards receiv'd by him; how Employ'd; and how, above my Capacity of deserving, Rewarded, is no Part of the present Case.[1]

But it is difficult to construct a plausible chronological account of these events. Tutchin's poem appeared on 1 August, *The True-Born Englishman* not until January 1701; yet strong circumstantial evidence shows Defoe already deep in William's confidence by the beginning of November.[2] Presumably, then, the poem was presented to the King in advance of publication, in a bid to gain his favour. Since William was in Holland from July to mid-October, that was probably where the vital events took place; and this would explain Defoe's comment in the

Preface to the poem, about being 'reproach'd in Foreign Countries, for belonging to a *Nation that wants Manners*'.[3]

This conjectural visit by Defoe to Holland would help to clear up another difficulty. The first edition of *The True-Born Englishman* included thirty lines attacking Tutchin personally under the name of 'Shamwhig'.[4] Since the continuity of the argument was greatly improved when these were omitted from later editions, they must have been interpolated. Apart from these thirty lines both Tutchin and his poem were completely ignored. What Defoe appears to have been answering is the whole chorus of abuse which over a number of years had been directed at the Dutch and foreigners in general and at the King in particular — a mounting crescendo in which Tutchin's was only the latest voice. Defoe's remark — '*who he was I then knew not*' — is curious, since Tutchin's authorship quickly became common knowledge.[5] Perhaps he took with him to Holland a copy of *The Foreigners*, hot from the press, before its authorship was known; or perhaps he was already in Holland, seeking access to the King, when he simply heard that such a poem had appeared.

Whether the conjecture that Defoe first gained access to William in Holland about August or September 1700 is correct or not, it seems clear that he himself must have taken the initiative in seeking to enter the King's service, the kind of bold stroke that would have been entirely in character. He would of course have needed a friend at Court to introduce him to the King; and by far the strongest candidate is William's chaplain, close companion and trusted adviser on Scottish affairs, William Carstares.[6] A few years later Defoe and Carstares were certainly on terms of close friendship, which may well have dated from the time when both men were exiles in Holland during James II's reign.[7] Carstares was probably the 'unquestionable witness' on whom Defoe relied for his assertion that William 'was a Prince of the greatest Piety, Sincerity, and unfeigned Religion'.[8] Defoe described an incident which had taken place eight years before 'at the great Battel of *Landen*, where the Night before the Battel, his Majesty lodg'd in his Coach, and in the morning had his Chaplain call'd into his Coach, to pray with him'; and this chaplain is known to have been Carstares.[9] Carstares may well have been Defoe's informant for a number of other incidents involving the King, at which Defoe cannot possibly have been present, though showing a puzzling knowledge of William's words and actions.[10] Carstares, discretion personified, was the last man to indulge in idle gossip, but may have shared with Defoe some of his memories of the master whom they both revered. He once ventured to wake William in the middle of the night, to beg him to reverse a disastrous political decision before the messenger could set out for Scotland.[11] This reminder that the chaplain's apartments probably communicated directly with the King's suggests how Defoe may have been able in the coming months, without arousing suspicion, to gain access on so many occasions to 'the Closet of a King'.[12] He covered his tracks so well that the author of *The True-Born Hugonot* had to imagine amatory adventures to explain why 'his own *Coachman* knew not where *he lodg'd*'.[13]

The two men who were so often to face each other in the royal apartments were united in their belief that the political issues of the day resolved themselves into a struggle between Protestantism and political liberty on the one hand, and 'popery and slavery' on the other. Yet in many ways the gap between them was immense — not merely in rank and past experience, but in personality. William, at fifty, had divided his life between the manoeuvres of the battlefield and those of high politics. Puny and hunchbacked, he was now visibly failing in health; but despite his declining energies and the embittering experience of recent years, he kept on his chosen course with stoical single-mindedness. Undemonstrative in manner, he was in fact a man of very strong feelings, which he usually, though not invariably, managed to control by an iron will. His confidence was never lightly given, but once given, was without reserve. Defoe, at forty, was full of robust health and nervous energy. A dissenting tradesman, now slowly rebuilding his fortunes after failing in business, he had travelled widely both at home and abroad, and was deeply read in history. A toad beneath the harrow, he had followed, with passionate commitment, the political convulsions of his own day; and he knew the mind of the man in the coffee-house. Above all, he was highly articulate; and the weapon he had to put at William's disposal was his pen. But first the King had to be persuaded that the prejudice which had paralysed his government in recent years could be overcome by skilful propaganda, aimed either directly at members of Parliament, or indirectly by stimulating and organising public opinion; and he had to be convinced that Defoe was the man for the task. Further, if such a campaign was to have any hope of success, the King, who had learned by bitter experience to put no trust in Englishmen, must be prepared to make him privy to his closest political secrets. We can only guess at what chemistry of personality brought the two very different men so quickly into mutual understanding. Defoe was certainly a convincing talker; but it must have taken more than this to win the King's confidence. Perhaps it was the boyish enthusiasm which still bubbled up in Defoe, despite all the vicissitudes of his life; or perhaps it was that, for all his self-confidence and self-sufficiency, he showed a hitherto little exposed side of his nature — a capacity for hero-worship and for dog-like devotion to a master who was really worth serving. At all events it is clear that within a few weeks of Defoe's introduction to William, the latter was freely discussing with him matters which he would not have confided to his ministers.

When William reached Hampton Court on 20 October after his return from Holland, his most pressing problems seemed to be the inevitable reconstruction of his government, and the settling of the Protestant succession, endangered by the death in the previous July of the Duke of Gloucester, the only surviving child of Princess Anne. Another cloud on the horizon was the failing health of Charles II of Spain; but William believed that he had provided against any harmful consequences by means of adroit diplomacy. One partition treaty had come to nothing through the untimely death of the principal beneficiary, the Electoral Prince of Bavaria, in January 1699. However, William had been able to negotiate a second partition treaty with Louis XIV, signed on 21 January 1700 by the Duke of Portland and the Earl of Jersey. According to this, Spain, the Spanish Netherlands and Spanish America were to go to the Emperor's younger son Charles, while Louis was to be compensated for the Dauphin's claim by receiving the Spanish possessions in Italy, subject to the proviso that the territory of Milan should be exchanged for the Duchy of Lorraine. It is true that there would be considerable opposition to the proposed partition. The Emperor would accept nothing short of the entire Spanish possessions for his son; and he felt that the growing resentment in Spain at any partition at all would strengthen his hand. In England, too, there was opposition for different reasons. It was argued that the increase of French power in Italy, and especially the acquisition of the Kingdom of Naples, would be fatal to English trade in the Mediterranean. In fact, there was a secret clause which would have removed this objection, a clause which neither party to the treaty found it expedient to reveal subsequently, by which Naples would have been exchanged for Savoy.[14] In any case, William believed that with the support of Louis the agreement would stand, that a general war could be averted and the balance of power maintained.

On 31 October news reached William that the Spanish King had died, leaving a will bequeathing his entire possessions to the sixteen-year-old Philip, Duke of Anjou, the younger son of the Dauphin. When he consulted the leading Tories, Rochester and Godolphin, each independently declared his preference for the will to the treaty, in the belief that, once in Madrid, Philip would fall under Spanish influence and shake off his grandfather's control; and when the news became public, this was the overwhelming view of the political world.[15] William however still pinned his hopes on his agreement with Louis, until on 4 November he learned that the latter had broken the treaty by accepting the will, and publicly recognising his grandson as Philip V of Spain. Defoe reported that William had greeted the news with the comment: '*et bien don[c], le Roy de France est Ruin[e] et l'Europe ausee*'.[16] Next day William wrote to Heinsius, the Grand Pensionary of Holland:

We must confess we are dupes; but if one's word and faith are not to be kept, it is easy to cheat any man. The worst is, it brings us into the greatest embarassment, particularly when I consider the state of affairs here; for the blindness of the people here is incredible. For though the affair is not public, yet it was no sooner said that the King of Spain's will was in favour of the Duke of Anjou, than it was the general opinion that it was better for England that France should accept the will than fulfil the treaty of partition . . . I am fully persuaded that, if this will be executed, England and the Republic are in danger of being totally lost or ruined. I hope that the Republic understands it thus, and will exert her whole force to oppose so great an evil. It is the utmost mortification to me in this important affair, that I cannot act with the vigour which is requisite, and set a good example; but the Republic

must do it and I will engage the people here, by a prudent
conduct, by degrees, and without perceiving it.[17]

In view of William's deplorable relations with Parliament during
the previous three years over the standing army and the Irish
forfeitures, this confidence in his ability to manipulate public
opinion is astonishing. It can only be explained by the trust he
was already placing in his new confidential agent, Defoe.

The latter now became, and was to remain for many years,
the most articulate defender of William's controversial treaty,
about which he claimed to speak with authority: 'I have had the
Honour to hear his Majesty speak of these things at large.'[18] He
recalled, on different occasions, how William had explained to
him 'his Reasons for making that Treaty, and some of the Views
he had in it for the future Good and Peace of Europe';[19] how
he had based the treaty 'upon a Supposition of the House of
Austria being divided into two Branches';[20] and how he had
heard 'his Majesty say, too Prophetically, *that* England *would
be glad to make Peace, upon worse Terms, after seven Years
war*'.[21] Sometimes he seems to be pitching his claims even
higher. When he wrote of 'that famous Treaty, which I had the
Honour to see, and something more in its Embrio', there is
some ambiguity, and he may perhaps mean only that he had seen
the actual text of the treaty.[22] Harder to explain away is his
reference to 'those Original Drafts, from which the late *Treaty
of Partition*, which he had the Honour to see form'd, was after
many alterations Concluded, and which he still has by him to
produce'.[23] Here he seems to claim to have been privy to the
original planning of the treaty; and this would mean that he
must have been in William's confidence at least eighteen months
before the death of the King of Spain, a supposition that would
raise insuperable difficulties. Perhaps in the course of instructing
Defoe about the aims of his policy William had entrusted him
with his own 'Original Drafts'. William's instruction was soon to
bear fruit. In contrast to the previous eighteen months in which
Defoe had been silent on political matters, the fifteen months
which began in November 1700 were to see an unprecedented
outburst of pamphleteering energy.

On 15 November there appeared what has the distinction of
being the first tract written by Defoe in the service of William
III: *The Two Great Questions Consider'd. I. What the French*

King will Do, with Respect to the Spanish Monarchy. II. What Measures the English ought to take.[24] Defoe argued that, if Louis XIV knew where his true interests lay, he would abide by the treaty rather than accept the will; and that in that event England should be prepared to enforce the treaty against the Emperor if need be. Yet even before the tract appeared it was generally known that Louis had in fact accepted the will and proclaimed his grandson as King of Spain;[25] in his preface, however, Defoe declared that he still thought it worth while to publish it. Now, as the French King's decision was known to William almost as soon as the death of the Spanish King, this seems at first sight fatal to the view that Defoe was in close touch with William when he wrote the tract. Closer examination, however, shows that all this was only an elaborate pretence. As the tract proceeds Defoe deals also with the possibility that Louis would abandon the treaty for the will, and he increasingly assumes that the French King was a threat to the balance of power and a potential enemy; he argues that England should 'put herself in a posture' — or, in modern idiom, re-arm — and that if Louis attacked either Spain or Flanders, we should seek allies and go to war. Reading between the lines, it is clear that Defoe knew all along the line that Louis would take, and only feigned ignorance so that he could appear in print at an early date while still apparently writing from an independent position 'without doors'.

Defoe's tract drew a prompt reply, *Remarks upon a Late Pamphlet*, written from an extreme isolationist point of view, though that of a 'grumbletonian' Whig rather than a Tory.[26] The demand for a 'posture' was attacked as a mere excuse to raise a standing army to undermine our liberties. What did it matter to us who was King of Spain? It is true that there would probably be war between France and the Empire, and that Holland would be the next victim. But England need not fear the combined might of France and Spain. We could rely upon our navy — or could we? For here the author launched into an attack on the shortcomings of the navy under its present administration. Again, if France controlled Spain, 'our trade may be embarrassed, but not so as to be totally destroy'd or undone'.[27] In fact, although on the face of it an attack on William's policies, the whole thing was really a subtle *reductio ad absurdum* of the isolationist position, presumably written by Defoe himself. But it contained no sarcasm; it was an attempt, not to expose William's enemies, but to influence them; and there must have been many who began to read it with approval, but finished with misgivings.

On 2 December, Defoe returned to the charge with *The Two Great Questions Further Considered, With Some Reply to the Remarks*.[28] This added little to the argument, though he now appeared to give a little ground: if the power of France could be checked without war, so much the better, 'let the King and the Parliament alone to the methods'.[29] A curious feature is an attack on a non-existent passage in the *Remarks*, a passage which he must have decided on second thoughts to omit.[30] Finally there appeared *Remarks upon the Two Great Questions. Part II. Wherein the Grand Question of all is Consider'd. Viz. What the Dutch ought to do at this Juncture?*[31] Here he stressed the danger the Dutch were in, but repeated his isolationist arguments, though with even less conviction than before: 'The Emperor and the *Dutch*, they must confederate together . . . and when it is the business of *England* to confederate, let her do so too.'[32] Once again, too, England's naval weaknesses were stressed. And so the mock battle raged, with a liberal sprinkling of personal insults to amuse the readers. The *Remarks* had accused the original author of being a sycophant, making his court to gain a place. In *Part II* we read that 'if I knew this honourable Author, I . . . should treat him as a FOE to my country'; and this tongue-in-cheek identification is later confirmed: 'I can tell who our Author is as well as *Tom C——l* himself', apparently a reference to Thomas Cockerill who had published Defoe's most ambitious work to date, his *Essay upon Projects*.[33] While they followed the mock struggle between Tweedledum and Tweedledee, few observed how the contestants were slowly edging to one side, imperceptibly drawing the spectators after them. This must have been the object of the whole operation, to insinuate that Louis XIV was threatening the balance of power, that England's interests were vitally affected, that war might be necessary, but that at all events we needed to strengthen our 'posture' and seek allies.

Meanwhile Defoe had produced a more straightforward defence of William's policy, in a tract whose theme is outlined in its running title:

A Letter to a Member of Parliament concerning the Present Posture of Affairs *in Christendom: First,* In Defence of the *Treaty of Partition.* Secondly, shewing the Great Prejudices that *Europe* in General, and *England* in Particular are like to receive from the Acceptation of the late King of *Spain*'s Will, contrary to the obligations of the said *Treaty.* In *Answer* to a *Letter* from him upon that Subject.[34]

After pointing out, amongst other dangers, how easy it would be for the French to gain control of Flanders, and from there to threaten the Dutch, he concluded: 'There is no other way for us to avert these Mischiefs, but by putting our selves (together with *Holland*) in a good Posture of Defence.'[35] In a final high-flown peroration he appealed to the nation to rally round their King, and to 'let the world know, in as publick and authentick a manner as we can, That we shall always be ready to concur with and second his Majesty to the utmost of our Power in such Engagements as He shall think it necessary to enter into abroad'. He concluded: 'Let us shew to all *Christendom*, by our Zeal and Cheerfulness in standing by so worthy a CHIEF, That we are not a Nation whose Alliance is to be neglected, and Enmity despis'd.'[36] Ostensibly dated 'Dec 1' this tract was apparently published shortly afterwards, when William had still not decided how he would handle his immediate political problems in England.

To say that William wanted to renew the war with France would be to oversimplify the issue. He would of course have preferred to attain his objectives without war, and at first was not altogether without hopes of achieving this. Ideally, he would have hoped for an early meeting of Parliament, a show of national unity, a generous grant of supplies to rebuild his army, and parliamentary support for a new alliance to resist the growing power of France. But a realistic view of the state of public opinion showed this to be impossible. Hostility to the very idea of an army, and personal hostility to William himself, meant that there was no hope of adequate supplies being granted to raise an army in time for a campaign next summer, or even to give teeth to William's diplomacy. Time, skilful propaganda and the pressure of events would be needed to bring public opinion round to William's point of view. He must have decided to devote the next twelve months to this purpose, a decision which, though perhaps inevitable, must still have called for great patience and moral courage, in view of his failing health.

Of the various political groups, only the Court Whigs and the adherents of Montagu and Somers could be counted on to support William's policies; and he had reservations about these. But no one else could be considered as the King's friends; and they were now the object of bitter attacks not only from the Tories, but also from the 'grumbletonian' Whigs. Montagu had been forced to resign, and Somers had been dismissed; and it would hardly be possible for William to employ them again in the foreseeable future. For the time being he had struggled on with a nondescript ministry, but the Tories were waiting impatiently to come into their inheritance. Though it seems to have been his intention, even before going abroad in the previous July, to bring them into the administration, it was not until some six weeks after his return to England that he finally took the plunge.[37] As Defoe later wrote to Harley:

> I remember Sir when haveing the honor to Serve the *Late King William* in a kind like this, and which his Majtie had the Goodness to Accept, and Over Vallue by Far, Expressing Some Concern at the Clamour and Power of the Party, at his Express Command I had the heart or Face or what Elce you will Please to Call it, to give my Opinion in Terms like These:
> 'Your Majtie Must Face About, Oblige your Friends to be Content to be Laid by, and Put in your Enemyes, Put them into Those Posts in which They may Seem to be Employ'd, and Thereby Take off the Edge and Divide the Party'.
> Twould be an Unsufferable Vanity to Offer you the Detail of That Affair . . . [38]

Whether or not Defoe's advice was as decisive as he imagined, early in December Godolphin returned to the Treasury and Rochester was appointed Lord Lieutenant of Ireland, while Montagu was kicked upstairs as Baron Halifax.

During the previous ten years Parliament had developed a seasonal rhythm, originally dictated by the requirements of William's campaigns. The sessions had opened in the late autumn, soon after William's return from Holland, and continued until the following spring. On this occasion William broke the rhythm; for not only did Parliament not meet in the autumn, but eventually, after William had been some nine weeks in England, it was dissolved on 19 December, and a new one summoned for 6 February. This may have suited both William and the incoming Tories, though for different reasons. William cannot have hoped for a swing big enough to enable him to bring back his old Whig ministers into office. But once he had accepted that time would be needed to win over public opinion, it was perhaps better to delay a meeting of Parliament in which strongly entrenched positions might be adopted. An election might well produce a marginally more amenable House of Commons. In other words, the King was concerned with measures, not men; and he had more to hope from 'the allaying of party heats' and the conversion of the moderate Tories to his point of view, than from a Whig victory.

In early January 1701, when the election campaign was getting into its stride, *The True-Born Englishman* at last appeared in print.[39] It began with an Introduction impugning the motives of those who criticised William's government; and then in Part I assigned to each nation its peculiar vice — in the case of England, ingratitude. It went on to outline the racial mixture in the ancestry of the English, and hence to pour derision upon the very idea of such a thing as a true-born Englishman. Part II returned to our national character, satirising further national vices, particularly drunkenness, but eventually coming round to our ungovernable nature. In the middle of this came the awkwardly interpolated attack on Tutchin as 'Shamwhig' — omitted from later editions. Then, referring briefly to the way William had freed the nation from oppression, it attacked the Anglican clergy for their inconsistent attitude towards the monarchy. After advancing the alternative Whig political theory to justify the Revolution, it returned to the way William had come to save the nation. Next Britannia was introduced to sing a panegyric on William. This led into praise for the Dutch, and a defence of William's reliance upon foreigners (Portland and Schomberg being singled out for praise), since the King could not rely on Englishmen. By a quick transition there followed a speech put into the mouth of Sir Charles Duncombe — an unsuccessful candidate for the Mayoralty that autumn and now seeking to represent the City in Parliament — in which he was made to boast of his ingratitude, treachery and attempts to win popularity by mass bribery. This led abruptly to the conclusion, summed up in the final couplet:

> For Fame of Families is all a Cheat,
> *'Tis Personal Virtue only makes us great.*

The immediate and immense success of the satire can clearly have owed little to the coherence of its argument, but was due in part to its vigorous but unpolished style, and perhaps even more to the bold effrontery with which it attacked some of the most popular attitudes of the age. One sign of its impact was the crop of replies which it provoked, even though one of these, *The English Gentleman Justify'd*, was only a mock reply, apparently by Defoe himself.[40] Such artificial stimulants to circulation were unnecessary. Not only did *The True-Born Englishman* run through ten editions in a few months (and another dozen in Defoe's lifetime), but it was seized on by the cut-price pirates and cried through the streets.[41] It was at first assumed that no Englishman could have written it, and it was laid at the door of the Irish free-thinker, John Toland; and although Defoe's authorship soon became known, this line of thought may explain the widely held belief that he was a Huguenot. Though not always relishing the notoriety he had achieved, he was really immensely proud of his success; and in future, if he wanted to identify himself as the author of a piece, it was usually as 'the Author of *The True-Born English-man*'.

Publication of the poem may have been deliberately timed to coincide with the general election. Its underlying theme — praise for William and ridicule for his enemies — as well as the attack on Duncombe, would fit in with this. On 4 January Defoe published an avowed piece of electioneering, *The Six Distinguishing Characters of a Parliament-Man*, which was in effect an appeal to the electors to choose members who would support the King in his resistance to Louis XIV by restoring the armed strength of the nation.[42] He was more explicit in identifying the King's enemies than his friends. The voters were urged not to choose Jacobites or those ill-affected to the present settlement, on the one hand, or atheists, Socinians, Asgillites or blasphemers on the other. His positive advice was somewhat vague: he recommended men of sense — 'a Gentleman may be a good Horse-racer, a good Sportsman, a good Swordsman, and yet a Fool of a Parliament-man'; men of years — 'he that sends a Boy to Market expects to make a Childs bargain'; and finally men of honesty and morals. Another tract which appeared about the same time, *The Present Disposition of England Consider'd*, asked who exactly were the King's friends, and gave an unequivocal answer: they were those who had been most generous in their loans to the King, who had established the Bank of England, who had carried through the recoinage and prompted the issue of Exchequer Bills to remedy the shortage of ready money while that operation was in progress. In other words they were the supporters of Halifax and his ally Somers, 'this great Man' who had been 'remov'd from the King's Ear . . . by the Advice and Counsel of false Friends'.[43] This tract reads very much like Defoe's work; and if so, it raises interesting questions, to be discussed later, about William's attitude at this time towards his former ministers, and about Defoe's role in their relationship.[44]

The same could be said of *The Freeholders Plea Against Stock-Jobbing Elections of Parliament Men*, which appeared on 23 January, as a commentary on the election then almost over.[45] Here Defoe deplored the unprecedented corruption, especially in the small boroughs, by the stock-jobbers of Exchange Alley who were profiting by the electoral rivalry of the two East India Companies — the New Company created by Montagu in 1698 as a Whig stronghold in the City, and the Old Company which, with the help of William's parliamentary enemies, had contrived to survive its intended destruction. Ten years later he recalled how 'Parliament Business was transferr'd to Exchange Alley . . . Here Elections were bought and sold . . . and a Thousand horrid Things practis'd, which made King *William* say, feelingly enough, *That if he did not put some End to the Difference of the two Companies, he must adjourn the Parliament to Exchange Alley*'.[46] Elsewhere Defoe says that this tract was laid first before the King and then before the Parliament, and claimed that 'it was his Majesty's Sense of the Consequence, that made him resolve to bring the two East India Companies to unite their Stocks'.[47] Negotiations, conducted by Halifax, eventually brought about a merger by the end of the year.

In *The Freeholders Plea*, while castigating the stock-jobbers,

Defoe had made a politic show of impartiality between the two East India Companies; but in *The Villainy of Stock-Jobbers Detected*, which appeared on 11 February, he was more openly partisan.[48] A run on the Bank of England, which had followed the success of the Whigs in the City election, was attributed to a deep-laid conspiracy on the part of those 'who have put themselves in direct Opposition to the Friends of the Government, and who always run retrograde to the King and the Nations Interest'. He specified the Old East India Company, and 'another sett of Men who are known to be in the same Interest' — principally goldsmiths, and particularly Sir Charles Duncombe, the mainspring of the opposition in the City to Halifax's Whig friends. Defoe had already published, on 6 February, his most direct attack, albeit moderate in tone, upon Duncombe and his associates: *The Livery Man's Reasons, Why he did not give his Vote for a Certain Gentleman either to be Lord Mayor: Or, Parliament Man for the City of London.*[49]

Though William can have placed no great hopes on the election as a means of securing a more friendly House of Commons, it did mean a delay of seven weeks during which politically effective public opinion could be influenced. This called for a succession of tracts, hammering home the same message, from differing points of view. Some time towards the end of December there had appeared *The Duke of Anjou's Succession consider'd, as to its Legality and Consequences; With Reflections on the French King's Memorial to the Dutch, and on what may be the Interest of the several Princes and States of Christendom, with respect to the present Conjuncture.* This was followed, some time during the following month, by *The Duke of Anjou's Succession Further Consider'd, As to the Danger that may arise from it to Europe in General; but more particularly to England, and the several Branches of our Trade.*[50] These tracts, which have all the hallmarks of Defoe's authorship, waste no time in defending the Partition Treaty, which was now a dead letter; it is the dangers of the present situation which are stressed. Since the Spaniards now 'had no other way left to them but to hug their Chains and make their unavoidable Slavery as easy to them as possible', the rest of Europe was threatened by 'this formidable Conjunction of the Sword of *France*, and the Purse of *Spain*'. With control of the Spanish Netherlands, Louis XIV would threaten the Dutch, whose independence it had always been England's interest to maintain since the days of Elizabeth. The Protestant interest was thus endangered; and with the Protestant succession in England still insecure, Louis would revive his efforts to replace James II on the throne. Similarly, French control of Spain would be fatal to our trade. Spanish wool would be diverted to France, and French woollen manufactures would replace ours in the Spanish market. By controlling Gibraltar and Cadiz, the French could shut us out from the Mediterranean and the indirect trade to Spanish America, thus depriving us of the bullion needed for our East India trade. The only reply to all this was for England to enter into 'amity and friendship' with the Dutch and the Emperor to resist the aggrandisement of the French King.

Perhaps to balance the predominantly mercenary arguments of this pair of tracts there appeared on 9 January: *The Danger of the Protestant Religion Consider'd, From the Prospect of a Religious War in Europe*, which began with a dedication to King William, a fulsome appeal to him to stand forth as the protector of the Protestant religion.[51] Since the power most aggrieved by Louis XIV's action was the Catholic House of Habsburg, the likelihood of a European war of religion might seem remote; but Defoe insisted that a coalition of Catholic powers was not as improbable as most people thought. He argued that the best way to prevent this was to divide the Catholic powers by forming an alliance with the Empire. This disingenuous special pleading, with its appeal to religious prejudice, at least gave him a chance to seize the standing army bull by the horns:

> They that would Enslave our Liberty by Standing Armies; and they that would leave us naked to our Enemies; or put us out of a Posture to help our Friends, are equally enemies to the Protestant Religion . . .
> I had rather see an Army in *England*, and run the hazard of our Liberties, than see the *Protestant* Religion in *Europe* trodden down for want of our helping to defend it . . .

This campaign of persuasion culminated in a tract which must have appeared shortly before the new Parliament met on 6 February. *An Essay on the Present Interest of England*, though sometimes attributed to George Stepney, has all the hallmarks of a typical Defoe tract.[52] Beginning with a defence of the Partition Treaty, it went on to argue not merely for a 'posture' but, for the first time, for war. The issue, it was claimed, was not one of war or peace; but of war now, with allies, or later, without. It insinuated that those who opposed military expenditure, whether in the name of liberty or of economy, were really crypto-Jacobites, who would also obstruct efforts to settle the Protestant Succession. Although no candidate was suggested as next in line after Princess Anne, derision was poured upon the idea that James II's son could ever become 'a Defender of the Protestant Faith and Liberties of *England*'. Returning to the coming war, it was proposed that the Archduke Charles should be supported by a Confederate army based on Portugal. In a remarkable anticipation of the conditions of the Peninsular War, more than a century later, Louis XIV's difficulties were outlined:

> . . . since from his own Frontiers thither, is a March of above 500 Miles over many Mountains rugged as the *Alps* through a Country barren and dispeopled, where such a force as he must bring, cannot subsist without Convoys from France.
> . . . he must have besides his Army in the Field, near half that number dispers'd at convenient distances to secure the march of his Convoys and Ammunition, which for the greatest part of so long a Tract must be carry'd on Mules Backs over mountainous and very narrow passes, where the very Peasants may intercept and plunder whatever is not strongly guarded.

England's part in such a campaign would apparently be to maintain sea communications, for 'the war we are to make must be altogether by Sea'. And now the carrot was used in preference to the stick. An expedition should be sent to the West Indies, 'and 'twill be the fault of our Commanders if all the French Colonies there be not rooted out'. He asked 'whether it ought not to be one of our great Aims by this War, utterly to extirpate the French out of *America*?' Further, such a war would open up the prospect of a direct trade with the Spanish colonies, eliminating many of the duties levied by the Spanish government as well as the profits of the Cadiz middlemen; and, introducing a theme more fully developed in the later pages of *Colonel Jack*, he asked: 'may we not thus during the War give a beginning to such a Commerce directly from our Plantations to the Spanish Continent, as may be continue'd after a Peace, to the unspeakable benefit of *England?*'[53]

At the end of the tract were printed documents illustrating the dispute about foreign policy between Charles II and Parliament in 1677, a topic which Defoe had touched on a month earlier in *The Six Distinguishing Characters of a Parliament-Man*:

> Former Kings would stand still, and see the French over-run *Flanders*, and Ruin our Protestant Neighbours, though the Parliament and People have intreated them to Assist them, and save *Flanders* from falling into the Hands of the French.
>
> Now we have a King who Solicits the People to enable him to preserve *Flanders* from falling into the Hands of the French.[54]

But it was already too late. A postscript to the *Essay* reports: 'Since the printing of which we have News from *Paris* that Orders are sent to Mareschal *Boufflers*, not only to take possession of all the Spanish Netherlands, but to disarm and seize the Dutch Troops in Garrison there; and we have reason to fear that those Orders are already executed.' This news had been trickling into England during the last days of January and the first few of February. The French troops, at the invitation of the Spanish government, had thus occupied the Barrier fortresses which had been the first line of defence for the Dutch on the borders of the Spanish Netherlands; and the Dutch had not dared to order their garrisons to resist. Without a blow, Louis had taken positions that enabled him directly to threaten the United Provinces. To William the danger now seemed acute, and Defoe spelled it out for the public in a brief but impassioned tract, *The Present Case of England and the Protestant Interest.*[55]

Parliament, having assembled on 6 February, was adjourned until 11 February, when William made a speech of studied moderation, simply asking them to provide for the Protestant Succession, and to guard against the dangers arising from the acceptance of Louis XIV's grandson as King of Spain. When the Commons had finished swearing their members, they framed on 14 February an entirely non-committal reply to the King's speech. There was clearly no sense of urgency; and perhaps as a result of this reply William and his intimate advisers — among

whom Defoe must be included — planned a campaign designed
to shock the Commons out of their complacency.

On the following day, Saturday 15 February, Mr Secretary
Vernon notified the Commons that he had received advice that
the French fleet was nearly ready to put to sea and land forces
on our coasts.[56] On the following Monday, 17 February, the
King sent to both Houses a letter supposedly written on 18
February, N.S. (7 February, O.S.) by the Earl of Melfort to his
brother the Earl of Perth, both of whom were attached to the
exiled James II's Court at St Germain. This letter, which Parliament was asked to believe had by some providential chance
found its way into the mail for England, where it had been
intercepted, discussed the high hopes of French support for a
Jacobite invasion:

> I told you, amongst other things the great fleet the king
> intends to put out this summer, the orders given, the money
> ready, the stores full, and everyone concerned active in their
> stations. There is no doubt but this fleet will be master of
> the sea for some time, if not all the summer, because the
> Dutch dare not stir till the English be ready, and they have
> long debates yet before they can be in a condition to act, if
> they have the will; and it is a question whether they will have
> it at all.[57]

The Lords ordered the Melfort letter to be printed, but the
Commons ignored it, apparently taking it for the forgery which
it undoubtedly was. Though too short to provide incontrovertible
evidence of Defoe's authorship, there are one or two characteristic touches, including one of his favourite similes — 'the fable
of the dog, who lost the substance for the shadow'. It is difficult
to see who else could have been responsible.

It has been charitably suggested that William must have been
imposed upon,[58] but the sequel shows that he must have been
party to the whole scheme. The next day, 18 February, he
passed to the Commons a Memorial from the States of Holland,
in which they called on England to honour the treaty of 1678
by which we were bound to send 10,000 troops to their aid if
they were threatened with invasion. In fact, no such request had
yet arrived from the Hague, and the 'memorial' had been concocted in England by William and the Dutch ambassador, van

Geldermalsen.[59] There is nothing to connect Defoe with this particular white lie, except that it was obviously part of a manoeuvre which he had master-minded.

For the third successive day, the shock tactics were repeated. On 19 February there appeared *The Apparent Danger of an Invasion. Briefly Represented in a Letter to a Minister of State*, supposedly by 'a Kentish Gentleman', but actually by Defoe.[60] Ostensibly dated from 'Mo——ds' on 14 February, it was an effort to create the impression that England's most vulnerable county was in fear of an imminent French invasion, against which we were virtually defenceless.

> The City Militia, I believe is our best; but what Discipline can Men have, who appear in Arms but once a year, march into the Artillery Ground, and there wisely spend the Day in Eating, Drinking and smoaking, in Storming half a Score Sir-Loins of Beef, and Vennison Pasties and having given their Officers a Volley or two, and like so many Iddle Boys with Snowballs, fooll'd away a little Gun Powder, return Home again as ignorant as they went out, and as fit to Fight the French at *Black Heath*, as one of our little *Yatches* is to engage the *Brittania*.

A puzzling variant of the running title reads: *The Apparent Danger of an Invasion, Briefly Represented in a Letter which is supposed to be writ by my Lord Melfort, to his brother the Earl of Perth; now commented on, and as that was, sent to the King and Parliament. Presented to a Member of Parliament.*[61] The *Apparent Danger* makes no mention at all of the Melfort Letter, which could not possibly have been known in Kent three days before it was presented to Parliament. But perhaps in the haste of the moment this had at first been overlooked, but then references to the letter had been cut out of the text, though not at first out of the title page. Whatever the explanation of this variant title, it leaves little doubt that the letter and the tract were both parts of the same propaganda operation in which Defoe and the King were both deeply involved.

Before the session was many weeks old it was clear that the Commons would not proceed harmoniously and speedily to vote the supplies which William needed to strengthen his hand. Instead they insisted on investigating what Jack Howe called the 'felonious treaty', and using it to attack Portland and William's ex-ministers, and through them the King himself. The dominant humour was party passion — the desire of the Tories to consolidate their power by completing the destruction of their Whig predecessors. On this issue many of the country Whigs would join them; and to such a man as John Tutchin this was 'the best of Parliaments'.[62] Prejudice against the foreigners whom William had employed and honoured, hatred of the Court Whigs who were believed to have enriched themselves corruptly while in office, and fear of a standing army which might be used to overthrow the nation's liberties, still in many men's minds outweighed any hypothetical danger from France. Defoe now set himself to use some of those very prejudices to win support for William's policy.

In the previous December, in *A Letter to a Member of Parliament*, he had put forward a detailed defence of the Partition Treaty, arguing that England's interests would have been far better protected under the Treaty than under the Spanish King's will, and that the new situation called for England to 'put herself in a Posture' of defence. Some weeks after the meeting of Parliament, perhaps in March, there belatedly appeared *Some Reply to a Letter pretended to be writ to a Member of Parliament in the Country in Defence of the Treaty of Partition.*[63] The Author of the *Letter* is attacked for defending 'those able Ministers, who designed to give the *Mediterranean* Trade and several Kingdoms to the French'; while his demand for a 'posture' is severely criticised, but on the unexpected ground that this would only be a half measure:

> Whoever declares against the necessity of a vigorous War, and are for Temporizing Measures, if I must allow them Honesty, I shall question their Understanding; and if their abilities are out of doubt, it is to be fear'd they are willing to accept of more titular Kings from *France* than one . . . Those who advise we should put ourselves in a Posture (as they call it) I . . . must look upon as the highest Flatterers; and the considering part of Mankind will certainly conclude they do not desire such Preparations and such Management of War as is likely to rescue the World from the Usurpations of *France*; but will suppose they want a pretty competent Army for some other Intent or Purpose, which they will not pretend to guess at.

An attempt is made to free the King from any blame for the hated treaty, and to lay it all upon his ministers. The tract concludes with an eloquent peroration, inviting William to 'consult with his People', since 'those that are most aggriev'd by the fatal Expedient of the Partition-Treaty are most able and willing to prevent the ill Consequences of it'; while 'whoever is wanting in raising a just Resentment against *France*, whoever disguises or diminishes our present Danger . . . whoever goes about to conceal or excuse past Miscarriages; . . . all these are equally guilty, and equally betray the last Opportunity of Settling our Government at home, or preventing our Ruin abroad'.

An even more ingenious attempt at intellectual Judo is made in *An Account of the Debate in Town concerning Peace and War. In Letters to a Gentleman in the Country*, probably published about the middle of March.[64] In the first of three letters, containing 'Reasons for a Peace', the author, who fears that a war may be necessary, reports a conversation with a 'Mr. P who is violently for a Peace'. The latter, however, gives as his reason only our unpreparedness: 'In the first place, we are in pieces among ourselves . . . Have we either Mony, or Credit, or Men, or Conduct for a War?' Eventually the two agree to accept the judgment of Parliament as to whether a war is necessary. In the second Letter, containing 'Reasons to believe the Court, is not for a War' the author declares that 'Many of you Gentlemen in the Country, who see things only at a distance, flatter your selves that the Court is at the bottom of all this Noise of the Necessity for a War, that they would have an Army again, and so hold on the present Juncture to blow the People up with Fears and Jealousies of imaginary Dangers, for which you fondly hope there's no Ground.' A 'Mr. S' is now introduced, to argue that the Court has deliberately neglected many steps it ought to have taken if there had been any real intention of resisting Louis XIV; and the inference is gradually insinuated, that there *is* a real national danger, to which the Court is wilfully blind, and from which only Parliament can rescue the nation. Finally in the third Letter, a 'Mr. R', a 'Place-Whig' is also brought into the discussion. However, it is at first 'Mr. S' who dominates the conversation, developing an orthodox attack on the Partition Treaty, and on its chief defender, the author of the *Letter to a Member of Parliament*. He claims that 'the last half of the Letter is not of a piece with the first . . . it is not consistent with one and the same Man to be for the Partition and War, or even the Posture of War'. Before long 'Mr. S' is attacking 'Mr. R' and the Court for supinely avoiding the war which they know to be necessary. Eventually 'Mr. R' offers an explanation of William's compliance with France, in the Partition Treaty and since: *'Caligula* us'd to creep into a Hole when it thunder'd, and piss on Jupiter's Statue when the Thunder was over . . . I own to you, that both I and others have observ'd a Change ever since *Charnock*'s Plot, and its the only Key we have for decyphering many things that have happen'd since.' He was even more explicit, for 'is not this Yielding to shun Fighting, the very Character of a Coward?' And the tract concludes with an impassioned plea to William to redeem his honour, 'even if he dies in the attempt'. Would anyone have dared to publish so savage an attack on William's personal character unless, like Defoe, he already knew that William was prepared to condone it to further the policy he had at heart? That Defoe thought it worth while to make such a wildly improbable charge illustrates the depth of prejudice in the minds of those whom he was trying to influence. The tract makes difficult reading today, for it can only be understood against the confused political background of 1701; but it is an exceptionally ingenious piece of work. On the face of it, it is an attack on William and all that he stood for; but the real message is steadily insinuated — that the country was in danger from the growing power of France. As Defoe later remarked: 'The Clamour Rais'd against the Treaty of Partition, was one of the Principal Arguments that brought some People to approve of this War.'[65] Even if few were actually convinced, many of William's enemies must have been becoming confused about the grounds of their hostility.

The question of the Spanish Succession had for the time being stolen the limelight from the equally important one of the English Succession.[66] William, a childless widower who had resisted all suggestions of remarriage, was now, though by no means an old man, in failing health. The next in line, Princess Anne, though not yet forty, also suffered from indifferent health. Despite her seventeen pregnancies, only one child of her marriage to Prince George of Denmark had survived early infancy — William, Duke of Gloucester, whose death on 30 July 1700 at the age of ten had left his mother as the only recognised successor to the throne. The former King James II, now in exile at St Germain, was in his late sixties; but he had a twelve-year-old son, James Edward, for the Jacobites to pin their hopes upon. It was thus important to secure the Protestant Succession without delay. The nearest alternative line also suffered from the disadvantage of being Roman Catholic. This was the House of Savoy, Victor Amadeus II having married Anna Maria, daughter of Charles II's daughter Henrietta and her husband the Duke of Orleans. It was thought that as the price of having one of the princes of the House of Savoy named as heir to the English throne, his parents would agree to have him brought up as a Protestant. William, however, had already decided to climb further back down the family tree to find a branch that was soundly Protestant. James I's daughter Elizabeth had married Frederick, the Elector Palatine, whose support for the Protestant cause had brought about the Thirty Years' War in Germany. Their daughter Sophia was now dowager Electress of Hanover, and her son George, Elector of Hanover since 1692, was a Lutheran Protestant who had staunchly resisted the ambitions of Louis XIV. It was upon this family that William's choice fell.

He well knew that his actions were so suspect to most of those active in politics that some finesse would be necessary to make his choice generally acceptable. Defoe mentions once telling the King of the wild ideas he had heard, that William was thinking of resigning his throne to the exiled James II; to which William replied with a smile that they must credit him either with very dull or very deep thoughts.[67] The latter was nearer the mark, as appears from the evidence of Alexander Cunningham, a Scot who was, like Defoe, secretly in William's service at this time:

> That he might prevail with the Princess to agree to the entail of the inheritance, he was not displeased to have a rumour spread, as if he was about to make the cession of the crown to another. He would also hold discourse in public concerning King James and his son; and inquire of those who came from abroad about the person and parts of the boy, and whether he was not a promising youth. The Princess Anne, hearing these things, and fearing that King William should resign his Kingdom and restore it to King James and his son, easily agreed with him about the substitution of heirs; but the

agreement was necessary to be kept secret until the opinion
of all the members of parliament could be known.[68]

The manipulation of opinion 'without doors' was Defoe's territory; and he helped to ensure that there was little effective
Jacobite opinion, even among the Tories, by a recently identified
tract: *An Argument, Shewing, That the Prince of Wales, Tho' a
Protestant, Has no Just Pretensions to the Crown of England.
With some Remarks on the late pretended Discovery of a Design
to steal him away.*[69]

But his best-known — and for long his only known — tract on
the Succession question is at first sight very baffling. In *The
Succession to the Crown of England, Consider'd*, which probably
appeared about February 1701, he cautiously advanced the
claims of a most improbable candidate: the Earl of Dalkeith,
son of the Duke of Monmouth.[70] Even if this had not been
quite contrary to William's thinking, Defoe must have known
that Dalkeith's claims could not be taken seriously. Presumably
this was a manoeuvre, with William's approval, to ease the
acceptance of the Hanoverian succession by drawing attention
to other and worse alternatives which would have excluded
Anne from the succession altogether. It is noteworthy too that,
even when pretending to urge the claims of Dalkeith, Defoe
acknowledged that the Hanoverians had a much stronger claim
than any other foreign dynasty.

Defoe's tract provoked a reply: *Animadversions on the Succession to the Crown of England Consider'd*, from an author
who had no difficulty in disposing of the case for Dalkeith, and
who argued strenuously in favour of the Hanoverians; who
yet found himself with suspicious frequency forced to agree
with the author whom he was attacking, and whose prose
rhythms and turns of phrase unmistakably identify him as
Defoe.[71] In a characteristic passage, he attacks the claims of the
Duchess of Savoy:

> In short, she's a *French* Branch engrafted into an *Italian*
> Stock, a Bigot to the Religion she has been unhappily brought
> up in, Imperious in her Temper from the Air she draws in,
> where she resides: and we have had such a melancholy knowl-
> edge of a *Trans-Alpinian* Constitution in the late Reign, that
> we have no great Encouragement to send beyond those

Snowy Mountains for a Queen to Rule us, *more Sabaudiano*,
i.e. by Fire and Faggot, and the most dreadful Persecutions.

The original tract must have been an Aunt Sally, set up as a
target for this reply. Further, the *Animadversions* identifies the
original author as 'the Gentleman who oblig'd his Countrymen
sometime since with the True-Born Englishman'. Defoe was
thus publicly designated as the author of the *Succession to the
Crown of England Consider'd*, an advocate of the claims of
Dalkeith, at a time when William had already committed himself
to the Hanoverians. He was thus shielded from any suspicion
that he was William's agent in this, or any other of his political
activities. The success of the ruse can be seen from the gibe in
The True-Born Hugonot (1703):

> Since *Hannover* the Nations Votes has won,
> And he dares speak no more for *Monmouth's Son*.[72]

At all events, the Hanoverian Succession was accepted by
Parliament without friction. In a rare display of outward
harmony, the motion was introduced in March by a Whig and a
Tory, and the Bill passed the Commons, *nemine contradicente*,
on 14 May, though the House was bitterly divided on other
issues. It is true that the Bill was loaded with clauses restricting
the powers of future monarchs, particularly those of foreign
birth. William swallowed the implied insult without a murmur,
and on 12 June royal assent was given to the Act of Settlement.
Perhaps it was in this connection that Defoe described how men
'laughed . . . at King *William*, and said that he durst not shew
any Resentment, was afraid to be angry, and the like'.[73] No
doubt the unanimous approval of the Hanoverian Settlement
outweighed all other considerations in his mind. Defoe wrote
later 'of the King my Master, who I have had the Honour very
often to hear express himself with great satisfaction, in having
brought the Settlement of the Succession to so good an Issue'.[74]
Despite the general agreement on the Hanoverian Succession,
and the gradual shift of opinion against Louis XIV, the temper
of the House was still unsatisfactory. Instead of making haste to
vote the supplies that William needed, they continued their
acrimonious inquest into the Partition Treaty, voting to impeach
not only Portland, the chief negotiator, but also Halifax, Orford

and Somers. Sir Christopher Wren now constructed funnels to carry the heat away from the House — not an ironic comment on the rising political temperature, but a recognition that the session would inevitably continue into the summer.[75] From the point of view of William, and of Defoe, the Commons were now completely out of hand.

This was the background to a return to the shock tactics which had been used at the beginning of the session. But this time it was with a difference; and an attempt was made to bring the pressure of public opinion to bear upon the Commons. On 29 April the magistrates of Kent met at Maidstone for the Quarter Sessions. According to Defoe's account, William Colepeper Esquire of Hollingbourne, having been elected chairman, was approached by several of the principal freeholders of the County to acquaint Parliament with the apprehensions of the people regarding a French invasion. Colepeper referred the matter to the Grand Jury, at whose request he drew up a petition — respectfully urging the Commons to lay aside their heats and animosities, and to turn their loyal addresses into votes of supply before it was too late.[76] This picture of a spontaneous upsurge of public anxiety is balanced by that of a Tory pamphleteer, who linked the whole campaign with Defoe's tract of two months earlier:

> The Malecontents in *London*, having joyn'd their wise Heads with some of the same Stamp in *Kent*, and contrived to form the Scene, out comes a Brisk Pamphlet, entitul'd *A Letter from Kent* to a *Member of Parliament* . . . This put the *Kentish*-men into a *Fright*, the *Fright* into a *Frenzy*, and all, as the Design was laid, run mad upon *petitioning* the Parliament to raise Forces to Guard their *Hop-Grounds* and *Cherry-Orchards* . . .
> . . . The *Chairman* having his Cue, refers the *Party* Complaints to the *Grand-Jury*; the *Grand-Jury* agree, and desire the Chairman to write them a petition: He very gravely retires to Word *A Petition that had been sent down from* London in his Verbis, *five Days before the Sessions at Maidstone: The Truth of which, there are not a very few Gentlemen in Town can attest.*[77]

No doubt there is truth in both versions. There is no smoke

without fire, but it is more evident when interested parties are fanning the flames and providing vents for it to escape. In view of the sequel, perhaps the Kentish Petition, too, was actually drafted by Defoe.

William Colepeper, accompanied by his younger brother Thomas, with Justinian Champneys, David Polhill and William Hamilton, Esquires, all young men of Whig sympathies, now went to Westminster, where one of the Kentish members reluctantly agreed to present the petition on 8 May. Later the same day Mr Secretary Hedges, by order of the King, delivered to the Commons a letter, genuine this time, from the States General, stating that they were in great danger from the French and requesting assistance in ships and troops according to the treaty of 1678. Predictably, the House reacted sharply to this double thrust, and the irrepressible Jack Howe complained that 'the King, the Dutch and the Kentishmen were all in a plot against the House of Commons'.[78] The Petition was voted scandalous, insolent and seditious; the petitioners were committed to the Gatehouse prison, and they were to remain in custody until the end of the session nearly seven weeks later. According to Defoe, but for the rough treatment meted out to the 'Kentish Worthies', there would have been further petitions; and to this extent the severity of the Commons achieved its object. But it may only have provoked a change of tactics.

On 15 May the Speaker, Robert Harley, received the famous document called the *Legion Letter*, or *Legion's Memorial*, attacking the Commons, in a deliberately insolent and provocative tone, in the name of the electors as a whole. Written by Defoe, 'in a hand that stood the wrong way', it was also soon printed and widely distributed.[79] He recounts; 'It was said that it was delivered to the Speaker by a woman. But I have been informed since, that it was a mistake; and that it was delivered by the person who wrote it, guarded about with sixteen Gentlemen of Quality, who if any notice had been taken of him, were ready to have carried him off by force.'[80] It is tempting to imagine a dramatic confrontation between Defoe and his future patron, Harley — once a Whig himself, now building a new Tory party from the various anti-Williamite factions, but already beginning to have misgivings about some of his more extreme allies. There was a tradition in the family of one of the Kentish Petitioners, David Polhill, that Defoe had indeed delivered the letter himself, disguised as a woman.[81] This would reduce the confrontation to the farcical level of Charley's Aunt. There seems no reason for Defoe to expose himself unnecessarily by coming face to face with the Speaker; and Luttrell's statement seems very credible, that the *Memorial* was found in the box of members' letters[82] — but placed there no doubt by Defoe in a woman's disguise, with sixteen gentlemen in the background, ready to rescue him, 'if any notice had been taken of him'.

When Harley read the covering letter, he can hardly have believed his eyes. It ran:

> Mr. Speaker — The enclosed Memorial you are charged with in behalf of many thousands of the good people of England. There is neither Papist, Jacobite, seditious, court, or party interest concerned in it, but honesty and truth. You are commanded by 200,000 Englishmen to deliver it to the House of Commons, and to inform them that it is no banter, but serious truth, and a serious regard to it is expected. Nothing but justice and their duty is required, and it is required by them who have both a right to require and power to compel, viz. the People of England. We would have come to the House strong enough to oblige them to hear us; but we have avoided tumult, not desiring to embroil, but to save our native country. If you refuse to communicate it to them, you will find cause in a short time to repent it.

The enclosed 'Memorial', addressed the 'Knights, Citizens, and Burgesses, in Parliament Assembled' in tones no less peremptory. They were told, for instance, that

> . . . though there are no stated proceedings to bring you to your duty, yet the great law of reason says, and all nations allow, that whatever power is above the law, is burthensome and tyrannical, and may be reduced by extra-judicial methods. You are not above the people's resentments: they that made you members, may reduce you to the same rank from whence they chose you, and may give you a taste of their abused kindness in terms you may not be pleased with.

The Commons were accused, amongst other things, of the illegal imprisonment of the Kentish Petitioners; 'voting the Treaty of Partition fatal to Europe, because it gave so much of the Spanish dominions to France, and not concerning yourselves to prevent their taking possession of it all'; 'addressing the King to displace his friends upon bare surmises'; 'delaying the proceedings upon capital impeachment, to blast the reputations of persons, without proving the fact'; 'suffering saucy and indecent reproaches upon his Majesty's person . . . by that impudent scandal of parliaments, John Howe'; 'neglecting to pay the nation's debts'; 'neglecting the great work of Reformation of Manners'; and finally, 'being scandalously vicious yourselves, both in your morals and religion, lewd in life and erroneous in doctrine'. Then, having told the Commons how to remedy these abuses, he concluded:

> Thus, gentlemen, you have had your duty laid before you, which 'tis hoped you will think of; but, if you continue to neglect it, you may expect to be treated according to the resentment of an injured nation; for Englishmen are no more to be slaves to Parliament than to Kings.
> Our name is LEGION, for we are many.

The effect of *Legion's Memorial* was even more electric than that of the Kentish Petition. The three tailors of Tooley Street were to become a laughing stock when they began their manifesto, 'We, the people of England'; but when Defoe signed his 'Memorial', 'LEGION, for we are many', no one laughed. The Commons asked the King to take care of the public peace, but there was no obvious culprit to victimise. Though the authorship was soon an open secret, proof was lacking; and several years later it was still possible for Defoe formally to deny it.[83] He followed it up soon afterwards with a ballad without a title, but similar in style to the *Encomium* in which he had attacked the previous Parliament two years before. His opening line, 'Ye True-Born Englishmen proceed' sounds like a defiant acknowledgement of his own authorship.[84] For the most part, it repeated in verse form the content of *Legion's Memorial*, and continued with comments upon the impact the latter had made:

> A strange Memorial too there came,
> Your Members to affront,
> Which told you Truths you dare not name
> And so the Paper 'scaped the Flame
> Or else it had been burnt.

> Some said the Language was severe
>   And into Passion flew,
> Some too began to curse and swear,
> And call'd the Author Mutinere,
>   But all men said 'twas true.
>
> But oh! the Consternation now
>   In which you all appear!
> 'Tis plain from whence your terrours flew
> For had your guilt been less you knew
>   So would have been your fear.
>
> In Fifteen Articles you're told
>   You have our Rights betray'd,
> Banter'd the Nation, bought and sold
> The Liberties you should uphold;
>   No wonder you're afraid.

Defoe even claimed that many Tory members, fearful for their safety in London, began to slip away to their homes in the country.[85] Perhaps this might have happened in any case as the session stretched on into the summer; but Oldmixon gives independent corroboration of the effect of the propaganda campaign:

> Though the 'Kentish Petition' and the 'Legion's Memorial' were seemingly treated with contempt by the Commons, yet there seemed now also some change in their air and language. They thought it policy to make the world believe that they were in the most perfect agreement with his Majesty's councils and conduct, and the most zealous for his honour and interest.[86]

On 12 June they at last reached the point of offering support for the alliances to be made by William with the United Provinces and the Emperor. The impeachments of the Whig Lords collapsed ignominiously when the Commons failed to appear on the appointed day — for there was no effective case to be made against them. At last the necessary supplies were voted, and on 24 June Parliament was prorogued, in an atmosphere of outward but hypocritical harmony.

The end of the session meant the release of the Kentish

Worthies, and maximum party advantage was extracted from this. Nahum Tate, the Poet Laureate, composed a poem in their honour. Their portraits were engraved, over the provocative motto, 'Non patriam auro' — 'They have not sold their country for gold.'[87] On 1 July they were entertained to a noble repast at Mercers Hall by some 200 gentlemen, and several noble Lords and Members of Parliament. According to a Tory account, next to the five Kentish Worthies was placed 'their Secretary of State, the author of the Legion Letter; and one might read the downfall of Parliaments in his very countenance'. The same author adds that

> . . . fame had brought a numerous crowd to be spectators. The journeymen and apprentices ran for one whole day from their masters. This was even as bad as a Lord Mayor's show . . . The most dissenting squeamish stomach could drink off its glass to the health of *Cinque Quatre*, i.e. to the five Kentish worthies and the four impeached Lords. It was resolved *nemine contradicente*, that the Parliament should be dissolved, and that the five worthies should be chosen in the next Parliament; two of them for the county, and the others for the most considerable corporations in Kent.[88]

The next day the Petitioners returned in triumph to their country houses. At Blackheath 500 mounted men waited to escort Polhill to Otford, while the rest of the party went on by way of Rochester to Maidstone. Defoe, who was with them, reports that there were bonfires that night, and enthusiastic shouts of 'A Colepeper! A Colepeper!' The Whigs set about using the affair as a springboard for a political counter-attack on a broad front; and Defoe kept it before the public with his *History of the Kentish Petition*.[89] During the late summer and autumn a series of addresses began to flow in from the counties calling for new elections, addresses which Defoe called 'the legitimate offspring of the *Kentish*-Petition'.[90] Whether he was personally involved is uncertain; but he did once claim that his service for William had involved him in travel throughout the country.[91]

A Tory pamphleteer complained that 'the *Mongrel Whigs* . . . were at the middle and both ends of this conspiracy against the House of Commons'[92] In fact the Whigs were only at one end;

at the other was King William; and in the middle was Defoe. This must have been the great secret which Defoe prided himself on never revealing — when, for instance he called himself 'this despicable thing, who scorn'd to come out of Newgate at the Price of Betraying a Dead Master'.[93] The whole episode fills a curious place in the history of public opinion as a political force; between, on the one hand, the activities of Pym and Shaftesbury, who had used it to strengthen their parliamentary base against the crown; and, on the other hand, those of Wilkes, who was foolhardy enough to challenge both King and Parliament. Here the King was in league with his former ministers to stir up opinion against the House of Commons, and to undermine those who were in office. This strange and rather furtive alliance between King and public against the Commons could only be a passing phase, appropriate to an uneasy stage in the nation's constitutional development, when the King had at last realised the necessity of choosing ministers acceptable to the majority of the House of Commons, but was still determined to keep control of policy in his own hands, and was ready to look elsewhere for advice.

On 10 September, Sunderland, the timid intriguer whose political judgment William valued, received a letter from the King in Holland, asking for such advice. Sunderland replied the next day, advising him to return to England without delay, to send for Somers and appoint a Whig ministry. On 15 September Sunderland wrote to Somers, enclosing William's letter and his reply, and discussing the best means of re-establishing the Whigs in power. He set high store by political propaganda:

> Among all the pamphlets which are come out, there ought to have been one, to have particularly explained the proceedings of the present Ministry which began at the King's return last year from Holland. The breaking the last Parliament; the late meeting of this; the care which was taken by them and their friends upon the death of the King of Spain to persuade the World that all was well, and that a war would undo us; how, by this management the French possessed themselves of Flanders, before the meeting of the Parliament; which was thought of so little importance in England, as not to be worth mentioning in the King's speech; all of which disheartened so our allies abroad, that the King of Portugal, despairing,

made a Treaty with France; and many Princes besides, thought it best to be neuter. The late meeting of the Parliament made it impracticable for England to be any use abroad this year either by Sea or Land, there not being time to conclude treaties with the Emperor and other Princes, without which war could not be declared.

When Somers replied on 20 September, he reported: 'A thing of that nature has been promised.' Writing again, on 1 October, Sunderland returned to the subject: 'but it is thought that nothing will be done without such a paper as has been before wished for'. Finally on 3 October Somers wrote: 'The paper desired would certainly have a good effect. It was promised, and it is believed to be ready printed. But for some reasons which the writer conceals, it has not yet appeared; and there is a doubt when it will.' The tract in question has not been identified, and seems never to have appeared at all.[94]

The independent-minded writer, whose contribution was looked on as so vital to the Whig cause, and whose support might be 'wished for' but not commanded, can only have been Defoe. He was now becoming known as the 'secretary of the Party'; and the political campaign with which he had been associated for several months would have been impossible without the organisation controlled by the Whig party managers; Somers's nominees still filled the county lieutenancies and magistrates' benches. On the other hand, Defoe would never have embarked on any major political manoeuvre without William's approval. But to suppose that the latter was working hand in glove with the Whig leaders to undermine the Tory ministers he had so recently installed in office would be an over-simplification. A campaign in favour of the Whigs might help to get William off the Tory hook; but he was no more anxious to be a prisoner of the Whigs than of the Tories. Reading between the lines of the circumspect references in the Sunderland—Somers correspondence, it seems clear that the Whig leaders knew well enough where Defoe's first allegiance lay, and that neither he nor the King was committed without qualification to the Whig cause. The withdrawal of the tract intended to expose the proceedings of the Tory ministers suggests that about the end of September Defoe had either received fresh instructions from William in Holland, or had changed his line in accordance with a previously

agreed policy of trimming the ship.[95] The emphasis was now to
be upon the 'allaying of party heats', and an attempt to achieve
some measure of national unity. In fact, if the Tories had been
prepared to drop the impeachments, William might have been
prepared to continue with the existing Parliament and keep
them in office. Such a pamphlet as Sunderland envisaged would
have helped to bring back the Whigs into power, but would
certainly have inflamed party feelings; and William's poor
health and Princess Anne's Tory sympathies pointed to yet
another political convulsion to come.

Developments overseas form the background to this change
of course. On the last day of June William had sailed for Holland,
free at last to negotiate alliances with the full approval of
Parliament. He had taken the Duke of Marlborough with him,
thus protecting himself from the charge of employing foreigners
to negotiate treaties where England's vital interests were at
stake. Negotiations had run smoothly, and on 27 August (7
September N.S.) the representatives of England, the United
Provinces and the Empire signed at the Hague what became
known as the Treaty of the Grand Alliance.[96] Since William had
been forced by his weak diplomatic position earlier in the year
to recognise Louis's grandson Philip as King of Spain, he could
not support the claim of the Habsburg Archduke Charles to
the whole of the Spanish inheritance, even if he had been willing
to do so. The allies however would insist on an undertaking
from Louis that the crowns of Spain and France would never be
united; the Emperor was to receive 'compensation' for his claims
to the Spanish throne, and was to gain the Spanish possessions
in Italy and the Netherlands; while England and the United
Provinces might retain whatever they could occupy of the
Spanish possessions in the New World. In Defoe's words, 'his
Majesty had a Partition Treaty in his view, even in the Grand
Alliance'.[97] He was still seeking to maintain the balance of
power, even after events had forced him into the opposite pan
of the diplomatic scales; and just as in the second Partition
Treaty he had insisted on two months for further negotiations
with Leopold, so now he insisted on two months for further
negotiations with Louis. These in fact never took place.

On 5 September (16 September N.S.) the exiled James II had
died at St Germain; and Louis, perhaps motivated by a quixotic
sympathy for the ex-King's family, recognised his thirteen-year-

old son as James III of England. As soon as William heard of
this breach of the Treaty of Ryswick he withdrew his ambassador from Paris and abandoned his intended negotiations. The
effect on opinion in England was equally dramatic. What Louis
had failed to do when he had accepted the Spanish throne for
his grandson, or sent French troops into the Barrier fortresses,
he achieved when he seemed to be choosing a king for England.
Addresses began to pour in, complaining of the French King's
bad faith, and urging an immediate declaration of war. Within
less than twelve months the current of opinion, which Defoe
had struggled so painstakingly and cunningly to divert, had
completely reversed direction. Whereupon, who should reappear
on the scene, once more struggling manfully against the current,
but Defoe? *The Present State of Jacobitism Consider'd*, one of
the few tracts which he acknowledged with his initials, minimised
the significance of Louis's action.[98] Again, in *Reasons against a
War with France*, he argued that only active support for the
Pretender would constitute a breach of the Treaty of Ryswick,
and he respectfully suggested that William had been too hasty
in withdrawing his ambassador without allowing Louis time to
make amends. We should only go to war with France if forced
to do so by a breach of the balance of power. If we had a
quarrel with anyone, it was with Spain, for accepting a Bourbon
ruler; and we might well fight to our advantage against Spain in
America. If Flanders must be recovered, this could best be
achieved as part of a bargain at the end of the war.[99] What is to
be made of this piece of special pleading, which contradicted
the whole tenor of Defoe's propaganda over the previous twelve
months, and which a far less able pamphleteer than he could
have demolished with ease? Was William, appearances to the
contrary notwithstanding, still pinning his hopes on negotiations
rather than war? The Emperor certainly feared that he might do
a deal with Louis. When in November the French occupied
Cologne, William refused Leopold's request for an immediate
declaration of war. But this was because Dutch preparations
were not yet complete and the English Parliament was not yet
pledged to fulfil the obligations of the recent treaty. In other
words, William was still paying the price of Parliament's dilatori-
ness over the previous twelve months. If the sudden war fever
in England forced a declaration of war before we were ready,
Louis might seize the tactical advantage and threaten the United

Provinces before England could effectively intervene. That it was all a matter of timing appears from the opening words of Defoe's tract:

> Of all the Nations in the World there is none I know of, so Entirely Govern'd by their humour as the *English*. There's no more to do to make way for any General undertaking, than by some wonderful Surprise to Rouse the Fancy of the People, and *away they go with it*, like Hounds on a full Cry, till they overrun it, and then they are at a Halt, and will run back as fast as they came on.

Three years later, in another of his parliamentary ballads, he attacked the attitude of the Tories to William's policies:

> Your want of Temper to the last
>   Did his Designs Defeat,
> Always too slow or else too fast
> Too backward, or in too much haste,
>   Too cold or else too hot.[100]

That William was now fully committed to war, at the right moment, seems clear from another important tract written in his interest, which must have appeared late in October or early in November. *Anguis in Herba*, full of characteristic Defoe expressions — the very title was one of his favourite Latin tags — chimes in exactly with his political position at this time.[101] The tract sought first to show that Louis XIV had aimed consistently at universal monarchy, concealing his aims, taking advantage of divisions between his opponents, and making and breaking treaties as it suited his interests. It next argued that his immediate difficulties would almost certainly produce a diplomatic initiative during the coming winter, whose only real purpose would be to disrupt the Grand Alliance; and that the steadfastness shown by the Empire and the Dutch, together with the bitter divisions in England, made the latter the inevitable target for such an initiative. It went on to discuss in detail any conceivable terms that Louis might offer, all of which would turn out to England's disadvantage. The conclusion then must be: '. . . let us heartily enter the War and depend on God for Success'. The aim, then, was to hold volatile public opinion steady on its belligerent course. Controversial party issues, if touched on at all, were handled in a non-provocative manner. Thus it was only mildly hinted that the unsatisfactory terms of the Partition Treaty were themselves the outcome of Parliament's action in reducing the standing army to a mere token force. Ostensibly written to appeal to those who had been anti-Williamite on all the divisive issues of the last four years, one of its aims was to instil at least a measure of understanding of the opposite point of view, and help to heal party differences. The hope was expressed that the unanimity of public opinion and the revived prestige of the King 'may let both Parties see that they have no way left to secure their own Reputation of being those Patriots they each pretend to be, but by heartily concurring' in all measures necessary for the coming war.[102]

William returned to England on 4 November still uncertain what course to take. It was only when the leading Tories refused an undertaking not to renew the impeachments of the Whig Lords, that he finally decided to dissolve Parliament on 11 November and issue writs for a new election. Godolphin at once resigned from the Treasury in protest, but others remained obstinately in office. Nor was William yet in a position to bring back Somers and Halifax, even if he had wished to do so. For the time being everything had to wait upon the results of the election, scarcely the best time for the parties to 'concur heartily'. The Whigs circulated a Black List of 167 Tories whose record they claimed was specially objectionable. Defoe was sometimes accused of being concerned in this, but he always denied it, warmly repudiating any such descent into personalities, which might involve insinuations which could not be substantiated.[103] *England's Late Jury*, however, a more selective attack upon twelve of those who had been most prominent in attacking William's policies, was in the same ballad metre that Defoe had used twice before for satires upon the Commons, and one stanza actually appears to have been reworked from the salvo he had fired at them in June.[104] About *Legion's New Paper* at least there can be no doubt. Here, without naming names, he renewed the attack on the outgoing House of Commons which he had made in *Legion's Memorial*, once more vigorously repudiating them in the name of the electors of England; for ' 'tis for your Sakes that is come to pass in *England* which was never heard of before, that the people should have recourse to the *King* to save them from being undone by the *Parliament'*.[105]

A more constructive contribution to the election battle came from 'the Author of, *The Duke of Anjou's Succession consider'd*' who we have already found reason to believe was Defoe. This was *The Dangers of Europe, from the Growing Power of France. With some Free Thoughts on Remedies. And Particularly on the cure of our DIVISIONS at Home: In Order to a Successful WAR abroad, against the French king and his Allies.*[106] Maintaining his criticism of the late Parliament, he justified its dissolution because of the disputes which so bitterly divided it; and told the electors that 'since the King hath graciously done his part, it's now incumbent upon the Nation to act theirs, in chusing such Men as will readily concur in what they would have had the late House of Commons do'. But he did his best to play down party issues:

> We have greater Concerns to mind than, whether the Whiggs or Tories shall be uppermost in Court or Parliament . . .
>
> It's things and not Men and Parties, that we must now have our Eye upon. We ought to be seeking for Expedients of Union, and not to spend our time in raking into past faults of Persons and Parties, which can have no other Issue, but to heighten our Divisions.

The storms of the previous session had given rise not only to bitter party warfare, but also to a more dignified debate on important constitutional issues, involving the relations between the two Houses, the right of petitioning, and the right of the Commons to order imprisonment without trial. One contribution, from a Welsh MP, Sir Humphrey Mackworth, and entitled *A Vindication of the Rights of the Commons of England*, drew a reply from Defoe: *The Original Power of the Collective Body of the People of England, Examined and Asserted.*[107] Apparently written before the dissolution, it was not published until 27 December, when the election was over. A dedication to the King, and the appearance of the initials, D. F., suggest that this was no ephemeral political tract, but was meant as a serious contribution to political thought. Compared with his *Reflections upon the Late Great Revolution* of a dozen years before, the differences are mainly ones of emphasis. The theological basis of the argument reappears, but in a more perfunctory way; and he now lays more stress on 'reason . . . the test and touch-stone of the laws'. He now contests the extravagant claims made, not on behalf of monarchs, but of the Commons. The original source of political authority is the people, who have a right to resume it to themselves if it is abused. However, he introduces a curious qualification, which he was often to repeat, without ever fully justifying it:

> I do not place this Right upon the Inhabitants, but upon the *Freeholders*; the *Freeholders* are the proper Owners of the Country: It is their own, and the other Inhabitants are but Sojourners, like Lodgers in a House, and ought to be subject to such Laws as the Freeholders impose upon them, or else must remove; because the Freeholders have a Right to the Land, and the other have no right to live there but upon sufferance.[108]

Defoe never followed up his apotheosis of the English free-holder with a thorough-going attack on the electoral system which represented him so imperfectly. From time to time throughout his writings he sniped at many of the features which a century later were to become the targets of radical criticism — bribery and corruption, drunkenness, intimidation and rioting at elections, the scandal of the decayed boroughs. Yet he never systematised his attacks, still less suggested any scheme for remodelling the parliamentary system, even as a hypothetical project. Defoe's radicalism, such as it was, was only a passing phase, hastily adopted to meet the situation of 1701, and equally quickly laid down. A more representative system might, in fact, have produced a more acceptable result in the election then just over. The counties and corporation boroughs for the most part returned Whigs; but the Tories still held sway in most of the smaller boroughs, and the parties in the new House of Commons would be delicately balanced.

When the new Parliament met on 30 December, William addressed it with an unusually long, powerful and effective speech. Shortly before this Sunderland had written to Somers: 'It would be well for the King to give order to two of his Cabinet to prepare the Speech, as the Duke of Devonshire and Secretary Vernon, and bid them consult in private Lord Somers, rather than bring to the Cabinet a speech already made.'[109] Despite this, it may well be that it was actually written, perhaps in consultation with Somers, by the man whose pen had so brilliantly served William's cause during the past year or so.[110] The speech began by stressing the 'high indignity' offered to William himself and to the whole nation, when Louis XIV had recognised the Pretender as James III; it went on to refer to the dangers to English commerce which flowed from the presence of a grandson of the French King on the Spanish throne; it pointed out how the eyes of all Europe were upon this Parliament, and 'all matters at a standstill until their resolution was known'. It continued:

> Therefore no time ought to be lost; you have an opportunity, by God's blessing, to secure to you and your posterity the quiet enjoyment of your religion and liberties, if you are not wanting to yourselves, but will exert the ancient vigour of the English nation; but I tell you plainly my opinion is, if you do not lay hold on this occasion you have no reason to hope for another.

The peroration urged them to lay aside 'the unhappy fatal animosities' which had divided and weakened them:

> Let me conjure you to disappoint the only hope of our enemies by your unanimity. I have shown, and will always show, how desirous I am to be the common father of my people; do you in like manner lay aside your parties and divisions; let there be no distinction heard of among us in future but of those who are for the Protestant religion and the present Establishment, and of those who mean a Popish prince and a French Government.

Not only did this speech play skilfully upon many strings which Defoe had touched in his recent tracts, but he several times recalled it in future years — once as 'that Honourable Speech which Graces our Houses now, as the best Picture an *English Heart can look on'*, and on another occasion declaring it to be 'justly celebrated, as the greatest, the best and most Emphatical Speech that ever Prince made'.[111] It is difficult not to feel that the speech *ought*, at least, to have been written by Defoe, a fitting climax to a brilliantly successful propaganda campaign.

Despite continued strong party feeling in the new House of Commons, there was at least a general consensus on the need for war; and the House, in response to William's appeal, pressed on without delay with the steps necessary for England to play her part in the next campaigning season.

Defoe could now lay down his pen, and for the first time for many months turn to his own affairs; and this easing of the breakneck momentum provides a breathing-space to consider his private circumstances. His house was somewhere in the large parish of Hackney, Middlesex, a few miles north of London, possibly in the hamlet of Kingsland to which he had removed eight or nine years before, after his bankruptcy; and he may still have been living with his mother-in-law, Joan Tuffley, and his brother-in-law, Samuel Tuffley. After eighteen years of married life he and his wife Mary now had six surviving children. Only the eldest, Maria, can yet have been in her teens. Then followed Hannah, Benjamin, Henrietta and Daniel, probably in that order. The youngest of all had been baptised in Hackney parish church on 24 December 1701, and named Sophia, perhaps after the Electress Dowager of Hanover who now stood second in the line of succession to the throne. We have no explanation for this piece of 'occasional conformity'; none of his other children is known to have had a church baptism. Presumably he was a regular member of some Presbyterian congregation, but it is not known whose meeting house he attended after the death of Samuel Annesley five years earlier. His views on Sabbath-keeping were strict. He considered that the worst blemish on King William's reign was an Act authorising coachmen to ply for hire on Sundays;[112] and he himself is never known to have written a letter on that day. How strictly he was able to observe his Sabbatarian principles under the exceptional pressures of the first six months of 1701 may be doubted. Nor is it likely that he was able, as head of the family, to conduct the daily Bible readings and impose the steady Christian discipline which he was later to recommend in *The Family Instructor*. He can have had little time to spare for his children; and the rest of his household must have found him a remote and baffling figure — spending long hours in his book-lined study scribbling they knew not what, and then disappearing abruptly for hours or days on end to unknown destinations, so that even 'his own *Coachman* knew not where he lodg'd'.[113] Nor could he have divided his time exclusively between his own study and 'the Closet of a King'.[114] He certainly maintained contact with the leading Whig statesmen. He had also to devise a safe means of communication with the printers and publishers of his tracts. He later told Harley how he had dealt with Robert Stephens, or 'Robin Hog', the fat and corrupt Messenger of the Press, who acted as the Secretary of State's agent in dealing with the book-sellers, and who usually took care to interpret his duties in a Tory spirit: 'His being a Rogue was Usefull to me, and I brib'd him allways to my Advantage.'[115] He knew too how to keep his own counsel: 'I have Learnt in all these things', he wrote, 'to make Agents without Acquainting them with Particulars.'[116] But his value to William depended on his ability to keep his finger on the pulse of public opinion; and this meant mixing freely among men of widely differing views, on the Exchange and in the coffeee-houses. He also declared that his service for William had involved him in travel throughout England, though it is difficult to see when he could have fitted it in — except perhaps in July and August 1701 during the campaign of ad-dresses urging the dissolution of Parliament.[117] There is no direct evidence that he went further afield than Maidstone.

He must also have found time to supervise his brick-and-tile works near Tilbury, his steadiest source of income, bringing him in some £600 a year. Though he told Harley that 'all the King's bounty to me was expended there', some must also have gone directly towards satisfying his creditors.[118] He claimed that in about ten years he reduced his debts, 'uncompounded', from £17,000 to little more than £5000; and only a little of this can be accounted for from his known resources.[119] Perhaps some of the gap was filled by the realisation of assets, and he must have received douceurs from the Whigs; but for the short while his service lasted, his main benefactor must have been the King, 'by whom I was beyond my merit bountifully rewarded'.[120] A few more years of such service would have seen his remaining debts paid off, for he still had plenty to offer his royal master.

By Article 6 of the Grand Alliance, England and Holland were entitled to keep whatever they could seize of the Spanish Empire in America; and Defoe had already suggested in *Reasons against a War with France* that this should be our major war objective.[121] Defoe the projector was ready with schemes for putting this idea into effect. One such scheme, perhaps based on Raleigh's unsuccessful quest for Eldorado, was to develop Guiana, the land around and to the south-east of the 'River Oroonoque'. Addressing the South Sea Company in 1719, he offered 'to lay before them a plan or chart of the rivers and shores, the depths of the water, and all necessary instructions for the navigation, with a scheme of the undertaking, which he had the honour about thirty years ago to lay before King William, and to demonstrate how easy it would be to bring the attempt to perfection'.[122] Though 'about thirty years ago' would take us back to the beginning of William's reign, such a project would make most sense in the context of a projected war with Spain, as was the situation in the early months of 1702. In any case the idea was not taken up. Several generations were to pass before there was any effective British colonisation in this area; while Defoe had to make do with the fantasy colony planted by Robinson Crusoe on his nameless offshore island near the mouth of the Orinoco.

His most original project was a proposal to send an expedition into the Pacific to seize the Spanish colony of Chile, which was too remote from the centre of their power in the New World to be easily defensible. The capital should be established at Valdivia, in the middle of a fruitful country which would yield rice, cocoa, wine, and further north, sugar and spices. The natives, who hated the Spaniards, would gladly accept our manufactures in return for gold, in which 'the Wealth of the Place', he declared, was 'Incredible'. A sister colony on the Atlantic coast would provide corn and cattle for the main colony, as well as a convenient port of call for ships before they passed through the Magellan Straits. Though 2000 miles apart by sea, the colonies could be linked by a postal service across the Andes, covering the 360 miles in about eight days. When he tried to interest Harley in the scheme ten years later, he assured him that 'No Eye Ever Saw the Drafft Except his Late Majtie and the Earle of Portland, and the Originalls were allways in My Own Hand'.[123] His knowledge of the country was of course entirely derivative, being based on Sir John Narborough's *Voyages*. In detail his plans were certainly unsound; he was characteristically over-sanguine about the resources of the area, and much of his topography was seriously inaccurate. Yet these schemes, he told Harley, 'the said King Approved Very well, and had Not Death prevented him, had Then Put in Practice'. Fortunately for

Defoe's reputation the project was abandoned; but it retained a powerful hold over his imagination, and more than twenty years later an overland journey from Chile to the Atlantic coast figured prominently in *A New Voyage Round the World*.[124]

An even bolder plan was to attack the Spaniards at the very heart, or rather throat, of their Empire. A force of thirty men-of-war, with some 8000 soldiers, was to be sent to the West Indies, where the help of some 2000 to 3000 buccaneers would be enlisted. The first objective was to seize Havana and gain control of Hispaniola; from this base, the key points on the mainland could be captured, notably Vera Cruz, through which the Mexican trade passed, and Cartagena, the chief port of the Spanish mainland on the southern shores of the Caribbean.[125] Thus the whole trade of the Spanish Empire could be intercepted, without the need of further conquests; thus achieving by English sea-power in wartime what the Scots Darien expedition predictably failed to achieve in time of peace. He added: 'I know there are some Popular Objections to this Attempt, and have heard those Objections debated before one, whose Judgment no Man will dispute.' So, despite 'the unhealthyness of the Country, and the Strength of the Spaniards', the plan seemed likely to go ahead; 'But the King died, between whose Hands this Glorious Scheme was in a fair Way of being concerted, and which, had it gone on, I had the Honour to have been not the first Proposer only, but to have had some Share in the Performance.' In the event, the West Indian expedition under Admiral Benbow was given much more limited objectives, much of the English war effort was diverted to attacks on Spain itself, and we are left to guess at what Defoe's 'Share in the Performance' might have been.

But Defoe cannot have thought that the war would be decided in the New World. He knew well enough that France must be defeated in Europe, and that the decisive theatre would be Flanders, where the bloodiest battles of the previous war had been fought.

> I must own I always thought, that to form a superior Force in *Flanders* to the *French*, and be thereby able to push them from their invincible barrier in *Flanders*, or bring them to a decisive Action there, was *the shortest way* to end this War . . . I have had the Honour to hear the Glorious Deliverer of this unthankful Nation, the abused and forgotten King *William*,

give it not as his Opinion only, but give Reasons for it too strong for any of our Objectors to answer . . .[126]

William's health could no longer stand up to the rigours of active campaigning; but he showed the excellence of his judgment to the end by putting the English forces under the command of the still unproven Duke of Marlborough, of whom he said, according to Defoe, that he had 'a warm heart and a cool head'.[127]

The phrase, 'a warm heart', comes unexpectedly from William; but Defoe seems, as no other Englishman did, to have penetrated the armour of the undemonstrative little King whom he served so devotedly. He told, on various occasions, not only how he had been 'heard', 'trusted', 'valued' and 'esteemed', but even, 'if I may say it with humblest acknowledgements beloved by that glorious Prince'.[128] He asserted from his own knowledge that he was 'a prince of the greatest piety, sincerity and unfeign'd religion'.[129] Sometimes William 'smiled' at what Defoe had to tell him, but more often he 'sighed'; for, 'After he was King of *England*, I am his witness that I have heard him say, He never compleatly enjoy'd himself, nor indeed, can I say, he ever had a happy hour.'[130] As Defoe observed with concern his royal master's failing powers, he came to believe that 'the grief of being tyed up, disappointed and suspected by a Nation he had done so much for, went very near his Heart, and hasten'd the fatal force of his other Infirmities to shorten his Life'.[131]

On 21 February William was riding near Hampton Court, when his horse, Sorrel, stumbled over a molehill. He was thrown and broke his collar-bone. He seemed to be making a good recovery, but complications set in which he had no reserves of strength to resist, and on 9 March 1702 he died. Defoe's sense of personal loss was no less for having been long anticipated. Three years later he wrote bitterly of how William's enemies had treated 'the late KING, to whom we owe . . . our Laws, our Religion, and our very being; I say, *by these Practices*, they had almost worn out his Weak Body, and more Vigorous Spirit, and almost broke his Heart, (for *their* Untoward and Ungrateful Behaviour contributed to *his End*, much more than did his FALL)'.[132] For Defoe, the rest of his life was really an anti-climax, and he never tired of recalling the memory of 'my dear and glorious master' — 'the best of Monarchs, and of Men to me'.[133]

13 Newgate, That Horrid Place!

The accession of Queen Anne saw a sharp change in the political climate. The Junto Whigs, Somers, Halifax and Orford, far from being restored to power, were dismissed from the Privy Council; and most of the principal offices of state passed into the hands of the Tories. The Queen's uncle, Rochester, recovered the post of Lord Lieutenant of Ireland which he had lost towards the end of William's reign; Godolphin returned to the Treasury in the more exalted post of Lord Treasurer; Nottingham, a narrow-minded Anglican, became principal Secretary of State; while elections held in July ensured Tory control of the Commons when Parliament met in the autumn. In one respect however Defoe had done his work well, with some help from Louis XIV. Whigs and Tories were equally determined to check the growing power of France, and war was declared on 4 May 1702. But other signs were less favourable. Though the Queen had declared her intention of maintaining the toleration of Dissenters, she had also expressed a wish to show special favour to the Church of England. A sermon preached at Oxford by Henry Sacheverell, in which he urged the Anglicans to hang out the 'bloody flag' of defiance to the enemies of the Church, served to canalise the feelings pent up by long years of frustration, and seemed to herald a new wave of persecution. Jacobitism once more became articulate, and few cared to remember or honour the dead King.

One of these few was Defoe, who gave vent to his feelings in *The Mock Mourners*, published on 12 May, a heartfelt eulogy of his dead master,[1] best summed up in the couplet:

> Posterity, when Histories relate
> His Glorious Deeds, will ask, *What Giant's that*?

He viewed the future with misgivings:

> Who shall the growing Gallick Force subdue?
> 'Twas more than all the World, but him, could do.

The military genius of Marlborough was still to be demonstrated, and the record of the English nobility inspired little confidence:

> For call'd by Fate to Fight for *Christendom*
> They sent their King abroad, and *staid at Home*.

But most of all he expressed his contempt for the Jacobites:

> But we have here an Ignominious Crowd,
> That boast their Native Birth and *English* Blood,
> Whose Breasts with Envy and Contention burn,
> And now rejoyce when all the Nations mourn:
> Their awkward Triumphs impudently Sing;
> Insult the Ashes of their injur'd King;
> Rejoice at the Disasters of his Crown,
> And Drink the Horse's Health that threw him Down.[2]

It was probably in June that there appeared *A New Test of the Church of England's Loyalty*, in answer to the charge that, whereas 'the Church of England has always brought up her Sons in an unspotted Loyalty and Obedience . . . the very Doctrine of the Dissenter is made up of Principles in their own Nature tending to Confusion and Rebellion'.[3] Writing for once in the person of a Dissenter, Defoe politely but firmly impaled his antagonists on the horns of a dilemma, pointing out that they had abandoned their own principle of non-resistance, by rejecting James II at the Revolution and accepting William III as King: 'crying up themselves for Fools, when we knew they were wiser Men, calling themselves Slaves, but when the Trial came, proving Stubborn, Refractory, *Liberty Mongers*, even as bad as the worst Whig or Phanatick of them all.' This was one of the least equivocal tracts that Defoe ever wrote, perhaps because he was for the time being detached from serving the fortunes of any great figure. He seems to have written nothing at this time on behalf of the Junto Whigs, with whom he had been co-operating during the previous year, and nothing designed to check the swing towards the Tories in the general election in July. He may even have been out of the country.

William's death had meant not only a deeply felt personal loss for Defoe, but also a return to financial insecurity. A volume of gaol records devoted to Fleet Prison appearances contains an enigmatic item:

> 20 May 1702. Dan ffoe before Mr. Justice Blenco to Moore spirited away by ff Southarn and Mottdishe.[4]

Francis Southarn appears to have been some kind of minor official — bailiff's setter, turnkey or constable; and it has been suggested that Defoe had been 'spirited', not out of custody, but into some private place of confinement kept by one Moore. All that can be said is that Defoe must once more have been vulnerable to pressure from his creditors. There may be a reference to this in his account, four years later, of 'A certain U[sure]r, not a mile from Southwark', who held two bonds of 'a very good Friend, and near Relation of his of nine years standing'. Though the bonds had actually been satisfied in 1696, the usurer declared that he could not find them, but promised to cancel them: 'They had Correspondency together, till 2nd of June, 1702, at which time he gave him a Note under Hand, That there remain'd nothing due to each other.' However, the usurer later made the bonds over to a third party, who intended to sue upon them. These details supposedly came from a correspondent; but Defoe added that 'the unhappy Author of this was a particular Sufferer'.[5]

Between July and November there is a gap in the record, which may conjecturally be filled by another continental visit, perhaps to keep out of the way of his creditors. He wrote: 'I have seen Places in the World reserv'd Neuter, when the Nations possessing them have been in actual open War — *Aix-la-Chappelle*, a City of Baths, apply'd purely for Health of the Body, has been exempted from the Concern of the War, when the Nations that possessed the Country, have been fighting in the most furious manner possible.'[6] The only time when Defoe could possibly have been at Aix when hostilities were in progress anywhere in the neighbourhood was in the late summer of 1702, when Marlborough was first establishing his reputation by capturing a whole string of French-held forts from Venloo to Liège, along the Maas to the west of Aix. No doubt visitors to the spa could mingle, not only with nationals of the rival states, but even with off-duty officers of the contending armies.

Defoe must have been home again by November, when there appeared another long poem, *The Spanish Descent*, inspired by news which had reached England in late October.[7] An expedition led by the Duke of Ormonde and Sir George Rooke, after failing ignominiously in its original objective of seizing Cadiz, had unexpectedly redeemed itself by destroying the Spanish treasure fleet in Vigo harbour. This lively account, poised between the heroic and the mock-heroic, can still be read with enjoyment; but it has little biographical significance.

It must also have been during the latter part of 1702 that a more important poem appeared, *Reformation of Manners*.[8] He was once more becoming concerned at declining moral standards. 'No sooner was King *William* Dead', he was later to write, 'than Universal Revels fill'd their Houses, and General Drunkenness began to Revive'; while maypoles, which had been set up in the licentious days of the Restoration but neglected during William's reign, were re-erected or repainted.[9] In his poem he now developed a theme he had already expounded four years before in *The Poor Man's Plea*, savagely portraying 'those, who pretending to suppress Vice, or being vested with Authority for that purpose, yet make themselves the shame of their Country, encouraging wickedness by that very authority they have to suppress it'. It has been plausibly suggested that his apparently random collection of victims may have been linked by membership of the various societies for the reformation of manners which were then flourishing. In penning these lively squibs Defoe seems to have been motivated not only by moral indignation, but also by a certain relish in depicting the vices he attacked; and for all his protestations that his targets were the vices rather than the men, he must have known that it was his attacks on well-known public figures that would sell his poem. Its very topicality, which appealed to his contemporaries, is the chief obstacle to modern appreciation; and his satirical portraits, apparently influenced by *Absalom and Achitophel*, are not really witty or pointed enough to survive in their own right, detached from the real figures they supposedly portray. His sketch of Sir Salathiel Lovell, the octogenarian Recorder of

London, is typical:

> L—— l, the Pandor of thy Judgment-Seat
> Has neither Manners, Honesty, nor Wit,
> Instead of which, He's plenteously Supply'd
> With Nonsense, Noise, Impertinence and Pride:
>
>   * * * * * * * * * * * * * * * *
>
> Definitive in Law, without Appeal,
> But always serves the Hand who pays him well.
> He trades in Justice, and the Souls of Men,
> And prostitutes them equally for gain
>
>   * * * * * * * * * * * * * * * *
>
> Fraternities of Villains he maintains,
> Protects their Robberies, and shares their gains.[10]

Even though he prudently warned his 'Satyr' against attacking 'Men of Posts' or parliamentary figures, 'Unless thou'rt well prepar'd for Martyrdom', he must have made many influential enemies; and within a few months he would regret his rashness.[11]

Perhaps it was an itch to get once more involved in politics 'within doors' that led him about this time to make, through William Paterson, tentative approaches to the Speaker, Robert Harley, the man who had managed the Commons in the Tory interest for the past three years, and to whom he had addressed his insolent *Legion's Memorial*.[12] This was less of a volte-face than might appear; for although as recently as June Defoe had listed him among the hard-line Tories,[13] Harley's political position had begun to change significantly during the last twelve months. As early as the previous November he had tried to arrange a secret meeting with William's confidant, William Carstares.[14] Now that the Tories were in power, his closest links were with Marlborough and Godolphin, whose overriding concern was the success of the war; and he was becoming increasingly uneasy at the more partisan activities of many of the Tories, who could think of little else but pursuing their vendetta with the Whigs or introducing new laws against the Dissenters. Perhaps already, with his instinct for the middle ground, he was feeling his way towards some kind of accommodation with the

Whigs, to free himself from his dependence upon the high-fliers of his own party. If Defoe was to resume his role as government propagandist which had brought him such self-fulfilment in the past, he would need once more to hitch his wagon to a star; and he was a skilful enough political astrologer to divine that it was Harley whose star would be in the ascendant in the years to come. However, before the year was out, his tentative approaches were swept aside by the most violent storm he was ever to experience.

The new House of Commons, predominantly Tory in character, had met on 17 October. On 1 November leave had been given to introduce a Bill against the growing practice of occasional conformity, and in the course of the month it passed through all its stages in the lower House. Its effect would be to disqualify from public employment anyone who, after qualifying by taking the sacrament according to the ritual of the Church of England, should subsequently attend any other form of religious service. The right of the Dissenters to worship in their own way was not directly threatened; they would merely be excluded more firmly than before from public life. But there were fears that this might be only the thin end of the wedge. By ensuring permanent Tory control of the borough corporations, this might lead to a permanent Tory majority in the Commons; and the consequences of that were incalculable. The narrow majority still held by the Whigs in the Lords could quickly be eroded by the appointment of new Tory bishops and the creation of new Tory peers. The Queen had indeed promised to maintain the toleration, but she had also made clear her wish to favour the Church of England. The Dissenters had only to look back twenty years to recall the last wave of Anglican persecution; and a few years later Defoe recalled a conversation which, whether real or imaginary, summed up their fears:

> *I knew a Person of the same* Principles *with the* High-Church, *who Discoursing with me upon the altering of the Lieutenancy throughout the Kingdom, was pleas'd to say*: Now, Sir, we have an Opportunity, and don't distrust our improving it: A little time and pain shall compel all to be of one Religion . . . it will not be long before all Dissenters will be out of *Office*, and the *Magistracy* in our own Hands; when that Damn'd *Liberty* of Conscience, *added he biting his Lips*, shall be

Snatch'd away, and they compelled to Conform . . . and as
for those who are *Obstinate*, I hope Queen *Mary*'s Bonfires
will blaze again in *Smithfield*, that they may all be extirpated,
and not a Soul left.[15]

The Bill had its origins among the grass-roots of the Tory
party, the country squires and parsons. In the government itself
it was welcomed by the narrowest Tory partisans, by Rochester
and Nottingham and by Sir Edward Seymour, but not by the
triumvirate upon whom the main burden of the nation's affairs
rested. Marlborough, Godolphin and Harley were more concerned with the conduct of the war than with party advantage.
Though of these only Harley had any personal concern for the
Dissenters, none of them wished to offend the dissenting financiers whose loans were needed to kept the armed forces supplied.
They did not want to see supplies delayed by interminable political wrangles, nor did they want to become prisoners of a
rampant Tory party. Their instinct was to lead from the centre,
and so divisive a measure threatened to destroy the centre. But
for them to oppose it openly would have been political suicide.
   The Bill was a particular misfortune for Defoe, who was
already on record as a critic of the practice of occasional conformity, which he had attacked in *An Enquiry into the Occasional Conformity of Dissenters, In Case of Preferment* (1698),
which he had reissued in 1700 with a new preface, and also in *A
Letter to Mr. How* (1701).[16] He had been concerned with the
question as a matter of personal conduct, and may have given
little thought to the possible political implications of his argument. Now however, he found himself in a very exposed position,
being blamed by his fellow Dissenters as 'the Man who has been
the Occasion of all this Persecution which is coming upon us, by
railing at Occasional Conformity'.[17] His public reaction was to
minimise the significance of the Bill. In November he published
another tract with a confusingly similar title: *An Enquiry into
Occasional Conformity. Shewing that the Dissenters Are no
Way Concern'd in it*, identifying himself as the author by attributing it to 'the Author of the Preface to Mr. Howe'.[18] He commented defiantly on his isolated position: 'So to me 'tis every
jot as wonderful to find no Body of my Mind, and yet be positively assured that I am in the Right.' He claimed that the Bill
was no real threat to the dissenting interest:

All those Gentlemen therefore who think that this Act will weaken the Dissenters, or wish it would, are manifestly Mistaken; it may distinguish them better, and I am perswaded will fortifie them in their Honest Profession; 'twill teach them, that if they will hold fast to the Truth, they must learn to live like People under the Power of those who hate them, and despightfully use them.

In a much briefer tract, *The Opinion of a Known Dissenter*, where he made a more serious effort to maintain anonymity, he even claimed that the vast majority of the Dissenters disapproved of occasional conformity, and enquired, 'How then can this Bill be aim'd at the Dissenters? We hold it to be a Novelty, an Abuse crept in among us, and we are glad to have it condemn'd by Authority.'[19]

In reality Defoe shared some of the worst fears of the Dissenters, and his anxiety betrayed him into the worst error of judgment of his career. *The Shortest Way with the Dissenters* played upon these fears, in what appeared to be a naked expression of Anglican intolerance, a vehement demand for the complete suppression of dissent.[20]

Heaven has made way for their destruction, and if we do not close with this divine occasion, we are to blame ourselves, and may remember that we once had an opportunity to serve the Church of England, extirpating her implacable enemies; and having let slip the minute that Heaven presented, may experimentally complain, *post est occasio calva.*

There are some popular objections in the way.

As first, the Queen has promised them to continue them in their tolerated liberty; and has told them that she will be a religious observer of her word.

What her Majesty will do we cannot help, but what, as head of the Church, she ought to do, is another case. Her Majesty has promised to protect and defend the Church of England, and if she cannot effectually do that without the destruction of the dissenters, she must of course dispense with one promise to comply with another.

* * * * * * * * * * * * * * * * *

I do not prescribe fire and faggot; but as Scipio said of

Carthage, *Delenda est Carthago*. They are to be rooted out of this nation, if we will ever live in peace, serve God, or enjoy our own; as for the Manner, I leave it to those hands who have a right to execute God's justice on the nation's and the Church's enemies.

* * * * * * * * * * * * * * * *

How many millions of future souls we save from infection and delusion, if the present race of poisoned spirits were purged from the face of the land.

'Tis in vain to trifle in this matter. The light and foolish handling of them by mulcts, fines, &c.; 'tis their glory and advantage! If the gallows instead of the counter and the galleys instead of fines, were the reward of going to a conventicle to preach or hear, there would not be many sufferers. The spirit of martyrdom is over; they that will go to church to be chosen sheriffs and mayors, would go to forty churches rather than be hanged.

If one severe law were made and punctually executed that whosoever was found at a conventicle should be banished the nation, and the preacher hanged, we should soon see an end of the tale. They would all come to church, and one age would make us all one again.

Such a vehement expression of religious intolerance was bound to raise a storm, and it broke at the very end of the year. If Lee was right in giving 1 December as the publication date, some three or four weeks must have elapsed before any public notice was taken of the tract; and it is difficult to imagine such explosive material smouldering for so long. All the other evidence suggests a publication date some three weeks later. It was later stated in court that the tract had been offered for sale in Bow parish within Cheap Ward on 22 December.[21] John Tutchin had discussed Occasional Conformity in his *Observator*, No. 69 (16–19 December), without mentioning *The Shortest Way*; but in No. 71 (23–6 December) he dealt with it, apparently as something newly published, and, addressing himself to the intriguing question of who could have written it, concluded that it must have been 'one of our Inferior Clergy'.[22] Tutchin, like everyone else, still took *The Shortest Way* at its face value. The Dissenters were aghast, and most Tory high-fliers delighted. It was said to have 'won applause' at both Universities; and Defoe himself later quoted a letter sent to a London bookseller by 'Esq. M———', a High Church country gentleman:

SIR,

I received yours and enclosed the Book call'd the Shortest Way with the Dissenters, *for which I thank you; and next to the Holy Bible and Sacred* Comments, *I place it as the most Valuable Thing I can have. I look upon it as the only Method, and I pray God to put it into the Heart of our Gracious Queen to put what is there propos'd in Excution.*[23]

It must have been late in December that Godolphin wrote to Nottingham, in an undated letter:

I had last night some talk with the speaker, and he has had a mind to speak to you about a book lately come out, called *a short way with the Dissenters.* He seemed to think it absolutely necessary for the service of the government that your Lordship should endeavour to discover who was the author of it.[24]

Presumably Harley too believed that *The Shortest Way* was by some high-flying Tory; and it was under this impression that the wheels of government were set in motion, and the Messenger of the Press, Robert Stephens, entrusted with the task of unearthing those responsible. The publisher, George Croome, had Jacobite sympathies, and must himself have been a victim of the fraud which had deceived the general public; but the manuscript had been brought to him by Edward Bellamy, a Southwark hosier, and an active Whig. On 2 January Bellamy was arrested, and on that day or the next named Defoe as the author.[25] On 3 January a warrant was issued for Defoe's arrest; but he had already gone to ground.[26]

But this must only be the record of how Defoe's authorship was formally established; for it seems to have been common knowledge before Bellamy informed on him. He himself declared that his tract, 'having amus'd the People a few Days, appear'd to be written by a *Whig*';[27] and only a week after his first mention of it, Tutchin was in no doubt:

The Author of this Book, was the Reputed Author of the

Legion Letter; the Secretary to that Party, who scandaliz'd
the best of Parliaments in a Black List, which justify'd all the
Cheaters in the late Reign under a Notion of being the Kings
Friends, who treated the five Kentish Worthies at *Mercers-
Chapel*, in Defiance of the Justice of that August and Honour-
able Assembly; this is the Party, which rail'd against *Standing-
Armies* and *Jure Divino*, in the reigns of King Charles II and
James II, and were for *Standing Armies*, Foreign Guards, and
making us a conquer'd Nation, in the Reign of King *William*
. . .[28]

The same issue of the *Observator* (No. 73, 30 December–2
January) hints that Defoe had already been taken up for
questioning: 'one Person was taken into Custody on that
Account, and made his escape from the Messenger' — according
to a later reference, by jumping out of a window.

By the time that *Observator* No. 75 appeared (6–9 January),
Defoe had published *A Brief Explanation of a Late Pamphlet,
Entitul'd, The Shortest Way with the Dissenters*.[29] He professed
surprise that anyone should have taken his tract seriously: 'If
any man take the Pains to reflect upon the Contents, the Nature
of the Thing, and the manner of the stile, it seems impossible to
imagine that it should pass for any thing but an Irony.' Yet no
one had recognised it for what it was: ''Tis hard, after all, that
this should not be perceived by all the Town, that not one man
can see it, either Churchman or Dissenter.' Not only here, but
on many future occasions, Defoe insisted that *The Shortest Way*
had been intended ironically; and it has been so regarded ever
since. It is true that some critics have been puzzled by an irony
that neither friend nor foe could recognise; and it has even been
suggested that he was not really capable of writing in that vein
at all. This is demonstrably not so, though his irony was usually
too obvious and heavy-handed rather than too subtle. Yet Defoe
sometimes offered a different interpretation of his tract, claiming
that he had written it to expose the High Church Tories by
getting them to acknowledge what had hitherto been hidden in
their inmost hearts; that it 'look'd so like a Brat of their own
begetting, that like two Apples, they could not know them
asunder'.[30] He even occasionally ran these two mutually inconsistent explanations in double harness — as if Swift's *Modest
Proposal* was designed to trap members of the Anglo-Irish

ascendancy into enthusiastic support for his project for breeding and rearing Irish babies for the dinner-table. Of Defoe's two explanations, the second is probably much nearer the truth.

One reply to his tract appeared so promptly that the author could still treat it as the work of a high Churchman: *Reflections upon a late Scandalous and Malicious Pamphlet entitul'd The Shortest Way with the Dissenters.*[31] The author argued that the purpose of *The Shortest Way* had been to set Protestants at each other's throats for the benefit of the Jacobites; and he appealed to moderate churchmen to use their influence to preserve the political rights of the Dissenters, as the best means of countering the schemes of the high-fliers:

> This the moderate Churchmen may easily perceive to be their Interest since any Man may see that there's a Set of Men in the Nation, who would fain be acting the same part over again, which they did in the Reign of King *Charles* and King *James* II when by the Intrigues of the Court and the High-Fliers, the Protestant Subjects were engag'd to worry one another with an unnatural, as well as unaccountable Fury, under the reproachful Names of Tories, Whigs and Trimmers, whilst a *Popish* Successor, and an Arbitrary Power came in like a Flood, and had well nigh swallow'd them all up.

All the indications are that this reply was written by Defoe himself. In other words, *The Shortest Way* was a brilliant piece of impersonation, intended as the target for a campaign in which he succeeded in firing only the opening shot, and one which aroused little notice because of the furore raised by his exposure. Once his authorship was known, he could never admit his real purpose, and could only defend himself with explanations which, however often repeated, never entirely carried conviction.

For a while Defoe lay in hiding in or near London, probably in the house of a Spitalfields weaver, Nathaniel Sammen.[32] Abuse was heaped on him from both sides. He could expect as much sympathy as a soldier who had crept into the enemy lines and opened fire on his own troops to show them where the enemy positions were. As he told the Dissenters a few weeks later: 'They are angry, because they take the Book as the Author meant it, and you, because you take it as he wrote it'; and he went on to ask the question which worried him most of all, even though he knew the answer well enough: 'but Pray why then is the Government angry with him?'[33] He was now an exposed pawn on the political chessboard. Nottingham, Rochester and their friends hoped to build their political future upon the destruction of the Whig party; and they hoped to extract from Defoe information which would enable them to blacken the memory of King William, impeach the Whig Lords, and crush the Whig party beyond hope of recovery. Hence the indignant postscript to his *Brief Explanation*:

> The Scandal of the *Observator* Charging the Author of this Book, with being the Author of the *Black List*, the *Kentish Feast*, the *Legion Paper*, and a World of other things, he knows nothing of, is a Baseness peculiar to himself. The Author challenges the said *Observator* to make out the least Shadow of any part of his Charge to be the Truth, and until he does, his Character Speaks for it self.

Nor indeed did Tutchin (*Observator* No. 75) offer any proof beyond hearsay: "Tis there indeed, said, he is the *Reputed* Author of these Things; and so much I have heard Hundreds of his Party (I mean the Modern Whigs) affirm at that time.'

Defoe was now desperately trying to make his peace with the government. He sent his wife to wait on Nottingham; and she was told that he should submit, and answer the questions that would be put to him. Perhaps Nottingham hinted at freedom from prosecution in return for the right kind of information. This was probably what Defoe had in mind when he proudly declared later that his wife, 'when my Lord Nottingham first Insulted her, then Tempted her, scorn'd so much as to move me to Complye with him, and Rather Encourag'd me to Oppose him'.[34] On 9 January Defoe wrote a long letter to Nottingham, the earliest of his letters to survive. He excused himself for fleeing from justice, on the grounds of 'a body unfit to bear the hardships of prison and a mind impatient of confinement'. He offered to answer in writing any questions which might be put to him; but a reference to 'former things which I have had no concern in, though I have the misfortune to pass for guilty by common fame' was hardly calculated to convince Nottingham that he would give the 'plain, full, direct, and honest answers' which he promised. He then tried to strike a curious bargain. If he pleaded guilty, and received some sentence short of imprisonment or the pillory, he would serve for a year in the Netherlands in any regiment the Queen might direct. But if the prosecution was dropped entirely, 'I will raise her Majesty a troop of horse, at my own charges, and at the head of them I'll serve her as long as I live'.[35] Nottingham was not impressed by this theatrical gesture. The *London Gazette* for 11 January carried an announcement, dated the previous day, of a reward for the apprehension of 'Daniel de Fooe', or as the name later appears, 'Daniel Fooe'. The *Gazette* for 14 January carried an amended notice, in which he was called 'Daniel de Foe *alias* de Fooe', and added a description:

> He is a middle sized spare man, about forty years old, of a brown complexion and dark-brown hair, but wears a wig, a hooked nose, a sharp chin, grey eyes, and a large mole near his mouth, was born in London, and for many years was a hose-factor in Freeman's Yard in Cornhill, and now is the owner of the brick and pantile works near Tilbury.[36]

The neighbourhood of London was now highly dangerous for him, but he remained there some time longer, still under attack from both sides. The hostility of the Tories he expected, but that of the Dissenters wounded him deeply. One of them, Col. W——ll, offered to act as hangman. Another, Mr S——, head of a club of Dissenters said that if he could find him, he would hand him over without claiming the reward.[37] Yet another, who met and recognised him, perhaps when taking the air after dark, 'would fain have got the 50 *l* but that he drew upon him, Frighted him out of his Wits and made him go down on his Knees and swear that if he ever met him again, he should shut his eyes till he was half a mile off him'.[38] Tutchin, without abating any of his criticism, was moved to protest at what he thought to be an unfair personal attack in a Tory reply to *The Shortest Way*. He wrote in his *Observator*, No. 78 (16—20 January):

> I don't know what Party stickles for Mr. *Foe*, all good Men condemn'd that Book. But the Party which is against him, and continues to Triumph over him, is the most despicable Party among the Sons of Men. To Triumph over Persons in

Affliction, and under the Frowns of a Government justly
incens'd, is neither the part of a Man nor a Christian.[39]

Perhaps it was this softening of Tutchin's attitude towards
him that encouraged Defoe to try to palm off another defence
of himself as Tutchin's work. This was *A Dialogue between a
Dissenter and the Observator. Concerning the Shortest Way
with the Dissenters*, which imitated Tutchin's method of discussion between 'Countryman' and 'Observator'.[40] Here 'Observator' tries to appease the incensed 'Dissenter' by explaining
once again Defoe's real purpose, praising his fair and generous
treatment of his creditors, and virtually apologising for attributing the *Legion Letter* to him without proof. However, when
the discussion touches on who were really William's friends, and
who his enemies, the 'Observator' gets the worst of the argument. But the tract was a defence of Defoe rather than an attack
upon Tutchin, who apparently felt no need to reply to it.
Unless the statement, 'the man is gone' was a deliberate red
herring, it seems that by the time the tract was published —
from internal evidence, probably late January or early February
— Defoe had found a safer and remoter place of refuge.[41]

Such clues as we have to Defoe's whereabouts during the
next few months all point to Scotland.[42] He must have travelled
under an assumed name, and avoided places where he was
known or likely to meet other travellers who might recognise him. The Great North Road would be much too dangerous;
and perhaps his route is reflected in the circuitous journey made
by Colonel Jack — also a fugitive from justice bound for Scotland
— through Puckeridge, Chesterford, Bourne End, Newmarket,
Brandon, King's Lynn, and thence across the Fens to Spalding
and Market Deeping.[43] Colonel Jack came into the Great North
Road at Stamford; but Defoe probably kept on through Lincoln
to Barton-on-Humber, where 'in an open boat, in which we had
fifteen horses, and ten or twelve cows, mingled with seventeen
or eighteen passengers, call'd Christians, we were about four
hours toss'd about in the Humber, before we could get into the
harbour of Hull; whether I was seasick or not, is not worth
notice, but that we were all sick of the passage, anyone may
suppose'.[44] Though Defoe had no contacts in Hull,[45] he might
have encountered merchants or seamen who knew him, and he
probably hurried straight on to Beverley. Here the sight of a

grave shared by two Danish soldiers, companions of those he
had seen years before at Chester — one killed in a duel, the
other executed for his death — may have aroused disturbing
memories.[46] After passing the Earl of Burlington's 'old built
house' at Londesborough,[47] and still avoiding the main roads,
he may have crossed the Cleveland Hills, where from Roseberry
Topping he could look across two whole counties to the
Cheviot, 'sixty Miles distant' on the Scottish border.[48]

Once on Scottish soil he was safe from the processes of
English law, and there is no reason why he should not have continued to Edinburgh, even though he was 'publickly known'
there;[49] but if so, there would surely have been some mention
of the fact in the public prints or correspondence of statesmen
who were interested in his whereabouts. He chose to lie low,
and perhaps went only a mile or two across the border, taking
refuge at the manse at Mordintown, the first township in
Scotland, just west of the road from Berwick to Edinburgh.
Alexander Lauder, the minister, certainly became well known
to Defoe, who called him a 'master of a good stock of learning,
and a double stock of reading'.[50] If Defoe had already started
work on his intended magnum opus, the very long poem, *Jure
Divino*, its unusually heavy annotation may have owed something to Lauder's library and his learning. He must also have
found some source of income, for he told Paterson in April, 'I
do allready Find Tis No very Difficult thing for me to get my
Bread.'[51]

Little of the news that reached him from England can have
been encouraging. On 24 February he had been indicted at the
Lord Mayor's Court at the Old Bailey for seeking to deny
religious toleration to the Dissenters, and the Sheriff had been
ordered to bring him before the next session of Oyer & Terminer in six weeks time. On 25 February a formal complaint
against *The Shortest Way* was laid before the Commons, and by
their order it was burned the next day in New Palace Yard. On
27 February, when Parliament was prorogued until the autumn,
the Queen's address urged the need for 'further laws for restricting
the great License which is assumed of publishing and spreading
scandalous Pamphlets and Libels'. Though the Lords had
successfully resisted the Commons, over Occasional Conformity
and other issues, it was only by the narrowest of majorities; and
the Tories had begun to use the Queen's favour to strengthen

their position in the Upper House, with four out of five new peerages created in March. Yet there was some comfort to be gleaned from the forced resignation of Rochester in the previous month; and it may have been Defoe's awareness of the tensions within the Ministry that prompted him to write in April to 'Mr. William Patterson in London', deploring his exile, thanking him for the concern he had shown at his plight, and hinting at his willingness to serve Harley.[52] Such overtures would be useless unless the latter was both willing and able to stifle the prosecution; but Defoe can have received no encouragement, for he now began to think in terms of a long exile.

Despite his assurances to Paterson, his financial position was again critical. He had in England a wife and six children to maintain. Although he had cleared many of his debts, he still owed £5000 when this disaster struck him, and he later estimated that it cost him, in one way or another, a further £3000.[53] His brick-and-tile works near Tilbury, which depended on his own active sales promotion, were vulnerable. He later blamed his fellow Dissenters for their failure, perhaps through the drying up of orders from people offended by *The Shortest Way*.[54] By a legal judgment, too, the tenure of his Essex estates was secure only until 29 September, when he could hardly hope to be in a strong position to re-negotiate with the mortgagees.[55] A still worse financial threat hung over his head. He had of course still been missing at the session of Oyer & Terminer on 7 April, and again on 12 May. Failure to appear at the adjourned session on 7 July might result in a sentence of outlawry, involving the forfeiture of any property held in his name. He had no intention of standing trial, but decided to risk a clandestine visit to London to sign legal papers, presumably to transfer his property to his wife's name or that of some trustee on whom he could rely. By May he was again on his way south.

Years later he described how 'a person', obviously himself, 'was obliged to come once more to London, to sign some writings for the securing some estate, which it was feared might be seized by outlaw, if the prosecution had gone on so far'; after which he intended to 'go away north to Scotland', But at Barnet he was twice awakened by the same vivid dream, that he was in his old lodgings in London, where he was arrested by two messengers. He told his dream to his brother-in-law, Mr R[obert] D[avis], who was with him; but despite misgivings they decided to continue to London. Next morning, after walking along the by-ways through Enfield Chase, his heart again failed him, and he took lodgings at Hornsey, intending to send his brother-in-law ahead to London, to enquire if there was any cause for alarm. But catching sight of someone he knew, but could not trust, he decided that Hornsey was too dangerous, and pressed on towards London. Failing to find private lodgings in Islington, he ended up at his former refuge, probably with Sammen, the Spittlefields weaver. Here, on 21 May, 'the next morning he was taken by the messengers, just in the very manner as he had been told in his dream'.[56] According to one account they had merely been conducting a general search for disaffected persons; but as the £50 reward was claimed and paid a few days later, to someone who preferred not to give his name, he must have been informed on.[57]

Defoe spent that day in the custody of the messenger. The following morning, Saturday 22 May, he was taken before the principal Secretary of State, the Earl of Nottingham, a tall, thin, dark, pedantic man, who 'examined him strictly' but clearly learned nothing of importance. He was then taken from the Secretary's office in a coach, under guard, to Newgate Prison, to which he had been committed to await trial.[58]

Moll Flanders recalled her feelings when she first entered Newgate:

> I was carried to *Newgate*; that horrid Place. My very Blood chills at the mention of its Name . . . 'tis impossible to describe the terrors of my mind, when I was first brought in, and when I look'd round upon all the horrors of that dismal Place. I look'd upon myself as lost, and that I had nothing to think of, but of going out of the World, and that with the utmost Infamy: the hellish Noise, the Roaring, Swearing and Clamour, the Stench and Nastiness, and all the dreadful croud of Afflicting things I saw there; joyn'd to make the Place seem an Emblem of Hell itself, and a kind of Entrance into it.[59]

Moll was a woman in fear of the hangman's rope. Defoe had only the 'infamy' of the pillory to dread; but his own apprehensions must have been almost as great, when the door of 'that horrid Place' closed behind him.

Defoe left no explicit account of his experiences in Newgate;
but in 1717 there appeared *The History of the Press Yard*, supposedly by 'one of the brethren of the Quill' who had endured
'a confinement of several months there' in 1715. Every test that
can be applied points to Defoe as the author, drawing on his
memories of a dozen years earlier.[60] The entrance to the Prison,
we are told, lay through a lodge, where he was surrounded by a
group of turnkeys and wardsmen, who eyed him like pickpockets sizing up a potential victim, passing remarks about irons
and fetters, to put him in a frame of mind to pay the various
sums extorted for petty favours. Next, however, he was thrown
into the Condemned Hold, the most noisome part of the whole
prison, with an open sewer running through it, and normally
used to house prisoners awaiting execution. Eventually the head
turnkey arrived and, with profuse apologies, escorted him back to
the lodge. Here it was explained to him that a gentleman such as
he was should not have been subjected to such treatment. For a
fee of twenty guineas, and a weekly payment of eleven shillings,
he could enjoy the comparative comfort of the Press Yard,
away from the squalor and obscenities of the Common Side
where common criminals were herded. One might have expected
that, as an exceptionally important political prisoner, Defoe
would have been spared this softening up process; but his statement that he had 'tasted the difference between the closet of a
King, and the dungeon of Newgate' suggests that he had indeed
seen the inside of the Condemned Hold.[61]

In the Press Yard, at the eastern end of the prison, were
'divers, large, spacious rooms . . . well supplied with light and
air, free from smells and well equipped'. The supposed author
of *The History of the Press Yard* had a room large enough to
hold three beds as well as several chairs and tables. But the
windows had bars as thick as his wrists, and the quiet was often
broken by 'the rattling of huge unweildy Keys, and the re-
verberating Sound of immense Iron Bolts'. A laundress could be
hired to do domestic work for a shilling a week, and exercise
could be taken in a paved passage between the side of the prison
building and the boundary wall. There was a good deal of freedom of movement within the Prison, and the Press Yard had its
own tap room. Here, on his first evening, the newcomer was
expected to pay an 'entrance fee' by providing wine and tobacco
for the inmates of the Press Yard, and this entitled him to

preside over a table at which most got drunk; and for this they were 'tried' and 'fined' the next morning at a mock court held by the turnkeys. The usual ways of passing the time — hard drinking, gaming and promiscuous fornication — held no attraction for Defoe, and he must have kept as much as possible to himself. Even so, he could not ignore all the 'dreadful croud of Afflicting things' that went on within the prison. Though he never produced an equivalent of Oscar Wilde's *Ballad of Reading Gaol*, he made Moll Flanders give a thumbnail sketch of a similar incident.

> The next Morning there was a sad Scene in the Prison; the first thing I was saluted with in the Morning, was the Tolling of the great Bell at St. *Sepulchres*, as they call it, which usher'd in the Day: As soon as it began to Toll, a dismal groaning and crying was heard from the Condemn'd Hole, where there lay six poor Souls, who were to be Executed that Day, some for one Crime, some for another, and two of them for Murther.[62]

The 'author' of *The History of the Press Yard* shared his room with a single companion; but Defoe must have had a room to himself. Here his wife, his two brothers-in-law and his old father could visit him, as well as his few faithful friends among the Dissenters and his political associates, and emissaries from more eminent political figures to drop hints and report back to their masters. Defoe himself invited three leading Presbyterian ministers to pray with him — John Howe, John Spademan and Robert Fleming — all probably old acquaintances from his exile in Holland many years before. All three refused.[63] John Howe had two years before been involved with him in a controversy, one which Defoe had gone out of his way to thrust upon him. All three were among those Dissenters who had blamed him for stirring up a hornet's nest by writing *The Shortest Way*. Hard words had been used on both sides, and he later recalled how he had 'the Honour to be insulted for it by worthy, grave Mr H——, Mr. S——, and Mr. F——, eminent *Dissenters*, as a Wrong to the *High-Church* Men . . . when I said they were ignorant, I said *less* than I ought; and that they had no reason to be angry, if I had said *they were Fools*'.[64] Defoe's indignation at their refusal to pray with him, expressed more than once in the coming weeks, may have been somewhat synthetic. They probably looked on his invitation as a manoeuvre to get them to identify themselves with his cause; and though this would not have impressed the authorities, it might have improved his standing with the Dissenters, and perhaps have helped to save his brick-and-tile works.

While Defoe lay in Newgate, Nottingham and his subordinates were going through the 'many papers and libels' which had been found in his possession — perhaps left in Sammen's house during his absence. Defoe later referred contemptuously to Nottingham's carelessness in passing over several of his political manuscripts and returning them amongst his personal papers.[65] What they were seeking, no doubt, was something that would enable them to compromise the Whig leaders or blacken William's reputation; but in this they were disappointed, for he had already burned many of his papers, probably several months before.[66] He was taken at least once more to be questioned by Nottingham. This must have been on a Tuesday or a Friday, for he later criticised the lack of security in the Secretary's office on post nights, when 'had I been a French Spye I could ha' Put in my Pockett my Lord N——ms Letters directed to Sir Geo: Rook and to the Duke of Marlboro' Laid Carelessly on a Table for the Doorkeepers to carry to the Post Office'.[67] Once, too, he was taken before the Privy Council, and there questioned about some papers, and in particular one containing questions about the delicate problem of the hereditary or parliamentary basis of the English monarchy: 'And one of the questions was this *Viz*. Whether her Majesty was not as much an usurper as King William. A great many objections were made to the rest of that paper, but when their Lordships came to this, and it was read, not a word was said.'[68] Presumably attempts were made at these interviews to get him to incriminate others, but without success.

On 5 June, after he had spent a fortnight in Newgate, Defoe was released on bail in the remarkably high sum of £1500, to appear at the Justice Hall, Old Bailey, at 9 o'clock on Wednesday 7 July. £500 of this was in his own recognizances. Of the four others, who each put up £250, one was his brother-in-law, Robert Davis, here described as a shipwright of Tilbury; the others were Joseph Whitaker, of Chicklane, St Sepulchre's, broker; Thomas Powell, of St Andrew's, Holborn, gentleman;

and Nicholas Morris, of Turnmill Street, St James Clerkenwell, baker.[69] Defoe later wrote, 'some few friends I had then too, who were engaged deeply enough as bail for me';[70] but nothing is known of his relations with these three Londoners who were willing to risk £250 on his good faith. Perhaps some of them were really acting on behalf of more eminent men who preferred to remain in the background — Halifax or Somers perhaps — who must have been gently perspiring at the thought that Defoe might decide to reveal all he knew, and who may well have thought it worth their while to place him under an obligation.

Defoe had just over a month of liberty before his trial. Part of his time must have gone on his business affairs, particularly his brick-and-tile works, though it is not known what stage of disintegration his business had reached. Our only item of information comes from a surviving fragment of yet another Chancery suit. Defoe's manager, Paul Whitehurst, had been sued by one Chapman for £53 6s. owing for 'small and strong drink' supplied for his workmen at Tilbury. To protect himself, Whitehurst had sued both Chapman and Defoe in Chancery. Defoe's reply, dated 3 July, declared that because of a disagreement over the account he had ordered Whitehurst to get his drink elsewhere, from one Miller of Dartford; he acknowledged that he alone was liable, and declared that Chapman would get his money when he came to a just account.[71]

Defoe had also his literary property to defend. On 17 April, while he had still been in hiding, there had appeared *A Collection of the Writings of the Author of the True-Born English-Man*, which included thirteen pieces in all, four of them in verse, only a small part of his already considerable output.[72] The pirate publisher was John How, who published the *Observator* for Tutchin. Two years later Defoe wrote scathingly of How's conduct in first stealing his property, and then trying to justify it by a legal technicality, complaining that 'when he finds an Author in Trouble, and unable to help himself; then like a thoroughpac'd —— Printer, he makes a whole prize of him at once, and prints his works altogether . . . and then Justifies it by a Statute Law, *that if he could find it would say*, An Author has no Right to his own Copy, because he was not Apprentice to *a Printer*'.[73] The publication of the pirated *Collection* must have been doubly unwelcome to Defoe. It had helped to keep his name before the public, when he would have liked to have been forgotten; and it robbed him of the financial benefits, such as they were, of his own writings, when he needed every penny that he could scrape together.

In reply he prepared *A True Collection of the Writings of the Author of the True-Born English-man*, to sell at 6s., compared with the 2s. 6d. for How's *Collection*.[74] For his extra outlay the purchaser would get a portrait of Defoe, engraved by M. Van der Gucht from a portrait by J. Taverner, which however revealed little of the man behind the self-confident front which he presented to the world. There were also eleven pieces not included by How, although this collection was still very incomplete. There was much that Defoe could not acknowledge as his own; but it would be wrong to read too much into the exact selection which was made. Among those omitted were several pieces which he had already owned by publishing them under his initials. These and others may well have been left out because no copy was available. More significant is the omission of two pieces which How had included. It would have been embarrassing to acknowledge *A Dialogue between a Dissenter and the Observator*, with its warm praise of Defoe put into Tutchin's mouth. *Lex Talionis* was also omitted, either because it really was not Defoe's work, but more likely because its theme, that Protestants abroad could best be protected by retaliatory expulsion of Roman Catholics from England, was itself a piece of religious intolerance, conflicting with his claim that 'rather a Spirit of Healing than of Sedition runs through the whole Collection, one misunderstood Article excepted'.[75] His Preface, marked by a tone of calm and dignified self-justification, aimed to appease his critics on two quite different counts. One was the charge on which he was to be tried, of seeking to arouse hostility between the Church of England and the Dissenters. The other arose out of his satire of the previous year, *Reformation of Manners*, in which he had savaged the vices of many of the City magistrates, some of whom would probably be members of the Court that would try him. Despite his other preoccupations, both themes bulked large enough in his thoughts to draw from him new pieces, echoing the titles of the offending works.

In *The Shortest Way to Peace and Union* he again protested that he had never intended to 'raise a feud between the Dissenters and the Church of *England*', but that his aim was rather 'a

healing Conjunction of Parties.'[76] Recognising that the origins
of Tory intolerance towards the Dissenters lay in memories of
the years of Puritan domination and fears of its return, he laid
stress on the weakness of the Dissenters, divided as they were
into four conflicting groups. Presbyterians, Congregationalists,
Baptists and Quakers were none of them strong enough
separately to challenge the Church or gain control of the State;
and they were so distrustful of each other, he argued, 'that 'tis
the True Interest of the Dissenters in *England,* to be govern'd
by a Church of *England* Magistracy'.[77]

An even more difficult task of appeasement was attempted in
More Reformation.[78] The censorious tone he had adopted in
Reformation of Manners had not only made him influential
enemies, but had provoked attacks on his own character.
Though he boasted in his Preface: 'God, I thank thee, *I am not
a Drunkard, or a Swearer, or a Whoremonger, or a busy Body,
or Idle, or Revengeful*', he freely admitted to more secret faults
than his enemies could find. In any case a satirist need not be
faultless, so long as he is not guilty of the vices he condemns.
He insisted that his attacks had been against vice, not against
individuals; only those whom the coat fitted need wear it. He
declared, '*the Lawyers have named me Twenty Men for my*
Clitus, *and abundance more for* Fletumacy', while

If one *Sir Harry* in the Lines appear,
All the Sir Harry's think themselves are there.[79]

But he knew well enough that many of his victims had been
only too clearly identified, and that at least one of them, Sir
Salathiel Lovell, the Recorder, would be a member of the Court
which would try him.

The placatory Preface to the *True Collection*, and its two
related pieces, were perhaps originally intended to influence the
jury at his trial; and it may have been doubts about the strength
of these cards that decided him to keep them in his hand and
delay publication. Legally his guilt was far from certain, but this
kind of trial was less a matter of law than of politics. With the
Tories now politically dominant in London, a hostile jury was
inevitable. But his fate really depended on decisions made at
government level. As the date of his trial approached he became
increasingly apprehensive. At one time he even thought of

absconding again, and some at least of those who had stood bail for him — or perhaps more eminent figures behind them — actually advised him to do so.[80] Behind the scenes, however, some kind of negotiations were going on with the authorities through his legal adviser, William Colepeper, the friend with whom he had co-operated at the time of the Kentish Petition. Defoe was promised, or believed that he had been promised, that if he pleaded guilty, he would be 'us'd Tenderly'. On Colepeper's advice, he decided to answer his bail, and 'to plead Guilty to the Indictment, Even to all the Adverbs, the Seditiously's, the Malitiously's, and the long Rapsody of the Lawyers et Ceteras'.[81]

At the appointed time, then, at nine o'clock on Wednesday 7 July, Defoe presented himself before the Court at the Sessions of Oyer and Terminer, at Justice Hall, Old Bailey. No detailed account of the trial has survived, but it is known that the Court was presided over by the Lord Mayor, Sir Samuel Dashwood, assisted by Sir Edward Ward, a Baron of the Exchequer, three aldermen, Sir John Fleet, Sir Edwin Clarke and Sir Thomas Abney, and by the Recorder, Sir Salathiel Lovell.[82] The prosecution, though only a formality, in view of Defoe's plea of guilty, was in the hands of the Solicitor-General, Sir Simon Harcourt, who was able to question and hector the defendant in the style for which he was notorious, before the Court considered — not the verdict, which was in no doubt — but the sentence.[83] To Defoe's dismay, it was a savage one. First, he was to pay a fine of 200 marks (£133 6s. 8d.); secondly, he was to stand in the pillory for an hour on three successive days, by the Royal Exchange in Cornhill, near the Conduit in Cheapside, and by Temple Bar in Fleet Street, with a paper on his head inscribed with his offences; and finally, he was to find sureties to be of good behaviour for seven years. Meanwhile he was again committed to Newgate, to await the execution of his sentence. This time no coach was needed, for Newgate Prison stood conveniently next door to Justice Hall.

The date set for Defoe to stand in the pillory for the first time was Monday 19 July, but the charade was far from over. For his part he drew up a petition to the Queen, which William Colepeper took on 11 July to present to Nottingham at Windsor. While he was waiting in the anteroom of the Council Chamber, an express arrived with news of the Fleet. Colepeper enquired whether Sir George Rooke, Admiral of the Fleet and a Kentish Tory, was with the Fleet or at Bath, a jibe which soon afterwards involved him in a brawl with another Kentish Tory, Sir Jacob Banks, within the precincts of the Palace. 'After this accident', Defoe tells us, 'his Lordship abated of his civility and good will when applied to on Mr. De Foe's behalf.'[84] Nottingham may already have taken an initiative of his own by hinting that Defoe might be able to obtain mercy by 'discovering parties'. The channel of communication was through Godolphin, then through William Penn, the Quaker, who sometimes acted as Godolphin's agent in delicate matters, and finally through William Penn, junior, who visited Defoe in Newgate. On 12 July Defoe wrote to the elder Penn, thanking him for his efforts on his behalf, but assuring him

> That in the Manner which they Proposed it I really had No Person to Discover . . . I Sollemnly Affirm that other Than what Passes in Conversation . . . I have no Accomplices, No Sett of Men, (as my Lord Call'd Them) with whom I used to Concert Matters, of this Nature, To whom I us'd to show, or Receiv hints from them in Ordr to These Matters, and Therefore to Put it upon Conditions of Such a Nature is to Offer me Nothing Attall.[85]

Defoe would seem to have closed the door firmly enough, but by the end of the week it again stood ajar. Perhaps his resolution had temporarily weakened; perhaps some genuine misunderstanding had crept in through the use of so many intermediaries; or perhaps he was simply playing for time and trying to raise the price of his silence. At all events, on 17 July Godolphin wrote to Nottingham, that Penn had been to see him on the previous day to tell him 'that *De Foe* was ready to make oath . . . of all that he knew & to give an Account of all his Accomplices in whatsoever he has been concerned, provided that by so doing, he may be excused from the punishment of the pillory, & not produced as an Evidence against any persons whatsoever'.[86] The Queen thought this important enough to justify the holding of a Cabinet Council next day, a Sunday, even had there been no other matters to discuss. On that day Penn wrote a brief urgent letter to Godolphin begging for at least a deferment of Defoe's 'disgrace', due to take place on the

Monday;[87] and Nottingham himself wrote to the Sheriff, Sir
Robert Bedingfield:

> I am commanded by the Queen to signify her pleasure to you
> that you must not put in execution the sentence for setting
> Mr. De Fooe in the pillory until Friday next.[88]

An almost farcical element now began to creep into Defoe's
tragedy. On Monday 19 July, Nottingham sent to the Keeper of
Newgate Prison to bring Defoe before him, only to be informed
that if he were taken outside the limits of London, this would
be technically an escape and that he could not then be compelled
to return. To get round this difficulty Nottingham wrote next
day to Sir Nathan Wright, the Lord Keeper of the Great Seal,
for a writ of *habeas corpus*.[89] On the Wednesday Defoe
appeared yet again before Nottingham, and on this occasion
actually signed a confession. But on the following day Godolphin
wrote to Nottingham: ' . . . as to Defoe, the Queen seems to
think, as she did upon your first acquainting her with what he
said that his confession amounts to nothing. However, she is
willing to leave it to the Lords of the Committee to let his sentence be executed tomorrow, or not until after Sunday, as they
think proper.'[90] On Friday morning, after consulting the Queen,
Nottingham sent yet another urgent note to the Sheriff:

> You may expect her Majesty's orders concerning Mr. Fooe
> this morning but I doubt not time enough to prevent his
> standing in the pillory today if that should be her Majesty's
> resolution, and therefore unless you hear from me again this
> morning, you will do well not to execute this sentence till
> Monday, by which time I shall acquaint you with her Majesty's
> final determination.[91]

Nottingham had decided on one further interview, this time
going himself to Newgate, accompanied by the Lord Privy Seal,
the Duke of Buckingham.[92] But Defoe, perhaps now satisfied that his influential Whig friends could shield him from the
worst horrors of the pillory, had firmly decided to choose that
briefer ignominy, rather than be branded for life as an informer.
During this remarkable confrontation, which probably took
place on Monday 26 July, 'Fear of Punishment' was reinforced

by 'Promises of Reward'; but the carrot was no more effective than the stick in persuading him to betray his friends.[93] The discussion seems to have degenerated into recrimination about past political issues. Defoe tells us that Nottingham reproached the memory of King William, by declaring that *'he purchased our Peace with the Ruine of our Trade'*;[94] and he commented scornfully on his adversary's rashness in arguing about the Partition Treaty when 'he had forgot to bring his maps'.[95] At the end of it all, Nottingham can have been in no doubt that Defoe was now adamant; while the latter must have known that he would have to endure the pillory.

On Tuesday 27 July Nottingham wrote once again to the Sheriff:

> I must acquaint you that her Majesty does not think fit to delay any longer the execution of the sentence upon Mr. Fooe, so that you must cause it to be inflicted without any further order.[96]

Defoe could pride himself that 'Neither by *Promises of Reward* or *Fear of Punishment* could they prevail upon him to discover anything, and so it remains a secret to this day'.[97] Writing to Halifax two years later, he called himself 'this despicable thing, who scorn'd to come out of Newgate at the Price of Betraying a Dead Master, or discovering those things which No body would ha' been the worse for'.[98] Later he was to write less delicately and more melodramatically: 'I have passed through the severest trial of this kind, and would I have been treacherous, what work should I have made of families: Nay, perhaps what blood might I have been the occasion of.'[99]

About noon on Thursday 29 July, Defoe was taken from Newgate and fixed in the pillory in Cornhill, near the Royal Exchange, almost within sight of Freeman's Yard, where he had once hopefully carried on his business as a hose factor. A pillory sentence usually involved, not merely the humiliation of public exposure, but subjection to the insults and missiles of a hostile mob. When Defoe's sentence had been imposed on 7 July there had been no reason to suppose that he would be an exception, since the tract for which he was to suffer had contrived to infuriate both sides. Yet within three weeks public opinion had

swung round in his favour, and the crowd which surged round the
pillory had come not to jeer but to acclaim him. An early sign
of this reversal of feeling had appeared soon after his trial,
when the essentially generous Tutchin had written indignantly
about it in his *Observator* of 10 July.[100] Defoe himself, the
supreme expert in the manipulation of public opinion, had
played his part. *More Reformation, The Shortest Way to Peace
and Union*, his dignified Preface to *A True Collection*, all
published since his trial, had helped to create the impression
that he had been misunderstood and savagely dealt with.[101]
Among those who knew or guessed what had been passing
'within doors' there must have been a growing realisation that
he had been resisting pressure to betray his friends. Such men as
Somers and Halifax could do nothing openly to help him; but it
is a reasonable guess that, through their friends in the City, they
helped to organise the demonstrations in his favour. Among
those present were said to be 'knights and aldermen . . . city
friends . . . the Dissenting tribe', as well as many of the great
unwashed.[102] According to one hostile account, 'That dirt
themselves protected him from Filth.'[103] Clearly Defoe's
friends were able to intimidate his enemies, or at least to keep
them at a distance from the pillory.

Some deliberate organisation is also implied by a sour comment about 'the *Party* causing his Books to be *Hauk'd* and Publickly *Sold* about the *Pillory*, while he stood upon it (in
Triumph!) for Writing them'.[104] In particular there was a new
poem, hot from the press, written by him in Newgate especially
for the occasion, and entitled *A Hymn to the Pillory*.[105] It
began:

> Hail *Hi'roglyphick* State *Machin*
> Contriv'd to Punish Fancy in:
> Men that are Men, in thee can feel no Pain,
> And all thy *Insignificants* Disdain.

After running through a brief roll of honour of 'Men of unspotted
Honesty' who had stood in the pillory before him, he lapsed into
satiric vein to suggest more suitable victims than himself — sometimes individuals, like the High Church clergymen, Sacheverell
or Sherlock, sometimes whole categories of offenders, such as

'Jobbers and Brokers of the City Stocks'. Finally with splendid bravado he defied those who had victimised him:

Thou Bug-bear of the Law stand up and speak,
    Thy long Misconstru'd Silence break,
Tell us who 'tis upon thy Ridge stands there,
    So full of Fault, and yet so void of Fear;
    And from the Paper in his Hat,
Let all Mankind be told for what:

* * * * * * * * * * * *

    And yet he might ha' been secure,
Had he said less, or wou'd he ha' said more.
    Tell them that this is his Reward,
    And worse is yet for him prepar'd,
Because his Foolish Vertue was so nice
As not to sell his Friends, according to his Friends Advice.

* * * * * * * * * * * * * * * * * *

Tell 'em the Men that plac'd him here,
Are Friends unto the Times,
    But at a loss to find his Guile,
    They can't commit his Crimes.[106]

About Defoe's feelings as he stood in the pillory we can only guess. Pope's epithet, many years later, was 'unabashed';[107] and we can be sure that he put on a bold front. Yet we may doubt whether he really relished his bitter-sweet triumph. He had never sought public applause. Indeed, anonymity had become almost an obsession with him, long before it became a political necessity. Like some creature living under a stone, his instinct when exposed to the light was to run for cover; but now, for an hour at a time, he was rigidly fixed in the full glare of publicity. When it was all over, the people 'expressed their affections by loud shouts and acclamations when he was taken down'.[108]

He had to face the ordeal twice more: on the following day, a few hundred yards further west in Cheapside; and finally on Saturday 31 July in Fleet Street near Temple Bar. Was the same scene repeated on each occasion? The surviving accounts suggest only a single demonstration. However, according to John Evelyn:

'There hapend the last weeke of this moneth so great & long continual Raine, as had not been known of late years, & the last day of it and the Sunday following 1. Aug: Thunder & lightning & raine . . . .'[109] It sounds as though on the Saturday at least, when Defoe was pilloried for the last time, the weather may have been bad enough to keep away onlookers, whether hostile or friendly. When there had been similar weather the night after the execution of Alderman Cornish in 1685, Defoe had taken it as 'a Token that God Almighty did not like the Work'.[110] If he drew a similar conclusion in his own case, he never ventured to say so. Perhaps it simply meant that when he returned for the last time to Newgate and welcome obscurity, it was not merely with aching neck and limbs, but also drenched to the skin.

Any elation he may have felt at his triumph in the pillory must in any case have quickly drained away into a mood of emotional exhaustion and dejection. Despite the comparative privacy of his room in the Press Yard, little separated him, physically or psychologically, from the lowest depths of human degradation and despair. But there is no reason to suppose that his habitual self-control deserted him; and no doubt he was soon applying himself with his usual resilience to piecing together the broken fragments of his life. His financial position was once again desperate. His business as a brick-and-tile manufacturer was ruined; and his debts, which he had reduced to £5000, had increased by this latest disaster to over £8000. Yet he could not get his discharge from Newgate until he had paid his fine of 200 marks. His experience of the last few years must have convinced him that he was a political animal; and it was the political scene that he scanned anxiously for relief. He must have noticed that while Nottingham had been playing cat-and-mouse with him, with Godolphin hovering in the background, there had been another cat taking no part in the game, but lying apparently asleep by the fire, though in reality watching every move out of the corner of his eye. This was the man of the future, or at least of the next few years, the Speaker, Robert Harley, to whom Defoe had already with a sure instinct made overtures. It would be through Harley that he would once again enter on 'a new scene of life'; but Harley was in no hurry. Meanwhile Defoe had to make the best of things in Newgate, and tell himself, as he had often had to do before, that 'there was no remedy but patience'. Had he turned his talents to autobiography he could have written with Robinson Crusoe:

> And thus I have given the first part of a life of fortune and adventure, a life of Providence's chequer-work, and of a variety which the world will seldom be able to show the like of.[111]

Abbreviations Used in Appendices and Notes

AH&J: An Appeal to Honour and Justice (1715).

AJ: Applebee's Journal.

AM&C: Atlas Maritimus & Commercialis (1728).

Arber's *Garner*: Edward Arber (ed.), *An English Garner* (12 vols, Westminster, 1903).

Bastian (1): F. Bastian, 'Daniel Defoe and the Dorking District', *Surrey Archaeological Collections*, lv (1958) 41–64.

Bastian (2): F. Bastian, 'James Foe Merchant, Father of Daniel Defoe', *N&Q*, ccix (March 1964) 82–6.

Bastian (3): F. Bastian, 'Defoe and Guy Miege', *N&Q*, ccxiv (March 1969) 103–5.

BL: British Library.

Boulton: J. T. Boulton (ed.), *Daniel Defoe* (London, 1965).

Cal.S.P. (Dom): Calendar of State Papers, Domestic.

Cavalier: J. T. Boulton (ed.), *Memoirs of a Cavalier* (Oxford, 1972).

CEG: Karl D. Bülbring (ed.), *The Compleat English Gentleman* (London, 1890).

CET: The Complete English Tradesman (1727).

CLRO: Corporation of London Record Office.

Col. Jack: Samuel Holt Monk (ed.), *The History . . . of . . . Col. Jacque* (Oxford, 1965).

Collection: A Collection of the Writings of the Author of the True-Born English-Man (1703).

Complete History: A Complete History of the Late Revolution from the First Rise of it to this present Time (1691).

DNB: Dictionary of National Biography.

Ellis: Frank H. Ellis (ed.), *Poems on Affairs of State: Augustan Satirical Verse, 1697–1704* (Yale University, 1970).

EuP: An Essay upon Projects (1697).

Evelyn, *Diary:* E. S. de Beer (ed.), *The Diary of John Evelyn* (Oxford, 1955).

Grimblot: P. Grimblot (ed.), *Letters of William III and Louis XIV and of their Ministers . . . 1697 to 1709* (London, 1848).

Hardwicke: P. Yorke, Earl of Hardwicke (ed.), *Miscellaneous State Papers from 1501 to 1726* (1778).

Hazlitt: William Hazlitt (ed.), *The Works of Daniel De Foe* (London, 1841—3).

Healey, *Letters:* George Harris Healey (ed.), *The Letters of Daniel Defoe* (Oxford, 1955).

History of Apparitions: An Essay on the History and Reality of Apparitions (1727).

History of the Devil: The History of the Devil, in Henry G. Bohn (ed.), *The Novels and Miscellaneous Works of Daniel De Foe*, vol. iii (London, 1854—6).

HMC: Historical Manuscripts Commission.

JD: Jure Divino (1706).

JPY: Louis Landa (ed.), *A Journal of the Plague Year* (Oxford, 1969).

Lee: William Lee, *Daniel Defoe: His Life and Recently Discovered Writings* (London, 1869).

Luttrell: Narcissus Luttrell, *A Brief Relation of State Affairs from September 1678 to April 1714* (Oxford, 1857).

Matthews, *Calamy Revised*: A. G. Matthews, *Calamy Revised* (Oxford, 1934).

Meditations: G. H. Healey (ed.), *The Meditations of Daniel Defoe* (Cummington, Mass., 1946).

MF: G. A. Starr (ed.), *Moll Flanders* (Oxford, 1971).

MJ: Mist's Journal.

Moore: John Robert More, *Daniel Defoe, Citizen of the Modern World* (Chicago, 1958).

Moore, *Checklist:* John Robert Moore, *A Checklist of the Writings of Daniel Defoe* (Bloomington, 1960).

New State: The New State of England (1691).

Newton: Theodore F. M. Newton, 'The Civet Cats of Newington Green', *RES*, xiii (1937) 10—19.

N&Q: Notes and Queries.

PCC: Prerogative Court of Canterbury.

PRO: Public Record Office.

Ramkins: The Memoirs of Majr. Alexander Ramkins, in James

T. Boulton (ed.), *Memoirs of an English Officer* . . . (London, 1970).

RC: J. Donald Crowley (ed.), *Robinson Crusoe* (Oxford, 1972).

RES: Review of English Studies.

Review: A. W. Secord (ed.), *Defoe's Review Reproduced from the Original Editions* . . . (New York, 1938).

Roxana: Jane Jack (ed.), *Roxana* (Oxford, 1964).

Secord: A. W. Secord (ed.), *Daniel Defoe: A Journal of the Plague Year and Other Pieces* (Garden City, NY, 1935).

Serious Reflections: G. A. Aitken (ed.), *Serious Reflections during the Life and Surprising Adventures of Robinson Crusoe* (London, 1895).

Somers Tracts: Walter Scott (ed.), *Somers Tracts* (13 vols, London, 1809—15).

State Tracts: A Collection of State Tracts. Publish'd during the Reign of King William III (3 vols, 1705—7).

Story: R. H. Story, *William Carstares, 1649—1715* (London, 1874).

Sutherland (1): J. R. Sutherland, 'Some Early Troubles of Daniel Defoe', *RES*, ix (1935) 275—90.

Sutherland (2): J. R. Sutherland, 'A Note on the Last Years of Defoe', *Modern Language Review*, xxix (1934) 137—41.

Sutherland (3): James Sutherland, *Daniel Defoe: A Critical Study* (Boston, 1971).

TC: Term Catalogue.

Tour: A Tour Through the Whole Island of Great Britain (Everyman, 1962).

True Collection: A True Collection of the Writings of the Author of the True Born English-man (1703).

VCH: Victoria County History.

Wing: D. G. Wing, *Short-title Catalogue of Books printed* . . . *1641—1700* (New York, 1945—51).

Appendix A: Defoe and Somers

Defoe's association with Montagu (Halifax) has documentary support, though from a slightly later date (1705—6) than is covered by this book (Healey, *Letters* (30), (33), (38) and (62), p. 147); but, perhaps as a result of a fire which destroyed most of Somers's papers in 1752, his connection with the latter remains purely a matter of inference. Defoe's admiration, however, is obvious from his advice to Harley in November 1704 to try to come to an understanding with him (Healey, *Letters* (22), pp. 68—9), and from the 22 lines in his praise in *Jure Divino*, Book XII, p. 4 (1706), where he is given pride of place among contemporary statesmen.

If the Sunderland—Somers correspondence of September/ October 1701 has been correctly interpreted above (chap. 12, pp. (256—8), Defoe must have been in touch with Somers at that time. It is significant that neither Sunderland nor Somers suggested that the latter should himself write the pamphlet which both agreed to be necessary, even though he had several pamphlets to his credit, some of them highly esteemed. The typical Somers pamphlet tends to be legally erudite, lengthy and with little popular appeal; and perhaps others which made more impact were 'ghosted' for him by Defoe, or written by the two men in collaboration.

If so, the first example may well have been the famous *Balancing Letter* (1697) which appeared early in the Standing Army controversy (see above, chap. 11, p. 207. In the opinion of his biographer, William L. Sachse (*Lord Somers* (1975), pp. 130—1) this was certainly his work, though the question is not actually discussed; but, as well as being uncharacteristically short for Somers, it seems to contain a fair sprinkling of Defoeisms (*State Tracts*, ii, pp. 585—9).

The clearest instance of collaboration seems to be *Jura Populi Anglicani* (pp. i—xiv and 15—64), which on internal evidence must have been written about August 1701, shortly before the Sunderland—Somers correspondence. The bulk of the tract deals with two legal issues raised by the case of the Kentish Petitioners — the power of the Commons to imprison (pp. 17—30) and the right of subjects to petition (pp. 30—53) — and must have been mainly the work of Somers; but the Preface and the last ten pages dealing with the political issues which had prompted the petition, read very much like Defoe — and incidentally cover very much the ground suggested by Sunderland as the basis of a separate tract.

It has already been suggested that both Somers and Defoe were in some way involved with William's last speech to Parliament (30 December 1701), described by Gilbert Burnet as 'the best speech that he, or perhaps any other prince ever made to his people'. The well-authenticated statement in his *History of my Own Times* [1823 edition, iv, 532—3, footnote (p)], that the 'original' was in Somers's own hand, is compatible both with a combined effort, or with a speech originally written by Defoe but channelled through Somers for the sake of appearances. See also chap. 12, pp. 263—4 above, and Appendix B (24).

Writing to Halifax on 16 July 1705 (Healey, *Letters* (38), p. 94), Defoe discussed the possibility that *The Memorial of the Church of England* might have been written by Dr James Drake: 'I Can Not forbear Assureing your Ldship, That however he Might be The Drudge or Rather Amanuensis in the work — his Master The Duke of Bucks is as plainly Pictur'd to me with his Pen in his hand Correcting, Dictating and Instructing, as if I had been of the Club with Them.' Perhaps this is a reflection of Defoe's own earlier dealings with Somers.

Appendix B: New Attributions

It has sometimes been claimed that Defoe's use of the English language was so idiosyncratic that pieces can be identified as his purely on the strength of words or expressions peculiar to him; but no one has ventured into print with a comprehensive list of such expressions, an undertaking that would call for a superhumanly extensive reading, not only of Defoe himself, but also of his contemporaries. But though such claims may have been overstated, this does not entirely invalidate the method. My friend's red hair, though far from unique, still helps to identify him. There are certainly many phrases and stylistic tricks that *are* characteristic of Defoe, without necessarily being exclusive to him (e.g. 'fire and faggot', 'under a necessity', 'in order to this', 'and the like'). There are also characteristic misspellings (e.g. 'Goal' for 'Gaol') and grammatical solecisms (e.g. 'neither . . . or'); favourite similes and metaphors ('like the dog in the fable', 'gilded pills'), or those drawn from his known interests (trade, seafaring); references to some of his hobbyhorses (begging as a trade, natives who 'barter gold for glass beads'); and the use of his favourite French phrases or Latin tags. Occasionally a longer passage can be closely matched in a known piece of his. There are also characteristic prose rhythms, easier to recognise than to define. As a rule, however, this kind of evidence, though useful, cannot be regarded as conclusive; nor, in view of his command of many styles and mastery of disguise, does the absence of such Defoeisms necessarily preclude his authorship.

An equally important test, especially where political issues are involved, is whether the case being argued is consistent with Defoe's known attitudes; and this has more force where the case was an unpopular one (*for* Standing Armies in 1697–8, or the

Partition Treaty in 1700–1). The view that Defoe was a mercenary hack, prepared to write on either or both sides of a dispute if he was paid to do so, is based on a misapprehension of his role as a political writer. There is often, it is true, a devious element in his work. Even in his earliest tracts, he sometimes pretends to be a member of the Church of England, presumably to gain a hearing from those who would not listen to a Dissenter; and by the year 1700 these tactics are more fully developed. Often he *appears* to be arguing against the cause to which he was committed; but this was only a ploy, to put his opponents off their guard before leading them off in the opposite direction. A variation of this method was to answer his own tracts, in order to introduce a mock battle, in which he made sure that his own cause came out on top; alternatively, to write a piece as an Aunt Sally, the target for a devastating attack; or again, to make his opponents look foolish by putting patently ridiculous arguments into their mouths. Others may have employed such devious methods; but no one took them as far as Defoe, or showed anything like the same tactical ingenuity or the same delight in sailing close to the wind. The typical Defoe tract was tailored to fit a specific occasion – so much so that he often complained of pressure of time, or introduced a 'stop press' comment to react to some new development in the situation. His tactical sense appears too in the fact that even when he directly attacked his antagonists' position, he seldom argued merely for victory, to win the applause of his own side by scoring points off his opponents. His tracts were nearly always directed *towards* the latter, or to some clearly visualised section of them, perhaps to win over doubting moderates, perhaps to drive a wedge between one section and another – Anglicans and Roman Catholics, for instance – perhaps merely to confuse them.

Another useful guide is the name of the publisher, where this is known. The significant ones at this period of his life are Richard Chiswell (at the beginning of William III's reign), and subsequently Richard Baldwin, and then his widow, Mrs A. Baldwin; for his verse, John Nutt is important. The likelihood that a piece is by Defoe is further increased if it is advertised at the back of a known Defoe tract (or later, in his *Review*) or alongside others from his pen in the *Term Catalogue*.

While the convergence of various criteria may establish a strong presumption of Defoe's authorship, it will always stop short of proof. Even to convince the sceptical would make undue demands on space. All that is aimed at below is to supplement the main text with more technical considerations, and to draw attention to points especially worth considering.

1. 'Foreword' and 'Prefatory Discourse' to Miege's *English Grammar* (1688) (chap. 7 pp. 126—7). I rely here on the almost *verbatim* extract from the 'Prefatory Discourse' in Miege's *New State of England* (1691), in a part of the latter compilation for which Defoe was actually responsible (see chap. 8 pp. 156—7 and Bastian (3)). Defoe's authorship of the 'Prefatory Discourse' is confirmed by a further slip: while England and the English language are normally discussed in the third person (presumably in deference to Miege's Swiss origins), the first person is once used: 'Neither are we troubled with Verbs reciprocal.' The ideas expressed correspond closely to those found in *EuP*, pp. 227—52.

2. *Some Short Considerations* (1689) (chap. 8 pp. 137—8). In *State Tracts*, i, 175—8. According to Wing, published 'for N.R.'. The passage quoted reappeared in a slightly compressed form in *A Complete History of the Late Revolution* (1691) for the main text of which Defoe was responsible (see Bastian (3)). As suggested in the main text, though the taut formality of the argument is untypical of Defoe, the political theory propounded and the interpretation of the Revolution correspond exactly to his ideas frequently expressed elsewhere. The high-flown peroration is characteristic of his early work. 'Post est Occasio Calva' reappears in *The Shortest Way with the Dissenters*, where the last word is incorrectly given as 'calvo'.

3 and 4. *A Discourse of the Necessity of Encouraging Mechanick Industry* (1690); *St. Paul the tent-maker* (1690) (chap. 8, pp. 146—8. In *State Tracts*, ii, 130—44, 145—58. *Discourse*, published by R. Chiswell, carried an advertisement for *St. Paul* 'now in the press . . . by the same Author'. *St. Paul*, published by R. Baldwin, carried advertisements for books 'printed for R. Chiswell'. In *TC*, Hilary (Feb) 1690 both are listed among the publications of Chiswell, who had published two other pieces for Defoe in 1689. In Holland, 'Even the children of four years old will earn their bread' (*State Tracts*, ii, 135): cf. Defoe's comments on Norfolk and the West Riding (*Tour*, i, 62; ii, 195).

5. *Taxes No Charge* (1690) (chap. 8, p. 148). *State Tracts*, ii,

116—29. Published by R. Chiswell. The title, perhaps derived from a famous tract of an earlier generation, *Killing No Murder*, anticipates Defoe's *Giving Alms No Charity* (1704). See the main text for the characteristically paradoxical views, and for links with Defoe's personal affairs, notably his borrowings to purchase Essex marshlands, and his visit to Northern Ireland in 1689—90. Among many Defoeisms, note 'The Moors who give us Gold for Glass-Beads' (*State Tracts*, ii, 123).

6. *Reflections upon the late Famous Petition* (1690) (chap. 8, pp. 154—5). In *State Tracts*, ii, 169—77. Pointers to Defoe's authorship, in addition to those mentioned in the main text, include familiarity with City politics, knowledge of a recently published work in French, and comment on those 'that first launch out into Chancery suits'. Defoeisms include the expression 'the World in a String'.

7. *A Discourse about Raising Men* (1696) (chap. 10, p. 195). In *State Tracts*, ii, 539—50. According to Wing, published by Richard Baldwin. The identity of the views with those expressed in the *Review* (20 Jan 1709) is discussed in the main text. Note also the praise for Louis XIV, because 'he put an end to Duels in *France*, by severe Laws, and a strict Execution of them', a theme on which he expanded in his *Review* (29 April 1704).

8. *A Modest Vindication of Oliver Cromwell* (1698) (chap. 11, pp. 208—9). In *Somers Tracts*, vi, 416—42. One of four pieces listed by Mrs A. Baldwin in *TC*, Easter 1698 (her first advertisement), the other three being known Defoe items. A remarkably prompt reaction to Ludlow's *Memoris*, which did not reach the *TC* until after the tract which attacked them. Defoe's early familiarity with this work appears from a reference in his *A Brief Reply to the History of Standing Armies*, which appeared about the beginning of the following December: 'two Volumes of *Ludlows Memoirs* . . . the government of a single Person opposed covertly' are listed among works produced by 'Socinians and Commonwealthsmen' against the government of William III; and this is the theme on which *A Modest Vindication* is based. Amongst plentiful Defoeisms, note 'Sylla' for 'Sulla' (p. ii), also found in M. Schonhorn (ed.), *A General History of the Pyrates* (London, 1972) p. 26. Defoe's titles include five other 'Vindications', one of them 'A Modest Vindication'.

9. *An Argument Proving . . .* (1698) (chap. 11, p. 216). Published by Mrs A. Baldwin. Among numerous Defoeisms, note

'gilded pills'; 'Quem Jupiter vult perdere prius dementat'. He often mentioned how James II 'returned from Feversham with the Huzza's of his People' (cf. *Review*, vi, 561–2; vii, 134; *AJ* 23 Oct 1725, in Lee, iii, 433).

10 and 11. *Remarks upon a Late Pamphlet Intitul'd, The Two Great Questions consider'd* . . . (1700); *Remarks* . . . *Part II* . . . (1701) (chap. 12, pp. 231–2). It is argued in the main text that these replies were really designed to raise doubts about the impact of Louis XIV's action upon our trade and national security. Defoeisms are plentiful. Of three Latin tags, two are favourites of Defoe, including 'Quos deus vult perdere prius dementat'. *The Two Great Questions Further Consider'd* (p. 17) attacks statements allegedly made in *Remarks* (p. 21); but they are not to be found on p. 21 or anywhere else in that tract. However, other cross references, to pp. 6, 9 and 14, are correct.

12. *A Letter to a Member of Parliament concerning the Present Posture of Affairs in Christendom* (1700) (chap. 12, pp. 232–3). I have seen the second edition (1700) in the Bodleian (Pamphlets 232). Support for the Partition Treaty was very scanty; and retrospectively Defoe was its most articulate defender, frequently claiming that William had personally explained to him his motives for making it. As this tract was the principal defence of the Treaty, it seems natural to attribute it to him. This is supported by numerous Defoeisms. 'What Measures we ought to take' (p. ii) echoes 'What Measures the English ought to take' in the title of *The Two Great Questions Consider'd* (1700), and anticipates 'What Measures the French King will take' in the title of *The Present State of Jacobitism Consider'd* (1701). See also *Some Reply to a Letter* (No. 19 below), ostensibly attacking this tract, but in reality seeking to nudge public opinion further along the same path.

13. *The Present Disposition of England Consider'd* (1701) (chap. 12, p. 237). In *State Tracts*, iii, 67–76. 'Publish'd in July 1701', but the Preface begins: 'The following Paper was printed the beginning of January last . . . But an injudicious Writer, by the name of a True Englishman, pretending after six Months Pause to give an Answer to it, under the Title of *England's Enemies Expos'd and its true Friends and Patriots defended &c.*, another Impression was thought necessary.' It went on to rebut the insinuation that the original tract was the work of a 'Noble Lord', and continued with what sounds like

an admission of authorship: 'The only Piece of Skill he shews, is by ranging this Paper with a Libel, call'd the Legion, to make them look like Companions.' Though Defoe still formally denied authorship of *Legion's Memorial*, his responsibility must have been an open secret, especially after his prominent role at the Mercers' Hall feast on the release of the Kentish petitioners. No doubt to advertise his links with the Junto Lords helped to divert attention from his much more significant relations with William.

14 and 15. *The Duke of Anjou's Succession Consider'd* (1700); *The Duke of Anjou's Succession Further Consider'd* (1700) (chap. 12, p. 238–9). In *State Tracts*, iii, 22–44; 45–67. The 5th and 2nd editions respectively were listed by A. Baldwin in *TC* Hilary (Feb) 1700/1, heading a group of eight, four others of which were by Defoe. I have been unable to examine the other two, both dealing with the Spanish Succession. Note the close analogy between the full titles, as given in the main text, and other Defoe titles, e.g. *The Succession of the Crown of England Consider'd* (1701), *The Succession of Spain Consider'd: Or, a View of the several Interests of the Princes and Powers of Europe* (1711), and especially *The Interests of the Several Princes and States of Europe Consider'd with respect to the Succession of the Crown of Spain* (1698). Note also '*Consider'd*' and '*Further Consider'd*' in a very recent pair of tracts. The case argued, while contrary to the consensus of public opinion, corresponds to Defoe's position. Defoeisms are plentiful. 'Since the writing of this' introduces a postcript to the first tract; 'Since the writing of whats above' occurs twice in the other. See also *The Dangers of Europe* (No. 23 below).

16. *The English Gentleman Justify'd* (1701) (chap. 12, p. 236). In Bodleian (Firth 2799.e.398). Published by J. Nutt. Though apparently a point by point rebuttal of the *True-Born Englishman*, the author in fact confines himself to insignificant cavils, and as the poem progresses increasingly expresses agreement, e.g.

> To your Wise Notions of a *Government*
> At least, (to all Material) I consent: (p. 54)

Praise of Whigs, and of William, is more heartfelt than that of Tories. He ends with a lukewarm and double-edged defence of Duncombe:

And if St. *Magnus* Dial cou'd but Speak,
She'd chime his Praises, tho' she Chimes them Weak. (p. 61)

The words of the original are often echoed, even when not directly referred to. Note also: 'I cavil at the title that it bears', and cf. ' . . . some will cavil at the Title' (*JD*, Preface, xxvi).

17. *An Essay on the Present Interest of England* (1701) (chap. 12, pp. 239—41). In *State Tracts*, iii, 154—82, no author being named. In *Somers Tracts*, xi, 195—218, where it is attributed to George Stepney. I have not traced any discussion of the authorship. Stepney (1663—1707), a schoolfellow and friend of Charles Montagu, now Baron Halifax, was a diplomat with special experience of the German courts, who was soon after this sent as ambassador to Vienna. Here he strongly urged the Emperor to intervene in Spain rather than in Italy; and as this tract stresses the advantages of a Spanish campaign. this may be the basis for the attribution. But the tract shows no knowledge of, or interest in, German diplomacy. Stepney was a poet, though an indifferent one; but I can find nothing else in prose attributed to him. The ideas and argument correspond exactly with the development of Defoe's propaganda campaign. Defoeisms are plentiful; and note, 'Since the printing of which . . . '.

18. The 'Melfort Letter' (1701) (chap. 12, pp. 242—3). In *Somers Tracts*, xi, 191—4. The grounds for the attribution, already discussed in the main text, may be summarised: (1) It was part of a larger propaganda operation, in which Defoe was undoubtedly involved, designed to shock the Commons into taking a serious view of the international situation. (2) The variant title of Defoe's tract, *The Apparent Danger of an Invasion*, quoted on p. 243, more specifically links the 'Letter' with Defoe's propaganda. (3) Although brief, there are two significant Defoeisms — 'his all is at stake' — 'the fable of the dog who lost the Substance for the shadow' (cf. 'Like the Dog in the Fable, grasping at the *Shadow* and lose the *Substance*', *Review*, 3 May 1709).

19. *Some Reply to a Letter . . . to a Member of Parliament* (1701) (chap. 12, pp. 244—5). In *State Tracts*, iii, 203—10. No fewer than 17 tracts in Moore, *Checklist*, have titles beginning with 'Some'. Content and method are both very characteristic of Defoe. Ostensibly an attack on the original *Letter*, its purpose was to nudge public opinion further along the same path (see No. 12 above). Defoeisms are plentiful.

20. *An Account of the Debate in Town* (1701) (chap. 12, pp. 245–6). In *State Tracts*, iii, 76–102. The content of this remarkable tract is fully discussed in the main text. Once again, while ostensibly attacking William, it actually supports the policy he had at heart. Thus, in content and method, it is highly characteristic of Defoe. The only Latin expression, '*hinc illae lachrymae*', was a favourite of his; and compare the comment on Sir Edward Harley (father of Robert Harley) in *State Tracts*, iii, 98, with a similar comment in the *Review*, 12 Dec. 1704.

21. *Animadversions on the Succession* (1701) (chap. 12, pp. 248–9). In British Library (8122.bb.35). This pamphlet first opened my eyes to Defoe's technique of waging mock battles by apparently writing on both sides of a controversy. How could Defoe, deep in William's confidence on the Succession question, have been so naive as to write in favour of Dalkeith? This reply makes sense of the whole manoeuvre.

22. *Anguis in Herba* (1701) (chap. 12, pp. 260–1). In *State Tracts*, iii, 312–42. Published by A. Baldwin. Sometimes attributed to Somers, and to Henry Maxwell, MP. The argument expresses Defoe's position at this time, now attempting to play down party divisions. The knowledge shown of the situation in Piedmont in 1680 (pp. 331–3) fits neatly with Defoe's suggested 'Grand Tour' in that year (see chap. 5, pp. 69–70). Defoeisms abound: '(Latet) anguis in herba' was one of his favourite Latin expressions (also 'the snake in the grass').

23. *The Dangers of Europe* (1702 for 1701) (chap. 12, p. 262). In *State Tracts*, iii, 343–73. 'By the Author of, *The Duke of Anjou's Succession consider'd*' (No. 14 above). Published by A. Baldwin. The theme, 'the Cure of our Divisions at Home', follows the line taken by Defoe at this time. Defoeisms are plentiful. Note the mention of William's 'Proclamation of Feb. 24 1697(8) against Profaneness and Immorality' (p. 54), a favourite topic of Defoe's; and also the very blunted attack on one of his own tracts, *Reasons against a War with France* (p. 43).

24. William's Last Speech (1701) (chap. 12, pp. 263–4). In *A Collection of all the Speeches . . . of . . . William III . . .*, published by J. Baker (1712), item 36. For the attribution to Somers, see chap. 12, pp. 263–4, above, and Appendix A. For Defoe's authorship, I rely on the frequency, warmth and accuracy of his later references to it (see chap. 12, note 111). As the

speech was sometimes framed and hung on the wall, this might explain Defoe's familiarity; but his reference in the *Review*, 13 Oct. 1705 was written when he was away from home, travelling in the north. *A Satyr Upon King William* (1703), for which John Dunton was responsible, but which in some unexplained way seems to incorporate material originating with Defoe, mentions or quotes the speech, in characteristic Defoe fashion, on four occasions.

25. *Reflections upon . . . The Shortest Way* (1703) (chap. 13, p.281. I have seen two versions, with differing title-pages: (a) BL, 698.i.27; (b) BL, 4135.aaa.3. Inaccuracies in the title-page of (a) are corrected in (b), which is also better printed. The impression of confusion and haste created by these discrepancies, is supported by the comment, 'I have no time to insist upon this Subject' [(a), p. 6]; and given the circumstances, this must reinforce the attribution to Defoe. Among other Defoe hobby-horses, note, 'our Lady of Loretto' (p. 3) and the 'Declaration for Sports and Pastimes' (p. 6). 'Argumentum ad hominem' was a favourite Latin tag. 'Beautefeu', a mis-spelling of 'boutefeu', can be matched by *'Beautfeus'* in *The Dangers of the Protestant Religion*, in *True Collection*, p. 238. Maximilian E. Novak, in 'Defoe's *Shortest Way with the Dissenters . . .* ', *Modern Language Quarterly*, xxvii (1966) 400, footnote 8, points out that Charles Leslie had suggested that Defoe was the author of the *Reflections*, but he does not pursue the point.

26 and 27. *The Locusts . . . Pts. I & II* (1704–5) (chap. 8, pp. 155–6). The BL copy, bearing the arms of the Hon. Thomas Grenville (1755–1846), is bound in with another Defoe piece, *The Experiment*, and has on the spine: DE FOE/EXPERI/ MENT/LOCUSTS/1705–4. This suggests some tradition of Defoe's authorship, but I have not found it assigned to him in any bibliography. *TC*, Trinity (June) 1704 listed the first part immediately after two known Defoe items, among five pieces 'sold by the Booksellers of London and Westminster'. *TC*, Hilary (Feb) 1705 listed Part II as 'printed for J. Nutt, near Stationers Hall: where may be had the First Part'; and *TC*, Michaelmas (Nov) 1705 listed both parts as sold by Nutt at 6*d*. each. Both parts were advertised in Defoe's *The Ballance* (published 8 June 1705), and in his *Little Review*, a supplement to his *Review*, from 8 June–13 July and 10–23 August 1705, when the *Little Review* came to an end. Part I traces the history of law, and

praises the English law and legal system, and only attacks
Chancery in the last few pages; Part II deals exclusively with
Chancery, first in a general way, but eventually by satirising
various personalities. This appears to be the only poem published
by Defoe in two parts. Perhaps he had been flying a kite, and
when no ill consequences followed the publication of Part I, he
felt it safe to publish the much more explosive Part II after
eight months; and when this was ignored, even to advertise both
parts, after some four months, in his own *Review*.

> How blest are we! *Treborius* now Controls
> The Chancery and *Scaevola* the Rolls (ii, 15),

with other comments about these two, only makes sense by
identifying *Treborius* with Sir John Trevor, Chief Commissioner
of the Great Seal from 14 May 1690 until 1693, and *Scaevola*
with Sir Henry Powle, Master of the Rolls from 1689 until his
death on 21 November 1692. This suggests that the poem was
written between May 1690 and November 1692, at a time when
Defoe was deeply involved in Chancery litigation, but set aside,
either through caution, or because Defoe was overtaken by his
financial troubles; and then taken in hand again, no doubt with
alterations and additions, a dozen years later. This might explain
why Trevor's character as a judge is justifiably praised under the
pseudonym of Treborius, while his personal character is savagely
attacked, also quite accurately, as 'T——r'.

28. *Some Plain Observations Recommended to the Consideration of every Honest English-Man; Especially to the Electors of
Parliament Members* (1705) (chap. 12, p. 269). This attack on
the record of those who had opposed the policies of William and
his 'friends' during the years 1695—1702, is highly characteristic
of Defoe with his 'Whig' rather than his 'moderation' hat on;
and by beginning with criticism of Tory hostility to three major
achievements of Halifax — the formation of the Bank of England,
recoinage, and the introduction of exchequer bills — he shows that
this tract was written directly in support of Halifax's political
friends. Though Defoe was now Harley's man, he had also
resumed relations with Halifax shortly before the election of
1705 (see Healey, *Letters*, 30, 33, 38). Though Harley ranked as
a Tory, Whig successes at the election would not have been unwelcome to free him from dependence on the high-fliers of his

own party. Yet, though he was not personally 'glanced at' in the tract, he had been largely responsible for some of the policies which were savagely attacked, and he is hardly likely to have connived at its appearance. Nevertheless, despite its brevity (eight pages), it appears to be unmistakably Defoe's work.

29. *The History of the Press Yard* (1717) (chap. 13, pp. 288—9). Published by T. Moor. Apparently first attributed to Defoe by Wilson, but rejected by Lee. Some works of reference have followed Wilson, e.g. Halkett and Laing, *Dictionary of Anonymous and Pseudonymous English Literature*, and *Catalogue of the Printed Books in Edinburgh University Library*; but it is omitted from Moore, *Checklist*. I have seen no discussion of the authorship. Ostensibly written by one of the 'brethren of the Quill' who had recently spent several months in Newgate for attacking the government of the day, it is a rambling and badly organised book, whose author tries to chase three hares at once. First, it is a lively account of life in the Press Yard, written by someone who had obviously experienced it at first hand; secondly, it is a journalistic investigation of the attitudes of the Jacobite prisoners who had been held there after their defeat at Preston; and finally, it is a defence of the government from imputations of undue severity towards the Jacobite prisoners. Defoe had of course spent several months in Newgate more than a dozen years before; visits to Newgate to interview Jacobite prisoners may have anticipated his later visits to interview common criminals; and he was secretly serving the government (see Healey, *Letters*, 234). This is supported by numerous Defoeisms, e.g. 'Goal' for 'Gaol', 'stiffle', 'Heights', 'Arcana's', and an old favourite: 'Quos Deus vult perdere prius dementat'. A reference to Newgate Prison as a 'Mansion House' can be matched in the *Review* (2 Sept 1707). An Attack on the Ordinary, or prison chaplain, Paul Lorrain (pp. 47—52), for profiting by the publication of prisoners' confessions, had been anticipated in *A Hymn to the Pillory* (1703). The stress laid on the failure of the Jacobites to defend the Ribble Bridge, as an explanation of their defeat at Preston (pp. 58, 74—82) foreshadows an incident in *Colonel Jack* (pp. 264—5). A long poem on 'IMPRISONMENT' (pp. 21—3) contains the lines:

> *Joy, that I by the best of Queens have stood,*
> *And dar'd to Vindicate the* Stuarts *Blood.*

It is difficult to see how anyone could have been imprisoned for
'standing by' Queen Anne. Perhaps this was a reworking of a
poem written by Defoe when himself in Newgate, when he
might well have expressed joy at standing by 'the best of Kings'.

Notes and References

Introduction

1. J. R. Sutherland, 'Some Early Troubles of Daniel Defoe', *Review of English Studies*, ix (1935) 275—90.
2. *Review*, ii, 485—6; *A Tour Through the Whole Island of Great Britain*, vol. i (Everyman, 1962) p. 306.
3. *An Essay on the History and Reality of Apparitions* (1727) pp. 373—6.
4. F. Bastian, 'Daniel Defoe and the Dorking District', *Surrey Archaeological Collections*, vol. lv (1958) 41—64.
5. See below, chap. 1, pp. 12—13; chap. 2, pp. 28—30; chap. 6, p. 95.
6. *Atlas Maritimus & Commercialis* (1728), Preface, p. ii.
7. See below, chap. 10, pp. 177—80, 182—3.
8. F. Bastian, 'James Foe Merchant, Father of Daniel Defoe', *N&Q*, ccix (March 1964) 82—6.
9. G. A. Aitken (ed.), *Serious Reflections during the Life and Surprising Adventures of Robinson Crusoe* (London, 1895) Preface, pp. ix—xiii.
10. J. Donald Crowley (ed.), *Robinson Crusoe* (Oxford, 1972) pp. 177—9; *Tour*, ii, 168—71.
11. G. A. Starr (ed.), *Moll Flanders* (Oxford, 1971) pp. 193—5; *History of Apparitions*, pp. 207—9; *The History of the Devil*, in Henry G. Bohn (ed.), *The Novels and Miscellaneous Works of Daniel De Foe* vol. iii (London, 1854—6) pp. 547—8.

Chapter 1

1. Exhibition Catalogue, *Daniel Defoe, 1660—1731, Commemoration in Stoke Newington of the Tercentenary of his Birth* (1960) p. 30, item 384.
2. George J. Armytrage (ed.), *Allegations for Marriage Licences issued by the Vicar-General of the Archbishop of Canterbury* (*Publications of the Harleian Society*, vol. xxx, 1890) p. 155.
3. For the publication date of *The Protestant Monastery* see John Robert Moore, *A Checklist of the Writings of Daniel Defoe* (Bloomington, 1960) item 486.
4. *RC*, pp. 63, 64, 69, 70, 112, 125, 133. See also *infra*, chap. 7, p. 116 and note 21.
5. *RC*, pp. 133, 278.

6. Guildhall Library. I have failed, however, to find any evidence to link the Foes with Fore street in this parish. See chap. 7, note 68.
7. Corporation of London Record Office, Assessment Boxes 25/MS 1, 56/18 and 7/12 show James Foe's presence there in March 1666/7, and on 21 Aug 1667 and 19 Feb 1668/9.
8. See Bastian (2).
9. Ibid. See Guildhall Library MS 6440/2 for James Foe's apprenticeship. For John Levitt see Guildhall Library MS 9325/2; MS 9327; also Portsoken Ward records in CLRO.
10. Guildhall Library, Butchers' Company Rough Annual Masters' and Wardens' Accounts, MS 6641/12 (1683–4). G. H. Healey (ed.), *The Letters of Daniel Defoe* (Oxford, 1955) Letter 9, p. 15.
11. Surrey Record Office, Kingston-upon-Thames; Dorking Court Book, 14 November 1671.
12. Wills of Elizabeth Marsh (PCC 146 Duke) and Henry Loxham (PCC 25 Reeve); PRO, Exch. B & A. Ldn. Chas II, No. 1049A, a reference given by A. J. C. Guimaraens, 'Daniel Defoe and the Family of Foe', *N&Q* (March 1912) 241, but who seems to have assumed that 'James Foe, merchant' was someone other than Defoe's father; will of James Foe (PCC 31 Poley).
13. Louis Landa (ed.), *A Journal of the Plague Year* (Oxford, 1969) pp. 11, 215, 9, 11.
14. James Foe is not found, however, among over 1800 names listed in *The London Directory of 1677. The Oldest Printed List of the Merchants and Bankers of London* (1878).
15. P. C. D. Mundy, 'The Ancestry of Daniel Defoe', *N&Q*, clxxiv (Feb 1938) 112–14, and further information kindly supplied by Mr Mundy.
16. Discussed more fully below, chap. 10, pp. 189–90, and notes 70–3.
17. See *The True-Born Hugonot* (1703) p. 5.
18. *VCH Northants*, ii, 486; his will, proved 1647 in Consistory Court of Peterborough, M.176.
19. F. Bastian, 'Defoe's *Journal of the Plague Year* Reconsidered', *RES*, xvi (1965) 158.
20. (a) Mary, daughter of Daniel and Rose Foe, baptised Etton, 1625. (b) H.F.'s 'only sister' in Lincolnshire (*JPY*, p. 9). (c) Will of John Abbott of St Saviour Southwark, gent (1693, PCC 104 Coker) mentioning 'cousin' James Foe and 'sister in law' Sarah Reynolds of Stamford, widow. (d) Defoe shows more interest in Stamford than anywhere else in Lincolnshire (*Tour*, ii, 104–9).
21. *Tour*, ii, 102, 109–10.
22. *VCH Hunts*, iii, 192.
23. Will of Solomon Fall, PCC 43 Evelyn, proved 20 Jan 1640/1.
24. The will of Thomas King (PCC 664 Wootton) mentions stepson Michael Foll and wife Rose. She had witnessed the will of her son, Daniel Foe in 1647, as Rose King.
25. A. W. Secord (ed.), *Defoe's Review Reproduced from the Original Editions* (New York, 1938) p. vii, Preface.

26. In his own will, and in a codicil, dated 26 June 1674, to that of Lady Mary Armyne (PCC 22 Dycer), referring to the manor and farm of 'Nanseclas', Bottlebridge, purchased from him.

27. Will of Thomas King, Orton Longueville, yeoman, proved 1641. Information kindly supplied by Cambridgeshire Record Office.

28. PRO, E 179/122/226, dated 15 Jan 18 Chas. II (1667) lists Bottle-bridge and Orton Longueville separately. No house in Bottlebridge had more than four hearths. Apart from Orton Hall (27 hearths) the largest in Orton Longueville was the Rectory (6 hearths). Edmund Spinks, ejected from Orton Longueville in 1662, lived in Bottlebridge; while Simon King, s. of Simon King of Woodhouse, Leics., who became Rector of Bottlebridge between 1651 and 1655, also ejected 1662, continued to live for over 30 years in Orton Longueville. I have failed to find any connection between Simon and Thomas King. See Matthews, *Calamy Revised*, pp. 209—10. For Lady Mary Armyne and William Pierrepont, see *DNB*. See also *VCH Hunts*, iii, 195—8.

29. G. A. Aitken (ed.), *Due Preparations for the Plague*, 1895 ed., pp. 93—111, especially pp. 93, 95, 96.

30. *Review*, vii, 98. See also *Review*, iv, 122, 125—6; v, 19, vi, 258, 599; viii, 210; *The Poor Man's Plea*, in A. W. Secord (ed.), *A Journal of the Plague Year and Other Pieces* (New York, 1935) p. 252; *Reflections upon . . . the Shortest Way* (1703), p. 6 [See Appendix B(25)].

31. *Review*, vi, 341.

32. *The Dissenters Answer to the High-Church Challenge* (1704) p. 43. See also *The Consolidator* (1705) p. 179.

33. *A Letter to Mr. How* (1700), in *A True Collection of the Writings of the Author of the True Born English-man* (1703) p. 327: 'I am of the same Class, and in the same Denomination of a Dissenter with your Self.'

34. Matthews, *Calamy Revised*, pp. 13—14; *The Character of the late Dr. Samuel Annesley* (1697), in *True Collection*, pp. 110—18; John Dunton, *The Impeachment* (1714) p. 13.

35. 'Friend William' in *Captain Singleton*, and Roxana's Quaker landlady.

36. There may be an obscure reference to the early days of Quakerism in *Review*, iii, 323: 'Riddle me Ree — As the Boys say, *Help Woodcock, Fox and Naylor*'. For William Woodcock, a Quaker active *c.*1655—60 see W. C. Braithwaite, *The Beginnings of Quakerism*, vol. i (1923) pp. 377—8; vol. ii, p. 18.

37. Jane Jack (ed.), *Roxana* (Oxford, 1964) pp. 210—330, esp. p. 311.

38. See *infra*, chap. 3, pp. 32—3 and notes 1—4.

39. (a) MS Jayne, in possession of the Lisbon Branch of the Historical Association; 'British Consuls in Lisbon, Part II, 1656—87', *5th Review and Annual Report* (1941) p. 319. Hardwick is listed as a member of the 'faction' of Richard Stanley who opposed the 'soberer merchants'. (b) 'Journal of James Jenefer, Captain of the *Suadades* of London, 1673', *HMC Dartmouth* III, pp. 23—7.

40. *Review*, i, 367; but see also *infra*, chap. 2, pp. 27—8 and note 45.

Chapter 2

1. John Strype, edition of Stow's *Survey of London*, vol. iii (1720) p. 64. See map between pp. 52—3.
2. *Review*, ii. 367.
3. Elizabeth is not mentioned again after her birth. The merchant in *JPY* who apparently represents James Foe had only two children. Robert Davis, sometimes said to be Elizabeth Foe's husband, was in fact the second husband of Mary Foe.
4. A poll-tax assessment list for Coleman Street Ward, March 1667 (CLRO Ass. Box 25/MS 1) shows James Foe and his wife as lodgers with 'John Ellsworth, factor', but the word 'lodgers' has been crossed out. See also Ass. Boxes 56/18 (1667) and 7/12 (1668/9). For Ellsworth/ Schapelinck see *Royal Commission on Historical Monuments (City)*, p. 34a, floor-slab in Dutch Church, Austin Friars, Strype, op. cit., vol. ii, p. 116; will of Ann Ellsworth, PCC 152 Noel (pr. 4 Oct 1700); and information supplied by Miss Julia de L. Mann.
5. *JPY*, p. 86.
6. E. Rogers, *The Life and Opinions of a Fifth Monarchy Man* (London, 1867) p. 32; H. P. Wheatley and P. Cunningham, *London, Past and Present* (London, 1891) pp. 339—40.
7. *Review*, i. 127. See also *Two Great Questions Considered* (1707) p. 22.
8. *JPY*, pp. 27, 29.
9. Ibid., p. 29.
10. *Review*, iv. 127; *More Short Ways with the Dissenters* (1704) p. 22.
11. Parish records of Allhallows, Bread Street, in Guildhall Library; will of Michael Stancliffe, PCC 135 Bath (pr. 1680).
12. *Tour*, ii. 83.
13. *JPY*, p. 1. See F. Bastian, 'Defoe's *Journal of the Plague Year* Reconsidered', *RES*, xvi (May 1965) 158.
14. *JPY*, p. 63.
15. PRO E/179/252/32 Hearth Tax, receipt dated 6 June 1668.
16. *JPY*, pp. 75—6.
17. *JPY*, p. 8.
18. See also *Review*, v, 558; *CEG*, pp. 39, 60.
19. *RC*, p. 25.
20. *JPY*, pp. 23—4.
21. *JPY*, pp. 103, 234, 241. See also *DNB* and Pepys *Diary* 29 July 1667.
22. Moore, *Checklist*, pp. 447, 449.
23. Bastian (as in note 13 above), pp. 158—60.
24. *JPY*, pp. 9, 13.
25. *MF*, pp. 179—87, 298—9.
26. See also *Review*, i[ix] , 13.
27. *JPY*, p. 13.
28. *JPY*, p. 100.
29. *JPY*, p. 86—8.
30. See Bastian (1), pp. 82, 84. Francis Foe, Vicar of Barkby, near Leicester, kept a school there. Henry Lox(h)am, of Belgrave, near Leicester,

gentleman, left his watch to James Foe (PCC 25 Reeve, 1678). See also J. Nichols, *History and Antiquities of the County of Leicestershire*, vol. iii (London, 1800) (Part 1), p. 184.

31. *JPY*, pp. 227—8.
32. PCC 82 Mico.
33. Thomas Vincent, *God's Terrible Voice in the City* (1667), a possible source for Defoe's *JPY*, described both the Plague and the Fire as judgments for sins.
34. *Review*, i[ix], 115.
35. *Mists's Journal*, 29 April 1721, in William Lee, *Daniel Defoe: His Life and Recently Discovered Writings*, vol. ii (London, 1869) 368.
36. Pepys *Diary*, 5 Sept 1666.
37. See Map of London after the Fire, by Wenceslaus Hollar, 1666.
38. *JPY*, p. 224.
39. *JPY*, p. 232. See W. G. Bell, *The Great Plague in London in 1665* (revised ed., London, 1951) pp. 152—3, with reference to *N&Q*, Second Series, viii, 288—9.
40. *JPY*, pp. 62—7.
41. *JPY*, p. 159. Royal Aid (25 Dec 1665—24 June 1666), CLRO Ass. Box 66/22.
42. *JPY*, pp. 89—91; St Stephen Coleman Street, Vestry Minutes, 29 Mar 1673, in Guildhall Library; his will, PCC 126 Hare (pr. 14 Oct 1684).
43. Will of Grace Heath (stepmother), PCC 40 Aylett (pr. 16 Feb 1654/5).
44. *Tour*, ii, 35.
45. *Review*, vii, 242.
46. Inferred from the will of Elizabeth Marsh, PCC Duke (1671). See *infra*, chap. 3, pp. 32—4.
47 *Tour*, i, 40—8.
48. *Col. Jack*, pp. 42—4. Will of John Cullum, PCC 131 Pett, pr. 7 Aug 1699.
49. (a) Suffolk Record Office, Ipswich: Hearth Tax, St Clements, adjoining entries: Tim. Grimball 3, Mr. Jo. Cullum 5 (Suffolk Green Books, No. xi, vol. 13). (b) PCC Admon., 20 July 1654, to John Cullum, husband of Abigael Cullum *alias* Grimble late of Ipswich. (c) George Whitehead held meetings at Tim. Grimble's house in January 1659 (W. C. Braithwaite, *The Beginnings of Quakerism* (London, 1923) pp. 382—3].
50. *The King of Pyrates*, pp. 9—10; *Captain Singleton, passim*.
51. *Review*, iii, 503.
52. *Review*, vi, 573.
53. Coleman Street Ward, 19 Feb 1668/9, CLRO Ass. Box 7/12. A. J. C. Guimaraens, 'Daniel Defoe and the Family of Foe', *N&Q* (March 1912) 241 mentions '1671, Jac. Foe, French Court, Broad Street Ward (Lay Subs. 252/23)'. There is ample evidence from Parish and Ward records that this was James Foe: Guildhall Library, MS 1303/1 (Scavengers Rolls); CLRO Ass. Boxes 34/2; 61/21; 11/9; 26/13. As James Foe does not appear in Ass. Box 57/7 (1671), that must be the year of his move.
54. Poll Tax, Broad Street Ward, 3 April 1678 (CLRO Ass. Box 11/9) shows: James Foe, wife and 2 children, Elinor Norman (servant).
55. *MJ*, 2 Aug 1718, in Lee, ii, 61—3.

Chapter 3

1. G. E. C[ockayne], *Some Notice of Various Families of the Name of Marsh* (Exeter, 1900) pp. 21—2; Bastian (1), pp. 53—8.
2. PCC 120 Mico.
3. Roger Marsh, PCC 157 Twisse; James Colbron, PCC 82 Grey; Henry Colbron, PCC 88 Aylett; Henry Lox(h)am, PCC 25 Reeve. For Loxham see J. Nichols, *History and Antiquities of the County of Leicestershire*, vol. iii (London, 1800) (Part 1), p. 184, and p. 177 for his wife.
4. *Col. Jack*, p. 76.
5. PCC 146 Duke.
6. Dorking Court Book, Surrey Record Office, Kingston-upon-Thames.
7. PRO, Exch. B. & A. Ldn. Chas II No. 1049 A.
8. Sutherland (1), pp. 281—3, with reference to PRO C8. 353/20.
9. Bastian (1), pp. 58—60.
10. Matthews, *Calamy Revised*, p. 198.
11. PCC 98 Vere.
12. *History of Apparitions*, pp. 373—6.
13. Survey of the Manor of Dorking, by William Foster (1649), copied by J. Hodskinson (1783) and H. Clifton (1891). Original in the possession of the Duke of Norfolk; photostat copy at Surrey Record Office, Kingston-upon-Thames. See *The Story of Surrey in Maps* (exhibition catalogue, 1956), item 47.
14. E. S. de Beer (ed.), *The Diary of John Evelyn*, vol. iii (Oxford, 1955) p. 154 (1 Aug 1655); vol. iii, p. 377 (9 Aug 1664); vol. iii, p. 561 (13 Sept 1670). J. Aubrey, *Natural History and Antiquities of Surrey*, vol. iv (London, 1718) pp. 164—7. For the date of Aubrey's visit, see Bastian (1), pp. 48—9.
15. *Tour*, i, 152.
16. *RC*, p. 37; for the way out of the cave, p. 103.
17. J. Timbs, *A Picturesque Promenade Round Dorking* (London, 1823) pp. 113—14, with reference to Nathaniel Salmon, *Antiquities of Surrey* (London, 1736), where however I failed to locate the passage quoted by Timbs. *RC*, p. 74.
18. *Tour*, i, 154—5.
19. *Tour*, i, 147—50, and Bastian (1), pp. 43—7.
20. Evelyn, *Diary*, iv. 76 (15 Oct 1675) — 'an exceeding dry Summer & Autumn'.
21. *Tour*, i. 152.
22. Salt MS 33. A copy is held by the Surrey Archaeological Society.
23. *Surrey Archaeological Collections*, xiii, 160.
24. Bastian (1), pp. 62—4.
25. *Serious Reflections*, p. 235.
26. *CET*, i, 189.
27. *DNB*, Sir Robert Viner.
28. *Tour*, i, 351.
29. *Cal. S. P. (Dom)*, 1671—2, pp. 308 (Wood), 436, 448 (Fisher).
30. *AM&C*, pp. 1—2.

31. *Review*, iii, 250. See also *Review*, vi, 71.
32. *Review*, vi, 57.
33. *Review*, ii, 170—1; and see also *Review*, vi, 372.
34. According to Mr P. D. Mundy, there had been two Wildbore—Foe marriages. John Foe, s. of Thomas Foe of Peakirk, was apprenticed (1638) to William Wildbore, citizen and clothworker. In 1650 he purchased the manor of Glinton and Peakirk from the suppressed Dean and Chapter of Peterborough, on behalf of John Wildbore, whose family had held the lease since 1597 (*VCH Northants*, ii, 493). Daniel Foe of Etton appointed his 'beloved friend', Randle Wildbore, as overseer of his will in 1647. Will of Nicholas Wildbore, citizen and draper, son of Randall Wildbore, late of Glinton, 1664 (PCC 77 Essex). *London Visitation Pedigrees, 1664* (Harl. Soc. Pub. Vol. 92), p. 92, for William Love.
35. *An Essay on the History of Parties* (1711) pp. 11—13.
36. *A New Test of the Church of England's Honesty* (1704) p. 19; and see also *A Fourth Essay at Removing National Prejudices* (1706) p. 19. See Basil Duke Henning (ed.), *The Diary of Sir Edward Dering, 1670—73* (New Haven, 1940) pp. 123—4.
37. *Review*, i[ix], 152.
38. H. M. Margoliouth, *Marvell's Poems and Letters* vol. i (Oxford, 1952) p. 317.
39. For Robert Wilde see *DNB* and C. E. Whiting, *Studies in English Puritanism from the Restoration to the Revolution, 1660—1688*(London, 1968) pp. 558—62.
40. *Tour*, i, 35.
41. *Tour*, i, 56.
42. Friends' Meeting House, Euston Road, London: Society of Friends, Quarterly Meeting of Suffolk (Woodbridge Meeting), Burials — which also shows that Mary Grimble of Ipswich, widow, d. 12 and was buried at Ipswich, 14 Dec 1691.
43. Henry Foe's will, PCC 33 Dycer, was proved on 13 April 1675.
44. *Tour*, i, 153—4, and Bastian (1), pp. 61—3.
45. Shiv K. Kumar (ed.), *Captain Singleton* (Oxford, 1969) pp. 61—2.
46. *Tour*, i, 149—50; E. Hockliffe (ed.), *The Diary of Ralph Josselin, 1616—1683*, Camden Third Series, vol. XV (London, 1908) p. 169.

Chapter 4

1. In addition to Morton's Academy, there were establishments kept by Edward Veale (Globe Alley, Wapping), Thomas Doolittle (Islington), Thomas Gale, later Thomas Rowe (Newington Green and Hackney). See J. W. Ashley Smith, *The Birth of Modern Education, The Contribution of the Dissenting Academies* (London, 1954) pp. 41—6, 56—61, 87—90.

2. *DNB*; Matthews, *Calamy Revised*, pp. 356–7; Lew Girdler, 'Defoe's Education in Newington Green Academy', *Studies in Philology*, 1 (Oct 1953) 573–91.
3. *The Present State of the Parties* (1712) pp. 293–333.
4. S. Wesley, *A Letter from a Country Divine to his Friend in London Concerning the Education of Dissenters in their Private Academies in several parts of the Nation* (1703).
5. Ibid., pp. 7–8.
6. Ibid., p. 8.
7. Ibid., p. 10.
8. *The Present State of the Parties* (1712) pp. 295–6. See also *Memoirs . . . of . . . Daniel Williams* (1718) p. 55.
9. *Review*, viii, 270. *The Two Great Questions Further Consider'd* (1700) p. 4.
10. G. A. Starr, *Defoe and Spiritual Autobiography* (Princeton, 1965). G. A. Starr, *Defoe and Casuistry* (Princeton, 1971), esp. chap. 1.
11. *CEG*, pp. 218–20.
12. *The Present State of the Parties* (1712) p. 318.
13. Ibid., p. 318.
14. (a) *Serious Reflections*, p. 226. (b) *Tour*, i, 143–4 (c) *Review*, viii, 739; *Jure Divino* (1706), Preface, p. xxvi; *The True-Born Englishman* (1701) Preface.
15. *JD*, vii, 14, footnote (a); *Serious Reflections*, pp. 265, 273.
16. *Review*, iv, 681–2, v, 246; vi, 291; vii, 107; viii, 525; i[ix], 151.
17. *An Elegy on the Author of the True-Born-English-Man* (1704) p. 33.
18. *JD*, i, 24, footnote (b); *Serious Reflections*, pp. 86, 106. See John McVeagh, 'Rochester and Defoe: a Study in Influence', *Studies in English Literature*, xiv (Summer 1974) 327–42, esp. p. 328.
19. *An Argument Proving . . .* (1698) p. 10. See Appendix B(9), for Defoe's authorship of this tract. For another Oldham quotation see *Review*, vii, 162.
20. *Tour*, i, 7.
21. *Meditations*. See *infra*, chap. 5, pp. 80–6 for a fuller discussion.
22. *Augusta Triumphans* (Tegg edition), p. 12.
23. *Tour*, i, 305; and see also *Tour*, ii, 111.
24. *Dunton's Whipping-Post* (1706). But see Theodore F. M. Newton, 'William Pittis and Queen Anne Journalism', *Modern Philology* (1935–6) 169, for the authorship of this.
25. *Review*, vii, 455.
26. *DNB*. F. Bastian, 'Defoe and Guy Miege', *N&Q*, ccxiv (March 1969) 103–5. For a comparison between Italian, French, Spanish, Dutch and English, see the Prefatory Discourse to Miege's *English Grammar*, discussed in Appendix B(1).
27. *Review*, vii, 455.
28. *The Storm* (1879 edition of Defoe's works), v. p. 273.
29. *Tour*, i, 56–7 (swallow); ii, 292–3 (gannet); *Review*, iv, 318–20 (flying ants, silkworms); *Caledonia*, pp. 13–15 and *AM&C*, pp. 9–10 (herring).
30. 'A Vision of the Angelic World', in *Serious Reflections*, pp. 259–78.

31. *Review*, vii, 499; *The Danger of the Protestant Religion*, in *True Collection*, p. 254.
32. *Review*, vii, 455.
33. S. Wesley, op. cit. (note 4), p. 6.
34. S. Palmer, *A Defence of the Dissenters Education* (1703); S. Wesley, *A Defence of a Letter* . . . (1704) p. 19; S. Palmer, *A Vindication of the* . . . *Dissenters* . . . *in Answer to Mr. Wesley's Defence* (1705) pp. 52—4.
35. *More Short Ways with the Dissenters* (1704) pp. 5—6.
36. *Review*, ii, 498. See D. Ogg, *England in the Reign of Charles II*, vol. ii (Oxford, 1934) p. 573, quoting *Commons Journals*, ix (31 Oct 1678) 530.
37. *Review*, ii, 497.
38. *Review*, ii, 498.
39. *Review*, viii, 153.
40. *Review*, ii, 498.
41. *Review*, iv, 530—1; and see also *Review*, i, 187; vii, 459.
42. *JD*, xi, 23, footnote.
43. *Review*, v, 118; *Tour*, i, 130—1; *The Freeholders Plea*, in *True Collection*, pp. 171, 176.
44. *Review*, ii, 170—1.
45. *Review*, vii, 297.
46. *Review*, vii, 297.
47. Quoted in Jane Lane, *Titus Oates* (London, 1949) pp. 226—7.
48. *Review*, i, 383.
49. *Review*, iii, 512; and see also *Review*, ii, 379; vi, 257—9.
50. *Tour*, i, 11; *MJ*, 17 Aug 1723, in Lee, iii, 172.
51. *CET*, i, 31. See also *Tour*, ii, 78—9, 220—2.
52. *Tour*, ii, 14, 148.
53. *Tour*, i, 75—6.
54. *CEG*, extract in Boulton, p. 248.
55. *CEG*, p. 13.
56. *CEG*, p. 65.
57. *CEG* (in Boulton), p. 249.
58. *CEG*, p. 60.
59. This theme is explored in Michael Shinagel, *Daniel Defoe and Middleclass Gentility* (Cambridge, Mass., 1968). See also G. A. Starr, *Defoe and Casuistry* (Princeton, N.J., 1971) pp. 86—90, and Peter Earle, *The World of Defoe* (London, 1976) pp. 158—60, 193—201.
60. *Meditations*, p. 4.
61. *History of the Devil*, iii, 546; and for a different version, *History of Apparitions*, p. 210.
62. *Meditations*, p. 4.
63. Ibid., p. 5.
64. In 'A Vision of the Angelic World', in *Serious Reflections*, pp. 296—8.
65. *More Reformation* (1703) p. 27; *Review*, iii, 258. For a different version see *Serious Reflections*, p. 87.
66. *Review*, vi, 341.

Chapter 5

1. *RC*, p. 6.
2. *RC*, pp. 10—13.
3. *RC*, p. 10.
4. *AM&C*, p. 59.
5. *RC*, p. 9.
6. *Tour*, i, 212.
7. *RC*, pp. 10—13. Many of the features common to the Portland Road incident and to Crusoe's Yarmouth storm also appear in the last two letters of *The Storm* (1704), both supposedly reporting shipboard incidents (one at Yarmouth) during the Great Storm of November 1703. I suggest that, unlike the other letters of this compilation, these two letters were concocted by Defoe.
8. *RC*, p. 7.
9. *RC*, p. 10.
10. *RC*, p. 38.
11. In addition to what follows in this chapter, there is a lack of hints of Defoe's presence in England for most of this year. *Review*, i[ix], 152, has a tale of how Charles II refused to allow the prosecution of the famous Whig journalist, Harry Care. He was in fact tried and convicted at Guildhall, though Charles apparently intervened to prevent his sentence from being carried out. See *Cal. S.P.(Dom) 1679—80*, p. 536, Newsletter, 3 July 1680. This strongly suggests Defoe's absence.
12. *RC*, pp. 4—6.
13. *Cavalier*, pp. 10—11.
14. *CET*, ii, 169.
15. *The Two Great Questions Further Consider'd* (1700) pp. 17—18.
16. *The New State of England* (1691) p. 277.
17. *Review*, vi, 20.
18. *RC*, p. 3. Defoe might, however, have taken the name from one of his sources for his *Memoirs of a Cavalier*. 'Creutzenach' features in *The Swedish Intelligencer, the Second Part*, pp. 77—82 ('Creutznach' in the Index).
19. 'Wintselsheim' may also have been influenced by Marlborough's title of Mindelheim.
20. e.g. *Review*, vi, 227.
21. *The Consolidator* (1705) pp. 153—4.
22. *Review*, iii, 454, See also *Review*, iv, 410; v, 182, 207; vi, 20; viii, 416; *The Two Great Questions Consider'd* (1700) p. 16.
23. *Tour*, ii, 63, 67.
24. *AM&C*, p. 68.
25. *St. Paul the Tentmaker*. See Appendix B (4).
26. *Roxana*, p. 105.
27. *AM&C*, p. 70. See also *History of Apparitions*, p. 267.
28. *Roxana*, p. 101. See also *Cavalier*, pp. 21—3, and *Tour*, ii, 63.
29. *Animadversions on the Succession* . . . (1701) p. 11. See Appendix B(21).
30. *Anguis in Herba*, in *A Collection of State Tracts. Publish'd during the*

Reign of King William III vol. iii (1705—7) pp. 331—3. See Appendix B(22). See H. V. Livermore, *A New History of Portugal* (Cambridge, 1966) pp. 324—5.
31. *AM&C*, p. 75.
32. *AM&C*, p. 71.
33. *Applebee's Journal*, 26 Jan 1723, in Lee, iii, 95.
34. *AM&C*, p. 72.
35. *Cavalier*, pp. 31—2.
36. *Roxana*, p. 103.
37. *Tour*, i, 332—3, 335.
38. *Serious Reflections*, pp. 130—1. This may be Defoe's own comment, but attributed to a third person since Crusoe had never visited Italy.
39. *AM&C*, p. 73. See also *History of Apparitions*, p. 182.
40. *Review*, v, 182.
41. *Cavalier*, pp. 32—4.
42. *Roxana*, pp. 6, 102, 173—81.
43. *Cavalier*, p. 34.
44. *Meditations* (5), p. 20.
45. *Review*, i, 383.
46. *Cavalier*, p. 34.
47. *History of Apparitions*, p. 373.
48. *Tour*, ii, 87.
49. *AM&C*, pp. 74—5.
50. *AM&C*, pp. 74—5; and see also *Review*, iv, 290, 460; *Tour*, ii, 35.
51. *AM&C*, p. 76.
52. *Col. Jack*, pp. 221—2.
53. *Review*, i, 41.
54. *Tour*, ii, 67. See also *Review*, iii, 226.
55. *Review*, i, 46. See also *Tour*, i, 195.
56. *Review*, i, 214—15.
57. *Cavalier*, pp. 87—93.
58. *Caledonia* (1706) p. 38, footnote.
59. *Review*, i, 117.
60. *Roxana*, pp. 84, 133, 134; *Tour*, i, 195; ii, 11.
61. *Tour*, ii, 344.
62. *Tour*, i, 165.
63. *Review*, iv, 358—60. Though Defoe claimed to have 'receiv'd it from one who was present at the Time', he also refers to 'the Minutes I took long ago of these things'. What follows may account for his reluctance to admit his presence in Paris at that time.
64. *Tour*, i, 176; and see also *Tour*, i, 333; ii, 87.
65. *Roxana*, pp. 84—5.
66. *Ramkins*, pp. 295—6.
67. Slightly distorting Jacob's curse upon Simeon and Levi, because 'in their anger they slew a man' (Genesis 49: 5—7); more accurately quoted, in a different context, in *Review*, vii, 451.
68. *Review*, i[ix], 67—8.
69, *Ramkins*, pp. 280—3.
70. *Cavalier*, p. 16.

71. *Col. Jack*, pp. 224—9.
72. *Ramkins*, p. 283; *Cavalier*, pp. 17—18; *Col. Jack*, pp. 229—31.
73. *Review*, vii, 223—4; *AM&C*, p. 22; *Tour*, ii, 255.
74. *Review*, i, 78; v, 185. See also *A Discourse about Raising Men*, in *State Tracts*, ii, 547 [attributed to Defoe, Appendix B(7)].
75. *Review*, Appendix to vol. I.
76. *Meditations*. See Moore, *Checklist*, 1. The best recognition of their biographical significance is in Michael Shinagel, *Defoe and Middle-class Gentility* (Cambridge, Mass., 1968) pp. 15—17.
77. But see note 82.
78. *JD*, iii, 10.
79. *RC*, pp. 87—8 et seq.
80. Roger Lloyd, 'The Riddle of Defoe', *The Church Times*, cxxxxvii (16 July 1954) 549, in Frank H. Ellis (ed.), *Twentieth-century Interpretations of Robinson Crusoe* (Englewood Cliffs, N.J., 1969) pp. 92—4.
81. *Serious Reflections*, p. 299; and see ibid., p. 80.
82. The words, 'See Page 125', beside the title, show that the first Meditation was in fact inspired by one of these sermons, in which the 'avenger of blood' and the 'city of refuge' were interpreted in a way which clearly struck home to Defoe.
83. *CET*, i, 53; and cf. the views expressed in *St. Paul the Tentmaker*, in *State Tracts*, ii, 145 et seq., attributed to Defoe in Appendix B (4).
84. See Rudolph G. Stamm, 'Daniel Defoe: An Artist in the Puritan Tradition', *Phil. Quarterly*, xv, no. 3 (July 1936) 225—46.

Chapter 6

1. *Review*, vi, 341.
2. *Review*, viii, 754.
3. Guildhall Library — Rough Annual Masters' and Wardens' Accounts of the Butchers Company (1671—89), MS 6441/1—17, esp. No. 9. See Philip E. Jones, *The Butchers of London* (London, 1976) p. 54.
4. CLRO, Return of Lodgers, June 1683, Coleman Street Ward, 3rd Precinct, Misc.MSS 87/4. *Royal Commission on Historical Monuments — London (City)*, p. 34a: Floor-slabs in Dutch Church, Austin Friars: Josyna Shapelinck, 1689/90; Anna Shapelinck, wife of John Ellsworth, 1700.
5. PCC 31 Poley, dated 20 March 1705/6, pr. 25 Feb 1706/7. See Bastian (2).
6. *Review*, iii, 22.
7. *CET*, ii (Part II), 162.
8. *Review*, i, 357.
9. *AJ*, 13 Nov 1725 in Lee, iii, 440—1.
10. *AJ*, 4 July 1724, in Lee, iii, 279—80. See also *Review*, ii, 26; i[ix], 105; and M. Beloff, *Public Order and Public Disturbances, 1660—1714* (London, 1938) p. 198.

11. *Giving Alms No Charity*, in Secord, p. 303. See also *Review*, iv, 26.
12. Timothy Cruso, *DNB*. I am not suggesting that Defoe did not know him. He named him first when listing the eminent products of Morton's Academy in *The Present State of the Parties* (1712) p. 320. But he may also have known other members of the family. Several references to the family in the registers of St Helens Bishopsgate, *c*.1655 spell the name 'Crusoe'.
13. 'Pedigree of the Family of Cruso', contributed by George W. G. Barnard, *The Genealogist*, New Series, xviii (1902) 246—52. Robinson, s. of Francis Cruso, mercer, was baptised at King's Lynn, 26 Feb 1732. He is described as upholder (undertaker), appraiser and auctioneer. Four of his descendants were also called Robinson Cruso.
14. *Review*, iv, 614. See also *Review*, iv, 622—4 and ii, 18.
15. *Giving Alms No Charity*, in Secord, pp. 315—16. *Review*, ii, 26.
16. CLRO, Poll Tax, Cornhill Ward, March 1691/2, Ass. Box 35/12.
17. *Review*, i[ix], 180.
18. *An Essay upon Projects* (1697) pp. 23—4.
19. *A Brief Case of the Distillers* (1726) pp. 15—21.
20. *Review*, viii, 307.
21. *Review*, i[ix], 193.
22. *Review*, viii, 14.
23. Healey, *Letters* (17), p. 206 and (18), p. 207.
24. *CET*, p. 8.
25. *Cal. S. P.* (Dom), 1682, p. 597. Newsletter, 30 December 1682.
26. *Review*, v, 454.
27. *RC*, pp. 45—58.
28. *Review*, iii, 6.
29. *Review*, vii, 527.
30. *AM&C*, pp. 60—1. See also *Review*, viii, 168, 203.
31. *Review*, viii, 175. *AM&C*, p. 64.
32. *RC*, p. 27; *Tour*, ii, 355; *AM&C*, p. 244. See also *Review*, ii, 110.
33. *A Fifth Essay at Removing National Prejudices* (1707) pp. 10—11. Both Singleton and Captain Merlotte in the *New Voyage* visited the Canaries. However, Defoe's account of the islands in *AM&C*, pp. 244—5, contains no convincing evidence of personal knowledge.
34. *AM&C*, p. 266.
35. *RC*, p. 27.
36. *Review*, vii, 114. See also, e.g. *AJ*, 31 March 1722, in Lee, ii, 505.
37. *AM&C*, p. 65. See also *Review*, i, 251.
38. *Review*, ii, 176; iv, 386; v, 90, 366; vii, 530; *Farther Adventures of Robinson Crusoe*, vol. i (1841 edition of works) item 6, p. 36.
39. *Review*, viii, 303.
40. *A Plan of the English Commerce* (1927 ed.) p. 146.
41. *Review*, iii, 45.
42. *CEG*, p. 34.
3. *The Interests of the Several Princes* . . . (1698) pp. 23—5. *Review*, i[ix], 173; *CET*, p. 27; *RC*, p. 247.
    M&C, p. 66; *Tour*, i, 168.

46. *AM&C*, pp. 71—2.
47. *AM&C*, p. 31; *Tour*, ii, 345—6. See A. W. Skempton, 'Canals and River Navigations before 1750', in *A History of Technology* vol. iii (Oxford, 1957) pp. 464—8.
48. *AM&C*, pp. 57—8.
49. *AM&C*, pp. 57—8.
50. *Review*, iii, 342.
51. *AM&C*, pp. 57—8.
52. (a) For earlier Stancliffe descent, see Burke's *Landed Gentry*. (b) W. B. Trigg, 'Scout Hall', *Transactions of the Halifax Antiquarian Society* (1946) p. 37. (c) Registers of All Hallows, Bread Street (Guildhall Library). (d) Wills of Michael Stancliffe, PCC 135 Bath (1680) and Samuel Stancliffe, PCC 136 Irby (1695), but throwing no light on Defoe.
53. Theodore F. M. Newton, 'The Civet Cats of Newington 'Green', *RES*, xiii (1937) 10—19; J. R. Sutherland, 'A Note on the Last Years of Defoe', *MLR*, xxix (1934) 137—41.
54. *Tour*, ii, 197—203.
55. J. Horsfall Turner (ed.), *The Rev. Oliver Heywood, B.A., 1630—1702, His Autobiography, Diaries, Anecdotes and Event Books* (Brighouse, 1882—5), *passim*, but especially, vol. iii, pp. 166, 174.
56. Matthews, *Calamy Revised*, p. 458.
57. *Royal Religion* (1704) p. 12.
58. *Review*, iv, 524. See also *Review*, ii, 445.
59. *The Dissenters Answer to the High Church Challenge* (1704) p. 11.
60. F. J. Dallett, 'Charles Lodwick', *N&Q*, cciii (Oct 1958) 452, and further information kindly supplied by Mr Dallett. Will of Walrave Lodwick, PCC 98 Laud, 1662.
61. See chap. 1, note 2.
62. Information from Mr F. J. Dallett. *Cal S.P. (Col), passim*. His will, PCC 37 Bolton, mentions a considerable number of friends, but not Defoe.
63. F. J. Dallett, loc cit. (note 60) with reference to PRO 0 5/1081, 68 and 681 and further information from Mr Dallett.
64. Charles Henry Pope, *The Pioneers of Massachusetts* (Boston, Mass., 1900—4) pp. 108—9.
65. *JPY*, p. 8.
66. PCC 104 Coker.
67. *Cal. S.P. (Col) (America and West Indies, 1681—5)*, p. 757, item 2033 (? Dec, 1684).
68. *Review*, iv, 504. See also *A Plan of the English Commerce* (1927 ed.) p. 266, and *Review*, i, 402.
69. *CET*, p. 84. For further evidence of Defoe's knowledge of the transatlantic trade, see *Review*, vii, 183.
70. Sutherland (1), pp. 279—80.
71. Information from Mr F. J. Dallett.
72. Geo. J. Armytage (ed.), *Allegations for Marriage Licences issued by the Dean and Chapter of Westminster, 1588 to 1699, Harl. Soc. Pub.*, xxiii (1886) 299 (20 May 1679).

73. *Catalogue of Pepsyian Manuscripts*, vol. i (Naval Record Society, 1903) intro., pp. 76—8. Quoted in A. Bryant, *Samuel Pepys: Saviour of the Navy* (London, 1949) pp. 150—3, with reference to Pepsyian MS No. 1490, pp. 143—52.
74. The Wright—Barham marriage was at St Olave Hart Street, London, on 20 March 1676/7. Will of Francis Barham, PCC 4 Bond, pr. 27 Feb 1695/6. See also will of John Cullum, Ipswich, mariner, PCC 131 Pett, pr. 7 Aug 1699.
75. PCC 115 Lloyd.
76. See chap. 7, note 48.
77. *Tour*, i, 105—8, 109—10, 136—8.
78. Abraham Sharp, *DNB*.
79. See chap. 1, note 2.
80. *The Farther Adventures of Robinson Crusoe*, vol. ii (1841 edition of works) item 6, p. 51.
81. Healey, *Letters* (39), p. 96.
82. Healey, *Letters* (10), p. 17.
83. *Wills and Administrations at Leicester, 1660—1750* includes ten Tuffley wills during that period. Henry Hartopp, *Roll of the Mayors of the Borough and Lord Mayors of the City of Leicester, 1209—1935* (Leicester, 1935) p. 135 for Charles Tuffley, Mayor in 1718. Like the Sarah, Giles and Charles Tuffley mentioned in John Robert Moore, *Daniel Defoe; Citizen of the Modern World* (Chicago, 1958) pp. 45—6, he can only have been a distant relative of Defoe's wife.
84. Healey, *Letters* (10), p. 17.
85. Will of John Tuffley, PCC 156 Lloyd.
86. e.g. *Review*, iii, 30.
87. Will of Samuel Tuffley, PCC 183 Romsey, dated 22 Oct 1714, pr. 3 Aug 1725. The figure of £12,000 is a very rough approximation, based on the size of Mary Tuffley's dowry, and John Tuffley's testamentary obligations as a citizen of London.
88. Wardmote Book of Cornhill Ward, CLRO MS 4069/2. For 'the usual time of chusing Parish and Ward-offices — *namely, the end of December*', see *AJ*, 4 April 1724, in Lee, iii, 249.
89. Moore, p. 87, with reference to *Spectator*, 9 Jul 1711, *Flying Post*, 28 July 1711, *Supplement*, 24 Mar 1711/12.
90. *Review*, viii, 470 (for 480).
91. *Review*, viii, 507 (12 Jan 1712).
92. Poll Tax, Cornhill Ward, Ist Precinct, 6 Mar 1691/2, CLRO Ass. Box 35/12.
93. *CET*, ii, 58. In Boulton, p. 237.
94. See H. W. Robinson and W. Adams, *Hooke's Diary* (London, 1935), *passim*.
95. Moore, *Checklist* (2). See Walter Wilson, *Memoirs of the Life and Times of Daniel Defoe*, vol. iii (London, 1830) pp. 645—6, footnote. See also *Review*, iii, 314, and *Serious Reflections*, pp. 189—90.
96. *An Appeal to Honour and Justice* (1715), in Boulton, p. 191. See also *Review*, i, 234.
97. e.g. *Reformation of Manners* (1702) and *JD* (1706), v, 15.

98. *Tour*, ii, 178.
99. *Review*, iv, 21, 347, 413.
100. *Serious Reflections*, p. 86.
101. *Review*, ii, 346; vi, 487.
102. *EuP*, pp. 228—30.
103. Carl Niemeyer, 'The Earl of Roscommon's Academy', *Modern Language Notes*, xli (Nov 1934) 432—7. See also B. S. Monroe, 'An English Academy', *Modern Philology*, viii (1910) 107—22; O. F. Emerson, 'John Dryden and a British Academy', *Proceedings of the British Academy*, x (1921—3) 45—58; Edmund Freeman, 'A Proposal for an English Academy in 1660', *Modern Language Review*, xix (1924) 291—300.
104. Moore, pp. 203—4, with reference to *Street Robberies, Consider'd* (1728) p. 57, *A Letter to the Dissenters* (1713) p. 33, *Rogues on Both Sides* (1711) p. 1.
105. *Review*, viii, 248.
106. *Review*, vii, 297.
107. *AJ*, 12 Sept 1724, in Lee, iii, 302, where the reference is actually to 'The Jovial Beggar'. This must refer to the production in December 1683 of Richard Brome's *The Jovial Crew*, with the alternative title, *The Merry Beggars*. See William van Lennep (ed.), *The London Stage, 1660—1800, Part I, 1660—1700* (Carbondale, 1965) pp. 30—1, 42, 151, 325, 377, 512.
108. *Review*, viii, 196.
109. *Tour*, ii, 13, note 1.
110. *Review*, i[ix], 152.
111. Ibid.
112. *Review*, viii, 713. See also *Review*, vii, preface, and *AJ*, 12 Sept 1724, in Lee, iii, 302.
113. *A Complete History of the Late Revolution* (1691) p. 8. For Halifax's views on Charles II, see 'A Character of King Charles II' (first published, 1750), in J. P. Kenyon (ed.), *Halifax, Complete Works* (Harmondsworth, 1969) pp. 247—67.
114. *Review*, viii, 724 — quoted by James H. Osborn, *John Dryden, Some Biographical Facts and Problems* (New York, 1940), where it is unconvincingly identified with the assault on Dryden in Rose Alley on 18 Dec 1679. See also *Review*, i[ix], 152.
115. See *Review*, vi, 94, for Defoe's version.
116. *Review*, viii, 206, and many other briefer references.
117. *Review*, ii, 498—9.
118. J. R. Western, *The English Militia in the 18th Century, The Story of a Political Issue: 1660—1802* (London and Toronto, 1965) pp. 67—8.
119. *An Argument Shewing*, in Boulton, p. 49. See also *Review*, vii, 150.
120. *Tour*, ii, 14. See Narcissus Luttrell, *A Brief Relation of State Affairs from September 1678 to April 1714*, vol. i (Oxford, 1857) p. 216 (Sept 1682), and Elizabeth D'Oyley, *James Duke of Monmouth* (London, 1938) p. 196.
121. *Review*, v, 466.

122. *JD*, iv, 27, footnote.
123. *A New Discovery of an Old Intreague* (1690) ll. 561—6.
124. *Review*, vii, 304.
125. *An Essay on the History of Parties* (1711) p. 13.
126. *Review*, vii, 98. See also *Review*, viii, 482.
127. *De Laune's Plea* (1706), Preface, p. ii.
128. *The Dissenters Answer to the High Church Challenge* (1704) pp. 14—15.
129. *De Laune's Plea*, p. 61.
130. Ibid., Preface, p. viii.
131. Ibid., Preface, p. ii. See William Jenkyn, *DNB*.
132. *Review*, ii, 485—6; *Tour*, i, 306.
133. *Review*,viii, 420. See also *Review*, viii, 582.
134. *AH&J*, in Boulton, p. 191. See also *Review*, i, 234.

Chapter 7

1. *Complete History*, p. 10. See also *New State*, ii, 135—6.
2. *The Present State of Jacobitism Consider'd* (1701) p. 21.
3. *Review*, vii, 308.
4. *AH&J*, in Boulton, p. 180.
5. *Cal. S. P. (Dom), James II, vol II (Jan 1686—May 1687)*, item 1833.
6. CLRO, Misc. MSS., 64/13, lists 10, all 'servants', in Cornhill Ward. The document is dated 14 July 1685.
7. *Review*, v, 194. See also *Review*, iv, 669.
8. *AJ*, 24 June 1721, in Lee, ii, 394. See Luttrell at relevant dates.
9. *Col. Jack*, p. 250.
10. Ibid., pp. 264—5.
11. *Tour*, i, 269.
12. *Tour*, ii, 35. See Miss H. C. Foxcroft, 'Monmouth at Philip's Norton, *Proceedings of the Somersetshire Archaeological and Natural History Society*, lvii (1911) pt. 2, 1—19.
13. *A Brief Reply to the History of Standing Armies* (1698) p. 12.
14. *Some Reflections on a Pamphlet* (1697) p. 21.
15. *Cavalier*, pp. 24, 25—7. Arthur W. Secord, in *'Robert Drury's Journal' and Other Studies* (Urbana, 1961) pp. 88—9, shows that a single sentence in Defoe's source is here padded out with 'fabricated' detail to fill several pages.
16. *The Apparent Danger of an Invasion* (1701).
17. *Review*, iii, 402.
18. *The Present State of the Parties* (1712) p. 319.
19. There are several references to him in *Cal. S. P. (Dom)*, *c.* 1683 for associating with Rye House plotters. See also note 20.
20. J. G. Muddiman (ed.), *The Bloody Assizes* (Edinburgh and London, 1929) pp. 53—72.
21. *RC*, p. 123.

22. *Review*, iii, 326. See also *A New Discovery of an Old Intreague* (1691) 1. 5.
23. *The Advantages of the Present Settlement*, in *State Tracts*, i, 271.
24. Wardmote Book, Cornhill Ward, CLRO MS 4069/2. See chap. 6, note 89.
25. Burial Register, St Michael Cornhill, in Guildhall Library.
26. *Review*, v, 78. See also *Review*, vii, 94; vii, 94, 533.
27. *Review*, vii, 598.
28. J. G. Muddiman (ed.), op cit., pp. 232—3.
29. *Col. Jack*, p. 266.
30. *A Plan of the English Commerce* (1927 ed.) p. 124.
31. *Tour*, ii, 159.
32. *Utrum Horum?* p. 42. See Bastian (3) for the attribution to Defoe.
33. *Giving Alms No Charity*, in Secord, p. 323.
34. *CET*, i, 131.
35. Shiv K. Kumar (ed.), *Captain Singleton* (Oxford, 1969) p. 38.
36. *Review*, ii, 135. *More Reformation* (1703) pp. ii, 38.
37. Quoted by Gordon Taylor, *Creative Writing in English*, ii, 7—9. Source not located.
38. *Tour*, i, 345. See also *Review*, ii, 62.
39. *AJ*, 19 Feb 1726, in Lee, iii, 460.
40. *AM&C*, p. 28.
41. *CET*, p. 48. See also *A Humble Proposal*, vol. iii (1843 edition) item 24, p. 5.
42. *AM&C*, p. 133.
43. *Tour*, i, 347—8.
44. *AM&C*, p. 115.
45. Rev. William Steven, *The History of the Scots Chuch, Rotterdam* (Edinburgh, 1832), also gives some details about the English Church there.
46. R. H. Story, *William Carstares, 1649—1715* (London, 1874) pp. 110—57.
47. T. C. Smout, *Scottish Trade on the Eve of the Union: 1660—1707* (Edinburgh and London, 1963) pp. 99—115.
48. (a) *Roll of Edinburgh Burgesses* (Scottish Record Society) p. 53, refers to his wife, Janet, d. of Mr William Livingstone, merchant. (b) *Marriages: Edinburgh Registers* (SRS) for his marriage, 2 July 1716, to Helen Russell, widow of John Hamilton, sometime factor in Campvere. (c) HMC *72 Laing*, ii, 238 has a letter dated 11 Mar 1733/4 mentioning 'Mr. Davis, the States' builder at Amsterdam'. Robert Davis had died ten years before, but this may have been a relative.
49. *Tour*, ii, 383—4. See *Register of the Privy Council of Scotland*, 3rd Series, viii, 403—4 (12 Mar 1684).
50. *The Consolidator* (1705) p. 105. F. R. J. Knetsch, 'Pierre Jurien: Réfugié unique et caracteristique', *Bulletin de la Societé de L'Histoire du Protestantisme Francaise*, tome 115, pp. 445—78.
51. *CET*, pp. 8—11.
52. *A Brief Case of the Distillers* (1726) p. 15.
53. Moore, p. 86, with reference to *Commentator*, 17 June 1720.

54. *RC*, p. 17.
55. Letter from James II to the Prince of Orange, dated Sept 1686, mentioning 'an Algerian man-of-war being come into Harwich': *Cal. S. P. (Dom) (Jan 1686—May 1687)* item 1019, p. 276.
56. *Review*, vi, 59.
57. F. R. J. Knetsch, loc. cit., p. 460; and the same author's 'Deux lettres des protestants captifs a Alger de 1687', cx (1964) 54—9.
58. *Col. Jack*, pp. 271—2.
59. *Cal. S. P. (Dom) James II, vol II (Jan 1686—May 1687)* item 1833.
60. e.g. *Review*, i, 114; *AM&C*, pp. 26, 142.
61. *Tour*, i, 122. See J. H. Andrews, 'Defoe and the Sources of his *Tour*', *Geographical Journal*, cxxvi, Part 3 (Sept 1960) 272.
62. Charles Morton, *DNB*; Charles Lodwick, see chap. 6, pp. 96—7 and note 63; David Clarkson, his will PCC 115 Lloyd.
63. PCC 156 Lloyd.
64. e.g. *Review*, ii, 325—6; v, 11; *JD*, iv, 14, footnote.
65. *Review*, vii, 7.
66. *Review*, viii, 422, 695.
67. Warmote Book, Cornhill Ward, CLRO, MS 4069/2.
68. Guildhall Library, MS 6446/1; MS 6443/1 fol. 26v; MS 7332. T. Wright, in *The Life of Daniel Defoe* (London, 1894) p. 85, quotes an entry in the Butchers' Company Records which gives James Foe's address as Fore Street, Cripplegate; and this has been followed by J. C. Thornley and G. W. Hastings (ed.), *The Guilds of the City of London and their Liverymen* (London, 1912) p. 152. This seems to be the origin of the new accepted view that Defoe was born in Fore Street. Though other details given by Wright are accurate, I have failed to find any mention of Fore Street in the Butchers' Company Records, and it would appear to conflict with other evidence. See also Philip E. Jones, *The Butchers of London* (London, 1976) pp. 54—5.
69. George Chalmers, *The Life of De Foe*, in *The Novels and Miscellaneous Works of Daniel De Foe*, vol. xx (Oxford, 1840—1). 2, footnote (a). This information is included among facts 'discovered, by searching the Chamberlain's books, which have since been burned'.
70. Cornhill Ward, Assessment 1688, CLRO Ass. Box 4/15.
71. Sutherland (1), pp. 280—1.
72. *AM&C*, pp. 30—1, 122. See also *A Discourse Concerning Mechanick Industry*, in *State Tracts*, ii, 136, attributed to Defoe in Appendix B(3).
73. *Serious Reflections*, p. 136.
74. *Review*, ii, 437—8. See also *Review*, vi, 295—6; i[ix], 8; *New State*, i, 282, ii, 135—6; *The Danger of the Protestant Religion*, in *True Collection*, p. 248.
75. Sutherland (1), pp. 275—91.
76. Guy Miege, *The English Grammar*, published by J. Wyat and advertised in *TC*, Trinity (July) 1688. See Appendix B(1).
77. *New State*, ii, 12—16.
78. Burial Register, St Michael Cornhill, Guildhall Library.
79. *The Advantages of the Present Settlement*, in *State Tracts*, i, 274.

80. *Letter to a Dissenter*, p. 3.
81. Moore, *Checklist* (4).
82. *Review*, viii, 422; and see *AH&J* in Boulton, p. 191.
83. *A New Discovery of an Old Intreague* (1690) Introduction.
84. *Review*, vi, 22.
85. *Complete History*, p. 36.
86. Ibid., p. 40.
87. *Review*, vi, 301.
88. *Complete History*, p. 42.
89. Ibid.
90. *Review*, vi, 598. Evelyn, *Diary*, 11 Nov 1688.
91. *Review*, ii, 273–4.
92. *Tour*, i, 294–8.
93. *Complete History*, p. 67.
94. *AJ*, 23 Oct 1725, in Lee, iii, 433. See also *Review*, vi, 561–2.
95. *Review*, vii, 134.
96. *The Ballance* (1703), p. 22. See Luttrell, 13 Dec 1688.
97. *Royal Religion* (1704), p. 20; *JD*, iv, 18, footnote (b); *Review*, iv, 631–2; *Tour*, i, 111–12; *CET*, ii (Part 1), 250–3; *The Advantages of the Present Settlement*, in *State Tracts*, i, 273.
98. *Complete History*, p. 78; and cf. *Review*, iv, 632.

Chapter 8

1. *Some Remarks on the First Chapter in Dr. Davenant's Essays* (1703) p. 20.
2. See Appendix B(2).
3. *Complete History*, p. 71.
4. *Some Remarks on . . . Davenant's Essays*, p. 21. See also *Review*, vii, 270; viii, 577–80; i[ix], 57.
5. *The Present State of Jacobitism Consider'd* (1701) p. 12; *The Six Distinguishing Features of a Parliament Man*, in *True Collection*, p. 273; *Review*, ii, 318, 411; vi, 470; vii, 304.
6. *Review*, iv, 576.
7. Moore, *Checklist* (6). The quotations are from pp. 34–5, 36–7, 40. *Reflections . . .* is also in *State Tracts*, i, 242–65.
8. *Reflections*, p. 66.
9. Moore, *Checklist* (7). In *State Tracts*, i, 265–80.
10. Wardmote Book, Cornhill Ward, CLRO, MS 4069/2.
11. Luttrell (7 July 1689), i, 556.
12. *Tour*, ii, 2–3. See *Survey of London*, vol. xvii (The Village of High-gate) pp. 50, 60.
13. *Tour*, ii, 10. See Luttrell (7 Oct 1689), i, 589; (14 Oct), i, 592; (9 Nov), i, 602; (24 Dec), i, 618.
14. J. Oldmixon, *History of England*, ii, 36, quoted in Lee, i, 23. See Luttrell (29 Oct 1689), i, 597.
15. Sutherland (1), pp. 275–91.

16. *EuP*, pp. 305—6.
17. *Review*, viii, 16.
18. *Review*, i, 369.
19. *Review*, viii, 577—80; and see also vii, 145. Such bills were under discussion between 1 July and 3 Aug 1689, and between 1 Dec 1690 and 2 Jan 1691. See *Commons Journals*.
20. Sutherland (1), pp. 286—9.
21. *Roxana*, pp. 164, 169.
22. *Tour*, i, 8—11, esp. p. 9.
23. A. D. Saunders, *Tilbury Fort, Essex* (HMSO, 1960); A. D. Saunders, 'Tilbury Fort', *The Antiquaries Journal*, xl (1960) 152—74.
24. M. Oppenheim, 'Maritime History', *VCH Essex*, ii, 291.
25. M. Oppenheim, 'Maritime History', *VCH Kent*, ii, 362—3.
26. See Appendix B(3).
27. See Appendix B(4).
28. See Appendix B(5).
29. See Luttrell (*c*. 25 Oct 1689), i, 596.
30. *Cal. Treas. Bks*, ix, (2) (1689—92), p. 533 (10 Mar 1689/90); ibid., p. 545 (19 Mar).
31. *RC*, pp. 39—40.
32. Wardmote Book, Cornhill Ward, CLRO MS 4069/2.
33. *Tour*, ii, 131.
34. *Tour*, i, 259.
35. Healey, *Letters* (46), p. 50.
36. *Tour*, ii, 273.
37. Luttrell (11 Jan 1690), ii, 5; Evelyn, *Diary*, (29 Dec 1689), iv, 654; (11 and 26 Jan 1690), v, 2, 4.
38. *Tour*, ii, 323—5.
39. *Tour*, ii, 326.
40. *Register of the Privy Council of Scotland*, 3rd Series, xiv (1689) pp. 58, 70—1.
41. *Marriages: Edinburgh Registers* (Scottish Records Society), 17 Nov 1718.
42. *Reformation of Manners*, in *True Collection*, pp. 88—9. See also *Review*, vi, 343. For further hints of Defoe's knowledge of Ulster see *The Parallel*, in *A Second Volume of the Writings* (1705) p. 382, and *Review*, vii, 223—4.
43. *Tour*, ii, 68—9, 255—9.
44. *Tour*, ii, 69—72. F. W. Robins, *The Story of Water Supply* (London, 1946) p. 164.
45. *Tour*, ii, 82—3. T. W. Whitley, *The Parliamentary Representation of the City of Coventry* (Coventry, 1892) p. 118 is not conclusive for the date of this riot. Trouble at elections was usual here, and Defoe was probably at Coventry during the 1698 election. See chap. 11, p. 215 and note 40.
46. *Review*, vi, 486.
47. *A New Discovery of an Old Intreague* (1691) ll. 439—50. About this time appeared *A Modest Inquiry into the Causes of the present Disasters in* England. *And who they are that brought the* French *Fleet*

into the English *Channel describ'd*, published by R. Baldwin, and subsequently reprinted in *State Tracts*, ii, 95—104. This powerful tract, exposing Jacobite activity in the Church of England, has many Defoe characteristics, but the evidence does not seem strong enough for a positive attribution.

48. See M. E. Campbell, *Defoe's First Poem* (Bloomington, 1938), *passim.*
49. *A New Discovery* . . . , ll. 286—7.
50. Ibid., ll. 389—90.
51. *Review, vi, 303.*
52. *See* Appendix B(6).
53. Moore, *Checklist* (9). See M. E. Campbell, op. cit, and A. M. Wilkinson, 'Defoe's *New Discovery* and *Pacificator*', *N&Q*, cxc (Nov 1950) 496—8.
54. *A New Discovery* . . . , ll. 561—6, and comments in M. E. Campbell, op. cit.
55. See Appendix B(26, 27).
56. *Locusts*, ii, 8.
57. Ibid., ii, 8.
58. Ibid, ii, 15.
59. Bastian (3).
60. *New State*, ii, 13.
61. *New State*, 2nd ed. (1693).
62. Bastian (3).
63. In *Utrum Horum?* See Bastian (3).
64. J. Dunton, *Life and Errors* (1705) pp. 248—64, discusses the *Anthenian Mercury* and its contributors, without mentioning Defoe. See Steven Parks, *John Dunton and the English Book Trade* (New York and London, 1976) pp. 76—83.
65. Moore, *Checklist* (10). 'Printed for James Dowley'; but this was a pseudonym for Dunton himself (see S. Parks, op. cit., p. 200), and Dunton, in his *Life and Errors*, p. 240, claimed that Defoe's ode had been written 'for me'.
66. J. Dunton, *Life and Errors*, p. 180.
67. J. Dunton, *The Impeachment* (1714) p. 13.
68. MS notes compiled by Rev. Josiah Thompson (Baptist Minister), 1724—1806, now in Dr Williams' Library.
69. Will of Walrave Lodwick, PCC 98 Laud, 1662.
70. Sutherland (1), with reference to PRO C7.373/22.
71. *Serious Reflections*, pp. 279—80.
72. *Memoirs . . . of . . . Daniel Williams* D.D. (1718) esp. pp. 5—15.
73. Story, *passim*. Healey, *Letters* (200), pp. 396—7.
74. *Royal Religion* (1704) p. 12.
75. *Review*, iv, 559.
76. *AM&C*, pp. 1—2.
77. Cornhill Ward, 6 Months Tax, CLRO, Ass. Box 15/23.
78. Cornhill Ward, Poll Tax, CLRO, Ass. Box 6/10.
79. Cornhill Ward, Poll Tax, CLRO Ass. Box 35/12.
80. Healey, *Letters* (10), p. 17.
81. Moore, p. 335.

82. Burke's *General Armory. Visitation of Kent, 1663—8*, Harl. Soc. Pub., liv (1906) p. 94 shows Michael Knight to have been aet.38 in 1663.
83. *Cal. S.P. (Dom)*, 1672—3, p. 95. Thomas Knight, Westerham.
84. *RC*, pp. 37—8.

Chapter 9

1. *London Gazette*, No. 2737 (1—4 Feb 1691/2).
2. *Review*, i, 369.
3. Cornhill Ward, Wardmote Book, CLRO, MS 4069/2. In the previous year he had been listed 20 out of 24 on the Grand Jury, his last appearance in these lists.
4. *EuP*, pp. 49—53.
5. *Review*, iii, 75; *EuP*, p. 225.
6. See chap. 7, p. 120 and note 51; chap. 8, pp. 143—4 and note 17.
7. See chap. 10, pp.180—1 and note 26.
8. *Tour*, i, 71, but I have failed to verify the year. Luttrell, ii, 472 (4 June 1692) mentions '200 colliers' caught in a storm, but says that they all came safe into Yarmouth Roads. J. R. Moore, *Defoe in the Pillory and other Studies*, pp. 89—90, discussing 'Dom Manoel Gonzales', which is based on the *Tour*, places the storm in 1696, as does H. J. Hillen, *History of the Borough of King's Lynn*, vol. ii (Norwich, 1907) p. 459; but I have failed to verify this year either. Defoe certainly had creditors at Yarmouth (see Healey, *Letters*, pp. 115, 123 and note, 401).
9. *CET*, pp. 66—7.
10. Theodore F. M. Newton, 'The Civet Cats of Newington Green', *RES* (1937) 10—19.
11. *CET*, p. 79.
12. Sir Charles Sedley, *A Ballad to the Tune of 'Bateman'*, in Harold Love (ed.), *The Penguin Book of Restoration Verse* (Harmondsworth, 1968) pp. 129—31.
13. Sutherland (1), pp. 281—3, places these events in 1691, but other evidence shows that they occurred in 1692 — e.g. Luttrell, ii, 468, 498 (28 May, 30 June 1692). See Montague Summers (ed.), *The Works of Aphra Behn* vol. i (London, 1915), Preface, pp. xxxiii—xxxvi.
14. *History of the Devil*, (*Works*, 1854—6), iii, 547—8.
15. *History of Apparitions*, pp. 207—9; *MF*, pp. 193—5.
16. Broad Street Ward, Poll Tax, 25 Jan 1692/3, CLRO Ass. Box 32/6.
17. *EuP*, pp. 16—18.
18. Sutherland (1), pp. 283—6.
19. For *Williams* v. *Williams*, see John Carswell, *The South Sea Bubble* (London, 1960) p. 18, with reference to Parch: W&M. Anno 1692, Carlton 269. However, his references to Defoe are seriously inaccurate.
20. M. Oppenheim, 'Maritime History', *VCH Cornwall*, ii, 496, 503.
21. *Cal. S.P. (Dom)*, 1690—1, p. 477 (8 Aug 1691).
22. *Tour*, i, 236—8.
23. *Tour*, i, 244.

24. *Tour*, i, 247.
25. *EuP*, p. 14.
26. *Tour*, i, 244. For a later reference, concerning a further grant to Trefusis, see *Cal. S.P. (Dom)*, 1703—4, p. 373 (23 Dec 1703).
27. *Tour*, i, 245.
28. *London Gazette*, No. 2796 (25—29 Aug 1692); Luttrell, ii, 551 (27 Aug 1692). Presumably the main body of the Dutch 'St Ubes' fleet had already passed by when the engagement took place. I have failed to trace any other engagement that Defoe could have seen, and have used this to date his visit to this part of Cornwall.
29. *Tour*, i, 238—9.
30. *Tour*, i, 237.
31. *Tour*, i, 103.
32. *Review*, ii, 85—7.
33. *CET*, pp. 175—7.
34. Newton, loc cit.
35. Healey, *Letters* (45), p. 115. See also *Review*, iv, 115—16, 118.
36. Pat Rogers, 'Defoe in Fleet Prison', *RES*, xxii (Nov 1971) 451—3.
37. *EuP*, pp. 13, 34—5. James Stancliffe was also interested in saltpetre: see *Cal. S.P. (Dom)*, Wm. & Mary, 1691—2, p. 227 (11 April 1692).
38. *Review*, viii, 263.
39. *EuP*, pp. 199—200. See also *Review*, iii, 82.
40. *Review*, v, 604.
41. *MF*, p. 64.
42. *CET*, p. 119.
43. *Review*, viii, 765.
44. *MF*, p. 66.
45. Cornhill Ward, *c.* Jan 1692/3, CLRO, Ass. Box 32/13 for Addis; 1694/5, Ass. Boxes 6/9 and 20/1 for Addis and Moyer. Richard Addyes, churchwarden, was buried at St Michael Cornhill, 15 Feb 1707/8.
46. Sutherland (1), p. 284, with reference to PRO, Register of Affidavits, Hilary 1692, No. 690 (24 Feb 1692/3).
47. Sutherland (2), pp. 137—41.
48. Healey, *Letters* (202), p. 401. See *RC*, pp. 27—8, where Crusoe shoots a sleeping lion.

Chapter 10

1. Newton, with reference to *Cal. Treas. Bks*, xiii, 151.
2. Healey, *Letters* (131), p. 263.
3. *Review*, vii, 455.
4. Healey, *Letters* (9), p. 15.
5. *CET*, pp. 343—4.
6. See notes 29 and 37 below. For further information: (a) Merritt: HMC, *MSS of the House of Lords*, vi, 119; ix, 101; *Gentleman's Magazine*, No. 665, for death of Solomon Merritt, Spanish merchant,

Dec 1739. (b) Dolliffe: HMC, *Lords MSS*, ix, 430 etc. for various references to Jas. Dolliffe, sen. & jun., Spanish merchants 1713—14; Jas. Dollyffe (Doliff, D'Olive) Director of South Sea Company, knighted 4 Oct 1714, d. 15 Feb 1715; *MJ*, 9 April 1720, in Lee, ii, 217, for an account of how Jas. Doliff Esq. foiled a highwayman who robbed him of a bank bill for £200, suggesting that Defoe was still in touch with him.

7. *Tour*, ii, 418—19.
8. *AM&C*, p. 137.
9. Sutherland (1), p. 286 with reference to PRO C6 499/41.
10. Newton, with reference to PRO C7 333/33.
11. *Tour*, i, 69—70; ii, 403, 404, 412, for landfalls; *Tour*, ii, 246—7 Scarborough); ii, 395—6 (Dundee); ii, 404 (Peterhead); ii, 413—15 (John o' Groats). Defoe's knowledge of these places appears to be first hand, and he often implies a seaward approach; but he shows no knowledge of their 'hinterlands'.
12. *AM&C*, p. 137.
13. *Caledonia* (1706) pp. 13—14, 16, 18.
14. J. T. Jenkins, *The Herring and the Herring Fisheries* (London, 1927), p. 68.
15. *AM&C*, p. 137. See Rev. John Brand, *A Brief Description of Orkney, Zetland, Pightland and Caithness* (1701, reprinted Edinburgh, 1883) p. 51
16. *A Humble Proposal to the People of England* (1729), in 1843 edition of his works, iii, item 24, p. 8.
17. *AM&C*, p. 50.
18. *RC*, p. 138.
19. See Brand, op. cit., pp. 74—5.
20. *Tour*, ii, 413.
21. *MJ*, 18 April 1719, in Lee, ii, 119; *AJ*, 26 Oct 1723, in Lee, iii, 198.
22. *AM&C*, p. 49.
23. Niels Nielsen, *Der Vulkanismus an Hvitarvatu, und Hofsjökull auf Island*, Medd. fra Dansk. Geol. Forening (Kbh., 1927) vii, 2.
24. Sutherland (1), pp. 283—6, with reference to PRO C7 373/22; C33/280/f.316; C6 499/41.
25. *EuP*, pp. 49—53.
26. Moore, pp. 90—4, with reference to *HCJ*, xi, 8, 25, 30, 31, 38, 59, 80, 84—5, 87, 102; *HLJ*, xv, 381, 382; and see *Review*, i, 370.
27. Sutherland (1), pp. 281—3, with reference to PRO C8 548/9; C8 353/20; C6.330.
28. Sutherland (1), pp. 286—9, with reference to PRO C5 170/49; C5 214/5; C33/296 f.213.
29. *Cal. Treas. Bks*, x(1) (1693—6) pp. 461—2.
30. *Cal. Treas. Bks*, x(1) p. 175 (28 April 1693) — *Desire*, 80 tons, 5 seamen, to Newfoundland; cf. ibid., p. 832 (19 Nov 1694), *Desire* of Newcastle, to Riga. See below p. 183 and note 37. It may be significant that the ship on which Crusoe made his fateful voyage 'was about 120 tun burthen, carried 6 guns and 14 men, besides the master, his boy, and my self' (*RC*, p. 40).

31. *AM&C*, pp. 153—4. See T. C. Smout, *Scottish Trade on the Eve of the Union* (Edinburgh and London, 1963) pp. 171—4.
32. *AM&C*, p. 60.
33. *Serious Reflections*, pp. 129—30.
34. *Review*, i, 142. 'Santo António Militar', in *Grande Enciclopédia Portuguesa e Brasiliera*. I am grateful to Mr G. V. S. Bucknall for translating this article.
35. *Tour*, ii, 418—19. See also *AM&C*, p. 137.
36. *CET*, p. 28, and *A Humble Proposal* (as in note 16 above). But see *Review*, iv, 633—5.
37. *Cal. S.P. (Dom)*, 1694—5, p. 378, 8 Jan 1695, where the owners' names are given as James Deliffe and Solomon Morret. *AM&C*, p. 137.
38. *AH&J* in Boulton, p. 168.
39. John Ehrman, *The Navy in the War of William III* (Cambridge, 1953) pp. 531, 538, 646.
40. *AH&J* in Boulton, p. 168.
41. Will of Francis Barham, senior, PCC 4 Bond, made 23 Aug 1694, pr. 27 Feb 1695/6.
42. *EuP*, pp. 109—10.
43. *Tour*, i, 128—41, *passim*.
44. *Tour*, i, 124.
45. *Tour*, i, 130—1. The Bramber election result was given in the *London Gazette*, 21 Nov 1695.
46. *Tour*, i, 131. See also *Review*, viii, 127; *Col. Jack*, pp. 56—7.
47. *Tour*, i, 132—3.
48. *Tour*, i, 133—4.
49. *Tour*, i, 135.
50. *RC*, pp. 125—8.
51. *Tour*, i, 140. See Richard Cromwell, *DNB*; also *VCH Hants*, iii, 417—22.
52. *Tour*, i, 139.
53. A. J. Holland, 'Naval Shipbuilding on the Hamble River before 1815', *Mariners Mirror*, xlix (1963) 21—7; and Ehrman, op. cit. (note 39), Appendix III, p. 632.
54. *Captain Singleton*, p. 3.
55. *Tour*, i, 136—9.
56. *AH&J*, in Boulton, p. 168.
57. *Cal. Treas. Bks*, x(3) (1693—6) p. 1198.
58. Ibid., p. 1200.
59. Pat Rogers, 'Defoe's First Official Post', *N&Q*, ccxvi (Aug 1971) p. 303, with reference to PRO T53/13/80.
60. Healey, *Letters* (107), p. 224, footnote 1.
61. Moore, pp. 287—9.
62. *AH&J*, in Boulton, p. 168.
63. *Review*, viii, 496. The Glass Duty Receipts from 29 Sept 1695 to 17 Aug 1697 were £24,953 0s 7¼d. (J. Davenant, *Discourses on the Public Revenues* (1698), i, 118, 227, 260.)

64. *Cal. S.P. (Dom) (1691—3)*, *passim*, shows him with a share in no fewer than 34 projects.

65. Luttrell, iii, 219.

66. *Post-Boy*, Nos. 63 (3 Oct 1695), 80 (12 Nov), 81 (14 Nov), 108 (28 Dec), 125 (25 Feb 1695/6), 129 (5 Mar), 133 (14 Mar), 134 (17 Mar).

67. 5 Wm. & Mary c.7. *Cal. Treas. Bks*, x(3) (1693—6) p. 533. See also Luttrell, iii, 380.

68. e.g. *A further account of the proposals made by T. Neale & D. Thomas for exchanging the blank tickets in the Million Adventure* (1695).

69. *Review*, v, 426. See also *Review*, vii, 106; viii, 765; and even the nearly contemporary *Essay Upon Projects* (published Jan 1697) pp. 184—7.

70. *Tour*, ii, 85.

71. *EuP*, p. 71.

72. *The True-Born Englishman* (1701), concluding couplet.

73. *The True-Born Hugonot* (1703), p. 5. John de Foo and Stephen de Fowe were listed among aliens in London in 1541, and Jesset de Foe in 1625 (*Publications of the Huguenot Society of London*, vol. X, i, 50, 52, 68; iii, 276). J. M. Cowper, in a brief note headed 'Robinson Crusoe', *N&Q* (1886) p. 158, mentions the occurrence of the name 'Defo' in Canterbury in the 1690s. I am obliged to Professor G. A. Starr for information about Daniel Defoe and Henry Defoe, weavers, transported in 1732 for a petty street robbery in London (*The Proceedings at the Sessions of the Peace, and Oyer and Terminer, for the City of London . . . in the Year 1732*, No. 5, pp. 139, 148).

74. Greenwich Hospital Minutes, 'Fabrick Committee', Vol. II (1695—1702), PRO Adm. 67/2 ff. 5, 60; Accounts of Greenwich Hospital, Works, PRO Adm. 68/670 (July, August 1696); 68/671 (August 1697).

75. Sutherland (1), pp. 286—9.

76. *Review*, ii, 34.

77. Lee, i, 32. For an account of the state of English brick manufacture at this time, see Nathaniel Lloyd, *A History of English Brickwork* (London, 1935) *passim*.

78. PRO Adm. 67/2; 68/670; 68/671 *passim*.

79. *Tour*, i, 96—7. Luttrell, iii, 83, discussed Morden's proposals, 25 April 1693. John Evelyn visited the College while building was in progress, 6 May 1695.

80. *Tour*, i, 334—5.

81. *EuP*, p. 115.

82. Spiro Peterson, 'Defoe and Westminster, 1696—1706', *Eighteenth Century Studies*, 12 (Spring 1979) 306—38.

83. *AM&C*, p. 115.

84. *OED* quotes Mrs Centlivre, *A Gotham Election* (1711): 'none of your hellish pantile crew'.

85. *Review*, v, 588; and see A. W. Lawrence, *Trade Castles and Forts of West Africa* (London, 1969) pp. 90—1.

86. *Review*, vii, 211—12.
87. *Tour*, i, 8.
88. Christopher Morris (ed.), *The Journeys of Celia Fiennes* (London, 1949) p. 122.
89. *Tour*, i, 9.
90. *Review*, iv, 317.
91. G. A. Aitken, Defoe's Brick-Kilns', *Athenaeum* (13 April 1889) 472—3.
92. *Review*, iv, 317.
93. Thomas Wright, *The History and Topography of the County of Essex*, vol. ii (London, 1836) p. 561, footnote. *Tour*, i, 139 (Itchen); i, 231 (Tamar); ii, 39, 40 (Severn); ii, 94 (Humber); ii, 255 (Mersey); ii, 311 (Forth).
94. *CET*, p. 28.
95. *CET*, pp. 32—3.
96. *Review*, ii, 112.
97. *Giving Alms No Charity*, in Secord, p. 325.
98. G. A. Aitken, (as in note 91 above).
99. *Review*, ii, 34. Healey, *Letters* (10), p. 17.
100. *Review*, iv, 317.
101. *The Villainy of Stock-jobbers detected* (1701) p. 4.
102. e.g. *Review*, iv, 509, 666; v, 43; vii, 54.
103. *Tour*, i, 101.
104. *Tour*, i, 99, 113.
105. *Tour*, i, 12, 122—3.
106. *Tour*, i, 346. See also *AM&C*, p. 19.
107. (a) *The Pretences of the French Invasion Examined* (1692) [Moore, *Checklist* (11)] ; (b) *An Answer to the Late K. James's Last Declaration* (1693) [Moore, *Checklist* (12)] ; (c) *The Englishman's Choice and True Interest* (1694) [Moore, *Checklist* (13)] .
108. See Appendix B(7).
109. *Review*, v, 509—12.
110 Moore, *Checklist* (16); *EuP*, p. 28.
111. *EuP*, pp. 36—7.
112. *EuP*, pp. 68—111.
113. *EuP*, pp. 112—78.
114. *EuP*, pp. 227—51.
115. *EuP*, pp. 252—81.
116. *EuP*, pp. 282—304.
117. *EuP*, pp. 178—90.
118. *EuP*, pp. 191—226.
119. *EuP*, pp. 305—11.
120. *EuP*, pp. 312—32.
121. e.g. see chap. 12, pp. 266—8 and notes 122—5; Healey, *Letters* (139, enclosure), pp. 278—85; *Tour*, i, 200—6, 355—60.
122. Moore, *Checklist* (14). In *True Collection*, pp. 110—18.
123. John Dunton, *The Impeachment* (1714) p. 13.
124. *Review*, ii, 388. See *HCJ*, 13 and 14 Nov 1696, and Luttrell, iv, 139 (14 Nov 1696).

125. *Review*, iii, 75, 77; and see *Review*, iv, 100.
126. *Review*, iv, 108, 111–12.
127. *Review*, iv, 115–16. See also *Review*, iv, 118, 122.
128. *Review*, vi, 119; *CET*, ii, 93; *MJ*, 3 Jan 1719, in Lee, ii, 88.
129. Sutherland (2), pp. 137–41.

Chapter 11

1. *EuP*, p. 258.
2. *An Argument Proving* . . . , p. 19. See Appendix B(9) for attribution.
3. *EuP*, p. 258. See also *Hymn to Victory* (1704); *Review*, iii, 479; viii, 347.
4. *Review*, iii, 327. See also *Review*, vi, 24. Defoe states that this was 'in print', but the piece has not been identified.
5. Lois G. Schwoerrer, 'The Literature of the Standing Army Controversy, 1697–1699', *Huntington Library Quarterly*, xxviii, No. 3 (May 1965) 187–212. Lois G. Schwoerrer, 'Chronology and Authorship of the Standing Army Tracts', *N&Q*, ccxi (Oct 1966) 382–90. See also J. W. Fortescue, *A History of the British Army*, vol. i (London and New York, 1899) pp. 383–90.
6. *Review*, v, 602.
7. In the absence of any full-scale biography of Montagu, I have relied on *DNB*, and on standard general histories of the period, as well as more specialised books and articles on various aspects of the economic life of the country.
8. Moore, *Checklist* (15).
9. See Appendix A.
10. G. Burnet, *History of his Own Times*, vol. iv (1823 ed.) pp. 366–9, esp. p. 368.
11. Moore, *Checklist* (18). In Boulton, pp. 36–50. Discussed in J. R. Sutherland, *Daniel Defoe: A Critical Study* (Boston, 1971) pp. 25–9.
12. Moore, *Checklist* (21).
13. Tallard to Louis XIV, 3 April 1698, in Paul Grimblot (ed.), *The Letters of William III and Louis XIV and their Ministers . . . 1697 to 1709*, (London, 1848) p. 343.
14. See Appendix B(8).
15. Moore, *Checklist* (17). See Sutherland (3), pp. 40–2.
16. *AH&J*, in Boulton, pp. 191–2.
17. The 2nd edition (20 Nov 1700) had a Preface to Mr How, signed D. F. Two years later came the crisis in Defoe's life arising from the Occasional Conformity Bill, and *The Shortest Way with the Dissenters*. See chap. 13 p. 275 *et seq*.
18. *Serious Reflections*, pp. 75–96. See footnote, p. 80: 'This was all written in King William's time, and refers to that time.'
19. Moore, *Checklist* (20). Sutherland (3), pp. 37–9.
20. *Review*, i, 353. Probably Defoe's own parish of St John's, Hackney.

21. D. Crane Taylor, *William Congreve* (London, 1931), chap. 8, 'Collier's, *Short View*'; chap. 9, 'The Stage Controversy', pp. 106—44; Appendix I, pp. 241—4, a bibliography of tracts on the subject.
22. Luttrell, iv, 379 (12 May 1698).
23. *The Dissenters Misrepresented*, in *A Second Volume Of the Writings* (1705) p. 350.
24. *Review*, iii, 294, 370, 381, 511.
25. *Review*, vi, 258—9.
26. *Tour*, ii, 148.
27. *Tour*, ii, 104. For the rebuilding of Burley, see H. J. Habbakuk, 'Daniel Finch, 2nd Early of Nottingham: His House and Estate', in J. H. Plumb (ed.), *Studies in Social History*, (London, 1955). Foundations were dug, 1695; main building erected, 1696—8; joiners, glaziers, plasterers, painters at work, 1698—9.
28. Healey, *Letters* (46), p. 117.
29. Evelyn, *Diary*, v, 286—8 (17 April; 1, 8, 19 May 1698).
30. *Tour*, ii, 283.
31. John Bell, postmaster at Newcastle, wrote to Harley on 1 Oct 1706, reporting Defoe's statement that he was already 'publickly knowne in Edinburgh'. *HMC Portland*, iv, 33—4, quoted in Healey, *Letters*, p. 130, footnote 2.
32. Healey, *Letters* (22, postscript), p. 47.
33. Luttrell, iv, 401 (12 July 1698).
34. *An Essay at Removing National Prejudices* (1706) pp. 20—1, implying knowledge of summer conditions before his first documented journey to Scotland. *JD* (1706) p. 6 shows similar familiarity with the Highland clan system.
35. *Tour*, ii, 219. Celia Fiennes reported in 1697 that Blacket had 'one of the largest Beeves in England' — Christopher Morris (ed.), *The Journeys of Celia Fiennes*, (London, 1949) p. 84.
36. *Tour*, ii, 227. See J. H. Andrews, 'Defoe and the Sources of his *Tour*', *Geographical Journal*, cxxvi, Part 3 (September 1960) 270.
37. *Tour*, ii, 183—5. Evelyn reported 'Greate and unseasonable stormes in many parts' on 24 July (v, 294); and 'Very cold, rainy & unseasonable weather' on 7 Aug (v, 296). I have failed to confirm the flood damage at Sheffield; but Thoresby records that on 13 December 1697 the near-by Calder was at its greatest height within living memory — 'higher than thirty-three years since'. [Rev. Joseph Hunter, F.S.A. (ed.), *Diary of Ralph Thoresby, F.R.S.* (1830)] .
38. *Tour*, ii, 174—7. See Andrews, loc. cit., p. 270 for confirmation that this visit must have been before 1702.
39. *Tour*, ii, 158, 177.
40. *Review*, iii, 176 (8 April 1706), where Defoe states that he had not been in Coventry for seven years previous to the election of the preceding year.
41. Moore, *Checklist* (22).
42. See Appendix B(9).
43. Moore, *Checklist* (19).

44. There seems to be nothing in these inconsistent with Defoe's authorship, but not enough evidence to establish it firmly. Further investigation may well suggest that Defoe may have been responsible for even more of the tracts in support of a standing army.
45. Grimblot, ii, 224. See also Burnet, op. cit., iv, 390—2.
46. P. Yorke, Earl of Hardwicke (ed.), *Miscellaneous State Papers from 1501 to 1726*, vol. ii (1778) p. 362.
47. Grimblot, ii, 224. footnote.
48. Ibid., ii, 229, footnote.
49. Ibid., ii, 224.
50. Frank H. Ellis (ed.), *Poems on Affairs of State: Augustan Satirical Verse, 1697—1704* (Yale Univ., 1970) pp. 43—57, contains introduction, text and notes. Two lines from the *Encomium* are quoted in *Review*, i[ix], 43.
51. *Somers Tracts*, xi (13 vols, London, 1809—15) 149—91.
52. Ellis, op. cit., note to *An Encomium*, ll. 36—7.
53. Luttrell, iv, 449 (10 Nov 1698).
54. 10 W. III cap. 17., quoted in *Review*, vii, 126.
55. Luttrell, iv, 543, 595 (29 July, 19 Dec 1699).
56. Luttrell, iv, 487 (25 Feb 1699).
57. *HCJ*, xii, 647.
58. In Ellis, pp. 157—80. Moore, *Checklist* (23). See Albert Rosenberg, 'Defoe's *Pacificator* Reconsidered', *Philological Quarterly*, xxxvii (1958) 433 *et seq*; Sutherland (3), pp. 93—6.
59. Healey, *Letters* (10), p. 17.
60. Letter from Robert Davis at Leith to the Earl of Oxford (Harley), 20 Oct 1713, with enclosure dated 25 Sept 1704. (HMC, 29 *Portland MSS*, v, 350—1.)
61. *Tour*, i, 206—7.
62. *Tour*, i, 209—10. For a reference to Rev. Samuel Bold, Rector of the near-by village of Steeple from 1682—1737, see *The Dissenters Answer to the High-Church Challenge* (1704) p. 11.
63. *Tour*, i, 213.
64. *Tour*, i, 214—15. See also *AM&C*, p. 104; and *MJ*, 12 May 1720, in Lee ii, 283, referring to a letter from Weymouth dated 6 May describing another good mackerel season.
65. *Tour*, i, 224—5.
66. *Tour*, i, 225—7.
67. Healey, *Letters* (40), p. 99.
68. See Note 60 above.
69. Hardwicke, ii, 362.
70. *AH&J*, in Boulton, p. 168.

Chapter 12

1. *AH&J*, in Boulton, p. 168.
2. See Ellis, pp. 43—6. *A Supplement to the Faults on Both Sides*

(1710), implies that Defoe's reply was written before the death of the King of Spain in October.

3. *The True-Born Englishman*, preface, in Boulton, p. 53. However, Defoe's statement: 'I gave my vote for Sir Thomas Abney', implies that he was in London at the time of the Mayoral election on 29 Sept 1700 (*A Letter to Mr. How*, in *True Collection*, pp. 328–9).
4. *TBE*, ll. 624–53, in Boulton, p. 69.
5. Luttrell, iv, 676 (10 Aug 1700).
6. Story, *passim*. See Healey, *Letters* (200), pp. 396–7 (Carstares to Defoe, 10 Feb 1713).
7. See chap. 7, p. 000.
8. *Royal Religion* (1704), p. 21.
9. Ibid., p. 15; Story, pp. 215, 231.
10. *Review*, iii, 629; *Tour*, ii, 10–11, 13 (and footnote), 15.
11. Story, pp. 234–42.
12. *Review*, viii, preface.
13. *The True-Born Hugonot* (1703), p. 12.
14. Stephen B. Baxter, *William III* (London, 1966) pp. 372–3, with reference to BM Loan 29/335 ff. 26–7 *sub* November 1700.
15. Ibid., p. 379
16. *The Felonious Treaty* (1711) p. 5.
17. Hardwicke, ii, 393–4. See Richard Lodge, *The History of England from the Restoration to the Death of William III. 1660–1702*, in W. Hunt and R. L. Poole (eds.), *The Political History of England*, vol. viii (London, 1910) pp. 436–42.
18. *Review*, viii, 353–4.
19. *The Felonious Treaty* (1711) pp. 4–5. See also *Review*, v, 619.
20. *Review*, viii, 353–4.
21. *Review*, i[ix], 140. See also *Review*, v, 291; *AH&J*, in Boulton, p. 192.
22. *Review*, viii, 59.
23. *The Succession of Spain Consider'd* (1711) p. 45.
24. Moore, *Checklist* (24). Sutherland (3), pp. 30–2.
25. Luttrell, iv, 703, 705, 706 (2, 7, 12 Nov 1700).
26. See Appendix B(10).
27. *Remarks . . .* , p. 19.
28. Moore, *Checklist* (25). Sutherland (3), pp. 30–2.
29. *The Two Great Questions Further Considered*, p. 20.
30. Ibid., p. 17, referring to *Remarks*, p. 21; but the offending passage does not occur anywhere in the *Remarks*. Other similar cross-references are correct.
31. See Appendix B(11).
32. *Remarks, Part II*, p. 7.
33. Ibid., pp. 2, 10.
34. In *State Tracts*, iii, 194–203. See Appendix B(12).
35. *A Letter to a Member of Parliament*, p. 24.
36. Ibid., pp. 25–6.
37. Keith Feiling, *A History of the Tory Party. 1640–1714* (Oxford, 1924) pp. 340–1.

38. Healey, *Letters* (22), p. 68.
39. In Ellis, pp. 259—309. Moore, *Checklist* (28). Sutherland (3), pp. 97—105.
40. See Appendix B(16).
41. *True Collection* (1703), Preface.
42. In *True Collection*, pp. 271—83. Moore, *Checklist* (26).
43. In *State Tracts*, iii, 67—75. See Appendix B(13).
44. See below, pp. 000—00.
45. Moore, *Checklist* (30).
46. *Review*, viii, 41—2.
47. *The Anatomy of Exchange Alley* (1719), quoted in Lee, i, 305. See also *A Fifth Essay at Removing National Prejudices* (1707) p. 34.
48. Moore, *Checklist* (33).
49. Moore, *Checklist* (32).
50. In *State Tracts*, iii, 22—44, 45—67. See Appendix B(14 & 15).
51. Moore, *Checklist* (27). Sutherland (3), pp. 32—3.
52. In *State Tracts*, iii, 154—182, and *Somers Tracts*, xi, 195—228. See Appendix B(17).
53. *State Tracts*, iii, 169—73; cf. *Col. Jack*, pp. 277—306.
54. In *True Collection*, p. 272. Moore, *Checklist* (26).
55. In *Somers Tracts*, xii, 593—5. See J. R. Moore, 'Defoe Acquisitions at the Huntington Library, *HLQ*, xxviii, No. 1 (Nov 1964) 54—5.
56. Luttrell, v, 18 (15 Feb 1701).
57. In *State Tracts*, ii, 72, and *Somers Tracts*, xi, 191—4. See Luttrell, v, 18—19 (18 Feb 1701). Appendix B(18).
58. J. E. Thorold Rogers, *The First Nine Years of the Bank of England* (Oxford, 1887), pp. 119—20 and footnote.
59. Luttrell, v, 19. Stephen B. Baxter, *William III* (London, 1966) p. 383.
60. Moore, *Checklist* (34).
61. In Huntington Library (HEH 326507). See J. R. Moore, 'Defoe Acquisitions at the Huntington Library', *HLQ*, xxviii, No. 1 (Nov 1964) pp. 53—4.
62. *Observator*, No. 73 (31 Dec 1702 — 2 Jan 1703).
63. In *State Tracts*, iii, 203—10. See Appendix B(19).
64. In *State Tracts*, iii, 76—102 [quotations from pp. 77, 81, 82, 90, 100, 101(2)]. See Appendix B(20).
65. *Review*, v, 618; and see Lodge, op. cit., pp. 436—42.
66. Most fully discussed by Defoe in *AH&J*, in Boulton, pp. 169—70. See also *The History of the Union* (1709) pp. 41—2.
67. *Review*, vii, 419; and see also *Review*, ii, 231; iv, 342.
68. A. Cunningham (translated from the Latin by W. Thompson), *The History of Great Britain: From the Revolution of 1688, to the Accession of George I* (London, 1787) i, 184—5. For Cunningham, see *DNB*.
69. Moore (as in note 61), p. 55.
70. Moore, *Checklist* (29).
71. See Appendix B(21).
72. *The True-Born Hugonot* (1703) p. 11.

73. *Review*, iii, 322.
74. *AH&J*, in Boulton, p. 170.
75. Luttrell, v, 26 (5 April 1701).
76. *The History of the Kentish Petitition* (1701).
77. *The History of the Kentish Petition Answer'd, Paragraph by Paragraph* (1701) p. 11.
78. *The History of the Kentish Petition*, in Hazlitt, iii, item 9, Preface (p. 5); and in Edward Arber (ed.), *An English Garner* (12 vols, Westminster, 1903) xii, 157.
79. In *Somers Tracts*, xi, 255—9, and Arber's *Garner*, xii, 179—86. Moore, *Checklist* (35). Quotation from *Legion's New Paper* (1701) p. 4.
80. *History of the Kentish Petition*, in Hazlitt, iii, item 9, p. 9.
81. W. Wilson, *Memoirs of the Life and Times of Daniel De Foe* (London, 1830) i, 396, footnote (R).
82. Luttrell, v, 50.
83. e.g., in *A Brief Explanation* (1703), postcript.
84. In Ellis, pp. 318—333; also in *Somers Tracts*, xi, 259—64. Moore, *Checklist* (36).
85. *The History of the Kentish Petition*, in Hazlitt, iii, item 9, p. 9 (in Arber's *Garner*, xii, 166).
86. Quoted in Hazlitt, iii, item 9, p. 5, footnote.
87. Luttrell, v, 68.
88. Quoted in Hazlitt, iii, item 8, pp. 9—10, footnote.
89. In *Somers Tracts*, xi, 242—54; Hazlitt, iii, item 8; Arber's *Garner*, xii, 157—78. Moore, *Checklist* (37).
90. *The Original Power* (1701), p. 2.
91. *Review*, viii, 57.
92. *England's Enemies Exposed, and its True Friends and Patriots Defended* (1701) p. 42.
93. Defoe to Halifax, 5 April 1705, in Healey, *Letters* (29) p. 82.
94. Somers Papers, in Hardwicke, ii, 447, 450, 451(2).
95. However, in *Review*, i, 393; iii, 158; iv, 103, Defoe followed a very similar line of argument to that suggested by Sunderland. See also Appendix A.
96. See A. D. Francis, 'Portugal and the Grand Alliance', *Bulletin of the Institute of Historical Research*, xxxviii (May 1965) 71—93 for a general discussion of William's diplomacy, 1700—2.
97. *Review*, viii, 391.
98. Moore, *Checklist* (38).
99. Moore, *Checklist* (39).
100. *The Address* (1704), stanza 25.
101. In *State Tracts*, iii, 312—42. See Appendix B(22).
102. Ibid., p. 319.
103. *Review*, i, 337. See also *Review*, i, 361; ii, 117; iii, 161—2.
104. In Ellis, pp. 343—52.
105. In *Somers Tracts*, xi, 264—72. Moore, *Checklist* (40). Quotation from *Legion's New Paper*, p. 13.
106. In *State Tracts*, iii, 343—73. See Appendix B(23).
107. Moore, *Checklist* (41).

108. *The Original Power*, p. 18. See also *Review*, iii, 429—31; *JD*, v, 3; *A Fourth Essay at Removing National Prejudices* (1706) p. 11, for an argument that a *single* owner of the land would be king.
109. Hardwicke, ii, 457.
110. See Appendices A and B(24). For comments on the speech, see H. D. Traill, *William the Third* (London, 1888) pp. 192—3, and Lodge, op. cit., pp. 448—9.
111. *A Supplement to the Faults on Both Sides* (1710) p. 33; *Review*, v, 610. See also *Review*, ii, 382; v, 607; viii, 435.
112. *Review*, viii, 210—11.
113. *The True-Born Hugonot*, p. 12.
114. *Review*, viii, Preface.
115. Defoe to Harley, 16 July 1705, in Healey, *Letters* (37), p. 92.
116. Defoe to Harley, 14 Aug 1705, in Healey, *Letters* (40), p. 100.
117. *Review*, viii, 570.
118. Healey, *Letters* (10), p. 17.
119. *A Reply to . . . Lord Haversham's Vindication* (1706) p. 7.
120. *Review*, viii, Preface.
121. See above, pp. 259—60. See also *Review*, viii, 202, 789—90.
122. Moore, pp. 223—4, quoting *An Historical Account of . . . Sir Walter Raleigh* (1720) p. 55.
123. Healey, *Letters* (171, enclosure), pp. 345—9.
124. *A New Voyage Round the World* (1724), in Hazlitt, i, item 8, pp. 73—86.
125. *Review*, vii, 511, 513.
126. *Review*, v, 198—9.
127. *CET*, ii, 80.
128. *A Reply to . . . Lord Haversham's Vindication*, pp. 8—9; *Review*, vi, 341; vii, 371—4.
129. *Royal Religion* (1704), p. 21. See also ibid., p. 12 and *Review*, iv, 67.
130. *Review*, vii, 419; *The Storm, An Essay*, p. 3, appended to *An Elegy on the Author of the True-Born-English-Man* (1704); *Review*, i[ix], 43.
131. *Review*, i, 398.
132. *Some Plain Observations . . .* (1705). See Appendix B(28).
133. *Review*, i, 386; *JD*, i, 26.

Chapter 13

1. In Ellis, pp. 372—97. Moore, *Checklist* (42). Sutherland (3), p. 105.
2. *The Mock Mourners*, in *True Collection*, pp. 60, 58, 49, 62.
3. Moore, *Checklist* (44). *A New Test*, in *True Collection*, pp. 398, 417.
4. Pat Rogers, 'Defoe in Fleet Prison', *RES*, xxii (Nov 1971) 451—3.
5. *Review*, i, 421—2.
6. *Review*, vii, 471.

7. In Ellis, pp. 467—84. Moore, *Checklist* (47). Sutherland (3), pp. 107—8.
8. In Ellis, pp. 398—448. Moore, *Checklist* (43). Sutherland (3), pp. 105—7.
9. Ellis shows that most of it must have been written in July, but the publication date is not known.
9. *Review*, ii, 330.
10. *Reformation of Manners*, in *True Collection*, pp. 70—1.
11. Ibid., p. 100.
12. Defoe to Paterson, April 1703, in Healey, *Letters* (2), pp. 5—6.
13. *A New Test of the Church of England's Loyalty* (1703) p. 28.
14. See letters from Harley to Carstates ('Monday at eight') and from Portland to Carstares (11 November) in Joseph M'Cormack, D. D. (ed.), *Carstares' State Papers* (Edinburgh, 1774), where they are tentatively assigned to the year 1700, but clearly must have been written in 1701.
15. *The Christianity of the High Church Consider'd* (1704) Preface.
16. According to Lee, the 2nd edition of *An Enquiry* appeared on 20 Nov 1700, and the *Letter* on 24 Jan 1701. See Moore, *Checklist* (17 and 31).
17. *A Dialogue between a Dissenter and the Observator*, in *A Collection of the Writings of the Author of the True-Born English-man* (1703) p. 221.
18. Moore, *Checklist* (48). Sutherland (3), pp. 42—3.
19. Moore, *Checklist* (49).
20. Moore, *Checklist* (50). Maximilian E. Novak, 'Defoe's *Shortest Way with the Dissenters*: Hoax, Parody, Paradox, Fiction, Irony and Satire', *Modern Language Quarterly*, xxvii (1966) 404 *et seq.* Sutherland (3), pp. 43—6. E. Anthony James, *Daniel Defoe's Many Voices* (Amsterdam, 1972) pp. 100—11.
21. Moore, pp. 120—1, with reference to City of London Records (Oyer & Terminer Roll for 22 and 24 Feb 1702/3). See also Moore, *Checklist* (50).
22. Pat Rogers informs me that the actual publication date was normally the later of the two dates given.
23. *The Dissenters Answer to the High-Church Challenge* (1704) pp. 37—8, quotes the letter. The sender is called 'Esq. M———' in *More Short Ways with the Dissenters* (1704) p. 2, and in *An Elegy on the Author of the True-Born-English-man* (1704) p. 23.
24. Healey, *Letters* (2), p. 5, footnote 3, with reference to BM., Add.MSS. 29,589 f. 400.
25. Luttrell, v, 253 (2 Jan 1702/3).
26. Healey, *Letters* (1), p. 1, footnote 1, with reference to PRO., S.P. 44/352/103.
27. *A Supplement to the Faults on Both Sides* (1710) p. 37.
28. *Observator*, No. 73 (30 Dec 1702—2 Jan 1703).
29. Moore, *Checklist* (51); but the publication date given there (28 Feb 1703, taken from Lee?) must be wrong, since Tutchin mentions it in *Observator*, No. 75 (6—9 Jan 1703), while Defoe himself mentions

Observator No. 73 in a postscript. Publication must have been in the first week of January. In *True Collection*, pp. 215—18.

30. *Review*, ii, 277.
31. See Appendix B(25).
32. Healey, *Letters* (21), p. 65, footnote 1.
33. *A Dialogue between a Dissenter and the Observator*, in *Collection*, p. 238.
34. Healey, *Letters* (10), p. 17.
35. Healey, *Letters* (1), pp. 1—3.
36. More fully treated in Moore, pp. 117—18.
37. Moore, p. 119.
38. *A Dialogue* . . . , in *Collection*, p. 225.
39. *Observator*, No. 78 (16—20 Jan 1703).
40. Moore, *Checklist* (52). Included in the pirated *Collection*, pp. 219—42, but omitted from Defoe's own *True Collection*, for reasons discussed below, p.292.
41. *A Dialogue* . . . , in *Collection*, p. 226.
42. (a) His letter to Paterson in April [Healey, *Letters* (2), p. 6] — 'whether Ever I am Restor'd to my Native Country Or Not'. (b) The story of his dream at Barnet (below, pp. 286—7) shows him approaching London from a northerly direction, with the intention of taking his family to Scotland. (c) In *Review*, vi, 195 (26 July 1709), he wrote that he had spent one whole winter in Scotland and part of two others. His long visit of 1706—7 accounts for one whole and one part winter. This is probably the other part winter.
43. *Col. Jack*, pp. 87—99.
44. *Tour*, ii, 94.
45. His agent for distributing pamphlets in Hull was 'Mr. Ibbetson' of Leeds. See Healey, *Letters* (46), p. 117.
46. *Tour*, ii, 239; *History of Apparitions*, p. 116.
47. *Tour*, ii, 234.
48. *Tour*, ii, 355. Defoe erroneously calls it 'Rosemary-Top', perhaps confusing the name with Rosemary Topping in the parish of English Bicknor, near Symond's Yat, an area which he seems to have visited.
49. See chap. 11, note 31.
50. *Tour*, ii, 283. See also *Review*, iv, 524; iv, 618; v, 353; vii, 772 (an advertisement for a book by Lauder). He was minister at Mordintown, 1695—1717.
51. Healey, *Letters* (2), p. 6.
52. Ibid., pp. 4—6.
53. Defoe's estimates of his further losses steadily increased, perhaps by accumulation of interest: *c*. May—June 1704 it was 'above £2500' (Healey, *Letters* (10), p. 17); by 24 March 1705 (*Review*, ii, 34) it was '£3000'; early in 1711 (*Review*, viii, Preface), 'above £3000'; by 5 Jan 1712 (*Review*, viii, 496) it stood at '£3500'.
54. *Review*, ii, 34.
55. Sutherland (1) with reference to PRO, C33/296 f. 213.
56. *History of Apparitions*, pp. 220—3. See Healey, *Letters* (21), p. 65, footnote 1.

57. Moore, p. 126, with reference to *Cal. Treas. Papers*, lxxxv, 154.
58. Moore, p. 126, with reference to *The Reformer Reform'd*, pp. 7–8; *Post-Man*, 25 May 1703; Nottingham's Letter Book, PRO, 44/352, f. 162.
59. *MF*, p. 273.
60. See Appendix B(29).
61. *Review*, viii, Preface.
62. *MF*, pp. 291–2.
63. *More Reformation* (1703), pp. 51–2.
64. *Review*, vi, 454.
65. Moore, p. 127, with reference to *Advice to All Parties* (1705) Preface.
66. Healey, *Letters* (171), p. 345.
67. Healey, *Letters* (14), pp. 38–9.
68. *Review*, vii, 90–1.
69. Moore, p. 128, with reference to Sessions Roll for 7 July 1703.
70. *Review*, i[ix], 184.
71. G. A. Aitken, 'Defoe's Brick-Kilns', *Athenaeum* (13 April 1889) 472–3.
72. Moore, *Checklist* (54).
73. *Little Review* (supplement to *Review*), 20 June 1705, pp. 18–19.
74. Moore, *Checklist* (58).
75. *True Collection*, Preface, p. iii.
76. Moore, *Checklist* (57).
77. *The Shortest Way to Peace and Union* (1703) p. 12.
78. In Ellis, pp. 547–84. Moore, *Checklist* (56).
79. *More Reformation* (1703), pp. iv, v, 42.
80. Moore, p. 128, with reference to *Review*, i[ix], 184.
81. Healey, *Letters* (3), p. 8.
82. Moore, p. 130.
83. *Review*, ii, 278; vi, 454.
84. *A True State of the Difference* . . . (1704) p. 5; *A Reply to* . . . *Lord Haversham's Vindication* (1706) p. 20.
85. Healey, *Letters* (3), p. 8.
86. Ibid., p. 7, footnote 2, with reference to BM Add MSS 29,589 ff.28–9.
87. Ibid., with reference to PRO, S.P. 34/3/3.
88. Ibid., with reference to PRO, S.P. 44/104/316.
89. Moore, p. 137 with reference to BM Add.MSS 29, 589 f.44.
90. Healey, *Letters* (3), p. 7, with reference to BM Add.MSS 29,589 f.46.
91. Moore, p. 137, with references to Nottingham's Letter Book, PRO Entry Book 104 f.318.
92. Moore, pp. 137–9; *The True-Born Hugonot*, pp. 18–19.
93. *Consolidator* (1705) p. 212.
94. *Review*, i, 386.
95. *The Felonious Treaty* (1711) p. 25.
96. Moore, p. 140, with reference to Nottingham's Letter Book, PRO S.P. Entry Book 104 f.320.

97. *Consolidator* (1705), p. 212.
98. Healey, *Letters* (30), p. 82. See also *Review*, v, 468, 586.
99. *Review*, i[ix], 158.
100. Quoted by Hazlitt, i, item 1, pp. xxvii-xxviii, footnote.
101. Published on 16, 22, 22 July respectively. See Moore, *Checklist* (56, 57, 58).
102. Moore, p. 141, with reference to *Heraclitus Ridens* and *The True-Born Hugonot*.
103. *The True-Born Hugonot* (1703) p. 4.
104. *The Wolf Stript*, p. 74.
105. In Ellis, pp. 585—605. Moore, *Checklist* (59). Sutherland (3), pp. 108—10.
106. The last word of the penultimate line, presumably a printer's error or a Freudian slip, was altered to 'Guilt' in later versions.
107. Alexander Pope, *The Dunciad* (1728) Bk II, l. 139.
108. Moore, p. 142; *The Consolidator*, pp. 68—9. See also *The Present State of the Parties* (1712) p. 21.
109. Evelyn, *Diary*, v, 543.
110. See chap. 7, pp. 116—17. *Review*, iii, 326.
111. *RC*, p. 304.

Index